The Framed Houses of Massachusetts Bay

THE FRAMED HOUSES OF
MASSACHUSETTS BAY, 1625—1725

ABBOTT LOWELL CUMMINGS

THE BELKNAP PRESS OF
HARVARD UNIVERSITY PRESS
CAMBRIDGE, MASSACHUSETTS, AND
LONDON, ENGLAND

Library of Congress Cataloging in Publication Data

Cummings, Abbott Lowell, 1923 –
The framed houses of Massachusetts Bay, 1625 – 1725.

Includes bibliographical references and index.
1. Wooden-frame houses—Massachusetts (Colony).
2. Architecture, Modern—17th-18th centuries—Massachusetts (Colony).   3. Architecture, Colonial—Massachusetts (Colony).   4. Architecture, Domestic—Massachusetts (Colony).   5. Architecture—United States—
English influences.   6. Historic buildings—Massachusetts.   I. Title.
NA730.M4C85   728   78-8390
ISBN 0-674-31680-0 (cloth)
ISBN 0-674-31681-9 (paper)

Designed by Mike Fender

To the memory of my grandmother, Lucretia Amelia Stow Cummings, who first awakened my interest in history

Preface

I T WAS a long-standing dearth of published information on the seventeenth-century domestic architecture of Massachusetts that led Clarence Ward of Oberlin College to suggest in 1945 that I make this subject the topic of a Master's Thesis. The work undertaken in the academic year 1945 — 1946 was accomplished largely through the use of secondary source material available in the Oberlin College library. Following my return to the east coast a few years later, I continued research in the same field, concentrating upon the houses themselves and the rich documentation within the area.

A significant amount of time was devoted to the verification of traditional dates for a majority of the important existing structures. Summary abstracts of the evidence for dating those houses mentioned in the text will be found in the appendix of volume 51 of the *Publications of The Colonial Society of Massachusetts*, for which I served as special editor. Included also are verbatim transcriptions of all the key building documents discovered in the course of my investigations.

Much of the material in the chapter on The House Plan is based upon recorded information concerning dimensions of houses built at Massachusetts Bay between 1637 and 1706, and in Boston between 1707 and 1729, as revealed in a cor-pus of official permits for building in timber. That evidence will be found in the Appendix of this book (tables 1 and 4). Of fundamental importance to the development of the same chapter are room-by-room inventories for Suffolk, Essex, and Middlesex counties from 1630 to 1660 (table 3 of the Appendix). This period covers roughly the mature life span of the first generation of settlers, and the documents themselves reveal both room usage and planning conventions. For the later years of the century, 1661 to 1700, a total of 107 inventories for rural Suffolk county have been analyzed and appear in a volume entitled *Rural Household Inventories* published in Boston under my editorship in 1964 by the Society for the Preservation of New England Antiquities.

Additional tables in the Appendix are concerned with timber felling grants (table 2) or reveal the chronological significance of comparative measurements for certain structural features discussed in the chapter on English Regional Derivations and Evolutionary Trends. These include scarf joints (table 5), and the spacing of floor joists (table 6). Although the several tables are not cited in the text, it will be clear what sections are supported by the documentary evidence.

In my efforts to synthesize and evaluate the vast body of existing information I wish to acknowledge the invaluable assistance and encouragement of many individuals who have helped to make the present work a reality. At the head of the list must be numbered those scholars and students in England and America who, because of similar interests in the subject of seventeenth-century vernacular architecture, have been a source of continuing inspiration. To them I have turned for specific information, for the testing of theories and hypotheses, and for that special nourishment which comes from enthusiasms shared. The ultimate satisfaction, of course, is the pleasurable experience of exploring an old house together, discovering its structural secrets, puzzling over its contradictions, and emerging with stronger conclusions than a solitary examination might have produced. For the many months of research in England, beginning in 1953, I owe a special debt of gratitude to R. W. Brunskill, Alan Carter, F. W. B. and Mary Charles, Sylvia Colman, Norman Davey, A. C. Edwards, Cecil A. Hewett, R. T. Mason, J. T. Smith, and to many other good friends and fellow members of the Vernacular Architecture Group who have patiently answered my inquiries and have arranged entry to houses I wished to study.

On this side of the Atlantic, and beginning with

the fruitful years of training under Clarence Ward of Oberlin College and Elmer Davenport Keith, both of whom are no longer living, my deep appreciation is extended to many friends and colleagues within the ranks of the Society of Architectural Historians, and particularly to Richard M. Candee, Cary Carson, John F. Cole, Frank A. Demers, Benno M. Forman, Elizabeth K. Frothingham, Daniel M. C. Hopping, Carrie B. Ladd, Bertram K. and Nina Fletcher Little, Charles E. Peterson, Morgan W. Phillips, Charles R. Strickland, Edward Thomas, Lura Woodside Watkins, and Daniel S. Wendel.

To the many libraries, historical associations, and record repositories which have been useful to me, including the Boston Athenaeum, the Essex Record Office in Chelmsford, Essex, the American Antiquarian Society, the Bostonian Society, the Colonial Society of Massachusetts, the Essex Institute, the Fairbanks Family in America, Inc., the Massachusetts Historical Society, the Massachusetts State Archives, and the Registries of Deeds and Probate together with the Courts for the counties of Essex, Middlesex, and Suffolk, I am endlessly grateful for constant cooperation. When this list is broadened to include the local historical societies as well it becomes impossible to recognize each in turn. Taking the part for the whole I should like to extend special thanks to Mrs. Elizabeth Newton and the Ipswich Historical Society and Mrs. Frederick C. Cheney and the Hingham Historical Society, representing the North and South Shores respectively and two of the richest towns at Massachusetts Bay in terms of surviving material from the first century of settlement.

The collections of the Society for the Preservation of New England Antiquities are the unfailing storehouse of information for any student of New England architectural history. The archival resources, documentary and pictorial, and the key seventeenth-century structures owned by the Society form in a real sense the cornerstone of the present work. My trustees and professional colleagues over the twenty-four-year period during which I have been privileged to serve this institution, and particularly the Society's former librarian, Daniel M. Lohnes, have been consistently helpful and utterly supportive.

It would be impossible to thank by name all those who have directed me to houses and information of which I was unaware and, above all, the many persons in England and America who have graciously opened their homes for my cellar-to-attic inspection. As the most fitting tribute, it may be said quite simply that I cannot recall a single early house to which in the course of thirty years of research and upon reasonable application I have been refused welcome entry.

Official gratitude is owing to the American Philosophical Society which made it possible with the support of a grant to invite Cecil A. Hewett to spend six weeks in Massachusetts in 1967 for the purpose of analyzing the American vernacular experience from the point of view of an English architectural scholar. I am deeply indebted also to Walter Muir Whitehill for continual encouragement and assistance which extended to within a few days of his unexpected and untimely death. Among these many courtesies none, perhaps, was more important than having secured a grant from the John Anson Kittredge Educational Fund to Lawrence A. Sorli for the execution under my supervision of the drawings which serve as illustrations in the text. The reader will recognize at once the infeasibility of developing the theme of the present work without the lucid and visually explicit statements which these drawings provide.

My former student John S. Garner prepared several of the floor plans, and William W. Owens, Jr., kindly volunteered to take the many fine photographs which bear his name. They are reproduced with his generous permission.

M. W. Barley of the University of Nottingham was kind enough to read the chapters pertaining to The English Background and The House Plan, and Mrs. Jane Garrett has read the manuscript almost in its entirety. Both have made helpful suggestions. James Marston Fitch, Jane Garrett, and Walter Muir Whitehill were my principal mentors, and to them I can never express sufficient appreciation for having kept my confidence buoyed aloft during what has seemed to many, I realize, an unconscionably long period of gestation.

To all of these, and to my secretaries, Kathleen Donovan and Helen E. Grady, who typed the major portions of the manuscript, my eternal thanks.

A.L.C.

Contents

Appendix Tables

Illustrations

Illustrations

The Framed Houses
of Massachusetts Bay

Men doe now build, as lokinge on a setled Com-
monwelth, and therefore, wee looke at posteryty
and what may be usefull or profitable for them.

—JAMES LUXFORD TO JOHN WINTHROP, 1637

Introduction

CONSCIOUSNESS OF AN architectural heritage has been one of the readily discernible elements in the rich cultural history of the Commonwealth of Massachusetts since the eighteenth century. This has resulted in the preservation here of the largest number of seventeenth-century houses in the nation. More than a hundred and fifty well-authenticated structures that span the first century of settlement at Massachusetts Bay have been identified within the limits of Suffolk, Essex, and Middlesex counties as originally defined.

The Reverend William Bentley, pastor of Salem's East Church from 1783 until his death in 1819, may be considered New England's first architectural historian. His diaries reveal a lively interest in not only the buildings erected during his lifetime but those of earlier periods as well. Repeatedly he takes us into the houses of the "first generation" and records in detail their salient features. Bentley's interest in early buildings was fundamentally antiquarian, and it was antiquarian curiosity that led Henry David Thoreau a half-century later, in 1859, to visit the seventeenth-century Hunt house in Concord when it was being demolished and to note "that the eastern two-thirds of the main house is older than the western third, for you can see where the west part has been added on."[1]

Memorial interest beginning in the second quarter of the nineteenth century accounted for a spate of town histories and family genealogies which reached a climax after 1876 when the Philadelphia Centennial focused new attention on our history and accomplishments. Even before the middle of the century it was the rare town history that did not contain some reference to the first houses built in the community or the ancient homesteads of prominent families, although the first separate publication on the subject was *A Paper on New-England Architecture*, read before the New England Historic Genealogical Society on September 4, 1858, by the Reverend Nathan Henry Chamberlain of Canton, Massachusetts. While Mr. Chamberlain's characterizations of the "quaintly-cornered, irregular-lined mansions of the colonial gentry" seem both superficial and cold to our modern ears ("all was plain, simple, austere"), there are also passages which underscore a rising tide of romantic sentiment:

One finds . . . in solitary rambles through old pastures sprinkled over with young pines, an irregular excavation, clothed with dark-green grass, from whose depths rise mullein and mothworth and tansy; while scattered about are damp, mouldy fragments of mortar or brick; while, around, a few decaying apple-trees stretch out their dry arms in the impotency of a fruitless age. Here once stood a Puritan home.[2]

Unquestionably romantic were the many drawings of early New England buildings by English artist Edwin Whitefield, who settled in America about 1838. These he published as color lithographs in a series entitled *The Homes of our Forefathers* beginning in 1879, including with each drawing a brief descriptive historical caption. The real roots of modern scholarship, however, can be found in the work of the late nineteenth-century antiquarians and a small group of early twentieth-century architects. In 1894, some thirty years before architectural historian Fiske Kimball published his *Domestic Architecture of the American Colonies*, with its emphasis upon documentary evidence, a relatively obscure writer named Alvin Lincoln Jones, in a work entitled *Under Colonial Roofs*, expressed a prefatorial hope "that his efforts to separate fact from tradition may merit the attention of those who prefer truth to fiction, whatever may be the judgment passed on other matters."[3] His text sets forth an extraordinary range of factual material which refreshingly offsets the many nostalgic tales that continued to pour from the pens of "colonial" romanticists.

Most impressively monumental of all turn-of-the-century efforts, however, is that of the Reverend Thomas Franklin Waters, who salvaged time somehow from a vigorous pastoral career to trace in detail the history of every seventeenth-century house-lot in Ipswich. The results were systematically summarized street by street, lot by lot in 170 finely printed pages appended to the first volume of his *Ipswich in the Massachusetts Bay Colony*, published there in 1905. Ipswich has consistently occupied a position of focal importance in the study of seventeenth-century architecture at Massachusetts Bay, for this community has preserved the highest density of houses from the first century of settlement of any town in New England. Mr. Waters identified the reason in 1898 when he wrote of the "sleepy, unprogressive life that has prevailed in old Ipswich for a century or more," by which "a large number of substantial mansions of the colonial type have . . . escaped the smart remodelling incident to vigorous prosperity."[4] Settled by some of the most influential men in the colony, Ipswich had nevertheless been foreordained to a role of diminishing importance. With an unsatisfactory harbor and largely bypassed by industry at a later date, the town tended to stagnate. James Birket, a merchant from Antigua, remarked in 1751 that "the houses here seem to be mostly old And upon the decline,"[5] while the Reverend William Bentley reported in 1803 that he found a few persons building, "but the houses are too much neglected, and their mossy tops are more numerous than in any other part of New England."[6]

After 1900 the number of students interested in the seventeenth-century buildings of New England began to multiply. Among the more prominent were George Francis Dow, Sidney Perley, who documented many of the early house lots of Salem, Beverly, Danvers and Marblehead,[7] and above all, William Sumner Appleton. These men worked closely with the architects, especially Joseph Everett Chandler of Boston and Norman Isham of Providence, Rhode Island, who had established reputations during the opening years of the twentieth century for a ready familiarity with the problems of restoration. Isham's *Early Rhode Island Houses* (in conjunction with Albert F. Brown) was published in Providence in 1895, and is precisely what its subtitle proclaims, "an Historical and Architectural Study." It is the first detailed analysis of seventeenth-century vernacular forms in New England.

For the student of Massachusetts' seventeenth-century architecture, however, there are but two serious works on the subject, both published in the 1920s. Fiske Kimball's *Domestic Architecture of the American Colonies and of the Early Republic* (though covering, as its title suggests, more than the seventeenth century) is the first study to stress the absolute necessity of an authentic chronology for those structures which are to play any part in the development of an evolutionary scheme. Fiske Kimball's work in 1922 and Norman Isham's *Early American Houses*, published by the Walpole Society in 1928 and devoted almost entirely to seventeenth-century Massachusetts, stand alone. Mr. Kimball's concern is fundamentally with style; Mr. Isham's with the analysis of construction. Aside from magazine articles, individual monographs, and cursory surveys in larger studies, nothing major has been produced since.

This paucity of information is all the more surprising in that there is such a wealth of study-reference material. In addition to the voluminous public documents, much of the record-keeping can be credited largely to the untiring efforts of a single man. The countless notes, observations, photographs, and measured drawings made, commissioned, or collected by William Sumner Appleton (1874-1947), founder in 1910 and lifelong corresponding secretary of the Society for the Preservation of New England Antiquities, represent a deep-laid factual foundation which no student can ignore. As early as 1919, when the seventeenth-century Browne house in Watertown was restored under his direction, Mr. Appleton had developed philosophical policies and methodical recording techniques which in many respects have not been surpassed in modern professional work.

Owing to the impressive increase in basic information, our understanding of seventeenth-century architecture in Massachusetts extends now far beyond the limits publicized by Isham and Kimball. The present work recognizes a profound debt of gratitude to these pioneers. It would have been impossible of achievement, however, without the work of William Sumner Appleton and the opportunity, extending over several decades, to explore the large number of houses whose innermost structural secrets had not yet been revealed to the earlier generation of scholars, but have been now through repair, restoration, or, unhappily, demolition.

CHAPTER I

The English Background

THE FIRST PEOPLING of Massachusetts from abroad was by Englishmen, with only a few exceptions. Throughout the seventeenth century there could be found a sprinkling of Dutch, Walloons, Germans, Portuguese, Jerseymen, and Irish, while an appreciable group of Scotch who came at the middle of the century following Cromwell's campaigns in the north of England and French Huguenots who arrived following the Revocation of the Edict of Nantes in 1685, together with an indeterminate number of Negroes, constituted significant minority groups within the total immigrant population. England contributed by far the largest number of colonists, however, and the timber-framed houses built during the century that followed the first settlement at Massachusetts Bay were fundamentally English. If there are occasional features, either structural or stylistic, which can be traced to some other national source, they were quickly absorbed into the mainstream of British thinking.

The immediate background of this dominant majority among the earliest inhabitants is thus a matter of basic concern. The observer must be able to recognize the evolutionary changes that occurred in postmedieval vernacular buildings during the reigns of Queen Elizabeth and the early Stuarts. He must know the exact level of de-

velopment and the character of these humbler English houses at the opening of the seventeenth century in terms of plan, construction technology, and regional stylistic differences if he is to understand fully the structures built by Englishmen in the New World throughout the first century of settlement. Whatever the religious, economic, and political motives for separation that lay behind the early migrations to New England, and whatever the changes and modifications made in inherited building practices by the colonists in America, their lives and attitudes in the Old World and in the new must be seen as part of a continuum. The men and women of the first generation, once transplanted to the western hemisphere, never wholly ceased to be English, and any study of seventeenth-century vernacular houses in Massachusetts fails at once if it does not seek to enunciate clearly the close relationship between the buildings at home in which the emigrants had grown up and those they erected here upon their arrival.

Which areas, then, sent the largest numbers of people to New England? English population densities had direct bearing upon migration statistics, and thus, generally speaking, the proportion of newcomers from each part of England tallies roughly with the bulk of that section's inhabitants

in 1630. "Populous counties sent many settlers; barren and sparse counties sent few."[1] In Massachusetts as elsewhere the majority of English colonists seem to have been drawn broadly from East Anglia and the southwestern counties. Beginning with the Pilgrims in 1620 the influx rose to a great crescendo in the decade from 1630 to 1640—that period called the Great Migration. The contemporary Edward Johnson estimated that more than 21,000 individuals had arrived by 1643.[2] While the exact starting point for only some 3,000 English heads of families among these pioneers have been located at present, the patterns which can be deduced from this group alone must have significance in suggesting origins for the many whose record is not so well known. Roughly 55 percent were recruited from those eastern English counties south of the river Trent, while an additional 37 percent were drawn from the western counties below the rivers Trent and Dee. In both cases the largest numbers are concentrated in groups of contiguous counties. For the eastern region, which includes London, heads of families for Suffolk, Essex, Kent, Norfolk, Hertfordshire, and Middlesex number 1,319. Highest concentrations to the west occur in Devonshire, Somersetshire, Dorsetshire, and Wiltshire, with a total of 563.[3]

The greater portion of these emigrants constituted that important element of rural society, the farmers, who in the sixteenth century were coming to be called yeomen. Below the yeoman in status came the husbandman, originally an unfree peasant who had his own home and land, and yet who stood, according to the dictates of the day, somewhat above the village craftsman in position. All alike shared in the upsurge of vitality under the Tudor monarchs. From the 1540s onward the yeoman and husbandman were in an enviable position. They had security of tenure with respect to their lands; their rents, established at an earlier period in time, were nominal; and above all, they enjoyed a situation in which expenses were relatively fixed while selling prices were rising steadily. "No yeoman with his wits about him could fail to accumulate money-savings on a scale hitherto unknown."[4]

The East Anglian counties of Suffolk and Essex had benefited in particular from the steady rise in national economic prosperity. In the northern areas the clothmaking industry developed and flourished. At the southwest, London provided an expanding market for Essex agriculture. The increasing prosperity was reflected in a widespread wave of building and rebuilding during the reign of Queen Elizabeth, when standards of living were on the rise and people were demanding more comfort and convenience. The phenomenon has been described as a "Housing Revolution,"[5] and by 1589 the situation called for parliamentary action. The preamble to an act of that year refers to "the erecting and building of great numbers and multitude of Cottages, which are dayly more and more increased in many partes of this Realme,"[6] though very often improvement of a medieval house, rather than complete rebuilding, was the order of the day.[7]

It was inevitable that these improvements in house construction in Tudor England aimed at greater comfort and convenience should percolate down the social scale and be reflected in even the most rural villages. Parson William Harrison of Radwinter in Essex sums it up with his reference in 1577 to "the inferiour Artificers and

most fermers, who have learned also to garnish their cubbordes with plate, their beddes with tapistrie, and silke hanginges, and their tables with fine naperie, whereby the wealth of our countrie doth infinitely appeare." The older men of his generation, he remarks, had noted several things which had been "marveylously altered in Englande within their sound remembraunce," among them the "great amendment of lodginge, for sayde they our fathers and we our selves have lyen full oft upon straw pallettes covered onely with a sheete under coverlettes made of dagswain or hopharlots . . . and a good round logge under their heades in steade of a boulster."[8]

It is not easy to realize how primitive in many respects the simple houses of rural England had been even as late as the beginning of Elizabeth's reign. Richard Carew, writing about Cornwall in the opening years of the seventeenth century, reported that the local husbandmen "in times not past the remembrance of some yet living," had dwelt in houses with "walles of earth, low thatched roofes, few partitions, no planchings or glasse windows, and scarcely any chimneys, other than a hole in the wall to let out the smoke."[9] And Edward Howes, who had earlier been a law student at the Inner Temple, wrote from England to John Winthrop, Jr., in Boston in 1632, "I like well the old English and still Irish buyldinge where the roome is large and the chimney or herth, in the middest. Certainly thereby ill vapour and gnatts are kept out, lesse firinge will serve the turne, and men had then more lusty and able bodies then they have nowe."[10] It is almost inevitable that among the many settlers who poured into New England during the 1620s and 1630s there must have been a few older persons at least who could recall a childhood in England in a cottage which had lagged somewhat behind its neighbors and had neither a chimney nor glazed windows. Indeed, Governor Winthrop recorded in 1632 that "Mr. Oldham had a small house near the wear at Watertown, made all of clapboards, burnt down by making a fire in it when it had no chimney."[11] For most colonists, however, and particularly for the younger men and women

who made up the major part of the Great Migration, such rude conditions must have been substantially beyond the range of everyday personal experience.

By 1630 a century of rapid change had witnessed in all parts of England and at all levels of society a proliferation of building improvements which significantly affected earlier house forms. In seeking out the specific examples that will have the greatest relevance for later developments at Massachusetts Bay it is important to examine concepts of living accommodation in general before we look at individual planning schemes in particular. The smaller timber-framed house, as it had evolved during the reign of the Tudors, was geared to the needs of a single family dependent upon a modest farm for a livelihood. At the core of the structure was the hall open to the roof, the common living room and meeting place of the household. More or less in the center of this area was an unenclosed hearth from whose fire the smoke meandered up and out through openings provided in the roof or at the gable ends. There were normally two opposite entrances, front and back. Thoroughly in keeping with a philosophy as yet untainted by formal classicism, these doors were located well off center at either end of a cross passage screened from the balance of the hall. Beyond the cross passage there were usually two rooms for domestic functions, one of which was apt to be the buttery in which drink was kept, while the other might be a pantry for provisions and table utensils. At the opposite, upper end of the hall additional space, when present, was given over to sleeping and polite uses, and in the case of both domestic services and sleeping the rooms themselves were often located in storied wings ranged at right angles to the hall block (figures 1 and 2).

Regional variations and evolutionary changes in the function and nomenclature of rooms are of particular interest. For the southern and southeastern counties the word chamber was early assigned by the peasantry to a ground-floor sleeping area. The term parlor, taken over from the upper classes, among which it meant a compartment reserved for secluded conversation and entertainment, began to be used in this area by the late sixteenth century to denote a principal ground-floor sleeping room. In the very simple houses where there was but a single such room it was called indifferently parlor or bedchamber, an ambivalence reflecting recent social change which would survive at Massachusetts Bay until after the middle of the seventeenth century.

In East Anglia the sleeping arrangements for adults were confined almost entirely to the ground floor and the newer expression parlor was used more commonly than chamber for these apartments. Essex people then, in fact, seldom referred to a lower room as a chamber, and while there may be some variation in terminology throughout the region as a whole, the word chamber by the opening of the seventeenth century was apt to describe an upper room.[12]

The service rooms make a special study in themselves. The baking of bread or cooking of meats in an oven did not appear until quite late, nor indeed did the kitchen itself. As first found in houses of all classes it took the form of a separate outbuilding. Suffolk and Essex, to say nothing of the counties farther west, were part of a region where, as the seventeenth century approached, the kitchen was still not regarded as part of the house. In a group of Suffolk inventories for 1582-1584, for example, less than a quarter of those with goods worth more than £20 had a kitchen,[13] and as late as 1592 the Essex will of one John Turner provided that his wife should

w'in two years after my decease make and build up at cost and Charges one kitchin howse as followeth that is to say in lengthe 30 foote in wydeth 18 foote one story a purlinde Rufe and cut Rufe ends with one partition in the same howse and thech and dawbe the same howse within the said Tyme.[14]

After 1625 the kitchen became more and more commonly a part of the house, though not invariably so. As late as 1635 – 1640, some twenty-two inventories for the village of Writtle near Chelmsford in Essex indicate that the kitchen

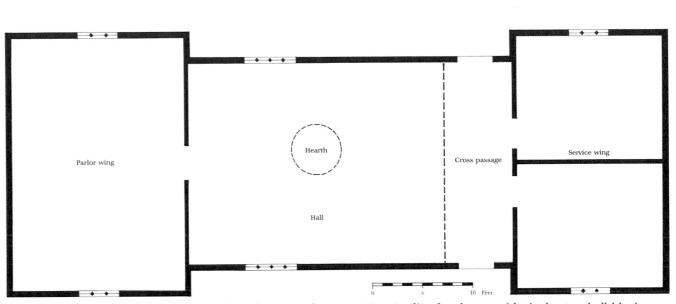

Figure 1. Ground-floor plan of characteristic early sixteenth-century East Anglian farmhouse with single-story hall block open to the roof and parlor and service wings.

Figure 2. Bailey's Farm, Mashbury, Essex, Eng. Two-story central hall block with parlor and service wings and integral chimney, sixteenth century, with seventeenth-century addition of central gable.

The English Background

was confined to the upper economic range. In the western counties this improvement in accommodation can be found at the turn of the seventeenth century despite the fact that cooking was still done in the hall. Here, too, the kitchen was thus becoming a part of the house, though it was often narrower and lower in height, as if still considered distinct.[15]

One of the most important developments of the sixteenth century in its effect upon the plan and form of the smaller farmhouse was the general adoption of the chimney where before the only fire had burned on an open hearth. Existing much earlier in structures of more ambitious character, the brick or stone chimney stack found its way into the hall of the yeoman's house during this period. Parson William Harrison wrote in 1577:

> There are olde men yet dwelling in the village where I remayne, which have noted . . . the multitude of chimnies lately erected, whereas in their young dayes there were not above two or three if so many in most uplandish townes of the realme, (the religious houses, and mannour places, of their Lordes alwayes excepted, and peradventure some great personages) but each one made his fire against a reredosse, in the hall where he dined and dressed his meate.[16]

The process had begun as early as 1500,[17] but lagged in the more remote counties. William Smith noted in 1585 that the farmers in the vicinity of Cheshire "till of late years . . . had their fire in the midst of the house, against a *Hob of Clay*, and their Oxen also under the same Roof," though he adds that "within these 40. years, it is altogethered altered: so that they have builded chimnies, and furnished other parts of their houses accordingly."[18] For the more progressive southeastern counties, Essex in particular, chimneys were increasing steadily in the sixteenth century. By 1601 Thomas Hinds of Ingatestone was presented at the manor court for lighting a fire in a room which had no chimney and was ordered to build one or pay a fine of ten shillings.[19]

A brick chimney in place of an open hearth,

Figure 3. Mayflower Cottage, Colne Engaine, Essex, Eng., 1620, with added lean-to. *Photo, Richard Cheek, 1975.*

with the obvious comfort and convenience its presence implied, "made it practicable to carry the . . . [second] floor across the whole of the house, thus converting the upper part of the hall into an extra chamber"[20] (figure 2). Henry Harning, an Essex vintner, for example, bequeathed to his wife in 1597 the life use of a "Capitall Mesuage or Tenement scituate in the parishe of St. Rundwall in Colchester," provided that she "build and make one dubbell Chimney betwene the hall and the parlour of the said mesuage or tenement And make A Chamber over the said hall."[21]

The emerging concept of an internal chimney with fireplaces that could provide heat for several rooms is readily understandable. More complex however, is the ultimate source of the simple

two-room plan with central chimney and lobby entrance in front of the stack, that form which is of particular interest in the development of American dwellings. The familiar hall/parlor formula with chimney serving both rooms was firmly rooted in East Anglia by the beginning of the seventeenth century and became common throughout several parts of England as the century progressed[22] (figures 3 and 4). Carried across the Atlantic by the first colonists, this well-established plan type set a pattern which has persisted through three and a half centuries and survives today in modified form in the modern American builder's vocabulary of styles as Garrison, Colonial, and Cape Cod houses.

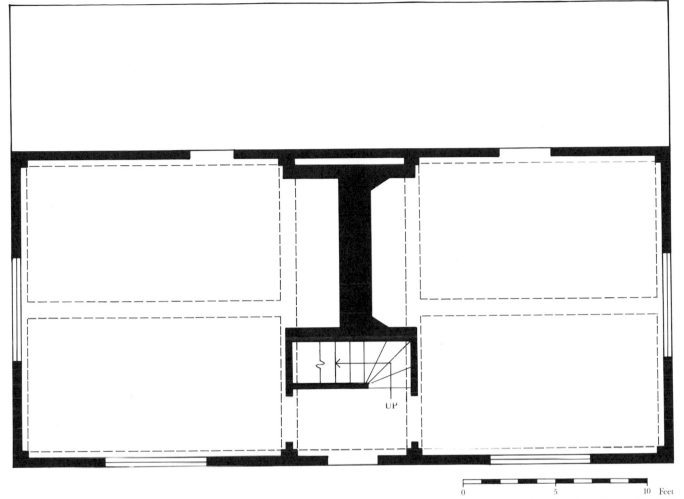

Figure 4. Mayflower Cottage. Ground-floor plan, original house. (Lean-to rooms not delineated.)

Speculation about the origins of the two-room plan involves a more intensive study of the various ways in which modest English houses were enlarged during the period of the Housing Revolution. A substantial part of the answer may eventually be found in medieval Suffolk dwellings among the many small houses without cross-wings which consisted initially of but two units— hall and service—under one continuous roof. Thorough analysis of a number of examples that were increased in size during the sixteenth and seventeenth centuries in response to changing social conditions has revealed that "the possession of a parlour, as a combined living-and-sleeping room, seems implicit in the alteration of these small houses: a sign both of increased opulence on the part of the occupants and of the decline in the importance of the hall as the centre of household activities."[23] The evidence of enlargement discloses a variety of solutions, but the lateral addition of a parlor to the simple hall house with service bay seems to have dictated a more or less uniform placement of the chimney stack on axis between the two principal rooms of the improved structure (figure 5). Often the new parlor block with two full stories was higher than the remainder of the building, proclaiming at a glance the changes which had taken place (figure 6). But there are many cases where a major internal alteration is concealed from the outside[24] (figure 7).

Is the reduction from a three-unit to a two-unit structure, also observable in Suffolk at this period, related to the introduction of the chimney and an increase in vertical space accommodations, eliminating the need to expand laterally? Or does it reflect the relegation of service rooms to subsidiary outshots? Certain it is that by the turn of the seventeenth century the central-chimney hall/parlor farmhouse in East Anglia was firmly established as a distinct building form. Whatever the answer to these questions as they affect English developments, we shall soon learn why the two-room, central-chimney plan—without a third unit or service bay—quickly became the preferred system in New England when we examine the transplanted Englishman in his New World environment.

We must consider one further closely related plan type, the single-room house, which was carried to America by the earliest settlers, existed side by side with the house of two-room, central-chimney plan, and in numerous cases also achieved two-room status through a process of elongation. Such houses in New England are, significantly, like many of the earlier English houses, indistinguishable on the outside from those which were of two-room plan at the outset. The single-room plan form has received scant attention from English scholars. Owing, perhaps, to its utter simplicity, and also to the fact that few early examples have survived, the structural characteristics and statistical incidence have not been studied extensively. Their once-common existence, however, is well documented from contemporary sources.[25] Further, the immediate and widespread appearance of such humble houses at Massachusetts Bay would indicate that the form was perfectly familiar to the first English settlers. Indeed, of eighty-five Lincolnshire probate inventories recorded for the year 1572, twenty-three can be interpreted as reflecting houses of one-room as against only seventeen of two-room plan, nearly all of them hall/parlor houses. By 1635 there were only nine one-room plans in contrast to fifteen examples having two rooms.[26] It is easy to see in these statistics a reflection of im-

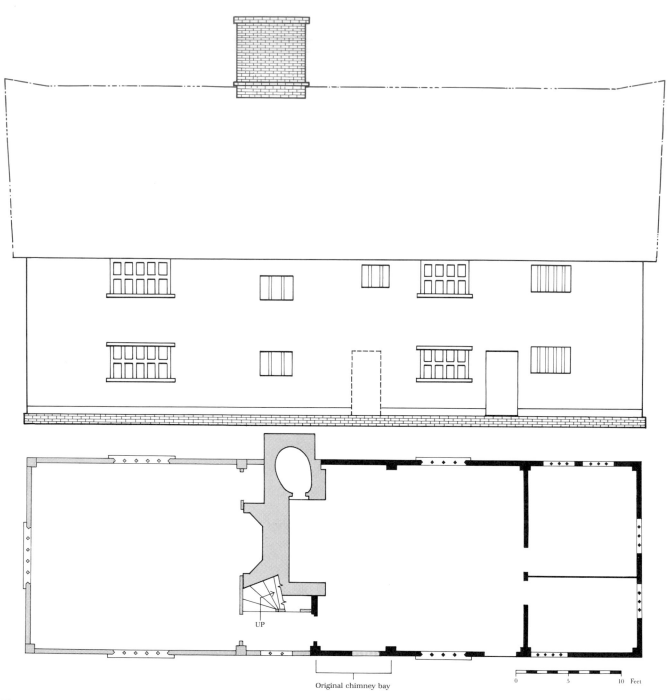

Figure 5. Swan Green Farmhouse, Cratfield, Suffolk, Eng. Elevation and ground-floor plan showing original house of ca. 1600 (at right) with hall, service rooms, end chimney bay, original (blocked) and later front doors, and addition of new chimney bay and parlor range, ca. 1625 or later.

Original chimney bay

0   5   10 Feet

Figure 6. Cottage near Brampton, Suffolk, Eng.

appear that the form was somewhat more complex than suspected, either in terms of impermanent inner partitions or makeshift outshots which have left little trace. In at least one or two examples at Massachusetts Bay some evidence for outshots does exist. Until, however, there has been more study of this neglected vernacular house form in England we are restricted to a minimum of data for comparative purposes. One explicit example can be found in Banham, Norfolk, part of that area from which so many of the East Anglian colonists were recruited. Here a small two-story house called Checquers Farm preserves its original single-room form with gable-end chimney bay, to which a smaller subsidiary addition has subsequently been made (figures 8 and 9). The house, which dates to about 1600 and is substantially well framed, provides in all major respects the evidence sought for an American prototype. The proportions of chimney and room bays are essentially those to be found among similar structures in New England, and the entrance is in the smaller bay before the chimney. For the most part, however, our sources of information for this important house form continue to be documentary.

Finally, we should note that the speed with which the bread oven was adopted as a part of the integral construction of the newly introduced

proved living standards which accompanied the Housing Revolution. And it is not hard to understand why so few have survived if, having been found less and less adequate, they were demolished or incorporated within enlarged structures.

Both in old and New England it may ultimately

Figure 8. Checquers Farm, Banham, Norfolk, Eng., ca. 1600, with modern addition (at left). *Photo, Richard Cheek, 1975.*

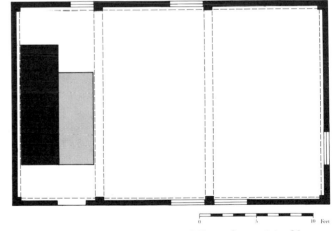

Figure 9. Checquers Farm. Ground-floor plan, original house. (Early chimney stack with probable addition unexcavated.)

chimney stack in the smaller English farmhouse remains open to some speculation. Although the proportion of rural bakers seems to increase after the middle of the seventeenth century, this is also a time when, "to judge from surviving houses, bread ovens are being installed in many [Lincoln-shire] farmhouses for the first time."[27] There is not evidence enough to show what had happened in England during the early 1600s, or at Massachusetts Bay for the second quarter of the seventeenth century. We are limited here in that there are so few original chimneys from before 1660. Those of the Fairbanks house in Dedham, ca. 1637, and the Whipple house in Ipswich, ca. 1655, are the only complete representatives, and it is probably significant that no evidence has yet appeared in either one to suggest that bread

Figure 7. Oak Farm, Whepstead, Suffolk, Eng. Hall/service house of probable sixteenth-century date with addition of parlor range and porch (at right) dated 1612. *Photo, Dennis H. Evans, 1969.*

ovens were an integral part of the original construction.

While there thus appear to have been some dwellings still of single-room plan at the lowest economic level, the characteristic smaller farmhouse from which most of the first emigrants to Massachusetts Bay set forth in the 1630s was fully developed by the close of the Tudor period and is found in East Anglia and the Midlands from the turn of the seventeenth century onwards. This was the house of two rooms on the ground floor, both chambered over, the chambers reached by a winding stair alongside the central chimney and often situated between the stack and the en-

Figure 10. Houchin's House, Feering, Essex, Eng., ca. 1600.

trance. A typical East Anglian inventory of the period, that for the estate of Richard Coliard, yeoman, of Thornage near Holt in Norfolk, taken in 1633, reveals an average pattern of room usage in a house apparently of two-room and probably central-chimney plan: the parlor contained, among other items, the best bed "of joyned worke" with curtains, a small framed table, "one chaire of joyners worke," a desk, and a window curtain. The second room is called the kitchen, a Norfolk synonym by this period for the hall when it was still used for cooking. The contents included a "framed table with a shorte forme and a chaire and 2 litle joyned stooles," "one cupboard of joyners worke," as well as a livery cupboard, pewter and earthenware, wooden dishes, two dozen "trenches," cooking utensils, a churn, beer vessels, and an old bible. In the chambers could be found a combination of bedding and storage, including household linen, two bedsteads with their furniture, an old trunk, six bushels of barley, a wheel and a pair of wool cards, a bushel of wool, and "2 bacon flickes."[28]

Parson William Harrison defines the structure of these early dwellings in broad terms when he writes in 1577 that "The greatest parte of our buylding in the cities and good townes of Englande consisteth onely of timber," and so it was particularly in Essex and Suffolk, where there was an absence of good building stone. The houses, even when not overambitious in scale, reflect the versatility as well as the limitations of timber framing. In contrast to later periods in which academic impulses quickened the renaissance of classicism both in England and America and cased the underlying house frame with applied ornament, we are dealing here with an almost fully exposed structure that reveals the carpenter's native skills.

At the heart of this study, then, lies the skeletal frame of the house itself, the timber core which defines plan and form (figure 10). Parson Harrison boasted in 1577 that "The auncient maners and houses of our gentlemen are yet and for the most part of strong tymber . . . in framing whereof our carpenters have beene and are worthilie preferred before those of like science among all other nations."[29] Oak was the traditional building material and its prodigal use aroused some fears of depletion in the sixteenth century. There seems, however, to have been little shortage in Essex at least until the closing years of Elizabeth's reign.[30]

The essential processes by which the house took shape, so far as we can determine, were perpetuated in the New World with very few modifications. The frame, as it "evolved through centuries of experience, was an ingenious equipoise of thrusts and stresses—firm, but not too rigid."[31] Ground-sills were sometimes laid on low foundation walls, sometimes without raised foundations. The timbers once felled were shaped with the axe and trimmed with the adz or sawn with the pit saw. Tenons were cut with a hand saw, mortices were made with an auger and squared with a mallet and chisel, and dowel holes were bored with the auger. The timbers were used soon after they were felled and were allowed to dry in situ, as is well attested by the character of the wood itself. Splits and checks will commonly be found in the larger timbers of oak, showing that they were used almost at once without benefit of thorough seasoning, in addition to which, contemporary incisions upon the surface of early wood will reveal, through microscopic in-

Figure 11. Derelict house near Kenton, Suffolk, Eng. Detail of gable end wall, probably seventeenth century. *Photo, Richard Cheek, 1975.*

Figure 12. Chester House, Knowle, Warwickshire, Eng. Detail of wattle and daub infill, mid-sixteenth century. *Photo, Christopher Owens, 1973.*

spection, that the marks were made when the timber was green and not yet dry. In further corroboration, Sir William Petre's surveyor wrote in 1566 of Chignall Hall in Essex that "it standeth nakedly without any defence from the winde and builded moostly with grene tymber, as yt semeth, for the houses [*sic*] yeld and shrink in every parte."[32]

The massive elements of the house frame, once assembled and prepared, were raised into place under the direction of the carpenters according to a carefully considered pattern or sequence of erection, a practice which persisted in rural New England until well into the nineteenth century. With the frame in an upright position the walls were made weathertight. The usual infilling of the walls of timbered houses was wattle and daub. The wattle in well-built houses was a close network made of sticks or riven staves firmly fixed between the studs, and either wedged into position or bound together. In poorer houses any

kind of hedge growth was used, often unbound. The daub, artfully prepared and making use of straw or the "cavings" from the threshing floor for binding, was then applied to the webwork, usually from both sides at the same time, and forced into the interstices. More layers were added until the panel was filled, and the surface was then finished with a coat of plaster and color washed (figures 11 and 12). The use of brick for the infilling of walls, often in herringbone patterns, did not become in any sense widespread in England until the seventeenth century (figure 13).

The roof of the small sixteenth-century English house consisted of pairs of common rafters, joined and pegged together at their apex without a ridge piece, and braced by a collar beam about a third of the way down their length, which is not unlike the manner in which roofs were framed in Massachusetts in the seventeenth century (and continuing in some instances into the nineteenth). The roof frame of the late medieval En-

glish house, however, was far more elaborate, and included one or more crown posts which rested on the tie beams and helped in turn to support a timber, known as the collar purlin, which ran the length of the roof under the collars. The crown post was normally braced into the collar purlin, and was often embellished in the more ambitious examples with a molded capital and base. The whole purpose of this construction was to impart longitudinal stability to the roof frame. In even the smaller open hall houses of the fifteenth and sixteenth centuries this soaring rhythmic expression of the carpenter's skill forms one of the chief delights of the building (figure 14). With the insertion of a chimney stack, accompanied by the almost universal flooring-in of the once open hall, this impressive structural display was hidden from view in dimly lit attics or sealed off entirely in the upper roof space. Once ferreted out, the early rafters with collars, collar purlin, and decorated crown posts, heavily soot-encrusted as a re-

Figure 13. Swans Hall, Hawkedon, Suffolk, Eng. Home of the first Abraham Browne of Watertown, Mass., ca. 1600. *Photo, Richard Burn, ca. 1959.*

Figure 14. Little Hall, Market Place, Lavenham, Suffolk, Eng. Detail of crown post and roof frame, fifteenth century. *Photo, Nedra Westwater, 1975.*

sult of the countless fires from the unenclosed hearth below, invariably betray the presence of a formerly open hall. This elaborate roof framing system, however, having through acknowledgment of the greater efficiency of side purlins become virtually obsolete by the second quarter of the seventeenth century, leaves no known traces among the transplanted English houses at Massachusetts Bay.

Like the insertion of the chimney stack the glazing of windows is, relatively speaking, a late

development in the small sixteenth-century English house. Parson William Harrison, writing of Essex in 1577, noted that "Of olde tyme our country houses in steede of glasse dyd use much lattis and that made eyther of wicker or fine riftes of oke in chekerwyse."[33] Windows in the simpler houses were small and entirely unglazed, their only refinement being a solid draw-shutter which could be pulled across the opening. Stout diamond-shaped oak mullions, set directly in the wall frame, provided some protection from intruders, but until late in the sixteenth century the choice was simple: an open window which admitted light, but also cold air, or a closed window and darkness. Glass was still somewhat rare, and

thus highly prized, when Wynkyn Grynrice, a Dutch shoemaker of Colchester, made his will in February of 1585 and provided that both "the waynscott and glase wyndowes in my howse wharin I nowe dwell shall nott be takyn owt of the howse."[34] Further, the original windows in the left-hand cross-wing of Raven's Farm in Woodham Walter, Essex, erected probably about 1600, were found during restoration in 1966 to have been still of the traditional open form with draw-shutters and diamond-shaped mullions, the latter, incidentally, discolored with soot where smoke had been allowed to belch forth (figure 15). For framed buildings as a whole in the more populous parts of England, however, the

Figure 15. Raven's Farm, Woodham Walter, Essex, Eng. Detail of original chamber window in service cross wing, ca. 1600. *Photo (during restoration), John E. Kimber, 1966.*

seventeenth century brought the luxury of leaded glazing to windows in many of the humbler houses.

Among the more striking exterior features of the modest postmedieval vernacular house, we may single out the not infrequent two-story enclosed porch, façade gables, and the projection of one story over another (figure 16). The use of the gable to break up a roof slope, "whether for attic accommodation or as a decorative feature, is a mark of late Elizabethan and Jacobean architecture."[35] Most conspicuous in important houses, it penetrated down to relatively small ones, and when oversailing the eaves was usually supported on variously shaped brackets which by the beginning of the seventeenth century tended to have a console profile (figure 17). The English call the familiar projection of one story over another a jetty, as did the seventeenth-century settlers of Massachusetts, though today in America the common designation is an overhang. This feature persisted throughout the seventeenth century in the Old World and the new and in its hewn, rather than framed, form can be found in isolated New England examples as late as the early nineteenth century. The ultimate and much debated origins have been explained in various ways. "The jetty was probably first used in towns where building space was more limited than in the country," we are told, "and the overhang provided a larger room in the upper storey,"[36] reaching almost absurd proportions as tall buildings in crowded towns, both in England and on the Continent, darkened the streets below with projecting upper stories which nearly converged. Urban contracts of the thirteenth and fourteenth centuries for jettied houses can be found, including a York contract in 1335 which calls for the building of a row of six timber houses with jetties on both sides.[37] Unless it can be shown that the

Figure 16. Church Hall, Broxted, Essex, Eng., ca. 1600, with earlier cross wing (at right).

Figure 17. Church Hall. Detail of bracket at cornice level. *Photo, Dennis H. Evans, 1968.*

Figure 18. House in Finchingfield, Essex, Eng., ca. 1600, with later additions. *Photo, Richard Cheek, 1975.*

jetty was as common from the start in the country as in the towns, one can see some real plausibility for the role which functions of space planning may have played in its evolution.

Purely structural reasons have been advanced, and these require careful scrutiny. It has been suggested, for example, that shorter posts were easier to obtain than long timbers, the full height of a house, though when superimposed, they would make a weak junction at floor level with the horizontal members. With projecting stories, however, shorter posts could be used satisfactorily, in addition to which the carpenter recognized such a system as a way of strengthening the frame of the house, for it gave him two places instead of one at which to make the necessary joints for the junction of posts with the horizontal girts.[38] These explanations, however, raise more questions than they answer. Certainly the jetty did not fundamentally strengthen the frame in such later postmedieval houses as Houchins Farm in Feering, Essex, of about 1600. Here the cantilevered crosspieces were simply lodged over and not framed into the girts, while at the opposite ends the rear posts, of a single three-story length, were weakened with just that multiplicity

of mortises which we are told this form of construction was designed to eliminate (figure 10).

In whatever importance we attach to the various theories put forward to explain the origin of the overhang, it must not be forgotten that we are dealing with timber and its inherent resilience, as opposed, for example, to nonresilient stone. Timber suggests cantilever possibilities. A formal development growing out of the nature of the material itself may have played some role at least at the beginning, and the results, which imparted an interesting play of light and shade to the wall surface, were found attractive and perpetuated. Pleasure in the appearance of a jettied house on the part of the client who could afford to pay for it

must have become a conscious factor,[39] and indeed, by the time of which we write, and for American expressions in particular, the question of origins is largely irrelevant. A seventeenth-century carpenter in Massachusetts would have been hard put to give any cogent explanation of the jetty's origins. Surely he continued a traditional English practice, and with respect to considerations of latter-day aesthetic appeal (in favor of purely functional reasons), it is noteworthy that the overhang at Massachusetts Bay appears almost invariably in those portions of the building where it will have good visual effect. It is, in fact, confined almost entirely to the front and/or exposed sides of the more ambitious dwellings.

Figure 19. House in Newport, Essex, Eng., sixteenth century, with seventeenth-century addition (at left).

For the English carpenter the jetty was affected in the early seventeenth century by the diminishing supply of timber. The great wave of new construction and conversion of older houses during Elizabeth's reign had markedly reduced the available supply of good oak, so that it became necessary to build on simpler lines.[40] The value of a load of timber had risen from 16s. 6d. in 1592 to as much as 21s. 2d. in the first decade of the next century, which understandably had its effects upon construction.[41] Robert Reyce, writing about 1603, tells us that in Suffolk

the carelesse wast . . . of our wonted plenty of timber, and other building stuffe, hath enforced the witt of this latter age to devise a new kind of compacting, uniting, coupling, framing, and building, with almost half the timber which was wont to bee used, and far stronger.[42]

Such a statement helps to explain, in part at least,

developments toward the end of the sixteenth century in which some two-story houses were being erected not with jetties but with all their walls reaching right up from foundation to roof. Examples of such houses without overhang in the late sixteenth and early seventeenth centuries can readily be found throughout East Anglia[43] (figure 18).

The diminution of timber in England and its consequent effects can easily be demonstrated in visual terms in houses such as that in Newport, Essex, where for the earlier portion, ca. 1500, we find massive studs closely spaced, and in an adjoining addition of about a century later, narrower studs spaced more widely (figure 19). Yet there is another factor to be taken into consideration here: throughout that period of social ferment which existed in Tudor England the joists, studs, and other framing members were more closely spaced by wealthy patrons for show. The

end of medievalism was lavish of timber, wasteful even, and now, in the seventeenth century, boastful overstatement was followed by restraint, aided and abetted by overriding factors of material economy.

Our transplanted English building practices in America coincide with the tag end of a remarkable centuries-long carpentry tradition in Great Britain. We may be grateful that a conservatism both rural and provincial and a plentiful supply of timber combined to preserve for a full century longer in New England a building style which, though its creative force was to some extent diminished, had nevertheless lost little of its native craftsmanship. The finishing of the timbers, their framing and jointing and decorative embellishment suffered but little in the best-built houses. At a comparable level for seventeenth-century England the picture has less surface appeal. While the humbler countryside farmhouse continued throughout this period to be derived fundamentally from earlier postmedieval models, as did its New England cousin, the lack of good building stuff proved a severe hobble.

Returning, however, to the still prolific years that marked the close of Elizabeth's reign, there is perhaps no more graphic picture of the English countryside, in Essex at least, than the maps drawn by John Walker, Sr., working between 1584 and 1616 (and in collaboration from 1600 with John Walker, Jr.). These colorful plats of estates and whole manors belong to the period immediately preceding the migrations to New England, and to a large degree reflect the environment as it was known to the earliest settlers during their childhood. While these maps, most of them for areas in northcentral Essex, have long been known, it has only recently been suggested that they may possess a hitherto unrecognized significance in the accuracy with which the cartographer has located and delineated buildings. Walker's representations of small vernacular buildings "show most accurately the general appearance of any one house—its type and the numbers and relative positions of such features as doors, windows, chimneys, wings and gables,"

Figure 20. Wells Cottage, Easthorpe, Essex, Eng., fifteenth or sixteenth century. (Before restoration.)

teenth century, at just that moment in history when the stage was being set for the exodus to New England. The English emigrants as a rule were people in early middle life who had been born at the beginning of that century or shortly after.[45] We have concerned ourselves with the mostly rural houses in which these settlers grew to man- and womanhood, the buildings that were freshest in their minds when they left England, and that many of them may have helped to build, alter, or repair.

"And now behold the severall Regiments of these Souldiers of Christ, as they are shipped for his service in the Westerne World,"[46] wrote Edward Johnson, a member of Winthrop's company, as that fleet set forth in the early spring of 1630. Although Endicott's settlement at Salem had occurred two years earlier, Winthrop's group constituted the first major influx of settlers at Massachusetts Bay. All alike, Johnson continues,

forsooke a fruitfull Land, stately Buildings, goodly Gardens, Orchards, yea, deare Friends, and neere relations, to goe to a desart Wildernesse, thousands of leagues by Sea . . . [where] the onely encouragements were the laborious breaking up of bushy ground, with the continued toyl of erecting houses, for themselves and cattell, in this howling desart; all which they underwent, with much cheerfulnesse, that they might enjoy Christ and his Ordinances in their primitive purity.[47]

While these sanctimonious phrases from the pen of a contemporary and participant in the New World venture furnish a principal motivation for the settlements in New England, more recent students have emphasized the economic motives that lay behind the mass migrations. The opening decades of the seventeenth century in England witnessed an increase in prices which operated more in favor of the large farmer than the small—with resulting unemployment and unrest. Craftsmen and husbandmen led revolts in the Midlands, while a decline in the cloth industry in East Anglia added financial pressures to the

as a comparison of existing buildings with the documentary evidence has revealed. In Walker's time nearly 60 percent of countryside houses were the single-story cottages of humble people. Nearly half of the remaining Walker houses are hall houses, with only one two-storied cross-wing containing a buttery and pantry on the ground floor and a chamber or chambers on its upper floor[44] (figure 20).

There is another important house form represented, however. In that detail from the map of the manor of Housham Hall, Matching, 1609, for example, which shows "Newlandes" (now, Newman's) End, we find a compact settlement of manorial tenants (figure 21). One notices at first glance the large proportion of single-story cottages with central chimneys. Ralph Rooke's house was a typical medieval hall house with one two-storied cross-wing. Of special interest, how-

ever, is that U-shaped range of buildings initialed E. G. for Edward Genninger. Two barns, an open cart shed, and still another out-building are shown in addition to the house itself, a two-and-one-half-story central-chimney structure with overhanging second story. A single-story outshot of some kind, a kitchen perhaps, is indicated at the right-hand end of the house. Such buildings represent in general outline the immediate forerunner of the seventeenth-century New England central-chimney house form.

In brief summary, then, we have traced those evolutionary aspects of the postmedieval English vernacular house that have the greatest significance for developments in the New World. We have laid particular stress upon the Housing Revolution in England, which reached a peak of building activity in the southeast during Elizabeth's reign and the opening years of the seven-

mounting bitterness associated with the religious persecutions in that area. Many of those who left England in the 1630s "had been torn from their deepest social ties by economic distress," though, indeed, "most of them, sympathetic to the cause of religious reform, feared persecution and sought a haven where they intended to build a godlier community."[48]

Among the predominantly middle and lower income emigrants we recognize the presence of a few persons of substance. The leaders of the exodus, men like Governor Winthrop, had indeed forsaken "stately Buildings" and "goodly Gardens." Nor is there a more poignant record of the initial hardships encountered upon their first setting down than that to be found in the opening lines of the letter written by Deputy Governor Thomas Dudley on March 12, 1631, to the Countess of Lincoln, in whose household he had served as steward: "I have . . . thought fit to commit to memory our present condition," he writes,

which I will do shortly, after my usual manner, and must do rudely, having yet no table, nor other room to write in than by the fireside upon my knee, in this sharp winter; to which my family must have leave to resort, though they break good manners, and make me many times forget what I would say, and say what I would not.[49]

Fascinating alike to the genealogist and social historian are the identities of the people who made up this heroic company—the man of quality and simple husbandman, the educated Puritan divine and the trained artisan. The names of Winthrop, Saltonstall, and Dudley are instantly familiar. But there are many others for whom history has accorded little or no recognition whatsoever. John Emery, for example, from Romsey in Hampshire, who set sail for the New World in 1635, aged thirty-four; Francis Bushnell from Berkshire the same year, aged twenty-six; William Carpenter, Sr. and Jr., from Wherwell in Hampshire, who arrived in 1638, the father then sixty-two, the son thirty-three; Ralph Mason from St. Olave's Southwark, aged thirty-five at the time of his leave-taking in 1635; and John Roper from

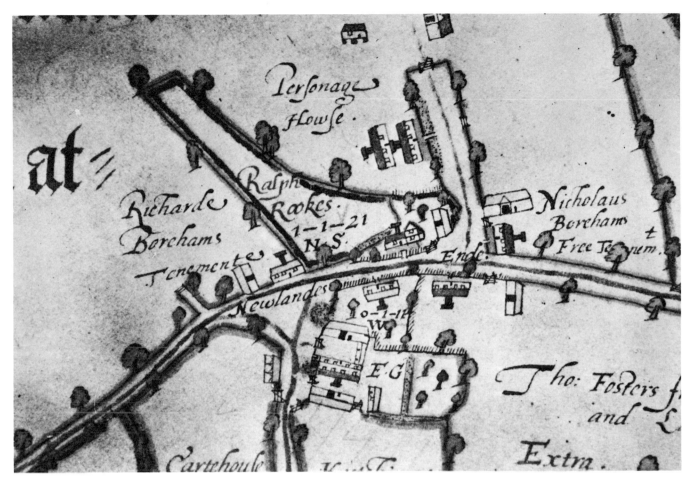

Figure 21. Manor of Housham Hall, Matching, Essex, Eng. Detail of "Newlandes Ende," 1609.

New Buckenham, Norfolk, aged twenty-six when his ship put into Massachusetts Bay in 1637.[50]

Why have we singled out these names from the embarcation rolls—names of men who seemingly share in common nothing more than that they were, with but one exception, all in their twenties or early thirties? They were also carpenters who had been born and apprenticed to their trade in old England—in all but a single case—*after* 1600. These and many others like them were the vital link in the transplantation of building ideas from the Old World to the new. These were

the men who wrestled with the unfamiliar environment as professional craftsmen and can be chiefly credited with whatever practical modifications and innovations occurred in the structures themselves. These were the men who trained a whole new generation which we may rightfully call the first native New England carpenters. And it was their tradition-rooted knowledge and acquired skills that established in this "howling desart" the building customs of postmedieval England that were to flourish at the vernacular level at least for yet another two centuries.

CHAPTER II

First Shelters and Indigenous Building Forms

THE EARLIEST New England writers, William Wood and Francis Higginson among them, lost no time in sending back to their friends at home verbose accounts of the areas selected for settlement. "The Bay of Massachusetts lyeth under the degree of fourty two and fourty three," wrote William Wood, "bearing South-west from the Lands end of England: at the bottome whereof are situated most of the English plantations." Although he points out that "it may be objected that it is too cold a Countrey for our English men, who have been accustomed to a warmer Climate," and that "The Summers be hotter than in England,"[1] he nevertheless parades before the prospective planter a beguiling catalogue of inducements, from which much is learned, incidentally, of the differences among the varieties of timber then available to the settlers.

Closely linked with the formal literature, much of it promotional, are the more intimate reports —the letters, later reminiscences, and above all, the vastly revealing day-by-day record of occurrences in Governor Winthrop's Journal. All alike stress the almost unendurable hardships experienced by the sea-weary colonists in the first months ashore, no matter at what time of year they disembarked. An average voyage took at least

twelve weeks, with only the basic necessities aboard ship. Further, and despite their best planning efforts, each successive vessel packed with newcomers sharply intensified the problem of keeping the whole company properly provisioned until the first planted crops brought forth their fruit.

Under such circumstances there could be little consideration of any but the most unaspiring forms of housing. As a consequence there was an interval of several months at least during which the settlers made shift to shelter themselves in ways which must have been largely unfamiliar and surely substandard in light of their accustomed lodgings at home. This phase is admittedly more interesting for its sociological than its architectural implications. It is important, nevertheless, to reiterate what is and what is not known about the earliest impermanent shelters at Massachusetts Bay, if only to correct long-standing misconceptions and to point up the sharp contrast these rude structures present to the professionally built timber-framed houses which the English erected just as soon as possible.

The simplest of the temporary shelters were makeshift indeed. The obituary in 1732 of Deacon Bartholomew Green, printer of *The Boston News-Letter*, mentions that his father, Captain Samuel Green, who landed at Charlestown in 1630, together with several others "were for some Time glad to lodge in empty Casks to shelter them from the Weather, for want of Housing."[2] Quite naturally, too, they may well have then and even later made use of caves, as reported by more than one nineteenth-century antiquarian. The Reverend William Bentley of Salem, for example, writes on Setember 9, 1817, when visiting Cape Ann that "Near Streightsmouth we were led to the Cellar over which once stood the house of Mr. Norwood an early settler, and on the opposite side the Cavern which was in use before the building was finished."[3]

Far more common were "Tents of Cloath" and "Canvis Boothes,"[4] which must have readily recommended themselves to the practical-minded emigrant who gave the matter any serious thought before venturing upon the New World. Edward Howes, for example, in contemplating his voyage, wrote from England to John Winthrop, Jr., on August 13, 1633, "I heare from you noe comendations of a tent which I conceive to be a necessary thinge with you. A man may buye one here for about ten pounds, and the fraight to you wilbe but small."[5] They were surely a familiar part of the landscape at the beginning.

The town records of Charlestown, for example, tell us that "The multitude set up cottages, booths and tents about the Town Hill,"[6] and Governor Winthrop records dejectedly in mid-winter 1631 that "The poorer sort of people (who lay long in tents, etc.) were much afflicted with the scurvy."[7]

Cottages are perhaps the most difficult of the temporary shelters to visualize and define. The term "cottage" by itself does not suggest precise architectural characteristics in England or America, and we can only guess what types of shelter the word was intended to describe. They cannot have been very substantial, for the Charlestown records, referring to the increase of scurvy, ascribe the cause to the settlers' "wet lodging in their cottages."[8] The question is further complicated by the not infrequent use of the terms "huts" and "wigwams" in the early documents. Edward Johnson, for example, writing about 1650, reports of the company's first landing at Charlestown that the colonists "pitched some Tents of Cloath, other built them small Huts, in which they lodged their Wifes and Children,"[9] and planter Roger Clap tells us that Winthrop's band "lived many of them in tents and wigwams at Charlestown, their meeting-place being abroad under a tree."[10]

References to huts and wigwams require careful scrutiny. It has been suggested that such habitations were not "uniquely the result of pioneer conditions in a new world, forcing the adoption of existing native types or the spontaneous creation of others adapted to the environment," but rather, a "transplantation . . . of types current in England, still characteristic then of the great body of minor dwellings in the country districts."[11] This principal is supported by illustrations of charcoal burners' huts in South Yorkshire and bark-peelers' huts from High Furness, presumably late nineteenth or early twentieth century in date.[12] Another modern example found near Sheffield was made of thin poles in the form of a cone, interlaced with brushwood and covered with sods laid with the grass toward the inside. Herein, perhaps, lies the crux of the matter,

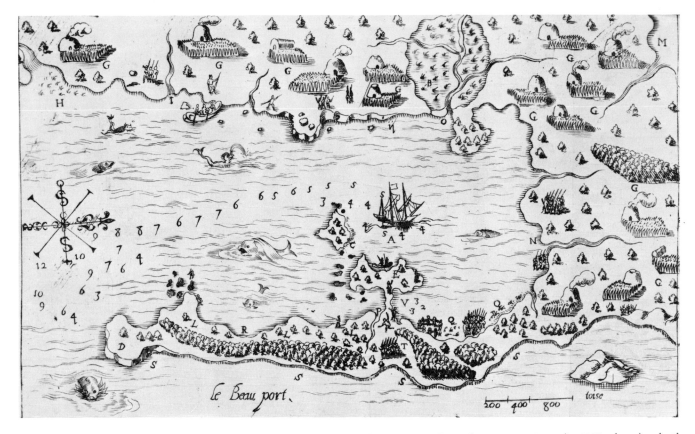

Figure 22. Harbor, Gloucester, Mass., in 1606, showing both round and arborlike Indian dwellings.

for such structures are described as "wigwam-shaped," borrowing a term from the New World. Nowhere, however, is it acknowledged that the wigwam of the indigenous New England Indian did not take the form of the tepee found among the American Indians of the western plains.

There remains, nevertheless, a more than reasonable possibility that the long vanished "huts" of the first English settlers in America do bear some direct relation to those impermanent sod houses of considerable antiquity which are known in certain areas of Great Britain. While no immediate parallel can be found in the early records for Massachusetts Bay, we can cite at least one circumstantial description of the period for purposes of comparison. Cornelius Van Tienhoven, secretary of the Province of New Netherland, wrote in 1650 that

Those in New Netherland and especially in New England, who have no means to build farmhouses at first according to their wishes, dig a

square pit in the ground, cellar fashion, six or seven feet deep, as long and as broad as they think proper, case the earth inside all round the wall with timber . . . floor this cellar with plank and wainscot it overhead for a ceiling, raise a roof of spars clear up and cover the spars with bark or green sods, so that they can live dry and warm in these houses with their entire families for two, three and four years.[13]

With no more adequate picture of these transient hovels, however, we can only suggest that the newly arrived Englishmen may indeed have borrowed from some long-familiar subvernacular building traditions in throwing together the rude structures which were to shelter them for the first winter at least.

Wigwams are another matter altogether. Those who contend that the colonists' primitive sod

Figure 23. Pioneer Village, Salem, Mass., 1930.

huts were of European derivation reason that they transferred to these the term "wigwam," which described the Indians' distinctive dwelling of poles and boughs or mats. There is actually some justification for such a theory in the contemporary statement by Edward Johnson that the English newcomers

> burrow themselves in the Earth for their first shelter under some Hill-side, casting the Earth aloft upon Timber; they make a smoaky fire against the Earth at the highest side, and . . . in these poore Wigwames they sing Psalmes, pray and praise their God, till they can provide them houses.[14]

The reference is unique, however, and one may convincingly argue that the English did in fact, adopt or adapt the Indian's native house form. They were surely curious about the behavior and artifacts of the native inhabitants and described the dwellings in particular detail (figure 22). Indian "houses" which the Pilgrims in nearby Plymouth Colony found on Cape Cod in 1620

> were made with long yong Sapling trees, banded and both ends stucke into the ground; they were made round, like unto an Arbour, and covered downe to the ground with thicke and well wrought matts, and the doore was not over a yard high, made of a matt to open; the chimney

was a wide open hole in the top, for which they had a matt to cover it close when they pleased; one might stand and go upright in them, in the midst of them were foure little trunches knockt into the ground, and small stickes laid over, on which they hung their Pots, and what they had to seeth. . . . The houses were double matted, for as they were matted without, so were they within, with newer and fairer matts.[15]

It was the task of the Indian women, writes William Wood in 1634, to build the wigwams, and in the summer time "they gather flagges, of which they make [the] Matts." These were "close-wrought mats of their owne weaving which deny entrance to any drop of raine, though it come both fierce and long, neither can the piercing North winde find a crannie, through which he can conveigh his cooling breath."[16]

How literally the first planters may have copied the native dwellings we shall probably never know. That they appropriated the term itself is beyond question. One Jonathan Gatchell, for example, reported in 1677 that he had lived in Marblehead when old John Goit first came there, forty years or more before, and that Goit first built a wigwam and lived there till he got a house.[17] Often the references are calamitous. One Finch, of Watertown, "had his wigwam burnt and all his goods," writes Governor Winthrop on September 30, 1630,[18] and Thomas Dudley a year or so later laments the inflammability of "English wigwams, which have taken fire in the roofs covered with thatch or boughs."[19] To what extent, if any, the term "English wigwam" represented modification of the native form is also open to question. The recreation at Salem Village in the 1930s of shelters modeled after the Indian wigwam may very well be accurate, though certain features are based entirely on conjecture (figure 23). It was assumed, for example, that an Englishman living in one of these structures during the winter season would more likely build a fireplace of stone or brick and a chimney of wood and clay than

The Framed Houses of Massachusetts Bay

"allow the smoke from his fire to find its way out through a hole in the roof in the Indian fashion," and that a door would have been installed as a suitable substitute for the Indian mat lifted upon entering.[20] Edward Johnson, however, writing about 1650, refers back to the period of earliest settlement in Cambridge "when they had scarce houses to shelter themselves, and no doores to hinder the Indians accesse to all they had in them."[21]

Yet to be found in connection with a seventeenth-century structure, but common enough in the eighteenth century, is the use of birch bark for the flashing of board joints, especially those of the roof, before applying shingles. Writing in 1634 William Wood refers to Indian "Cannows . . . made of thinne Birch-rines, close ribbed on the in-side with broad thinne hoopes,"[22] and clearly, this practical application of so plentiful a natural commodity in New England must have been obvious to the colonists. We can only conjecture whether its later use among English-descended carpenters has some direct derivation from Indian practices. In any event, students of vernacular building in England have not as yet encountered the phenomenon there.

Nor must we forget the continuing presence of the Indian wigwam at Massachusetts Bay after the "English wigwam" had been abandoned by the European settlers for the traditional English framed house. While radically reduced in numbers through a "mortality" which raged during the presettlement years and by the later Indian wars, the native population remained a distinct part of the picture throughout the seventeenth century, and the wigwam of the aborigines was a not uncommon ingredient of the landscape. The town records in Dedham, for one example among many, make reference in 1664 to "Noannets wigwame" on the north side of the Charles River,[23] and at an even later date Samuel Sewall records in 1688 the tragic death of three Indian children, who "being alone in a Wigwam at Muddy-River [Brookline], the Wigwam fell on fire, and burnt them."[24]

An early dwelling form about which very little is known, the "palisado" house with walls constructed of upright sticks of timber, is mentioned in the records of both Plymouth Colony and Massachusetts Bay. The Reverend John Lothrop tells us, for example, that when he arrived at Scituate, "which was aboute [the] end of Sept. 1634," he found only nine houses in that infant community, "all which [were] small plaine pallizadoe Houses."[25] And when the three Sprague brothers who had landed first at Salem arrived at Charlestown in the summer of 1628, "they found but one English palisadoed and thatched house."[26] In Plymouth Colony in 1647 a thief entered the house of one John Crocker "by putting aside some loose pallizadoes on the Lords day," though the term as used here may refer only to palisado fences surrounding a given property.[27] This was perhaps the case with that early building in Revere which Samuel Maverick reports about 1660 was "yet standing there which is the Antientest house in the Massachusetts Government. a house which in the yeare 1625 I fortified with a Pillizado and flankers and gunnes both belowe and above in them."[28] Further, the Essex County court records in 1641 refer to a defective fence in which were found "some pallizadoes loose and some rotten."[29] Nevertheless, we have descriptions of walls composed of pales at an early date in England,[30] and more important yet, there is a mid-nineteenth-century description of some such construction which had survived at Yarmouth on Cape Cod until about 1840:

This house was built by taking large sticks of timber for sills and plates, boring two paralled [sic] rows of holes in each, about six inches apart, excepting where doors or windows were to be placed, and filling between [the vertical pales] with stones and clay.[31]

Lacking both the structures themselves and more extensive documentation, the question raised by the term "palisado" may be passed over. It is perhaps more to the point to stress here how quickly the colonists sought to provide themselves wherever possible with proper housing. Francis Higginson found when he came to Salem in the summer of 1629 that there were "about half a score houses, and a fair house newly built for the Governor [John Endicott]. . . . We that are settled at Salem," he adds, "make what haste we can to build houses, so that within a short time we shall have a fair town."[32] And at Charlestown, despite the initial discouragements, Governor Winthrop in July of 1630 "ordered his house to be cut and framed,"[33] one of the earliest unequivocal references at Massachusetts Bay to building practices which would soon become the rule.

Thereafter timber-framed houses sprang up almost at once as soon as new communities were settled in every part of the Massachusetts Bay area. By mid-century, twenty years after his arrival, Edward Johnson could write that "the Lord hath been pleased to turn all the wigwams, huts, and hovels the English dwelt in at their first coming, into orderly, fair, and well-built houses, well furnished many of them, together with Orchards filled with goodly fruit trees, and gardens with variety of flowers."[34] While surviving structures are most often found in open country and in the smaller towns, we must be keenly aware at all times of the city which became the central core and capital of Massachusetts Bay. The settlers at Charlestown, we are told, found no good sources of water, a fact which contributed to the general state of poor health. At which point there enters the narrative one William Blaxton, a Master of Arts of Cambridge University, who had sought out the solitude of the New World some years earlier and established himself across the river on the western slope of what is now Beacon Hill. When affairs had reached something of an impasse in Charlestown, it was Mr. Blaxton, "dwelling . . . alone, at a place by the Indians called *Shawmutt*," who informed Winthrop of an excellent spring there. Whereupon the governor and the larger part of his company "removed thither; whither . . . the frame of the Governor's house, in preparation" at Charlestown, was carried also. Here, the early chronicle continues, as that first summer of 1630 ripened into autumn, the people "began to build their houses against winter; and this place was called Boston."[35]

CHAPTER III

The House Plan

OUR KNOWLEDGE OF house plans for the earliest period at Massachusetts Bay is based on a few extant buildings, an equally small number of building contracts, and room-by-room inventories. To the extent that they form a restricted body of evidence, they cannot help us in determining the incidence of plan types. Only the inventories can be said to represent a comprehensive sampling, though one cannot stress sufficiently the dangers in attempting to erect houses upon foundations imagined from these reports of household contents.

The two most common plans in contracts, inventories, and the actual houses from the first century of settlement are the single-room and two-room plans, though both may have been more complex than we have realized (figures 24 and 25). For the simpler of these there is recorded evidence in the form of a contract in 1640 between John Davys, joiner, who sailed from London for Boston in April 1635 when he was twenty-nine years of age, and one William Rix. Davys agreed to build a framed house for Rix in the vicinity of the present Haymarket Square in Boston, "16 foot long and 14 foote wyde . . . the Chimney framed without dawbing to be done with hewen timber."[1]

The typical house of one-room plan for the ear-

liest decades and into the eighteenth century remained more or less uniform. Of at least seventy dwellings for which dimensions are given in documents from 1637 to 1706, thirty-nine were obviously of this variety. Only two were less than fifteen feet square. Seventeen measured from twenty-two to twenty-eight feet in length (clearly including a chimney bay) with a width for the most part of eighteen to twenty feet, dimensions which readily coincide with the oldest surviving houses of unquestioned one-room plan in the area: the Deane Winthrop house, Winthrop, ca. 1638–1650 (24' × 18'); the Austin Lord house, Ipswich, built before 1653 (25' × 18'); and the Whipple house, Ipswich, ca. 1655 (27½' × 19').

It is tempting to categorize this basic form as one having peculiar appeal for persons of limited means and few material possessions, and the probate records tend to confirm such a claim. For the counties of Suffolk, Middlesex, and Essex during the period 1630 to 1660, ten estates out of thirteen representing houses almost surely of one-room plan range in value from £15 to £163. Of twenty-seven inventories which list estate totals for houses of two-room plan, only four fall below £100; the remaining twenty-three range between £112 and £1,506.

The one-room plan cannot be associated ex-

clusively with persons of moderate means, however. Well-to-do John Whipple of Ipswich, a deputy to the General Court, apparently found the one-room plan a practical starting point. Indeed, a significant proportion of surviving seventeenth-century two-room, central-chimney houses at Massachusetts Bay commenced life as dwellings of single-room plan. Clearly, the immediate need for shelter under pioneer conditions, with no other housing available as was the case in England, seems to have dictated for many of the settlers at every class or economic level a simple single-unit dwelling for a start, to be soon enlarged as their situation in life improved.

Without exception the earliest surviving houses of one-room plan at Massachusetts Bay have been added to, and most of them were enlarged not once but several times. The first extension was normally in a longitudinal direction, and the first colonists were surely familiar with this contemporary English concept. As early as 1638 Samuel Cole of Boston sold to Captain Robert Sedgwick of Charlestown "all that parte of the new house wherein the said Samuel lately dwelled . . . and the old house adjoyning," the language of the conveyance suggesting a house which had been enlarged in a longitudinal direction.[2] In 1652 William Heath of Roxbury left to

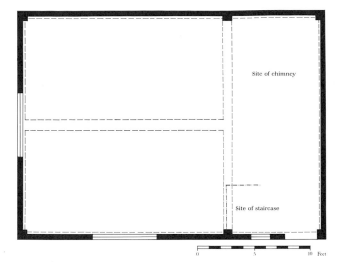

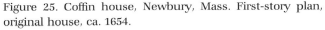

Figure 25. Coffin house, Newbury, Mass. First-story plan, original house, ca. 1654.

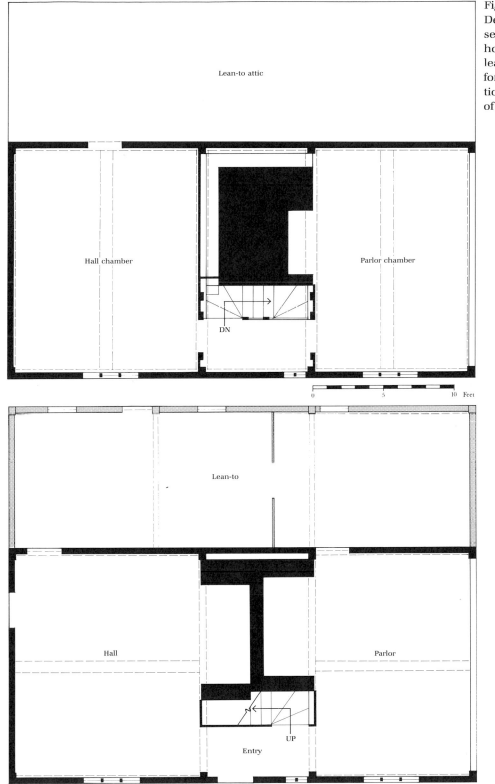

Figure 24. Fairbanks house, Dedham, Mass. First- and second-story plans, original house, ca. 1637, with rear lean-to added probably before 1668. (Room designations suggested by inventory of 1668.)

his wife "the newe end of my house that I nowe dwell in both above and below" and to a son the "old end of my dwelling house."[3] And in a 1659 building contract for an addition to an existing house, William Averill, carpenter, agreed to undertake for Richard Jacob of Ipswich "one Bay of building of 18 foot square and 13 foot in the stud." For reasons best known to the carpenter and his client the older house was to be moved over and the addition erected upon its site. Testimony offered in connection with a suit to compel Averill to live up to the terms of his contract dwells not unexpectedly upon the complications which this decision produced.[4]

Although inventories for the period 1630 to 1660 show only thirteen houses of presumed single-room plan as opposed to thirty-five of two-room, basically hall/parlor disposition, the buildings themselves tell a different story. Among a total of 144 houses erected before 1725 at Massachusetts Bay in which the structural evidence has been observed and recorded, eighty-two, more than one-half, were built originally on a one-room or half-house plan, all but a mere handful of which were later enlarged by the addition of one or more rooms, usually in a longitudinal direction. Clearly, then, a number of the structures with a two-room layout in the inventories achieved that status through growth. Further, the

The House Plan

Figure 26. Ivory Boardman house, Saugus, Mass., probably after 1725. Demolished ca. 1925.

distribution of dates among the 144 houses reveals that practical-minded New Englanders in established towns and newly settled communities as well continued to build one-room or half houses and then enlarge them throughout the seventeenth century and indeed well into the eighteenth century, although numerous later examples of the form have come down to us basically unaltered (figure 26).

We should not conclude, however, that houses of two-room plan evolved invariably from single-room beginnings. The two-room, central-chimney plan was fully developed in England by this period, and New England's earliest surviving frame dwelling, the Fairbanks house in Dedham, ca. 1637, falls into this classification (figure 24). Its outer measurements are thirty-four feet nine inches by sixteen feet six inches, similar to the seventy houses at Massachusetts Bay for which relatively uniform dimensions are recorded between 1637 and 1706. Of twenty houses of apparent two-room, central-chimney plan, the width is consistently sixteen to twenty feet, while the length is thirty to thirty-five feet in ten examples (one of which was a poorhouse built by the town with a width of only fourteen feet) and thirty-six to fifty feet in fifteen examples. Of the latter, nine are to be found among those eleven

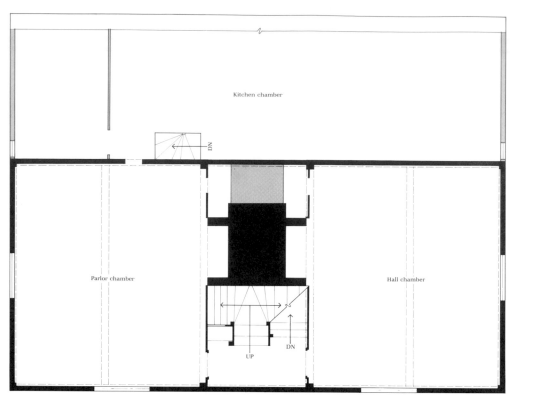

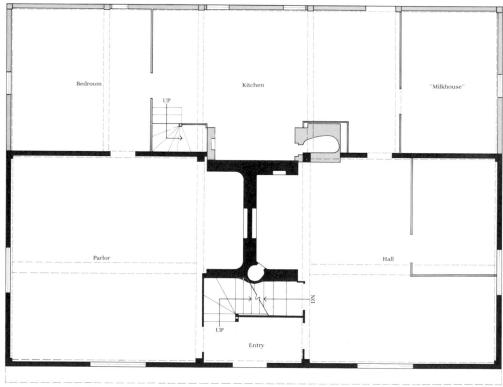

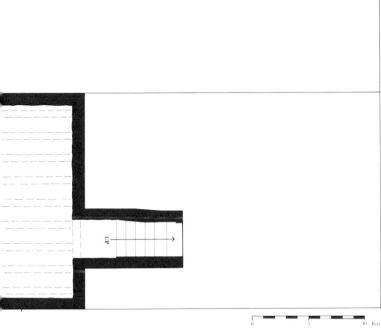

Figure 27. Boardman house, Saugus, Mass. First- and second-story and cellar plans, original house, ca. 1687, with rear lean-to added before 1696. (Room designations suggested by inventory of 1696.)

houses built by communities for their minister.

Variants of the standard two-room, central-chimney plan existed. One such emerges clearly from the letter written by Samuel Symonds to John Winthrop, Jr., in 1638 concerning the house which Symonds wished to have built on his farm in Ipswich. "I am indiferent," he wrote, "whether it be 30 foote or 35 foote long 16 or 18 foot broade." This would have brought it in any event to virtually the same overall dimensions of the Fairbanks house, though there were distinctive differences between these contemporary structures of two-room plan, especially in the position of the chimneys. "I would have wood chimneys at each end," continued Symonds, and he was willing to let them be "all the breadth of the house, if you thinke good." He then specified two doors "to be in the middle of the howse one opposite to the other," an arrangement reminiscent of earlier rather than later postmedieval planning.[5] The introduction of the central or axial chimney into the East Anglian farmhouse, and its almost universal acceptance in New England as reflected in the plan of the Fairbanks house, led at once to a rethinking of the placement for a back door, which earlier in England had been located opposite the front entrance at the far end of the cross passage. At the Fairbanks house the hall to the left has an original doorway in the rear wall near the corner post, while at the Boardman house in Saugus, ca. 1687, an original exterior doorway in the hall to the right, leading at present into the later rear lean-to, is not far from the chimney post (figures 24 and 27).

Another solution occurs in connection with the seventeenth-century house in Salem built by Abraham Cole. His will of 1715 describes a structure of two-room, central-chimney plan, and a court deposition in 1754, made by a person who had lived in a neighboring house before 1692, informs us that "there were two steps or stairs without the East end of said Coles house upon the raised way . . . which led into a Door at said end of said house."[6] Similarly, the White-Ellery house in Gloucester, erected ca. 1710, has an original doorway forty-four inches wide in the end wall of the integral lean-to. In terms of surviving physical evidence, however, such arrangements are not common. A second egress located in the rear wall of one or another of the principal rooms or of the lean-to seems to have been the more common situation.

The plan of Symond's farmhouse in Ipswich has flexibility in the definition of interior space:

> The staiers I thinke had best be placed close by the dore. It makes noe great matter though there be noe particion upon the first flore. If there be, make one bigger then the other. . . . In this story over the first, I would have a particion, whether in the middest or over the particion under I leave it; In the garrett no particion.[7]

The hall of the Fairbanks house is thirteen feet two inches wide by fifteen feet eight inches deep while the parlor at the right was only eleven feet wide as first built. Here, then, is early documentary and actual proof of the dimensioning of rooms to accommodate the functional needs of the occupants. Despite the fact that the Blake house in Dorchester, ca. 1650, is quite symmetrical, with the hall and parlor each measuring fourteen feet four inches in width by nineteen feet four inches in depth, one normally finds some degree of asymmetry through the seventeenth century and even later.

The present stairs at the Fairbanks house, which ascend in front of the chimney, are later, and indeed, the present entry, seven feet three inches wide within the posts by six feet deep, is sufficiently cramped to have permitted only a very narrow staircase (figure 24). Nevertheless, if the clapboardlike siding of oak applied to the east wall of the stairwell is early, then the presence of a pre-existing, similar stairwell is assured. The absence of any floor overhead in the second-story entry in front of the chimney suggests that the attic has always been accessible, as it is to this day, by ladder only. There is very little structural indication among existing houses that ladders were used to get from the first to the second story. Such may have originally been the case, however, at the Fairbanks house and for some of the less well-constructed buildings of the period which have not survived. While we know little of the character and quality of the house belonging to Jonathan Hardman in Ipswich, a court case in 1650 would suggest that if not in an unfinished state, its appointments may well have been as primitive as the manners of its occupants. Dorothy Prey, aged about sixteen years, deposed that one John Bond had come to Hardman's house and that he had drunk too much wine or beer, so that he could not sit upon his stool. On a subsequent occasion Bond had taken her in his arms and carried her forcibly out of the kitchen into another room on the same floor. There was a short ladder of about four or five rounds that went up into the room overhead, continues the deposition. She ran up this ladder, but the boards not being laid on the upper floor, she "went"

Figure 28. Coffin house, Newbury, Mass., ca. 1654, with eighteenth-century additions.

down into the room from which she was first taken.[8]

The main stairs of the Fairbanks house, though later, occupy a location opposite the front entrance. This position was to become absolutely traditional in Massachusetts, and is clearly derived from English practice, despite the fact that the stairs in many contemporary East Anglian farmhouses are often found behind the stack. The choice of a site for the stairs at the front of the house was probably influenced by the vital role the chimney was to play in a cold climate. When additions were projected at the back of the house, the logical place for the new fireplace was butting up against the rear surface of the chimney where, in so many English examples, the stairs and/or a passage will be found.

While in New England the stairs were almost invariably erected in front of the chimney, one notable exception existed at the Coffin house in Newbury, ca. 1654, where there is a small window to the left of the present door between the two

stories which must have originally lighted a stairwell[9] (figure 28). A patch of disturbed boarding in the floor of the chamber lends further support to the argument, but there is no other trace of this exceptional arrangement, for which, quite naturally, English precedent can readily be found, and the present stairs of later date ascend in the normal position against the chimney.

The Blake house in Dorchester, of central-chimney, two-room plan, is only slightly larger than the Fairbanks house, measuring thirty-nine by twenty feet nine inches, and its chimney bay measures seven feet two inches in width within the posts. The half-house, on the other hand, reveals significant differences in the width of the chimney bay. In the Deane Winthrop house in Winthrop, for example, and the Pierce house in Dorchester, ca. 1650, the original end-chimney bays measure only five feet two inches and five feet in width, respectively, within the posts. While such narrow bays could easily accommodate a chimney with fireplaces of sufficient depth to serve both the room below and its chamber, and the remaining space in front of the stack could

with some ingenuity be fitted with a staircase composed all of winders and a miniscule entry as well, it was surely a short-sighted concept. The entries of the Deane Winthrop, Pierce, and Whipple houses, and others as well, had to be widened when enlargements were projected at the chimney end of the original house and the chimney itself was increased in size (figure 29). In some of the earlier houses with a restricted chimney bay, the planning arrangements for this space may have been exceptional. Mortises in the chimney tie beam of the Deane Winthrop house, for example, suggest that the area in front of the chimney was floored over at the start—which means, of course, that one must look elsewhere than against the stack for original access to the attic. In any case, the chimney bay as a general rule continued to be narrower in the house of single-room or end-chimney plan, one of the narrowest on record being that of the John Holton house in Danvers, erected probably about 1700, which is only thirty-nine and one half inches within the posts.

For the period 1630–1660 only thirteen possible examples are found in the inventories which suggest a one-room plan. The actual proportion was probably much larger. Many of the simpler inventories without mention of rooms, which record the possessions of persons at the lower end of the economic scale, probably represent hall houses of one-room plan. The term hall, which designates an all-purpose area for cooking, eating, and living, is thoroughly consonant with English practice. As late as the 1630s cooking equipment could still be found there, despite the fact that the kitchen had increasingly become an integral part of the house. In six of the thirteen inventories of one-room plan the best bed is located in the chamber, which here in most cases probably meant an upper room, while four at least place the best bed in the hall or lower room, with the cooking gear and furniture for daily use. And in six of these houses of presumed single-room plan where either the best bed or simply bedding is found in the chamber, grain and/or storage items will be found there as well.

Of the remaining eighty-nine room-by-room inventories between 1630 and 1660, the majority reflect either houses of two-room plan, with or without additional service rooms, or more ambitious houses. One assumes that the simpler two-room examples were of the central-chimney variety, which is the case with nearly all extant seventeenth-century timber-framed houses of two-room plan. The earliest inventory for the Fairbanks house is not until 1668. The two principal rooms of the original central-chimney portion are called the hall and parlor, terms which were more or less standard throughout the period. The rooms above are described as hall chamber and parlor chamber (figure 24). The hall, upon rare occasions, will be referred to as the "fire room," and at least one later Roxbury inventory of 1693 describes a house consisting of parlor and "Dwelling roome" with a chamber over each.[10] The parlor then, as later in the nineteenth century, was the "best" room, and consistently included the occupants' more valuable furnishings. It was also the room which contained the parents' bed.

While the single-room plan was conceived of normally as a hall house, and the single-room unit added on the opposite side of the chimney thus logically became the parlor, this was not invariably the case. The Story house in Essex, ca. 1684, reveals one set of complications which might arise when the reverse process occurred. The single lower room of the dwelling as first erected functioned apparently as a hall, and its fireplace was furnished with an oven in the front corner. When, in the early eighteenth century, the house was enlarged and extended, the new room became the hall. Its fireplace, backing onto the original stack, was also furnished with an oven— or more correctly, utilized the existing hall oven with a new opening broken through the latter's rear wall and the original opening bricked up (figure 30). The earlier hall was then presumably converted to the function of a parlor.

Taken as a whole, inventories for houses of two-room plan between 1630 and 1660 reflect ongoing evolutionary changes in the living habits of

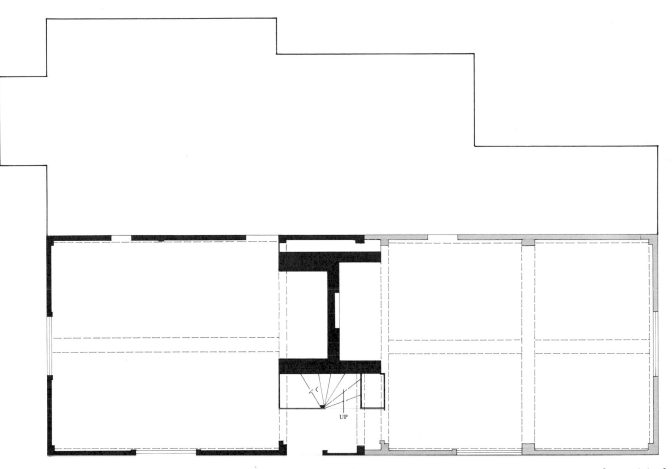

Figure 29. Whipple house, Ipswich, Mass. First-story plan, original house, ca. 1655 (at left), with parlor range added before 1683. (Lean-to rooms not delineated.) (Above)

Figure 30. Story house, Essex, Mass. First-story plan, original house, ca. 1684 (at right), with hall range and service bay added ca. 1725. Demolished 1957. (Below)

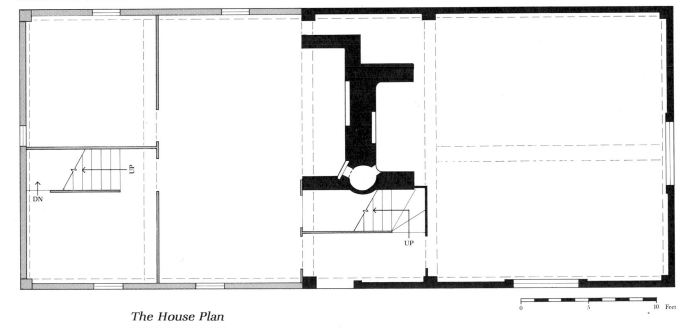

The House Plan

the occupants which are thoroughly in keeping with trends in old England. Of thirty-five inventories, twenty-two reveal the presence of cooking equipment and sometimes bedding in one of the two ground-floor rooms, with bedding of highest value for the head of the household and more formal furniture in the other room, including unlocated chambers. Upper chambers, when they occur, are normally given over to bedding of less value and storage of barrels, skins, grain, provisions, yarn, spinning and weaving equipment, and "lumber," that archaic term for odds and ends. In seven cases in which the chambers are clearly identified as second-story, however, the best bedding is found there, together with suitably formal furnishings. These individual differences may easily reflect regional practices in England. In the far western counties, for example, the upstairs chamber, whether over the hall or another room, was during the sixteenth century the principal sleeping room.[11] By the early seventeenth century, in southeastern England at least, the parlor had become the principal ground-floor sleeping room, and this continues to be its chief function in Massachusetts as reflected in the inventories for houses with a plan of two or more rooms. William Bentley, the Salem diarist, noted in 1812 that during the seventeenth century "no families or heads of families lodged on the second stories."[12] Indeed, the ground-floor parlor remained the master bedroom for the head of the family into the eighteenth and even in some cases into the nineteenth century in rural areas.[13] Any occasional variation, beyond a possible derivation from English regional practices, may best be explained in socioeconomic terms. It is only among the most and least well-to-do (the latter particularly when occupying houses of one-room plan) that we find the principal ground-floor lodging room for the head of the family deserted in favor of upper apartments. Those examples in the higher economic bracket would seem to foreshadow social usages which we associate with the more formal houses of the eighteenth century.

The most impressive fact derived from a review of inventories is the number of instances, thirteen in all, in which the term kitchen has replaced that of hall, a process which has been described as a "new habit" in Norfolk in the 1630s. For Sussex also two inventories of 1632 can be cited in which the room for living and cooking that one would expect to be called the hall is now called the kitchen. "These are the earliest instances of what later became a widespread [English] practice, to downgrade the hall to a kitchen where it continued to be used for cooking."[14] Massachusetts was not far behind. The home of John Winthrop, Jr., in Ipswich, inventoried about 1635, consisted of a parlor which contained the best bed and a "kyttchin" with fireplace implements and cooking equipment. There were chambers over each with bedding.[15] For the second half of the century, 107 rural Suffolk County inventories between 1661 and 1700 reveal the presence of cooking equipment in the hall or its equivalent in only seventeen houses where the other principal living room is the parlor and in only one case where there was also a kitchen. This example occurs not unexpectedly before 1670. During the same period at least ten additional houses disclose the presence of cooking paraphernalia in a buttery or a lean-to, presumably stored there for use in the hall. Significantly, however, these same items, often accompanied with fireplace implements, are found in that room called the kitchen in forty-one houses, of which twenty-seven are fundamentally of two-room plan. In all but five cases, in fact, these are parlor/kitchen houses. Here the hall has clearly become the kitchen in name if nothing else.

When we examine those enclosed spaces which were subsidiary to the mass of the house or an appendage to it, we find that the planning vocabulary of the seventeenth-century builder was by no means restricted to a limited range of stock solutions. The inventories, while admittedly incapable of conjuring up precise tectonic shapes, do nevertheless suggest unusual house forms and planning arrangements, whether of one build or several, and these include especially the service rooms which appear almost at once at

Massachusetts Bay. The house of Thomas Beechar at Charlestown, for example, contained in 1637 a hall and kitchen with a chamber over each and a "milkhows" as well with a room over that.[16] The hall to the left of the entrance at the Fairbanks house is important for the evidence it preserves of two adjoining original doorways in the northwest corner (figure 24). That in the west end wall near the rear corner post was apparently an inner doorway from the start. Did it lead originally to a small outshot containing a service room? If so, later additions here have obliterated the evidence. The door frame in the rear wall, chamfered and weathered on its outer surface, was an exterior door. It now gives access to the lean-to which must have been added soon to the original house. We cannot be certain of the first uses of this lean-to, but they almost certainly included service. The one-room and two-room plans were answerable to all of the settlers' immediate needs except that of cold storage for food. It is not clear how consistently solutions to this problem at Massachusetts Bay were based upon logic of the Old World, where multiple service rooms were customary in even the very modest seventeenth-century English farmhouse. In a sampling of 189 inventories for mid-Essex between 1635 and 1700 which represent for the most part hall/parlor houses, the buttery is an almost invariable feature, while the dairy or milkhouse can be found in fully one-half of the dwellings appraised. Fifty-six of the inventories reveal a single buttery as the only service room; eighty-four show the presence of a dairy or milkhouse in addition to one or more butteries. There are, in fact, forty inventories at least which include more than a single buttery, distinguished as "best butterry," "strong beare buttrey," "small beare buttrey," "dish buttery," and so on. The contents, other than drink vessels, are almost always cooking implements, especially pots and pans and eating utensils, including pewter. The milkhouse will contain dairy equipment and often a powdering tub for salting meats. Cheese lofts or cheese chambers are mentioned occasionally for the storage of that commodity.[17]

A comparison of contemporary seventeenth-century English and American farmhouse inventories points up at once some interesting contrasts with respect to service rooms. While one might readily expect to find both the buttery and dairy or milkhouse present in the first-built houses at Massachusetts Bay, and even an occasional example of more than one buttery, as in the case of George Barrell, whose Boston home, inventoried in 1643, contained both a buttery and "an other buttry,"[18] the overall statistics, nevertheless, paint a different picture. There is a surprisingly low incidence of service rooms in the earliest houses in and around Boston—at least by name. Among the total of 102 room-by-room inventories between 1630 and 1660, there are only thirteen butteries and but five dairies or milkhouses. Not a single example can be found of a house with both a buttery and a dairy.

Among the earliest butteries at Massachusetts Bay, we find at least that the contents correspond with those of comparable English inventories during the period. Michael Bacon of Dedham, whose estate was appraised in 1649, had a buttery that contained, in addition to beer vessels, a melange of pots, pans, kettles, a skillet, ladle, chafing dish and four silver spoons, pewter, bowls, trays, scales and weights, and linen yarn.[19] Moreover, among a number of the mid-Essex English inventories for houses with a buttery only and no dairy, it appears that the buttery absorbed the functions of milkhouse, and reflections of this practice are readily found at Massachusetts Bay. The contents of the buttery in the home of Ensign Francis Chickering of Dedham, for example, included in 1658 three barrels, a brewing tub, three keelers, two sieves, "4 Chesfulls 2 Cheese breads," a tray, pails, tubs, sixty pounds of butter "in a firkin," measures, and thirty trenchers.[20]

In some cases, and not unexpectedly in a pioneer society, the more specialized functions of buttery and dairy seem to have been absorbed into the larger working areas of hall or kitchen, as in the 1646 inventory of Matthew Whipple's house of two-room plan in Ipswich, where the hall included in addition to the cooking and eating equipment and tools an assortment of cheese "mootes," "two cheese breads," sieves, barrels, firkins, keelers, and a churn. Similarly, John Cutting in nearby Newbury, whose goods were appraised in 1659, had a brewing tub, drink vessels, and powdering tubs in his kitchen, in addition to the normal cooking and eating gear.[21] For the latter half of the seventeenth century, too, among the 107 room-by-room inventories for rural Suffolk County, it appears that dairy equipment was located in only two instances in a dairy or milkhouse as opposed to its appearance on nine occasions in a buttery and twenty in the hall, kitchen, or lean-to.

In light of the small number of butteries and dairies mentioned by name in the inventories at Massachusetts Bay, it is significant that the lean-to will generally contain provisions and other items peculiar to these service rooms. The home of John Fleming in Watertown, for example, contained in 1657 a parlor, lodging room, and hall, together with a lean-to furnished with a cheese press, churn, tubs, keelers, and cheese motes.[22] At the Fairbanks house, in addition to all of the original rooms, there is mention also in 1668 of "the Roome called the new house," which is thought to be the present lean-to of obvious early construction. Its contents include just such items one would expect to find in a service room: three keelers, one half bushell, one half peck, one cheese press, two cheese fats, and farm tools as well.[23]

It is clear, then, that the English concept of service rooms did indeed survive among the transplanted settlers in the New World, though modified by frontier practicalities. There is much greater innovational significance, however, in the single most striking contrast to emerge from any comparison of English and American seventeenth-century vernacular houses. This was the almost immediate and widespread adoption at Massachusetts Bay of the underground cellar as a suitable area for both provisions requiring cooler temperatures and items appropriate to the buttery. The cellar as an excavated area beneath the house frame was a relatively novel feature in the smaller farmhouses of seventeenth-century East Anglia. The first mention of any such among a total of 248 mid-Essex inventories between 1635 and 1749 is not until 1686, and there are only ten additional examples.[24] At Massachusetts Bay, on the other hand, fully one half of the houses in the inventories between 1630 and 1660 include cellars, while among the structures themselves there is scarcely a survivor from the seventeenth century without an underground cellar. Occasionally there was more than one. Estate appraisals of Richard Webb of Boston in 1659 and Thomas Wells of Ipswich in 1666 mention "both" cellars,[25] and two cellars are identified in the first inventory of the Fairbanks house taken in 1668.

There was usually but one cellar, however, located normally under the parlor in a house of two-room, central-chimney plan. Although there are references now and again to trap doors into the cellar,[26] access in virtually all seventeenth-century houses is by stairs leading down from the hall underneath the main stairs. Such an arrangement called for a basement stairwell in front of the chimney foundation (figures 27 and 31). The cellar excavation was otherwise rectangular, unless interrupted for an exterior entrance. As early as 1638, in connection with his farmhouse to be built in Ipswich, Samuel Symonds had written to John Winthrop, Jr., "it were not amisse to leave a dore-way or two within the Seller," and his directions for placement would suggest the front of the house, a location for the cellar bulkhead which became common as the century progressed.[27]

In explanation of the rapidity with which the English settlers incorporated the somewhat unfamiliar cellar into their planning schemes, we can only assume that quite soon after arrival they came consciously to grips with the problem of keeping provisions cool but not frozen in subzero temperatures during mid-winter. They must have realized that the cellar is somewhat warmer than an unheated room above ground level in freezing weather. Indeed, the Reverend William Bentley of Salem had advanced much the same theory in 1812 when he observed that "our first settlers by

Figure 31. Boardman house, Saugus, Mass. Detail of cellar stairwell and chimney foundation, ca. 1687. *Photo, William W. Owens, Jr., 1974.*

putting the sills of their houses under ground, provided for the warmth of their cellars and their rooms."[28] In any event, it can be argued that the widespread adoption of the cellar furnishes a principal reason for the absence, particularly by name, of the traditional buttery and dairy or milk-house. Documents reveal consistently the presence below grade of items appropriate to those service rooms. In 1639, for example, Thomas Lechford records an agreement concerning the sale of a farmhouse and outhouses at Mount Wollaston

in which it was stipulated that the grantor should have "one of the cellers for milke."[29] In the cellar of the home of Henry Ambrose of Boston in 1658 we find beef, pork, brewing vessels, and a barrel of tar, while the appraisers of the estate of Michael Metcalf, Jr., of Dedham, in 1654, listed for the cellar a collection of powdering tubs and milk and beer vessels, despite the fact that the house also contained a buttery. Its only contents, however, were a spinning wheel and "some few smale things."[30] The two cellars of Jonathan Fairbanks' house were described individually in 1668 as "the Working Celler" in which there were "2 vises and one turning lath and other small things" and "Another Celler" which contained four beer vessels,

three tubs, one chair, five keelers, three trays, one old cupboard, cheese, butter, beef, and tallow.[31] For more than 100 rural houses in Suffolk County between 1661 and 1700, drink and its appurtenances, when mentioned, were located in the buttery in only three instances as opposed to twenty-six in which these same items were found in the cellar. Similarly, dairy equipment appears here in fifteen examples, and only twice in a dairy or milkhouse, while salting tubs for meat were quite consistently located in the cellar (twenty-nine examples in contrast to ten in all other rooms of the house put together).

The cellar thus became a fixed feature of the New England house, and in the eighteenth century it often included formal structural provision for a dairy or larder. Long before this time, however, with the rigors of first settlement behind them, the colonists had returned increasingly in their thinking to the problem of service rooms above grade. In this evolving process we can point to but a single example of a house with the conventional English disposition of service rooms. That portion of the Story house in Essex added early in the eighteenth century to the original seventeenth-century one-room, two-and-a-half story structure resembled the characteristic East Anglian arrangement (figure 5), except for the introduction of a staircase between the two rooms beyond the main body of the added hall (figure 30). The room in the front corner containing the stairs was presumably a buttery, as early shelving would suggest. The original function of the room of equal size behind it is less clear, though it may originally have been a semisubmerged dairy. The complex as a whole—allowing for the late date and consequent possibility of a coincidental significance only—is the one unequivocal example at Massachusetts Bay of a traditional English arrangement which the earliest settlers failed to retain in the development of their own provincial house plan.

The more typical solution for service rooms, particularly as the century wore on, was the lean-to extending the entire length of the house at the rear, as revealed in the Boston builder's contract

The Framed Houses of Massachusetts Bay

of 1679 which specified a house thirty-four by twenty feet with a lean-to ten feet wide at the rear "to reach throughout the whole length of said house."[32] The rear lean-to at the Fairbanks house in Dedham is probably the oldest surviving example of this characteristic appendage (figure 32). Its picturesque outline arouses curiosity about origins. From the sixteenth century onward the multiplication of the ground-floor service rooms in the postmedieval English house had become a matter of axiom. Extension of the working part of the farmhouse took priority over adding to the upstairs rooms. By the later decades of the seventeenth century, the "saltbox" profile seems to have become relatively standard at Massachusetts Bay, and among the few unaltered examples of such additions made before 1700 we can readily distinguish certain developed usages from the architectural fittings of the rooms themselves. When the lean-to extending the entire length of a central-chimney house was divided into three distinct areas, a large room in the center and two smaller rooms at either end, one of the latter seems to have functioned as a buttery or dairy. After 1700 this area is often easiest to identify because of the presence of shelves or because of its half-submerged position. For much of our information, however, we must rely again upon the documents, for example such deeds as that by which Peter Oliver, merchant, in 1655, sells a dwelling house in Boston "containing two lower roomes, and two upper roomes, a leantoe, a buttery at one end of the leantoe and a shead or out house."[33]

The William Boardman house in Saugus, ca. 1687, formerly known as the "Scotch"-Boardman house, had soon acquired through addition a lean-to extending the entire length of the structure at the rear (figure 27), and by 1696 there is reference to the "Milkhouse," which one assumes was the small service room at the cooler, northeast corner of the lean-to.[34] This location became standard in the eighteenth century for the buttery or dairy, which was not infrequently located halfway between the cellar and ground floor. When situated at the first-floor level, it can be

argued that the desire for proximity to a warm lean-to kitchen in subzero weather overcame the earlier objections to a milkroom at grade level.

From this seventeenth-century ambivalence with respect to the handling of wet and dry provisions and storage of food and its paraphernalia, there emerged ultimately a solution which we have honored until well into the twentieth century. This was the inclusion among the service rooms of a cool all-purpose "pantry" directly off the kitchen, designed fundamentally for the storage of pots and pans and eating utensils and certain foodstuffs as well, including those requiring lower temperatures. Though the temperance movement of the nineteenth century drained the buttery of its drink and the modern refrigerator solved overnight the problem of cold storage, and although somehow in the process the more colorful terms of "buttery" and "dairy" were supplanted, the room itself, in size and location, survived other more radical evolutionary changes in

Figure 32. Fairbanks house, Dedham, Mass. Rear view, ca. 1637, with seventeenth- and eighteenth-century additions.

usage. Once its position and functions were thoroughly accommodated to the New England experience, a tradition was defined, and where today in remote farmhouses and country villages the pantry still lingers in use, one may expect to find the electric refrigerator crowded into one corner.

By the late seventeenth century the location of the kitchen was fixed as the large middle room of the lean-to, which at the Boardman house measures twenty-one and a half feet wide by twelve feet nine inches deep (figure 27). Presumably the early fireplace here was introduced when the lean-to was added. We have noted an early acceptance at Massachusetts Bay of changing concepts in England by which the kitchen took on new status as the center for the preparation of meals while the hall became fundamentally a sitting room. That the kitchen, on the other hand,

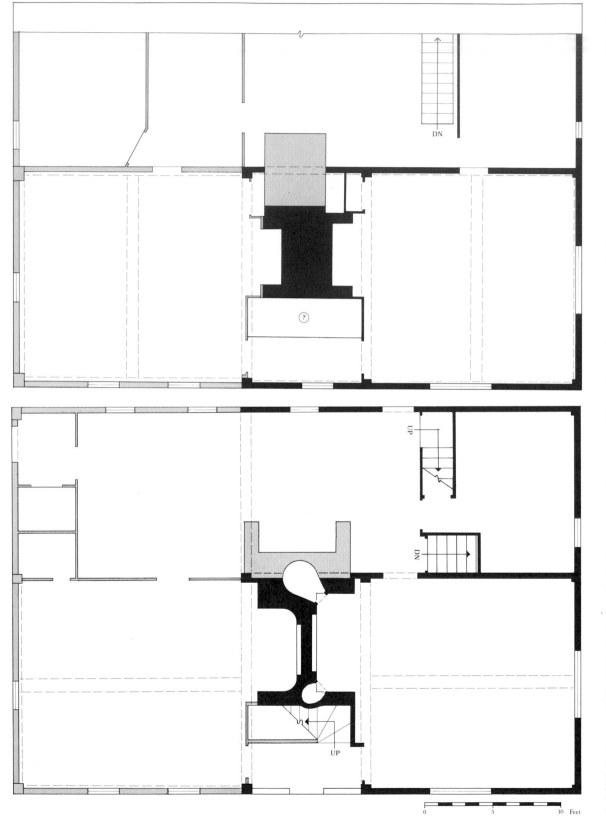

continued in some cases to occupy a secondary or subordinate position with respect to the preparation of meals is interestingly demonstrated at the Cooper-Frost-Austin house in Cambridge, the original eastern half of which is thought to have been built about 1689 with an integral lean-to (figure 33). The present fireplace with its separate flue in the lean-to was an addition to the original stack, which contained an oven in the hall. The earliest designation and purpose of this room without a fireplace as first constructed remains somewhat in doubt. One likely use was that of storage space for cooking utensils which were to be used in the adjoining hall. At the death in 1718 of Samuel Cooper, the builder and first owner, this space was described as the kitchen, equipped with both cooking and eating utensils as well as "a pair of Iron doggs" and a spit, implying that the fireplace had by then been introduced.[35]

By the middle of the eighteenth century the lean-to kitchen had become the undisputed area for preparation of food, though occasional exceptions can be found. The Hapgood house in Stow, ca. 1726, of two-room plan, acquired apparently before the Revolution a rear lean-to which never had a fireplace added to the central brick chimney stack of the original house, and such is the situation at the much earlier Fairbanks house in Dedham. The kitchen as an architectural entity and not merely a term, however, had become firmly incorporated in the house proper before the end of the seventeenth century. English kitchens were also apt to be no longer in a detached building at this late date, although the kitchen area in new houses "might be narrower or lower than the rest of the building, and evidently thought a distinct part of it."[36] This statement by an English student has immediate comparative significance for the development of the kitchen in the lean-to of the characteristic seventeenth-century house in New England.

In 1718 the second and smaller of the existing two rooms in the original lean-to of the Cooper-Frost-Austin house was described only as "the little Room" (figure 33). The contents, however, help us to visualize clearly its usage. In addition to two chests, there was no more than a bedstead and bedding.[37] Plentiful evidence exists in the eighteenth century to confirm the widely acknowledged purpose of this second, smaller room of the conventional lean-to. Located usually at the warmer end and immediately adjacent to the kitchen, it was ideal for the oversight of older, infirm persons, invalids, or for a confinement.

The rear lean-to almost invariably included a secondary staircase. Ascending steeply, the single run with winders was normally enclosed and placed with strict functional regard for the fact that one emerged at the head of the stairs into a lean-to attic with restricted headroom. The location of the staircase between kitchen and bedroom in the Cooper-Frost-Austin house, or kitchen and buttery in other cases, represents the more common arrangement (figure 33). That in the lean-to of the Boardman house is exceptional (figure 27), although the angle formed by a partition and the projecting jamb of an added fireplace would seem a perfectly logical site for a run of stairs composed all of winders. The position selected in this case provided again for emergence in the second story along the rear wall of the original house, where attic headroom reached its highest point.

As fully developed, the characteristic later seventeenth-century house plan at Massachusetts Bay consisted of two rooms ranged on either side of a central chimney, usually with corresponding chambers above. There was a hall which had evolved in function as a living room, though still not infrequently used for the preparation of meals, and a parlor which contained formal pieces of furniture and the best bed for the parents. The chambers above were given over to sleeping arrangements for other members of the family and to storage. The one-story lean-to with sloping roof, which represented a compact addition at the rear of this simple and functional com-

Figure 34. Whipple-Matthews house, Hamilton, Mass., 1680–1683, unrestored. *Photo, Malcolm E. Robb, ca. 1914.*

plex, contained a warm downstairs bedroom and a buttery or dairy adjacent to a working kitchen in which, increasingly, meals were prepared. Before the end of the century the lean-to at the rear began to be incorporated as an integral part of the frame of the main house, one of the earliest examples being the Whipple-Matthews house in Hamilton, built between 1680 and 1683 (figures 33 and 34). The practice became increasingly rooted during the first quarter of the eighteenth century.

Both the documents and structural evidence, however, reveal the presence of lean-tos and additions which bore differing relationships to the mass of the house as a whole. The Boxford town records, for example, in 1701, contained a vote for building a parsonage forty-eight feet long and twenty feet wide, with a "back Roouem" sixteen or eighteen feet square,[38] and a contract for erecting a house forty feet long and twenty feet wide for the Latin schoolmaster in Boston that same year specified a kitchen sixteen feet long and twelve feet wide.[39] These appendages, covering only a part of the rear wall, may have taken the form of the familiar back lean-to, but such was not the case when the town of Cambridge granted timber to William and Jason Russell in 1682 for a dwelling house twenty-six feet long "with a leanto at the Ende of It."[40] Much earlier, in 1639, there is reference to an agreement by which William Brackenbury of Charlestown was permit-

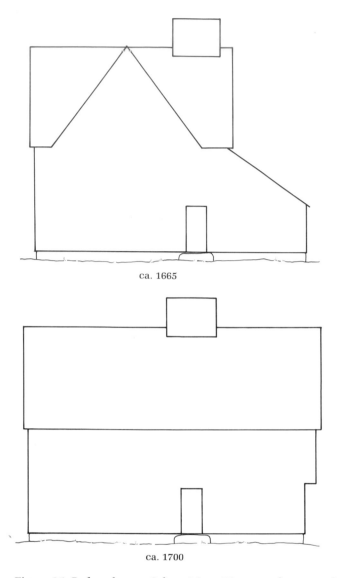

ca. 1665

ca. 1700

Figure 35. Gedney house, Salem, Mass. Diagram of structural growth, ca. 1665 and ca. 1700.

ted "to make a leanto unto the outside end of the parlor" of a dwelling house in that community, "not stopping or hindering any light or lights of the same parlor or other rooms of the same house."[41] Furthermore, it is significant that while the majority of surviving seventeenth-century houses would appear to belong to the typical group which we have just described, not a little of the evidence for variation comes from these same houses and suggests that they were not so "typical" at the beginning after all.

The Gedney house of about 1665 on High Street in Salem is an excellent case in point. The structure has presented to several generations of passers-by the profile of an early house with characteristic rear lean-to. Of central chimney plan, two and a half stories high, the only modification of the traditional form is the lean-to itself, added about 1800 and of two stories rather than one, in addition to which this late lean-to contains an entirely separate but also central chimney stack. When Eleazer Gedney, the builder and first owner, died in 1683, the house consisted of a hall and hall chamber (both with fireplace equipment), "parlour or lento," kitchen (with fireplace equipment), "Loft over it" and "litle Leantoo," garret, lean-to chamber, and cellar.[42] The language of the inventory confirms our knowledge of the original plan and form of the house, which was unusual. The left-hand portion, a full two stories high with attic, is that which contained the rooms designated as hall, hall chamber, and garret. The room to the right of the central chimney was smaller, only a single story high, and was covered with a lean-to roof at right angles to the mass of the house (figure 35). This was the "parlour or lento" of the inventory. Such an arrangement admittedly produces little change in the traditional central-chimney house plan except that a room roofed in this way was necessarily limited in width, and there were, of course, consequent changes in the floor plan as one proceeded from story to story. The inevitably narrow lean-to chamber would thus find its place above the "parlour or lento." Concerning the kitchen and "litle Leantoo" we can only assume that they were at the rear of the building. There is some structural evidence for earlier appendages here, although the present lean-to has effectually obliterated nearly every trace of their form and character. Long before this late addition, however, probably just before or after 1700, the "parlour or lento" had been raised to a full two stories, giving the house its traditional oblong form (figure 35).

The Gedney house in Salem is by no means an isolated phenomenon. A few blocks away stands the Samuel Pickman house, erected before 1681.

Physical evidence confirms the original or very early existence of a lean-to here at right angles to the mass of the house proper. As in the case of the Gedney house the lean-to was subsequently raised to a full two stories, and the same process was repeated at the Goldsmith-Pickering house in Wenham, ca. 1700.

Given this seventeenth-century end lean-to plan variant, for which ample precedent can be found in contemporary English work, what can we assume was its prevalence at Massachusetts Bay? There is no hard and fast answer, although the inventories shed some light on the matter if we accept as significant those consisting of two rooms and a single chamber identified terminologically as belonging to one or the other of the rooms in question. When there is mention of a hall only, for example, together with a parlor and parlor chamber, it is not hard to visualize a schematic layout consisting of two principal rooms, one above the other, with chimney bay, and a lean-to at right angles to the latter. There are many New England examples, later than the seventeenth century, showing just such an architectural arrangement.

Closely related to this problem is the fact that between 1630 and 1660 a number of houses emerge from the records with a single room and chamber (or two rooms and chamber) but no indication as to whether the chamber was above or ranged alongside of the ground-floor rooms, except perhaps where there is mention of grain, which was often kept in upper stories. Some of these chambers were apparently on the ground floor and would have been disposed longitudinally in a single range with the other rooms as one often finds in East Anglia, or at right angles in an ell or lean-to. The designation chamber as used in England in the opening years of the seventeenth century could mean either a ground-floor or an upper room, though in Essex, at least, the term was not used for ground-floor rooms, and the same had been largely true of Suffolk in the late sixteenth century. While the term chamber normally referred to an upper room in late seventeenth-century New England, a further indication, perhaps, of the diffusion of East Anglian influence, we cannot be sure that the first colonists, recruited from more than one area in the British Isles, always made such a sharp distinction. The appraisers of the estate of Edward How of Watertown in 1644 mention a "Lodging Chamber" that included bedding, and identify in addition to the parlor, hall, and dairy certain possessions which were "upp ye Chambers." Similarly, in 1645 Thomas King of Watertown had besides his hall a "lodging chamber" and "other lodging Roome" as well as grain and bedding "uppon the Chamber."[43] The terms lodging chamber and lodging room used here seem to describe ground-floor rooms, and in Kent, at least, in the 1630s, the lodging chamber was indeed to be found there. The Kentish "bedchamber" was also apt to be a ground-floor room,[44] although the popularity of this term is not noticeably great in the period 1630 to 1660 at Massachusetts Bay. At least one house, however, that of Michael Bacon of Dedham in 1649, contained a hall (with best bed), bedchamber (with slightly less valuable bedding), buttery, meal house, hall chamber, garret, and "chamber over the bedd chamber."[45]

To whatever degree our conceptualization of the houses of the first settlers must be modified by or reconciled with traditional English planning conventions, it is clear that earlier terminology had undergone a significant Americanization by the final decade of the seventeenth century, when there can be found no more than fourteen unlocated chambers among 107 rural Suffolk County houses appraised between 1661 and 1700. Only two of these contained the best bed.

We must note also that smaller rooms were sometimes partitioned out of larger ones. In Gloucester, for example, in 1663, a slander case turned upon whether or not one John Meager had kept a young lady "in his cabin all night." The term occurs from time to time, and is further defined here by Thomas Jones, who deposed "that the cabin of John Meager was one room divided by boards into two."[46] An arrangement of this sort can be found at a later date at the Boardman house in Saugus where the hall has been subdi-

Figure 36. Whipple house, Ipswich, Mass. Detail of parlor ceiling frame, before 1683, showing change in chamfer pattern and nail-hole evidence along lower edge of transverse summer beam, suggesting former presence of a board partition. *Photo, William W. Owens, Jr., 1974.*

vided with a vertical featheredged board partition, presumably in the early eighteenth century (figure 27). In some cases the subdivision of larger rooms may have been contemporary with original construction. From what can be seen of the original frame of the Pierce house in Dorchester, the dimensions of the room to the right of the narrow chimney bay are somewhat unusual. The distance from chimney girt to the transverse summer beam is thirteen feet, five inches, while the space beyond this unit, measuring to the end wall of the house, is but eight feet, eight inches. Both upstairs and down there are later partitions along the summer beams which divide the total space into separate rooms. The partition in the upper story was in place, apparently, as early as 1744, when an inventory mentions the "West Chamber" (added to the original house), "East Chamber," and "Middle Chamber," which could only be that portion of the original house that

measured thirteen feet, five inches in width.[47] A similar condition, with the larger portion of the ground-story room measuring eleven feet, four inches and the smaller, beyond the transverse summer beam, measuring nine feet, six inches, exists in the later half of the Whipple house in Ipswich, added to the original dwelling before 1683, and here there is evidence for an early board portion (figure 36). The documents suggest no consistent use for these inner rooms, and we have no direct evidence that the buttery was at times in the seventeenth century a subdivided element in a larger room, as will be found in certain areas of England.[48]

The projecting porch was but a spatial extension of the chimney bay beyond the front plane of the house. Despite the fact that early seventeenth-century English precedent can readily be found for this elaboration of the entry (figure 7), there is little or no indication of its presence outside of Boston until after the middle of the century. Only a mere handful of examples can be found before 1660. These occur in connection with ambitious houses belonging to well-to-do or prominent members of the urban community. Herein lies the readiest explanation for the absence of a feature which in plan and elevation must have seemed superfluous, even luxurious, under pioneer conditions—except to the leaders of the colony. Governor John Winthrop's inventory in 1649, for example, mentions a porch chamber with garret over it.[49] The bulk of evidence, however, falls within the more settled period of 1650–1700, and often involves the addition of porches to existing houses, implying "improvement."

There was very little deviation from a standard formula for the projecting porch, although one Boston deed in 1664 describes a "house being fortie two foote Long, with two porches and a Leantoo which makes it twentie Eight foote wide,"[50] and in 1658 one Captain Walden in Boston was granted permission "to sett upp two pillars under his porch."[51] We are hampered fundamentally by the fact that not a single projecting two-story porch has survived from the seventeenth century.

All extant examples are nineteenth- or twentieth-century recreations.

Characteristic dimensions are laid down in a contract of 1657 by which John Norman, house carpenter of Manchester, agreed to build a parsonage in Beverly, thirty-eight feet long and seventeen feet wide, "with a portch of eight foote square and Jetted over one foote ech way."[52] A year later, in 1658, Norman contracted with Dr. George Emery of Salem to build a porch "seven ffoot 4 enches stud 8 ffoot of frame braced and tenneted in to the stud [and] jetted over 14 enches . . . three wayes and to cover it and shingle the gutters."[53] Both contracts, in that they refer to the jetting of the porch, almost certainly imply a full two-story gabled elevation, and this would consistently bear out surviving physical and early pictorial evidence (figure 37). For those seventeenth-century houses which have revealed traces only of a two-story porch—for example, the Corwin or Witch house in Salem, ca. 1675, and the Appleton-Taylor-Mansfield house, the so-called Ironworks house in Saugus, ca. 1680—it is often difficult to determine how far the frame projected. Nor are we entirely well informed as to how the porch and entry were subdivided, if at all.

With respect to full-scale additions or integral elements of the house plan which were something more than just appendages, in particular

Figure 38. Turner house, Salem, Mass., ca. 1668, with seventeenth-century addition.

the ell or wing, we are largely limited for evidence to buildings which have survived or for which there is good pictorial evidence. Among the earlier examples is the full two-and-one-half-story addition of single-room plan probably made by John Turner before 1680 to the conventional central-chimney house which he had erected in Salem about 1668 (figure 38). This ell with its own chimney added along fully one-half of the south front measured twenty-one feet, five inches, by twenty-two feet, and provided a vertical file of

rooms consisting of parlor and parlor chamber. These rooms were of more formal proportions, with higher ceilings, making it necessary to step up from the old house into the new chamber and attic. Like the original structure, the south ell was furnished with façade gables.

The Turner house was enlarged further before the end of the seventeenth century through the addition of a second wing or ell at the rear. An inventory of 1693 mentions over and beyond all the readily identifiable rooms of the main house a "New Kitchen" and kitchen chamber, being in all likelihood those rooms contained in an ell centered at right angles along the rear line of the

original structure that appears in a crude plot plan of the property executed in 1769.[54] The present lean-to, for which no authoritative evidence exists, and the wing beyond it to the north were added when the house was restored between 1908 and 1910.

The rear ell was not uncommon in urban areas. At least two examples are known from pictures,

Figure 39. The Old Feather Store, Boston, Mass., 1680. Demolished 1860. *Stereographic view, 1860.*

the Old Feather Store in Boston of 1680 (figure 39) and the Philip English house in Salem, ca. 1690. Photographs and drawings of these well-known landmarks, long since demolished, reveal a similarity in plan and form, with the ells so placed

that the buildings were fundamentally L-shaped. The wing of the Old Feather Store was furnished with a façade gable, and Bentley tells us in 1793 that a similar gable once ornamented the ell of the English house.[55] The latter building was also furnished with a two-story porch in the angle formed by the main house and the ell.

Contemporary with the construction of the Old Feather Store is the still extant Paul Revere house in Boston, ca. 1680, with a two-and-one-half-story rear wing, again at right angles and so placed as to make an L-shaped plan (figure 40). The angles are not entirely regular, however, for the house with its ell was apparently built to conform to the restricted boundaries of the property. This had been the case also with the Old Feather Store, deeds for which indicate that the lot lines had been established as early as 1666: thirty-one feet on North Street, thirty-nine feet on Market Square, and only ten feet along the ancient dock.[56] Following the sweeping fire of 1679 along the water front, new construction here was pushed out to the very limits of these lines. The ground story diminished sharply at the gable end on Market Square, a situation which the builder sought to correct at the second-story level. Thus the overhang at the front corner was a conventional twenty inches or so; at the rear corner, on the other hand, the chamber story projected several feet, and required the additional support of a brace, clearly visible in early photographs and drawings of the house (figure 39).

The conformity of the Paul Revere house to its boundaries is more prosaic, but on the basis of these two examples we may assume that the compact streets of seventeenth-century Boston contained not a few such eccentricities. Additional evidence is to be found in a group of timber building permits for the city which date from 1707 to 1729. With such limited knowledge of early urban buildings in New England, these permits furnish valuable documentary information if little else. One notes with interest the number of kitchen ells, many of which, the records would suggest, were ranged as extensions in a lateral direction. Of even greater significance, however, is

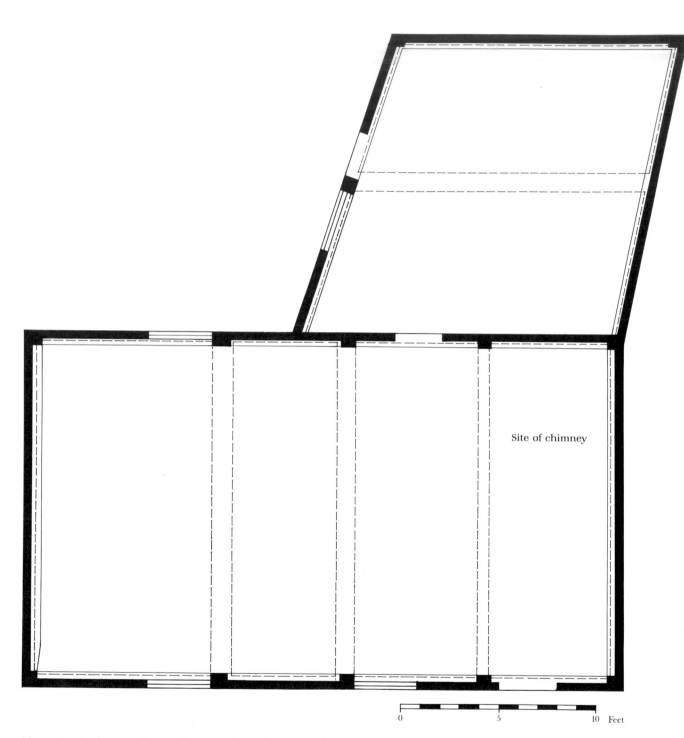

Site of chimney

Figure 40. Paul Revere house, Boston, Mass. First-story plan, ca. 1680.

"dwellinge house with a kitchin and barne" in Salem, the owner's will making clear that the kitchen was unconnected.[57] The practice in Boston at a later date may simply reflect an understandable effort to disengage those portions of the structure more readily subject to the hazard of fire in crowded neighborhoods. The separate kitchen, so common in the warmer southern colonies, is almost never found in rural situations at Massachusetts Bay, for obvious climatic reasons. When found here during any period, for example at the later Royall house in Medford, described in 1739 as an "Out Kitching" (the building itself of brick still extant),[58] its presence can usually be explained by some extenuating factor. In this case, Isaac Royall had come north from Antigua with a retinue of slaves, and was undoubtedly importing planning concepts from another climate when he rebuilt and enlarged an older house purchased in Medford in 1732.

There are departures among the timber building permits from the normal length-breadth ratio for the seventeenth-century framed houses of rural Massachusetts Bay, and there are at least two examples of houses with dimensions which imply irregular angles imposed by constricted house lots. Nevertheless, one is impressed with the number of plans in which the length is approximately twice the width (just under one half the total number). Many, in their correspondence with the normal ratio for rural houses, would suggest a two-room plan, while others readily imply the typical one-room house plan. To be sure, there is mention of a chamber over a passage, and other unusual features can be found in Boston deeds as well which conjure up some of the more picturesque aspects of seventeenth-century London before the fire, but the close correlation in dimensions between urban and rural houses at Massachusetts Bay as reflected in these Boston building permits is noteworthy.

There are, on the other hand, distinctive differences between the siting of houses in town and in the country. Where open space permitted, the builder and client preferred a sunny, southern exposure. Among a total of 125 houses where the

the appearance, even in small numbers, of the separate or detached kitchen in Boston at the beginning of the eighteenth century. They were not common in urban areas in the seventeenth century, although there is reference in 1661 to a

The Framed Houses of Massachusetts Bay

original orientation has been noted, ninety-eight face more or less due south. Of the remainder, all but two or three are located in compact towns or in urban situations, though even here, the house was often sited on its lot to face south with the gable end turned to the street. In-town building sites were apt to be more valuable, and narrow frontages have also played their role in dictating placement of the house with its gable end to the street. The plan in all important respects remains unchanged when thus turned at right angles, though we do not have sufficient evidence to suggest how often the parlor or superior end of the house was situated next to the street, as one often finds in English practice. And in Boston, at least, the inability to flex at all times in a lateral direction led to the introduction of the cellar kitchen. Such a feature is implied in a Boston building contract of 1679,[59] and physical evidence of an original cooking fireplace survives in the cellar of the Paul Revere house.

The house of single-room plan with chimney bay, one-and-a-half and two-and-a-half stories in height, and the house of two rooms ranged on either side of a central chimney, both with contemporary or soon-added lean-tos, were present from the outset, and other somewhat more involved forms were present as well. In 1676, the unpopular Edward Randolph, about to embark for New England, was furnished with statistical estimates which he was to confirm or disprove. From these we learn that there were then, as it was supposed, some 1,500 families in Boston with fifteen merchants worth about £50,000, and five hundred persons worth £3,000 each. No house in New England, the document continues, contained more than twenty rooms, and not twenty in Boston had more than ten rooms each.[60] Surely there is little evidence to contradict this statement. In town and country alike, the timber framed houses of the community leaders and more affluent citizens impress us only in terms of a relatively modest increase in the number of rooms and elaborateness of furnishing. At the upper end of the scale, however, we find before the middle of the century the presence of ambitious framed houses. It is not easy to visualize their now long-vanished features. Beyond the Turner house in Salem, we have only the inventories which hint at complexities of plan and even, as early as 1669, such advanced social concepts as the separate "dyning Roome,"[61] and whose contents, carefully enumerated, give us a word picture at least of their provincial sumptuousness. Such was the commodious home of the Reverend John Cotton, Boston's celebrated divine, who had come from Boston in Lincolnshire. Situated at the entrance of what was later to become Pemberton Square, this house with its porch and chambers, three parlors, a hall and kitchen, and a "Gallarie" as well, together with "the grownd before and backside and other side of the hill," was valued at £220 in 1653, and we learn further from Mr. Cotton's will that the structure itself had developed through enlargement. Reference is made to "that south Part of my house, which Sir Henry Vane built, whilst he sojourned with me," which would fix a date for this portion before Vane's departure from New England in 1637.[62] Such documents bespeak a degree of elegance which was fully commensurate with the tastes and aspirations of the ruling elders and an emerging mercantile "aristocracy." That so little tangible evidence of these exceptional architectural flights has survived to the present century must be accounted one of the sadder accidents of American history.

CHAPTER IV

The Builders and Their Resources

IT HAS PERSISTENTLY been repeated that the early colonists built their own houses—that every farmer was his own carpenter. As early as 1827 Erastus Worthington had written of Dedham that

> The society which has not a joiner, a carpenter, a blacksmith, or a shoemaker, must necessarily be very deficient in articles of the first necessity. It was however several years before any of these kind of artificers came into the town. . . . It is an obvious fact therefore, that the first houses in Dedham were chiefly built without them.[1]

Nothing could be further from the truth. In the very town of which Worthington speaks we have record at the outset of a blacksmith, tailor, shoemaker, weaver, and one who had "knoweledge in Marshiall afayers," as well as three or four carpenters and a joiner.[2] For any but the crudest of shelters the trained carpenter's skill was essential, and it is important to realize that we are dealing consistently throughout this study with a professional product. The very simplest houses at Massachusetts Bay were carpenter-built, and carpenters loomed from the start as one of the largest groups of building artisans in the seventeenth century.

In general terms this situation simply perpetuated conditions which had existed in rural England for several generations. Where statistics concerning trades and professions are readily available, for example in a study of Worcestershire wills and inventories for the period covering roughly the century between 1550 and 1650, we find a total of some ninety-six carpenters as opposed to no more than seventeen joiners, fifteen masons, and four bricklayers.[3] This ratio of five or six carpenters to one joiner becomes seven to one at Massachusetts Bay, with its unprecedented demand for new construction. Known building craftsmen who arrived at Massachusetts Bay before 1650 included 175 carpenters as opposed to 25 joiners and 25 masons and bricklayers.

Of startling significance is the median age of the immigrant carpenter. Of 146 carpenters arriving at Massachusetts Bay before 1650 whose ages can be estimated, 91 percent (a total of 133) were in their twenties and thirties or were servants, apprentices, or recently married with young children, while only ten or a dozen were well into their middle years, the oldest recorded age being sixty-two.

The large number of carpenters present among the colonists would argue for a careful examination of their role. What was their training? How thoroughly specialized were they? What laws governed their activity? What was their relationship to the client? To begin with, we have far too little knowledge of the background in England of our earliest American carpenters to be able to particularize all aspects of their training. The greater proportion of these men came from small villages or nonurban communities where, traditionally, the young aspiring builder was apprenticed to an established master-workman for a period that spanned most of his teens. Seven years seems to have been the normal time, and it is interesting to observe the large number of incoming carpenters at Massachusetts Bay during the earliest years who give their age as twenty-one or twenty-two and had apparently completed their apprenticeship.

Later, in 1660, and owing unquestionably to unique labor conditions in the New World, the Boston selectmen complained that "many youthes in this Towne, being put forth Apprentices to severall manufactures and sciences, but for 3 or 4 yeares time, contrary to the Customes of all well governed places," had not unexpectedly become "uncapable of being Artists in their trades," and more important yet, had revealed an "unmeetnes" at the expiration of their term "to take charge of others for government and manuall instruction in their occupations." It was ordered, therefore, "that no person shall henceforth open a shop in this Towne, nor occupy any manufacture or science, till hee hath compleated 21 years of age, nor except hee hath served seven yeares Apprentice-ship."[4]

Contracts provide us with the terms which under normal circumstances governed the relationship between master and apprentice. In 1666, for example, John Queire of County Cork, Ireland, "Of his owne free will" bound himself to Job Lane of Malden "to learne his Art . . . in the Trade of a Carpenter and in such other Country imployment in reference to husbandry" for the full term of seven years. During this period Queire promised to serve Job Lane faithfully, to keep his "secrets," to obey his lawful commands, and not to waste or lend his goods. At a more personal level, he agreed not to "play at any unlawful game whereby his Master may have any Losse," not to haunt taverns, ale-houses, or places of gaming, nor, further, to commit fornication or "Contract Matrimony within the said term." Lane, for his part, was to teach and instruct John Queire "in the Art and Trade of a Carpenter and in Husbandry," to provide him with meat, drink, clothing, washing, lodging, and all other necessities, and when his training was complete, to give him "Two Sutes of Apparrell, the one for Working dayes the other for Lords dayes fitt and Convenient for such an Apprentize."[5]

During the basic period of training the youthful novice was taught to know the various kinds of timber he would use and their particular properties, seasoned and unseasoned; to make careful selection of the trees which would provide him with the proper units for his frame; and to estimate quantities in volume, weight, and running length. He became experienced in the cutting and felling of these trees; in the shaping of the individual pieces through riving, sawing, and hewing; in finishing and embellishing their surfaces; and in sawing and planing boards. He learned the dynamics of timber-framing: the measuring, scribing, and cutting of the all-important joints and the reasons for selecting one particular joint or framing scheme over another; the logic asso-

ciated with the numbering and assembly of the matching units; and finally, the mechanics of rearing the frame, an awkward but highly disciplined aspect of his craft. Immediate experience in this intricate operation began at a relatively early stage in the apprentice's career when, as a light-weight boy, he clambered to a perch aloft from which he could insert the pins in a joint and drive them home. Later, as a nearly full-fledged builder, he was charged with the greater responsibility of directing or assisting to direct the labors of the raising crew.

Once arrived at Massachusetts Bay the carpenter and his skill were in great demand, especially at the beginning. Francis Higginson had written home to friends in Leicester from Salem in September 1629 "Of all trades, carpenters are most needful; therefore bring as many as you can."[6] Governor Winthrop had sensed the need in advance and had sought to recruit carpenters before his company sailed for Massachusetts Bay in 1630. "Let John enquire out 2: or 3: Carpenters," he wrote to his wife from London on October 20, 1629, and surely the urgency must have communicated itself to the artisans themselves and strengthened a number of resolves. A few months later, in January of 1630, the Reverend Nathaniel Ward wrote to Winthrop from Stondon in Essex,

I intreate yow to reserve roome and passage in your shipps for 2 families, A carpenter and Bricklayer, the most faithfull and dilligent workmen in all our partes. One of them hath putt of[f] a good farme this weeke and sold all, and should be much dammaged and discouraged if he finds no place amoungst yow. He transports himselfe att his owne charge.[7]

Promotional literature such as William Wood's in 1634 also provided strong inducement. Among the men who would be "most fit for these plantations," he specifies "an ingenious Carpenter, a cunning Joyner . . . and a good brick-maker, a Tyler and a Smith." Any person with skill in these trades, he continues, "needs not feare but he may improve his time and endeavors to his owne benefit."[8]

Nevertheless, the shortage of skilled labor continued to outstrip the demand for services in the face of a staggering amount of new construction. In answer to repeated requests for carpenters who might be persuaded to emigrate, Thomas Gostlin wrote tersely from Groton in Suffolk to John Winthrop, Jr., on June 11, 1633, "I could get none."[9] The results, of course, were inevitable. By November of 1633 Governor Winthrop complained that "The scarcity of workmen had caused them to raise their wages to an excessive rate, so as a carpenter would have three shillings the day, a laborer two shillings and sixpence, etc." As concern among the public had increased, he continues, the court ordered that "carpenters, masons, etc., should take but two shillings the day."[10]

Actually the official records at Massachusetts Bay reveal that steps had been taken almost at once to regulate wages. On August 23, 1630, it had been ruled that "carpenters, joyners, brickclayers, sawers, and thatchers" should not take above two shillings a day. A month later, on September 28, this law was amended to the extent that "noe maister carpenter, mason, joyner, or brickelayer shall take above 16d. a day for their worke, if they have meate and drinke." On March 22, 1631, in a more lenient mood the court ordered that the restraints previously fixed be removed and that wages of builders "and other artificers . . . shall nowe be lefte free and att libertie as men shall reasonably agree." It is the ensuing abuse of this relaxation and the tightening of regulations to which Winthrop refers. Again the law was repealed on September 3, 1635,[11] and once again by the following year Winthrop reported that prices of commodities had risen and that carpenters had gone back to charging three shillings per day.[12]

Rather than follow the ups and downs of wages in the early years of the colony as they relate both to economic trends in general and the demand for skilled workmen in particular, we turn instead to the question of specialization among building artisans. To what extent did an urban guild-oriented psychology continue to flourish in the

New World; to what extent was a more loosely conceived English rural apprenticeship system perpetuated among the largely nonurban immigrants at Massachusetts Bay; or did the older, European order soon come under attack in response to unique conditions in provincial America? The answer would seem to lie in the documents rather than in the artifacts. We find among many of the earliest newcomers a highly specialized diversification of skills, consistent with our knowledge of urban vocational habits in England at the time. By 1650 Edward Johnson of Woburn, born in 1598 in Hernehill Parish, Canterbury, in Kent, and trained there as a joiner, noted that the crafts at Massachusetts Bay had "fallen into their ranks and places . . . Carpenters, Joyners, Glaziers, Painters, follow their trades only . . . Masons, Lime, Brick, and Tilemakers . . . are orderly turn'd to their trades."[13]

In both town and country there are continuing references throughout the century to specialization, as for example in the legal deposition of Richard Jacques in 1679 concerning the house which his father, Henry Jacques, a carpenter of Newbury, had built five or six years earlier for Henry Ellis at Boston. In the summer his father raised the frame, he reported, and the structure was finished before winter set in, so that the masons did not have to wait for their work.[14] In 1673 an agreement with a plasterer is mentioned among other items contracted for in the completion of a meetinghouse in Salem,[15] and in Manchester, when the selectmen settled accounts with the committee charged with building a parsonage in 1699, there remained £2-6-10 owing to "the glasers for glasing the abov sd hous."[16] Surely in urban areas we may expect a clear-cut pattern of specialization. In 1701 the Boston selectmen made separate arrangements with the members of several building trades in the erection of a house forty feet long by twenty feet wide for the Latin schoolmaster in that city. John Barnard, housewright, was to perform the carpentry work and was instructed, incidentally, to "provide a Raysing Dinner for the Raysing the Schoolmasters House at the Charge of the Town not exceeding

the Sum of Three pounds." Concurrently the selectmen contracted with John Goodwin for "the masons worke of the house now to be built," and on October 30, 1703, Thomas Child, a London-trained painter-stainer, was engaged to paint the house and fence.[17] Similarly, in 1707 we find record of payments made to "Workmen About the House" of Michael Shute in Boston, namely, Benjamin Browne and Joseph Ryal, carpenters, James Varney, mason, Moses Peirce, glazier, Samuel Robinson, painter, and William Manly, paver.[18]

There is some indication, at least, that the equally recognizable phenomenon of diversification, or the blurring of craft distinctions, can be traced to a breakdown in the inherited system of specialization. Writing much later, in 1806, the Reverend William Bentley of Salem refers to a conversation with an older person who

represents that the arts were better understood in the first generation at Salem than in any succeeding. The first settlers were from old countries and were men of enterprise. In a new Country they had only the necessities of life to provide for. . . . He was acquainted with those who knew them or most of them. An ingenious Carpenter made rakes, a good mason laid cellar rocks and bricks in clay. A good painter became a glazier of glass windows set in lead. They taught what they practiced not what they knew.[19]

A far larger body of evidence exists, however, to suggest that a well-established English tradition of the ambidexterous rural artisan—ancestor, if you will, of the nineteenth-century Yankee jack-of-all-trades—was brought to the New World by a predominantly country-bred group of immigrants and perpetuated in the social structure of Massachusetts Bay. If this rural English tradition was in any degree inhibited by lingering restraints imposed by the guild system, here we must acknowledge that the colonial experience, as suggested by Bentley, hastened and intensified the disintegration of these controls. Edward Johnson himself, presumably guild-trained as a joiner, is known to have built a bridge in Woburn

in 1642 and to have constructed a boat to explore the Merrimack River in 1652.[20] Thomas Eames, whose English origin is not known, had arrived in Dedham by 1640 at the age of twenty-two and is referred to in that year as a brickmaker.[21] He had moved to Medford by 1652, where in 1660, described as a "Brickelayer, and maker of bricke," he took as apprentice one Joseph Mirrible, agreeing to instruct him "in the art and trade of a bricke layer, and brickemaker . . . as also to learne him to write, and so farr in Arethmaticke, as may enable him for the keeping of the reckonings and accounts of one of Such a Trade."[22] Later, however, when a resident of Sudbury in 1664, and still called "mason, and brickemaker,"[23] he is credited with building the timber-framed meetinghouse in Sherborn in 1674–1675. Following the burning of his house there during an Indian raid on February 1, 1676, Eames enumerated among his losses five pounds worth of carpenter's and joiner's tools.[24] Similarly, a 1664 inventory of the immigrant carpenter, Stephen Fosdick of Charlestown, includes a full complement of carpenter's and joiner's tools and "a parsell of turning tules And a Laeth" as well,[25] while John Emery, the Newbury carpenter who came to Massachusetts Bay from Romsey in Hampshire in 1635, also possessed "Carpenter and turners and Joyners tooles" at his death in 1683.[26]

From building documents we learn further how versatile many of the builders were. In 1659, for example, William Averill of Ipswich, carpenter, agreed to construct an addition to the house of Richard Jacob in that town. Besides framing a single bay, eighteen feet square, and providing clapboards and shingles, laying them together with three floors, and making four windows, partitions and doors, he promised as well "to make a table and frame of 12 or 14 foot Long and a joyned form of 4 foot Long and a binch Behind the table."[27] An even more diversified record of the early carpenter's work is found in the account book of Joshua Buffum of Salem who was brought to the New World as an infant. Together with such predictable items as the making of a "mantelltree," framing and boarding a house, and raising a corn barn, there are entries for masonry work and miscellaneous construction as well:

for Engenes [Indians] helpe aboute making morter (1679)
for windos making and stayeres making
for Irone worke beside casmentes and selere dore
for worke a boute his drain (1695)
for a brick mould
for sitting his gat postes and maken the gate (1700)

In addition to all of this he built a "Bridge at the Mills belonging to the Trasks" in 1685, and in 1688 contracted to erect a sawmill in Salem for which, as the accounts show, he not only dug the foundation but did the iron work as well.[28]

Francis Perry of Salem, to take another example, born about 1608, had arrived at Massachusetts Bay by 1631, and was described as a wheelwright in 1651.[29] He referred to himself later as carpenter for the infant ironworks established in Saugus, and deposed in 1653 that he had made many things for the agent's house on the company's account, including one great press, and had set up two dressers. During the same year he submitted bills for three days' work with his sons "fetching Stuffe for the finnerrye wheeles Coverreinge," and three days' work "mackeing morter for the finnerey Chimneye"; for clapboards, for cutting the anvil block, for making a bridge for carting mine, for felling a tree for the hammer beam, for "his teeme and hands brei[n]geing the hammer Beeme to the workes," and for the work of one Roger Tiler who helped him "mackeinge and fitteinge the furnace Beeme and placeinge it, beeinge fower weekes worke."[30] Nathaniel Pickman of Salem, carpenter, who came from Bristol in the mid 1630s, then aged about twenty-one, billed Captain George Corwin in 1678/9 for several typical carpentry items, such as mending the fence in the garden, one window in the hall chamber, for putting in a groundsill in the warehouse, for eleven days clapboarding the house, for making the cellar doors, and, in addition, for making "mrs Hathorns childs Coffen."[31]

With respect to other members of the building profession, we find in such seemingly specialized contracts as that drawn in 1675 by Jonathan Corwin of Salem with Daniel Andrews of the same town, mason, for work "to be bestowed in filling, plaistering, and finishing" Corwin's house, the so-called Witch house on Essex Street in Salem, that the trades of mason and bricklayer are now confounded. Andrews agreed to dig and build a cellar, to underpin the house, and to make stone steps into the cellar. In addition it was specified that he would "take downe the Chimneys which are now standing, and to take and make up of the brickes that are now in the Chimneyes, and the stones that are in the Leanetoo Cellar . . . and to rebuild the said Chimneys with five fireplaces . . . also to fill the Gable Ends of the house with bricke, and to plaister them with Clay."[32] Even in Boston by the late seventeenth century these professional labels seem to have been applied interchangeably, and William Clough, for example, between 1680 and 1702 calls himself mason in some documents and bricklayer in others, documents which reveal that he was performing the services of stone mason and bricklayer upon demand.[33]

As for the joiner, the situation is more complicated. The William Rix house contract of 1640 directed the joiner, John Davys, to construct a framed house sixteen feet long and fourteen feet wide, and to clapboard the walls and build a framed chimney "with hewen timber."[34] More than one early joiner possessed the tools for rough carpentry work, yet it was the carpenter who, in addition to hewing, erecting, and finishing the house frame, was normally expected to make doors and windows, to board and clapboard the walls and shingle the roof, to make the stairs, to lay the floors, and to hew the manteltree. The Salem selectmen, for example, when agreeing with "Jno Scelling" to finish the Townhouse in 1677, specified shingle, clapboards, floors, windows, stairs, and all other things "needfull with respect to Carpenters worke."[35] Whenever partitions are mentioned in the documents the carpenter is instructed to make them as well. Furthermore, where fully consecutive

building contracts exist, as for the Latin schoolmaster's house in Boston, there is no mention of a joiner. Thus in the case of the handsome molded sheathing and trim in the chambers of the Boardman house in Saugus, ca. 1687, we must acknowledge that Boardman, the client, a joiner by profession, raised in the immediate environs of Boston, may have relied on the carpenter for these details of finish, although creasing planes which were used to mold the edges of board trim can be found in both carpenters' and joiners' inventories.

With the opening of the eighteenth century the situation begins to change. William Paine, joiner, was paid for work at the house of George Mountjoy in Braintree in 1698, and when Robert Gibbs of Boston erected "Four Brick Tenements" in Cornhill, two in 1712 and the other two in 1716, there is mention of "the Slating . . . And all the Masons Bricklayers Housewrights and Joyners worke,"[36] records which look forward to the coming importance of interior woodwork in the eighteenth century. For more rural areas it is not unusual by the 1720s to encounter, as we do in the account book of the joiner Joseph Brown, Jr., of Newbury, all the familiar furniture items, including bedsteads, cases of drawers, joint stools, chests, cupboards, table tops, and "a Great Chair mended and botomd," in addition to accounts in connection with work he did on houses. We find, for example, "bording and shingeling" in 1725, "by Laing flore in Garrit and Round Chimly" in 1726, "by Leting in Jyce," "by makeing garrit stayers" and "by makeing a par[ti]tion" in 1728, and "by 1100 of Clabords and Sheaveing spliseing and joynting them" in 1729. Beginning with the late seventeenth century, stair balusters must be accounted for as well, and while turners were present during the period, Joseph Brown, Jr., also, apparently, owned a lathe, for he charges on occasion for "turning Rounds."[37] In a similar vein, Ezra Clapp of Milton, whose profession is not given, billed the town in 1695/6 "for making a kasment and frame," "for turning 27 banisters," and "for a peace of planke for the south dore sill [of the meetinghouse] and putting of it in."[38]

With respect to both house frame *and* trim we can report with assurance that the records uniformly refuse to support the popular attribution of such work to shipwrights. The claim seems to be based on romantically inspired explanations of the picturesque irregularity of line in so many early houses and must be considered mythical. Quite to the contrary, the few documents we have which link the labors of house carpenter and shipwright furnish just the opposite proof. William Bennett, for example, an Essex County carpenter, deposed that about 1647, when John Winthrop, Jr., had established a salthouse in Salem, he had been employed there "upon Carpintry worke some times for Mr. Winthrope and some times hewing Timber for ship or vessells use upon the Comon Lands Adjacent Mr. Winthrope,"[39] while John Elderkin of nearby Lynn, a carpenter and millwright who removed about 1650 to the New London, Connecticut, area, is reputed to have built a ship there in 1661.[40] The house erected about 1665 by Eleazer Gedney in Salem, standing then at the water's edge, is clearly the product of experienced house carpenters. Mr. Gedney was a shipwright, and the relatively small lot of land on which the house stands, about half an acre, was near his shipyard. A deed of 1697 refers to "the buildplace" here where "Mr. Eleazer Gedney was wont to launch his vessels."[41] The property passed ultimately to Gedney's son-in-law, also a boat builder, and it is amusing to note that at some point, perhaps in the early eighteenth century, when a strengthening of the junction of a tie beam with its supporting post was found necessary, the very practical device used was a ship's knee, of which a number were presumably strewn about the yard.

Concerning more general aspects of the profession, builders and their employees, then as now, were hard-working or lazy, successful or indigent, pillars of their communities or continual troublemakers. Samuel Bennett of Lynn, for example, a house carpenter who came from England in 1635 at age twenty-four, was forever involved with the law, saying scornfully that he cared neither for the town nor its order, and

being admonished for sleeping in time of service or for taking away a cart and pair of wheels. He was characterized by one of his contemporaries as "stout and insolent" and even more forthrightly by another as "the verryest Rascoll in new England."[42] Trouble could arise as a result of the culture barrier as well. One William Fisher, carpenter, had arrived in Boston in 1675 as servant to Mr. Thomas Hobson of Bristol in England, and could find no taker for his indentured time. John Hull complained to Hobson later that Fisher "had not bene wonted to our Countrey Carpenters way and that williame was much more in words then in deeds and greatly adicted to Company."[43]

As for quality, what about the mystique which makes a paragon of the early craftsman? Were these men infallible? Timothy Hawkins, carpenter, for one admitted humbly in 1640 in a petition to the General Court, that having built a house "for the Country" at Castle Island he was aware of "some smale foult in the postes, yet now the same being viewed by workmen it appeareth that there is some other default therein . . . for which he [is] much grieved."[44] Of a different temperament, and incapable of self-criticism, apparently, was John Wilcott of Newbury, continually before the courts to answer charges of shoddy workmanship. Practicing both as millwright and carpenter he was assailed with reports of contracts not properly performed, floors laid so loose that a man could put his hand in, split boards used which did not come together at the edges, a windmill "not soficiently undarpined" nor tightly covered, with vanes, arms, sails, and upper running gears inadequate, and tasks undertaken for which he was not judged to have the requisite skill. For all these accusations he had nothing but truculent retorts. Witnesses testified in 1680 to having heard Wilcott's son say that they did not care "If the Divell had the windmill" as long as they got their money.[45]

The soundness and well-executed detail of the great majority of surviving seventeenth-century structures, however, are the most telling arguments in favor of the average builder's ability. At

the upper end of the spectrum we have nowhere, perhaps, a clearer insight into the level of professional achievement of the New World carpenter than that found in the circumstantial agreement executed in 1657 with Thomas Joy and Bartholomew Barnard, two Boston carpenters, for the erection of a "very substantiall and Comely" edifice, the first Boston townhouse. The contract reveals clearly an unusual measure of attainment among certain seventeenth-century artisans. The structure was to measure sixty-six by thirty-six feet, "set upon twenty one Pillers of full ten foot high between Pedestall and Capitall . . . placed upon foundation of stones in the bottome." There were to be jetties, three gable ends on each side, "A walke upon the Top fourteen or 15 foote wide with two Turrets, and turned Balasters and railes, round about the walke," and all this "according to A modell or draught Presented to us, by the said Tho: Joy, and Barth: Bernad." The specifications reflect a concern for craftsmanship of the highest order and reliance upon the professional builders' judgment as well, for Joy and Barnard were responsible not only for the "modell or draught" but also for "finding things necisarie and meet for the said Building viz: Timber in everie respect and of everie sort, substantiall and meet according to Proportion and Art."[46] The language of the contract may have been simply pro forma; its content, however, suggests the full expectation of the client that here were two seventeenth-century Boston carpenters at least who could perform at a thoroughly sophisticated level.

We cannot stress too heavily the fact that the earliest English carpenters brought with them not only the acquired knowledge of their trade but also their familiar building tools. Indeed, Francis Higginson, writing back to England in 1629, before the mass migrations had begun, urged all prospective emigrants to "be sure to furnish yourselves with things fitting to be had, before you come . . . all manner of carpenters' tools, and a good deal of iron and steel to make nails, and locks for houses . . . and glass for windows, and many other things, which were better for you to think of them there than to want them here." A year later, in 1630, having composed a "Catalogue of such needful things as every planter doth or ought to provide to go to New-England," he enumerated "1 broad axe, 1 felling axe, 1 steel handsaw, 1 whipsaw, 1 hammer . . . 2 augers, 4 chisels, 2 piercers, stocked, 1 gimlet, 1 hatchet, 2 frowers [frows]," as well as "Nails, of all sorts."[47]

These recommendations were aimed at the average planter. An inspection of the immigrant carpenter's tool chest reveals how well the professional builder was outfitted. From an early legal action, for example, we learn that Edward Jones of Wellingboro in the county of Northampton, "on or about the first day of May Anno 1639" delivered "on London Bridge" into the hands of his son, Edward Jones, then a carpenter's apprentice bound for Boston, a box of clothing and tools. These included "one broade axe, one narrow axe, one adds [adz], one twyebill, one dozen of awgers from two inches and halfe to halfe an inch and an inch, two paire of chisells, one gouge, two paire of smoothing plane Irons, two joynt irons, one hollowing iron, one halfe round [and] one rabbetting iron."[48] A similar array of tools was owned by Peter Branch "of Halden in Kent in owld England Carpenter," whose will is dated June 16, 1638, and "who dyed aboard the Shipp called the Castle in his voyage to N.E." a short time later: "a Tiller of Whipp Sawe, 3 Chalk lynes, Augers and 4 owld Chiseles, a wrest to sett a Sawe withall, a plane, a bitt and a Chisell, 7 Augers, 2 sockett wedges and a sledge, 3 Axes . . . and 3 broadaxes and a hatchett, a Matock and a hammer, a Carpenters Case, a whipp sawe, 2 handsawes, 3 handsawes, one thwart sawe [and] one thousand of nayles."[49] And for Essex County at a slightly later date we have the estate appraisal for Michael Carthwick of Ipswich, carpenter, taken in 1647, which includes "a hatchett, 2000 of nailes, one large handsaw, 7 axes, one twibill, one long saw, one hand saw, 5 augers, 4 augers, 2 ham[mer]s and a holdfast and 16 planes, 9 chissells, several small chis-

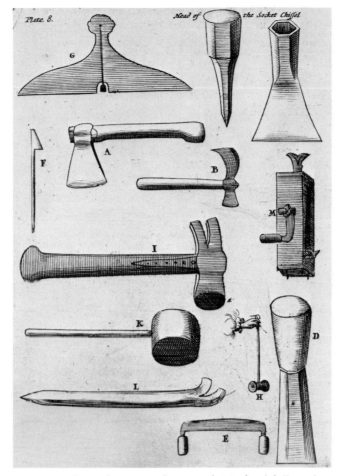

Figure 41. Plate 8 from Joseph Moxon's *Mechanick Exercises* (London, 1683), showing carpenters' tools, including A. ax, B. adz, D. ripping chisel, E. drawknife, and M. jack.

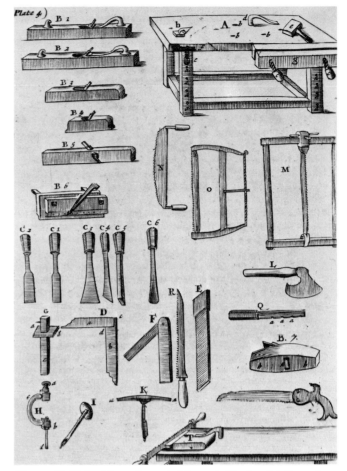

Figure 42. Plate 4 from Joseph Moxon's *Mechanick Exercises* (London, 1683), showing joiners' tools, including B. planes, C. chisels, C6. gouge, H. piercer, I. gimlet, K. auger, L. hatchet, M. pit saw, N. whip saw, O. frame saw, and (unlettered, above the bench), hand saw.

sells, a shave, a little square, a little sawe and a hatchett, an auger and a frame sawe and hand saw, a frow, a mattock and a square, a beetle ring and 4 wedges," as well as "several tooles sold to Jo: Catcham" and "Tooles laid by for willm Addams."[50]

Such additional items as "2 owld wimbles" (ca. 1640), "three draweing knives" and "one crosse cut sawe" (1640), "a lath frowe" (1643), "one payre of pinchers" (1662), "a breast wimble with bitts" (1667), and "2 perser bitts" (1644) are recorded.[51] The implements themselves are in nearly every case readily identifiable[52] (figure 41). Thus we recognize, in turn, the narrow felling ax, the ponder-

ous broad ax for trimming square the fallen timber, and the long-handled, broad-bladed adz used in smoothing the surfaces of a beam. The hatchet was then a small variety of the broad ax for dressing the surface of the wood, while the T-shaped twibil, double-headed, was employed in cutting mortises.

The wide-bladed hand saw resembles the carpenter's hand saw of today except for the open shape of its handle as opposed to the modern hollow grasp, and was used for general work in shaping and fitting. The frame saw is also easily identified as the thin saw blade strained upon an oblong wooden frame. In its larger form the frame

The Builders and Their Resources

Figure 43. Plane initialed L. C. and dated 1666 which descended in the Curtiss family of Stratford, Conn. *Photo, Einar M. Larson, 1969.*

saw was universally employed in sawing logs longitudinally into boards, sometimes but not invariably over an open pit, with two men, each managing one of the narrower ends of the frame. The late seventeenth-century author Joseph Moxon, in fact, identifies and illustrates this form as a pit saw (figure 42). The cross-cut or thwart saw, operated then, as now, by two men, each holding one of two vertical wooden handles, was less important because it simply cut across logs and did not make boards. Moxon describes this implement as a whip saw. Contemporary documents, however, by mentioning the cross-cut and whip saw in the same breath, suggest that the two were differentiated in some way. A sixteenth-century continental source illustrates the sawing of boards from a log by means of an unframed saw equipped with tillers or horizontal handle bars.[53] Since the Branch inventory and an Essex County inventory of 1678 link the whip saw with tillers,[54] we may hypothesize that the term was used among the first New England settlers to describe an unframed pit saw in one form or another.

Moxon illustrates both the semicircular gouge and the chisel and distinguishes a variety of the latter which have been used immemorially by the carpenter to edge, notch, hollow, and mortise woodwork. Similarly, he shows us the small gimlet or wimble, the larger auger, and the wooden piercer, or brace, with its metal bit—all of them associated with the drilling of holes. Planes, which he considers to be more properly joiners' tools, were also in widespread use among seventeenth-century carpenters with many and varied "irons" for smoothing, rabbeting, and molding (figures 42 and 43). Among these we may mention in particular the creasing plane, which is thought to have been the implement used to create the delicate decoration that we identify today as "shadow molding." In 1665 John Slater and Robert Knight of Marblehead agreed to "Bord the fore side of the Metting howse" and plane the boards and rabbet them, and to "ranne the Eigdgeges [edges] with the Creas plainge."[55] Another important paring or surfacing tool, to be classed rather with the plane than the adz, was the draw knife or shave, furnished at both ends with handles at right angles to its straight blade.

Finally, we recognize the frow, a thick-backed knife hafted at right angles upward from a dull blade, designed to be clubbed through squared or quartered logs in order to split out clapboards, shingles, and lath. Heavier timber had to be riven by wedge splitting, for which purposes iron wedges were pounded through the log with the beetle, a wooden mallet, the cylindrical head of which was iron-ringed.

Most of these tools were brought from England, although domestic manufacture must have begun almost at once. William Wood, concerned like Higginson with advice to the prospective planter, had urged the settlers in 1634 to bring "all manner of tooles for Workemen . . . with Axes both broad and pitching axes. All manner of Augers, piercing bits, Whipsaws, Two-handed saws, Froes, both for the riving of Pailes and Laths, rings for Beetles heads, and Iron-wedges," despite the fact, as he adds, "all these be made in the Countrey: (there being divers Black-smiths)."[56] One record, at least, of domestic manufacture can be found in 1663 when Stephen Fosdick of Charlestown mentions "the felling ax that goodman Cutler made mee," probably John Cutler, an early Charlestown blacksmith.[57]

Surely no "tool" or technological device was of greater value to the builder or more important to the beginning economy of the colonies than the sawmill.[58] It is important to recognize, however, in the buildings themselves, the evidence for hewing and pit sawing as well. Saw pits are mentioned almost at once in the communities which made up the Massachusetts Bay Colony. At Dedham, when the building of the meetinghouse was undertaken in 1637, two shillings and six pence were allowed "for digging of Pitts 12: foote in length 4½. foote broad [and] 5: foote deepe," and the carpenters were "to have for makeing of pitholls 12d. the payer."[59] While no systematic effort has been made to gauge the proportion of pit-sawn timber to those building units which have been hewn or mill sawn, extant structures erected during the course of the seventeenth century and documents as well testify to the continuing presence of sawyers and use of the pit saw[60] (figure 44A).

It is clear, nevertheless, that the volume of sawmill lumber increases sharply throughout the seventeenth century. Much of this can be credited to the many local mills in the Massachusetts Bay area, which must at the very least have answered the individual communities' demands. In Dedham, in fact, during the very year of 1659 that a committee appointed by the town drew up articles of agreement with Lieutenant Joshua Fisher and Eleazer Lusher and provided encouragement for building and managing a saw mill on the Neponset River, the town also granted the Natick Indians liberty to finish "the sawe mille that is in good part allready built by the Indians" and to enjoy "the free use of the streame for that use" with land adjoining, "and allso to make use of such pyne or Ceader Timber as they shall cutt at the said mille."[61]

While such building units of smaller scantling as studs, common rafters, collars, and floor joists are often found to be sawmill sawn, especially in the later decades of the century—the earliest known examples being the wall braces of oak in the Pierce house, Dorchester, ca. 1650, and the floor joists of the oldest portion of the Whipple house in Ipswich, ca. 1655 (figure 44B)—the sawmill's greatest activity seems to have been in the cutting of plank and boards, which had become a chief commodity in trade. The sawmill of Edward Gilman in Exeter, New Hampshire, was producing prodigious numbers, about four score thousand of boards and planks for three fourths of the mill in 1650 and part of 1651, and about 60,000 in 1652 and 1653. If the mill had been properly furnished, we are told, it would have cut much more. A good deal of this, apparently, was being shipped to Boston.[62]

A number of contemporary accounts mention the abundant building materials found in the virgin territory of North America by the English settlers.[63] William Wood, for example, in 1634, assured the prospective planter that "the Timber of the Countrey growes straight, and tall, some trees being twenty, some thirty foot high, before they spread forth their branches." For the benefit of "mechanicall artificers" he goes on to identify and discuss the varieties present. "The chiefe and common Timber for ordinary use is Oake, and Walnut," he writes. "Of Oakes there be three kindes, the red Oake, white, and blacke; as these are different in kinde, so are they chosen for such uses as they are most fit for, one kind being more fit for clappboard, others for sawne board, some fitter for shipping, others for houses."[64] Thomas Morton, who arrived at Massachusetts Bay before Winthrop's company, also mentions more than a single variety of oak. There were "two sorts, white and redd, excellent tymber for the building both of howses and shipping, and they are found to be a tymber that is more tough then the oak of England."[65] Neither of these writers, however, identify which specie was considered best for the individual functions described. Generally speaking, and despite the fact that furniture makers in

Figure 44A. Boardman house, Saugus, Mass. Detail of joists in hall chamber ceiling, showing marks of the pit saw, ca. 1687. *Photo, William W. Owens, Jr., 1974.*

Figure 44B. Whipple house, Ipswich, Mass. Detail of joists in hall chamber ceiling, showing marks of the power-driven saw, ca. 1655. *Photo, William W. Owens, Jr., 1974.*

Figure 45. Giddings-Burnham house, Ipswich, Mass. Interior wainscot door, probably before 1650. *Photo, William W. Owens, Jr., 1974.*

The Builders and Their Resources

Figure 46. Pierce house, Dorchester, Mass. Detail of original clapboards, rear wall, ca. 1650. *Photo, William W. Owens, Jr., 1974.*

Essex County at least seem to have preferred the red oak with its greater porosity and knot-free expanse of trunk,[66] white oak was apparently the more popular material for house frames, perhaps because of its imperviousness to rot.

We are too limited in our knowledge of those houses built during the middle of the seventeenth century to determine how often oak was used for finish trim. Recalling that doors and partitions in even the smaller English houses of the period were normally of oak, we might expect to find similar conditions here at the first. Yet there is but a single piece of evidence in the form of a wainscot door of oak found in a reused position in the Giddings-Burnham house in Ipswich, ca. 1680, and dating probably to the period of an earlier house on the property (figure 45). John Josselyn, on the other hand, who visited New England in 1663, suggests that red oak was not uncommon for such purposes.

> When they have cut it down and clear'd it from the branches, they pitch the body of the Tree in a muddy place in a River, with the head downward for some time, afterwards they draw it out, and when it is seasoned sufficiently, they saw it into boards for Wainscot, and it will branch out into curious works.[67]

John Evelyn reported to the Royal Society in 1662 that the "*Chestnut* is (next the *Oak*) one of the most sought after by the *Carpenter* and *Joyner*,"[68] and Thomas Morton, writing in 1622, notes that "there is very great plenty, the tymber whereof is excellent for building."[69] William Wood speaks of chestnut only in passing, though it was indeed used occasionally in the construction of the seventeenth-century New England house frame. One documentary reference at least can be found in 1712 when the Boston selectmen contracted with Edward Foster of Dorchester to build a barn forty feet long and thirty feet wide at Deer Island, "the frame thereof to be all of Oak

Timber Excepting the plates which are to be either of Oak or Pine." A short time later they agreed "that where Mr. Edwd. Foster is obliged by Covenant to put Oke Timber in the Frame of the Barn at Deer Island, Chestnut Shall be Accepted in Sted thereof."[70]

William Wood, in describing the cedar, tells us that it "is a tree of no great growth . . . [and] is more desired for ornament than substance, being of colour red and white like Eugh. . . . It is commonly used for seeling of houses, and making of Chests, boxes, and staves."[71] Thomas Morton found an "abundance" of cedar upon his arrival at Massachusetts Bay in 1622, "and if any man be desirous to finde out in what part of the Country the best Cedars are," he writes, "he must get into the bottom grounds, and in vallies that are wet at the springe of the yeare."[72] The swamp cedar does indeed seem to have been preferred, as we learn when the town of Dedham in 1648 granted to John Kingsbury "ceader timber in the common swamp to supplye him in his finishing his house," and in 1656 granted Daniel Morse "two Seders to make Clabbord out [of] in . . . the Swampe."[73] The original clapboards on the rear walls of the Fairbanks house in Dedham, ca. 1637, and the Pierce house in Dorchester (figure 46), preserved by the early addition of lean-tos, are of cedar. Use of this material for clapboards, coinciding with the entries in the early records, is significant, and would indicate that oak clapboards, which have survived in a number of cases, were not the invariable rule in the seventeenth century.

In 1663 John Josselyn wrote of the white cedar that "this Tree the *English* [at Massachusetts Bay] saw into boards to floor their Rooms, for which purpose it is excellent, long lasting, and wears very smooth and white; likewise they make shingles to cover their houses with instead of tyle, it will never warp."[74] Few if any original seventeenth-century roof shingles have come down to us. The documents, on the other hand, are not silent. The selectmen of Dorchester, for example, in 1670, granted to Ensign Daniel Fisher of Dedham and his brothers "soe much Seare Ceder as they shall make use off for Shingle . . . in a Swamp or Swamps neer pole-plaine," and Edward Randolph reports in 1676 that the timber-framed building which then constituted Harvard College was covered with shingles of cedar.[75] Elsewhere, in Andover Town Meeting it was ordered "that noe man shall have libertie after the first of January 1675 to sell, or transport any Cedar out of the towne, either in shingles or otherwise."[76]

The New England ash, wrote William Wood in 1634, "is much different from the Ash of England, being brittle and good for little, so that Wallnut is used for it."[77] Whatever the extent of its use in house building in sixteenth- and seventeenth-century England,[78] it seems clear that our settlers did indeed avoid it, and no more than one or two references to its use have been found. The Reverend William Bentley of Salem, for example, on June 5, 1799, called upon an eighty-three-year-old man in Swampscott whose "House was built for his Grandfather in 1660." Of this structure he wrote: "An ash frame now firm."[79] Similarly, we have not as yet identified in any significant measure the extent to which larch may have been used, though Josselyn writes in 1663 that cedar, oak, "and the Larch-tree are best for building. Groundsels made of Larch-tree will never rot, and the longer it lyes the harder it growes."[80]

As for the ubiquitous New England pine, William Wood is succinct. "The Firre and Pine bee trees that grow in many places," he writes, "shooting up exceeding high, especially the Pine. They doe afford good masts, good board, Rozin and Turpentine."[81] The almost exclusive use of this wood for finish trim, including doors, window sash, boarded partitions, and floors, can be overwhelmingly demonstrated in the seventeenth-century houses of Massachusetts Bay which have come down to us. In fact, vertically boarded partitions of pine, found almost from the start, occur far more commonly in New than in old England, and suggest an innovational significance related to its ample availability. Pine was also used on occasion for shingles, as we find in Wenham, where the selectmen in 1700 granted Nathaniel Walderne "so much Timber pine or

Figure 47. Whipple house, Ipswich, Mass. Detail of hall summer beam, ca. 1655. *Photo, William W. Owens, Jr., 1974.*

Figure 48. Cooper-Frost-Austin house, Cambridge, Mass. Detail of chimney tie beam and fireplace wall, hall chamber, ca. 1689. *Photo, William W. Owens, Jr., 1974.*

hemlock as may make shingle anuf for the shingleing ye west end of his hous."[82] We have very little information about the shingling of walls as opposed to clapboarding, and it is virtually impossible to surmise whether the builders at Massachusetts Bay were apt to prefer cedar for the roof and pine for wall shingles, or whether these Wenham records, which include at least two additional references to pine or hemlock shingles during the period, reflect a purely local situation.

The prevalence of pine as a part of the frame is also hard to gauge. The various structural components of the seventeenth-century house are usually of oak or occasionally chestnut, especially the posts, braces, and studs, but the massive summer beams in the earliest portion of the Whipple house in Ipswich are of pine (figure 47). Later in the century as well pine is not infrequently found as part of the frame, particularly in the case of girts and summers. With oak predom-

inating at first in any examples where pine also is used, as in the case of the Whipple house, the balance shifts during the first half of the eighteenth century in favor of pine, which ultimately in the later eighteenth and nineteenth centuries replaces oak in the frame to a large extent. As early as 1697, in fact, the selectmen of Wenham granted Thomas Fiske "pine Timber for building his hous and for planke and board," suggesting more or less an exclusive use of pine for the frame,[83] and if, as supposed, this town grant relates to the now extant Captain Thomas Fiske house (the Claflin-Richards house, so-called), we find that all major units, except the posts and ground-story chimney girt, in the frame of the earliest pine-planked portion are of pine.

The ultimate logic of selection may have been based largely on local practicalities. The Whipple-Matthews house in Hamilton, built between 1680 and 1683, for example, is not easily explained on any other grounds. The posts, studs, and braces are of oak, as are the end and chimney tie beams, the girts of the integral lean-to, and the floor joists. The summer beams, on the other hand, together with the front, rear, and end girts of the main house and the rear wall plate, a single stick forty-five feet long, are all of pine. The roof is mixed, with principal and common rafters of pine, collars of oak, and oak for the principal purlins in the front slope, while the same members in the rear slope are of pine. The preference for pine here may have been related quite simply to its length and straightness. The chimney tie beam of the original portion of the Cooper-Frost-Austin house in Cambridge, ca.1689, however, is of oak, and quite markedly crooked (figure 48). Perhaps the builder was stubbornly clinging to tradition in his selection of material. It seems hard to imagine that a long straight piece of pine could not have been found. As it was, the frame had to be adjusted to the curve of the stick.

It has been argued that one reason, at least, for the adoption of pine may have been the gradual depletion of oak owing to continued building needs as the seventeenth century wore on. Yet as late as 1698 commissioners appointed to investigate colonial naval stores reported that they found in the forests of Massachusetts and New Hampshire "vast quantities of white pine fit for masts of all dimensions, and of excellent white oak for timbers of all sorts."[84] Early and unprecedented pressures upon the consumption of oak, nevertheless, may very well have been a perceptible factor in the acceptance—hesitant at first—of native New England pine for use in the house frame.

The first settlers at Massachusetts Bay had left England at a time when timber depletion was becoming a widespread problem. John Norden, an early seventeenth-century surveyor of His Majesty's English forests, voiced concern in the guise of a "Bayly": "for you see this country inclinable to wood and timber much: yet within these twenty yeeres they have bene diminished two parts of three: and if it go on by like propor-

tion, our children will surely want."[85] In spite of what must have seemed like inexhaustible forest reserves, the colonists in New England moved quickly to regulate the supply. Nearly all of the town records for those communities clustered about Massachusetts Bay contain recurring orders throughout the century aimed at the conservation of local timber resources. Dedham may serve as a typical example. In 1636, the first year of settlement, it was ordered that if any man felled without permission a tree "of six Inches thicknes in the Carfe" or of any scantling above six inches any place within the town, except upon his own property, he was to be fined twenty shillings for each tree so felled. "Wood reeves" or overseers were appointed to enforce these ordinances and for the further "preventing of the Waste of Timber," any one who let a grant of building stuff lie unimproved more than six months after felling was to forfeit it all to the town. Allowances were strictly supervised. In 1669, to cite one or two among many, Anthony Fisher, Jr., was permitted to take "7: or 8: tunne of timber upon the common Lande for the building a house in Towne," while his fellow townsman, John Mackintosh, was summoned before the selectmen in 1664 to explain why he had felled timber on the town common "without leave" to build himself a barn. Such grants could also serve as remuneration of a sort, as when the selectmen in 1640 stipulated that Jonathan Fairbanks "maye have one Ceder tree set out unto him to dispose of wher he will: In consideration of some speciall service that he hath done for the towne." They added quickly, however, that this grant should not be "a president for others to obteyne the like without some speciall cause guiding therunto."

Timber allowances will be found sprinkled throughout the Dedham town records for the balance of the century. In the meantime, the selectmen revised the ground rules from time to time as new problems arose. In 1651, for example, it was realized that fire wood was "now much spent." To accommodate the townspeople and in order "to preserve such Oake trees as at present or heere after ar like to be usefull Timber for the

supplye of building," it was ordered that the inhabitants could fell and take from the common land only such fuel as they might need for their own burning, provided that they be such trees "as by reason of the Rottennes crookednes or other defect ar unfitt for Timber." This order prohibited the felling of young oak trees as well. A different problem altogether was posed by the sale of building timber from this town for use in Boston, which had virtually no natural supplies of her own. By 1669 the practice had become a matter for concern, and on the 27th of February in that year the selectmen moved to regulate the exportation of "any oake Timber being one foote or more." A schedule of fines was imposed with one half of the proceeds to the informer and the other half to the selectmen. Shortly thereafter Daniel Pond, a carpenter, admitted to the authorities that before the publication of this order he had felled "about 8 Tunnes of Timber for building a house at Boston," and having thus openly presented his case was allowed to proceed upon the payment of sixteen shillings "in merchantible building nayles."[86]

Other Massachusetts Bay communities were also engaged in the business of exportation. Hingham on the South Shore had profited greatly by transporting timber, plank, and masts for shipping to Boston, as well as cedar and pine-board to other towns and to remote parts, "even as far as Barbadoes."[87] Boston had early become the center for traffic in building materials well beyond the limits of New England. One Abraham Palmer, for example, received "aboard the may flower of Boston" in 1652 "a frame of a howse at the price of forty pounds seventeene shillings which I am to sell at the barbadoes," while a decade later, in 1662, the *Golden Falcon* of London was freighted in Boston "with Beames for houses boards, pipestaves, tarr and other Lumber from said Boston to Terceraes."[88] With respect to such activities one can well appreciate the anguished request by the commissioners and selectmen of Boston on August 18, 1679, that the transportation of boards and other building timber out of the Colony be prohibited for a time "in regard of the townes occasions thereof being layd wast by the late fire," which had destroyed virtually the entire trading center of the city.[89]

While such conservation measures later in the seventeenth century may be readily understandable, those for the earlier years require careful scrutiny. The reasons which led the first settlers to establish a timber rationing system are not entirely simple. We shall probably never know just how abundant were the supplies of building trees which they found upon their arrival. The early writers for the most part are rhapsodic on the subject, and surely in light of conditions in England by 1620 the wooded New England coast must have presented something of a feast for famished eyes. Thomas Morton, for example, says of his first visit in 1622: "I did not thinke that in all the knowne world . . . [Massachusetts Bay] could be paralel'd, for so many goodly groves of trees." Yet it is Morton who has described more thoroughly than any other writer the prevailing Indian custom of burning over the country "twize a yeare, viz: at the Spring, and the fall of the leafe." The reason, he writes, is because the land "would other wise be . . . all a coppice wood, and the people would not be able in any wise to passe through the Country out of a beaten path." He is principally concerned, however, with the fact that "The burning of the grasse destroyes the underwoods, and so scorcheth the elder trees that it shrinkes them, and hinders their grouth very much." If one wants to find large trees and good timber, he adds, it will not be on the upland. Rather, one must seek for them, "(as I and others have done,) in the lower grounds, where the grounds are wett."[90]

Whatever the available amount of wood suitable for building at Massachusetts Bay, one must recall that long before the first settlements in North America there were well-developed concepts of forest management in England designed to cope with the problem of building supply and demand over an extended period of time. Planning for future uses and rationing of timber were undoubtedly a far more everyday component of the English emigrant's thinking than we have realized. In Cambridge, Massachusetts, in fact, as late as 1666 the time-honored English nomenclature is preserved when Samuel Reyner was appointed on April 9 of that year to be "Surveyor of the woods and commons on that quarter where he liveth, and to enforme the Select men from time to time, as he shall find any stroy to be done thereon."[91] Local variations in the rate of depletion of English forests may have had some slight impact upon attitudes among the first settlers. Suffolk and Norfolk, for example, seem to have experienced shortages earlier than Essex, though here, too, one can identify pocketlike areas where it was necessary by the late sixteenth century to go further afield for building stuff, as opposed to wood for fuel. Quantitative analysis of specific early English buildings, moreover, has provided an exact indication of the number and size of trees necessary for their construction, and demonstrated that it took a great many trees to support sustained building activities over an appreciable period of time.[92]

In the New World there were no pre-existing dwellings which could be repaired or enlarged. The volume of new building, especially during the first two decades when several thousand peo-ple had to be housed at once, must have produced soon the specter if not the actuality of depletion. As early as January 1637 the town of Salem ordered "that henceforward noe sawyer clapboard cleaver or any other person whatsoever shall cutt downe saw or cleave any boards or tymber within our lymits and transport them to other places," because, as the recorder explains, "we have found by experience that the transporting of boards and clapboards from our plantation hath . . . bared our woods verie much of the best tymber trees of all sorts."[93] Since the colonists did not demonstrate immediately a willingness or, for that matter, an ability to push very far beyond the coastal waterways to tap the richly wooded hinterlands, it could be argued that timber rationing found consistently in nearly every community at Massachusetts Bay reflects more than anything else the English settlers' long-evolved and deeply ingrained attitudes about the limited availability of building trees. They were surely not selfishly blind to the problem. Perhaps no single piece of evidence is more revealing than the entry of December 27, 1667, in the Dedham Town Records in which the efficacy of existing regulations was questioned and attention focused once again on the fact "that great waste is made in the wood and timber in the Common Lande of the Towne," and this they judged "very prejudiciall at present but especially for the succeeding generations which it concerne us to consider."[94]

CHAPTER V

Assembly and Rearing of the House Frame

OUR FIRST CONCERN in analyzing the seventeenth-century house frame must be the identification of the individual members and their correct terminology. Traditional nomenclature for the several timbers in the frame is derived variously from the building jargon of the carpenter, the layman, and the architectural historian, and is not always technically explicit. The expression summer beam, for example, has been in use for several centuries, and has always had specific meaning for carpenter and layman alike. One assumes that its appearance in contracts and other documents is for the very reason that it *did* have such an exact connotation. The client then as now looked at the work in progress and was satisfied that the frame of his new house looked sound and workmanlike and was content to call the salient features by their familiar names. It is unlikely that anyone discussed with his carpenter the fact that the word summer beam can be properly applied to structural members with quite different functions.

Then, too, words are subject to changes in meaning. A technical term in carpentry inherited from the past which defines a structural component no longer used will not uncommonly be applied to some other member that has come into general use. Historically speaking, "this occurred more often than new terms for new components were coined."[1] Thus we may find flagrant and not always comprehensible terminological contradictions. The early nineteenth-century English architect Peter Nicholson, for example, invests the term sleeper, as do his New England contemporaries Asher Benjamin and Edward Shaw, with the same meaning which it is consistently given in seventeenth-century American documents, namely, that of a floor framing member at foundation level,[2] while Richard Neve defines the sleeper as a roof member, an oblique rafter that lies in the gutter,[3] and Joseph Moxon, a few decades earlier, calls it a purlin.[4]

Our designations for structural members, whether derived from early sources or folk parlance, can amount to little more than a convenient system for identification. What is more important is understanding the technical function of each member in the frame, and, when no other terminology is available, finding the language which most precisely describes that function. We begin, then, at the bottom of the house frame and proceed upwards.

GROUND-SILL

The ground-sill is the horizontal timber laid along the foundation into which the wall members are framed (figure 49). The sill, as it is sometimes called in short form, may also receive the frame members of the ground-story floor, consisting normally in the seventeenth century of a carrying beam with its joists, or may rest directly upon sleepers without jointing. This causes the sill to appear in the lower-story rooms of the house and was considered by an earlier generation of architectural historians to be proof of exceptional age.[5] The practice, however, can be found throughout the seventeenth century, and occurs as late as about 1715 in the frame of the progressive Parson Barnard house in North Andover. In function the ground-sill provides basic support for the house frame as a whole.

POST

The posts, being the principal means by which the structure remains upright, divide the carcass into bays, and have as their primary function in all but exceptional cases the support of the individual roof frames (figure 49). Corner posts (the term found in Boston as early as 1654)[6] mark the outer angles or corners of the house. Those posts at the front and rear of the building which limit the space the chimney is to occupy are invariable and may perhaps best be described as chimney posts, though that designation has not been

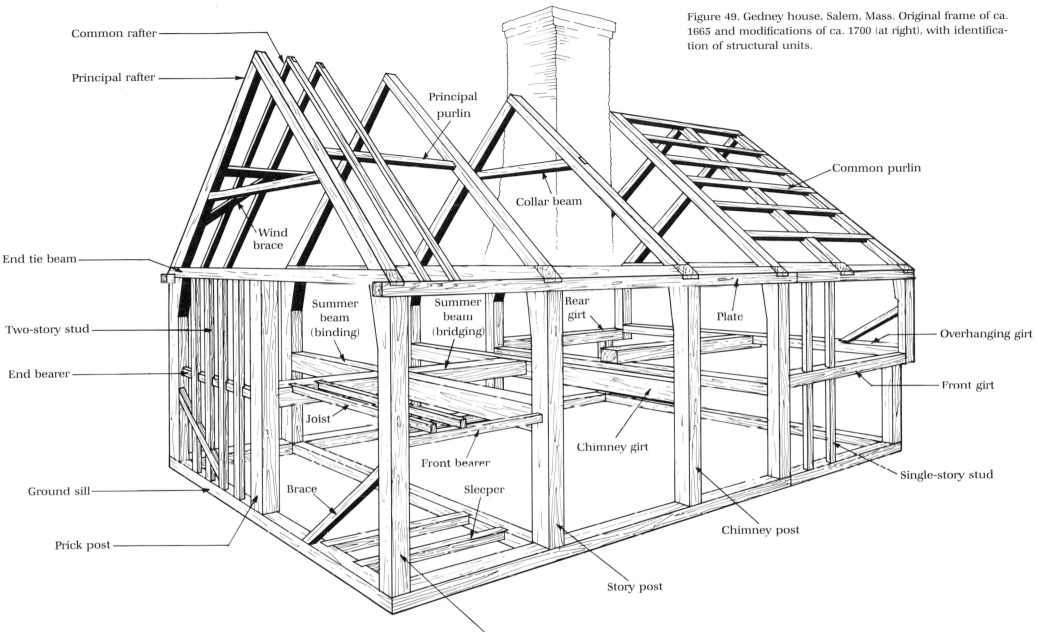

Figure 49. Gedney house, Salem, Mass. Original frame of ca. 1665 and modifications of ca. 1700 (at right), with identification of structural units.

Labels in figure: Common rafter; Principal rafter; Principal purlin; Common purlin; Collar beam; Wind brace; End tie beam; Summer beam (binding); Summer beam (bridging); Rear girt; Plate; Overhanging girt; Two-story stud; Front girt; End bearer; Joist; Chimney girt; Ground sill; Front bearer; Single-story stud; Brace; Sleeper; Prick post; Chimney post; Story post; Corner post

found in early documents. Not invariable are the posts sometimes found at the front and rear of the building which support transverse summer beams. It is probably to such a member that Increase Mather refers in his account of a bolt of lightning which struck a house in Marshfield, Plymouth Colony, in 1658, and "rent into shivers . . . one of the main posts of the house into which the summer was framed."[7] These intermediate posts in the front and rear walls may be referred to as story posts (wall posts where only of one-story height), while the English mill-wright's term prick post may be used for the post found under a gable.[8] Joseph Moxon, writing about 1680, defines prick posts in house carpentry as the units framed in "between Principal-Posts [corner posts], for the strengthning of the Carcass,"[9] and this meaning seems implied in a later barn contract of 1743 in Ipswich which specifies "two prick posts in Each Eand."[10]

In their fundamental support of the roof frames and in order that the tie beam of the roof might be securely seated, each of the posts in the front and rear walls of the house frame was normally set, as Moxon also notes, "with one of its narrowest sides towards the Front,"[11] and with a perceptible flare or jowl at the top (figure 50).

Assembly and Rearing of the House Frame

ary function they receive the wall covering both inside and out, and may also, when trenched for bearers, help support the second-story floor.

The stud can be of one- or full two-story length, the latter being found in the Fairbanks house, Dedham, ca. 1637, and in the oldest portion of the Whipple house, Ipswich, ca. 1655. In 1638 Deputy Governor Samuel Symonds, a native of Great Yeldham, Essex, suggested a similar construction for the house he wished to have built on his farm in Ipswich when he directed that the side-wall bearers "must not be pinned on but rather eyther lett in to the studds, or borne up with false studds."[12] While the two-story stud can be found occasionally in the later seventeenth century and even in the eighteenth, it does not appear to have become in any sense universal, despite certain economic advantages in its use. The "false studds" mentioned by Symonds, are not easily explained.

GIRT

The term girt appears both as a noun and as an adjective. In modern parlance we speak of front and rear girts, first- and second-story end girts, and chimney girts as well (figure 49). None of these qualifying terms has been found as yet in the contemporary record. Nor can we be entirely certain what variety of girt was being described when the town of Billerica in 1667, having ordered "That ther shall be a house [for fortification] built of stone and brick," twenty-six feet long and twenty-two feet wide, specified walls nine feet high to the underside of the plate, and "a floore, lying one foot below the plate, with crosse runners, the long girt lying cross the house."[13]

The front and rear girts, those horizontal timbers introduced into the wall frame midway between ground-sills and top plates, serve primarily to maintain the transverse frames erect and parallel and, by shortening the lengths of studs, to render the wall more rigid. They may also, as a secondary function, carry the ends of joists and thus help to support the second-story floor. The first-story end and chimney girts are technically

binding beams, a term we find as early as 1624 when Sir Henry Wotton writes that "Oake, and the like true hartie Timber being strong in all positions, may bee better trusted in crosse and traverse worke, for *Summers*, or guirding and binding *beames*, as they tearme them."[14] The binding beam must not only be transverse but must join upright posts as well. In principle these units help to stabilize the frame from vagary due to downward compression. While unlikely in reality, such compression could in theory cause the buckling inwards or outwards of the upright posts and studs. Both first-story end and chimney girts may also, as a secondary function, carry the ends of floor joists.

Those units which earlier writers have described as second-story end and chimney girts are properly tie beams,[15] and as a part of the roof frame are more appropriately considered within that context.

Finally, a second system of wall support, described in the following section, provided the seventeenth-century builder with an alternative to proper girts, and it is here that we find meaning for the specific directive in seventeenth-century building contracts that "the house or fframe is to bee a Girt house" (Marlborough, 1661), or that a given piece of building is to be "gert worke" (Dorchester, 1669).[16]

BEARER OR SIDE BEARER

The term side bearer refers to the horizontal member of smaller cross section which takes the place of front, rear, and end girts in houses where the studs are a full two stories in height (figure 49). The bearer is pinned to the stud which has usually been trenched to receive it, and has as a principal function the support of the second-story floor joists. This framing device may well be derived from solutions hit upon during the late sixteenth century in England, when later floors were introduced into formerly open halls upon bearers tacked to the existing walls. While the practice was thus in all likelihood rooted in expediency, there were economic advantages, too, which the client at least was presumably quick to

Figure 50. Pierce house, Dorchester, Mass. Detail of rear story post, hall chamber, ca. 1650. *Photo, William W. Owens, Jr., 1974.*

STUD

The term appears commonly and refers to those vertical units of smaller cross section set at stated intervals between the posts (figure 49). Like the posts the studs help support the roof, and thus resist downward compression. As a second-

grasp. The bearer was not only of smaller scant-ling than the regular girt, but the time and expense involved in preparing mortises and tenons for both studs and joists could be eliminated. Samuel Symonds seems to have appreciated this fact when he writes in 1638 of his farmhouse to be built at Ipswich: "I thinke to make it a girt howse will make it more chargeable then neede."[17] At a later date, early in the eighteenth century, one English writer, concerned also with costs, points out in terms of then current practice that "The Carpenter's Work to build a Barn in the Country that hath one single Stud, or one heighth of Studs to the Roof, is two Shillings a Foot, but if it have a double Stud and a Girt, 'tis worth two Shillings and Six-pence."[18]

SUMMER BEAM

The summer beam, one of the larger elements of the house frame, can be as wide as eighteen inches.[19] It is certainly one of the most important members in a purely visual sense (figure 49). As such it excites continual curiosity as to the origin of the term, which has considerable antiquity and was used by generations of English builders before the first settlements in North America. The accounts for the construction in 1338 of a timber-framed building in Cambridge, for example, refer to "somers" and "gistes" (joists), and there are references in Latin during the same century. At Trinity Hall, Cambridge, a contract in 1374 refers to *sumers et giystes pro solariis* and in 1357 corbels were inserted in a wall at Nottingham Castle *ad supponendum someras subtus gistas arearum*,[20] suggesting a possible derivation from the Latin *summus*, meaning literally the uppermost, highest, or topmost, but also in terms of rank or degree the greatest. The Oxford English Dictionary, on the other hand, argues for a root in the ancient Anglo-French word *sumer* or *somer*, meaning a packhorse, and presumably by extension in a building situation a burdenbearer. By the time our first colonists set sail for the New World the term had become a commonplace, and throughout the seventeenth century it consistently describes that major frame unit which ran

through the ceilings of their principal rooms. While contemporary definitions are explicit, for example, "the sommer or beame which lyes overthwart the great chamber" (Boston, 1638) and "A Beam full of Mortises for the Ends of Joists to lie in" (1726),[21] they do not give any hint of the complexity of the summer beam's functions.

Among the early houses at Massachusetts Bay, we may distinguish between summers that function as binding beams, those that are bridging agents, and those that, at the second-story level, are tie beams. The first-story summer is fundamentally a binding beam if it runs in a transverse direction and connects upright posts, in which case, like the first-story end and chimney girts, it helps to stabilize the frame from downward compression. Its direct involvement in the support of the floor above is a secondary function, as we find in the Gedney house, Salem, and later half of the Whipple house, Ipswich, added before 1683, where the binding beams support bridging timbers which in turn carry joists, or as in the Balch house, Beverly, of undetermined seventeenth-century date, the Samuel Pickman house, Salem, built before 1681, and the Parson Barnard house, North Andover, in which the binding beam itself receives the floor joists.

The summer beam as a bridging unit in either a transverse or longitudinal direction has as its primary function the support of the floor. It will normally be found at Massachusetts Bay running from chimney girt to end girt and is supported by them. Variations can be found, however, for example, in the left-hand (original) room of the Whipple house, Ipswich, in the right-hand end of the Austin Lord house in Ipswich, erected before 1653, and presumably also in the Fairbanks house, Dedham. In these cases the first-story hall summer beam as a bridging agent housed in the chimney girt is supported at the other end by a yoke framed into the studs (figure 51). At the Blake house, Dorchester, ca. 1650, the summers running in a longitudinal direction in both stories are supported at their outer ends by prick posts. And in those houses with an overhang, the summer as a bridging unit lying in a transverse posi-

tion may project over the first-story wall to help support that of the second story, as at the Hooper-Hathaway house in Salem, ca. 1682. As a bridging agent lying in a longitudinal position the summer beam derives from sixteenth-century building practices, when chimneys and floors were inserted in formerly open halls. Since the existing frame could not be sprung apart to receive the summer, the simplest solution was that of letting one end of it into the transverse girt at the lower end of the hall and lodging the other end in the masonry of the newly introduced chimney. Thus it will be seen that the longitudinal summer beam was to all intents and purposes a relatively recent development at the time of the first English settlements in North America.

While at least two examples of overhanging second stories that made use of the diagonal dragon beam survived into the twentieth century (Sun Tavern in Boston and Manning house in Ipswich, both probably late seventeenth century in date), none are now extant (figure 52). The term itself can be found in contemporary documents, for example in a contract of 1696 for an addition to a shop in Boston, where we are told there were to be "Foure dragon Summers att each corner one to beare said building, That is to jett, Eighteen Inches on the street att each end."[22] In function the dragon furnishes one method of support for the corner post of the second story when it overhangs at both the front and end of the house.

The choice that governed the selection of one of these binding and bridging structural systems over another involves conjecture. We may yet find that there is English regional significance in the variant discovered at the Blake house, to say nothing of the curious yoke arrangement at the Whipple and Austin Lord houses. In the latter case, however, economy is one obvious answer, and it is noteworthy that the summer as a binding beam, involving as it does additional posts and sometimes additional bridging units as well (material cost factor) and a larger number of joints (time/expense factor), implied a more costly house. Thus with the exception of the Salem area, which is subject to special considera-

Assembly and Rearing of the House Frame

Figure 51. Whipple house, Ipswich, Mass. Details of yoke supporting hall summer beam in gable end wall, ca. 1655.

tions, we are not surprised to find the summer as a bridging agent employed more commonly at Massachusetts Bay, particularly in the less ambitious houses.

JOIST

Floor joists are those slender units framed into summer beams and girts and tie beams (or supported upon the two latter), across which the floor boards are placed (figure 49). Their fundamental purpose, in other words, is the support of floors, a function implied in a number of contemporary contracts which instruct the builder "to Frame and fix Substantially a floore of Summers of Oake with Joyce therein" (Boston, 1696) and "to Lay three flors with Joys and bord" (Ipswich, 1659).[23] Moxon, it should be added, writing about 1680, notes that the "*Floor*, in *Carpentry* . . . is as well taken for the Fram'd work of Timber, as the Boarding over it."[24]

SLEEPER

The term sleeper distinguishes that unit which performs at foundation level the floor support function associated with the joist (figure 49). Jonathan Corwin of Salem, for example, in contract-

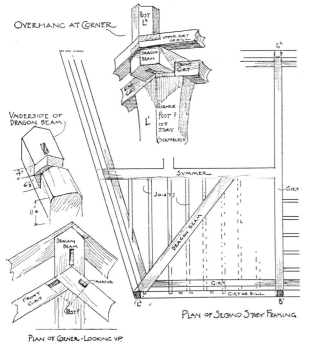

OVERHANG AT CORNER

UNDERSIDE OF DRAGON BEAM

PLAN OF CORNER-LOOKING UP.

PLAN OF SECOND STORY FRAMING

Figure 52. Sun Tavern, Boston, Mass. Details of overhanging second story, probably late seventeenth century. Demolished 1912.

ing for a house with Thomas Flint in 1679, mentions the "Joyce" as well as "Sleepers for the Lower ffloore," and the Town of Cambridge, in a grant of timber to Daniel Cheever in 1686, specified "some sleepers for his house over his seller."[25] One assumes that the distinguishing characteristics were the sleeper's larger cross section and its employment in the frame without the intermediary agency of a bridging unit.

TRIMMER

Moxon, about 1680, defines and illustrates the function of the *"Trimmers* and *Trimming Joysts"* and their relation to the *"Stair-case,* and *Chimny-way."*[26] In a characteristic New England situation, the trimmer would be found running between the chimney girts or the end and chimney girts to frame the stairwell and to receive the trimmed joists at right angles that support the floor of the second-story entry above. Actually, however, the term is not found at Massachusetts Bay, probably because the practice itself almost never appears here. The George Giddings house and now-de-

molished Story house, both in Essex and both dating to the late seventeenth century, are among the very few exceptions where this correct procedure has been observed. In virtually all other cases, including ambitious houses, there is no trimmer. Instead, common joists are framed into the girts flanking the chimney, with a requisite number simply omitted to form a stairwell.

BRACE

The function of the wall brace, which can either be in compression or in tension and which runs diagonally from an upright post to a horizontal member, is primarily that of maintaining the frame square (figure 49). Similarly the wind brace, so-called, in the roof frame, through triangulating the junction of two timbers, serves to maintain the angle they form. Symonds writes in 1638 that he "would have the howse stronge in timber though plaine and well brased."[27]

PLATE (TOP PLATE, WALL PLATE)

Moxon, writing about 1680, describes the plate as "A piece of Timber upon which some considerable weight is framed . . . Hence *Ground-Plate.*"[28] In practice, the term seems to have been largely restricted in seventeenth-century America to the horizontal units laid along the tops of walls which received in turn the feet of the common rafters (figure 49). Moxon himself uses the term wall plate, and this expression seems to have been current among carpenters at Massachusetts Bay as well. John Wilcott of Newbury, contracting to build a house at Bradford in 1663, agreed to "daub" the ends of the house and the sides "unto the wall plates" with clay.[29]

As the crowning members of the front and rear walls of the house carcass, the wall plates receive the full weight of the roof trusses and must withstand the tendency to rotate and overturn from any outward thrust of the rafters. To accomplish this the triangular roof-frame was ingeniously conceived at an early date as a dynamic entity, the lowermost element of which would rest upon and lock the wall plates through the use of a tie joint.

TIE BEAM

The tie beam, a transverse member and essentially a part of the roof structure, receives the principal rafter feet and, as we have just seen, is secured to the front and rear wall plates by means of a dovetail joint on its under surface (figures 49 and 53). This joint, which is so fashioned to prevent withdrawal, is ancient, and is called by its time-honored name in 1699 when three local carpenters contracted to build a wooden bridge over Concord River in Billerica, and agreed that "the poasts of each shoare arch [were] to be put into the cells with A duftail tennon."[30] For additional security, the shouldered post which carries the wall plate and tie beam is furnished at the top with a stout tenon which enters the tie behind the dovetail. All transverse units so framed at the junction of carcass with roof are tie beams, and while referred to loosely as chamber summer beams, chimney girts, and end girts, they should more properly be described as summer ties, chimney ties, or end ties. The primary function of the tie beam is thus to resist any adverse effects arising from the spread or extension of the principal rafters at their base. The tie beam may also, as a secondary function, carry joists and thus help to support a floor.

Referred to simply as beam by Neve in 1703 it is described as "a piece of Timber, which always lies cross the Building, into which the Feet of the principal Rafters are Framed."[31] The Boston shop contract of 1696 specifies the erection of "a beame with Two Cornerposts,"[32] and there is reference in Boston in 1638 to "the sommer or beame which lyes overthwart the great chamber."[33] Not until the nineteenth century do we find the term tie by itself, when in the 1830s the New England trained Asher Benjamin defines the word as that piece of timber "placed in any position acting as a string or tie, to keep two masses together which have a tendency to spread to a more remote distance from each other."[34] While Peter Nicholson may have been among the first to use the full term tie beam,[35] Batty Langley at a much earlier date wrote that the beam "on which the principal Rafters are framed" was intended

Assembly and Rearing of the House Frame

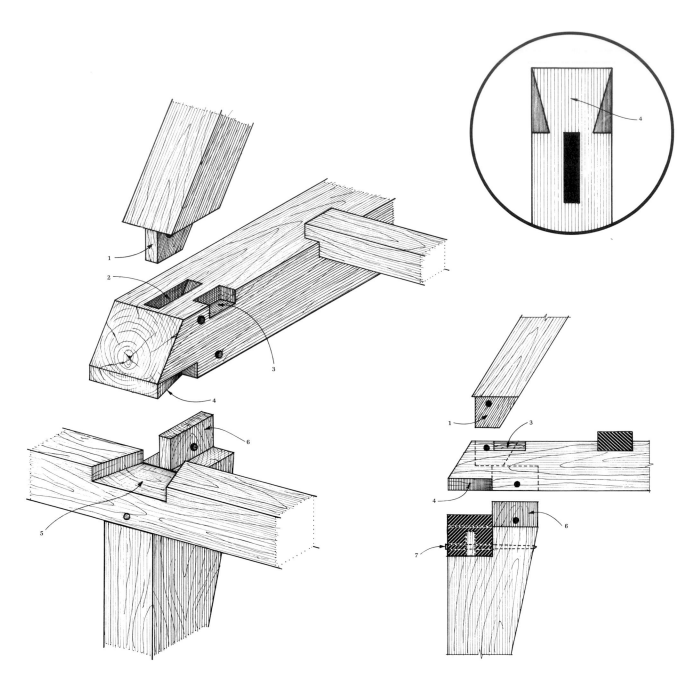

"to prevent the Thrust of the Roof from forcing out the Walls on which the Roof is placed, and to tye in the Walls."[36]

The tenon atop the post which enters the mortise of the tie beam is described by Neve as a *"Teazle Tennon"*[37] (figure 53).

RAFTERS

Rafters, which are roofing members, consist of two sorts (figure 49). Principal rafters, of heavier section than common rafters, occur at bay or transverse intervals and give the roof its basic skeletal form. They are so called by Moxon[38] and by Samuel Sewall in Boston in 1714, when he describes a bolt of lightning which struck the house of Col. Vetch and "Split the principal Rafter . . . to the purloin."[39] Common rafters are of smaller scantling and are intermediary to the principal rafters. Their primary function is to support the horizontal boarding of the roof. They are occasionally called spars, as for example in 1638 when Samuel Symonds wrote that he wished "to have the sparrs reach downe pritty deep at the eves to preserve the walls the better from the wether."[40]

PURLIN

The purlin also consists of two sorts, as commonly found at Massachusetts Bay (figure 49). We may distinguish first the principal purlin, that horizontal timber which is framed into the principal rafters and over which the common ʀafters are lodged, or, in rare cases, into which they are tenoned. The basic purpose is to provide lateral stability to the roof frame, and, in supporting rafters, to maintain the slopes of the roof in a single plane. Common purlins consist of horizontal units of relatively slim scantling which occur normally in sets of three or four, including a purlin at the roof ridge, and are not tenoned but trenched into the rear slope of the principal rafters. The length of common purlins may vary, although any break in a sequence almost invariably coincides with a rafter. While imparting some degree of longitudinal stability to the roof frame, their principal function is the support of the vertical

Figure 53. Fairbanks house, Dedham, Mass. Assembly of post head, plate, tie beam, and principal rafter, ca. 1637, with identification of framing details: 1. tenon, 2. mortise, 3. cog, 4. dovetail, 5. trench to receive dovetail, 6. teazle tenon, and 7. pin.

roof boards. They seem to have been referred to as ribs, although we do not know how commonly. In 1699 permission was granted to Joseph Fowler of Wenham to take from the common "a few small Trees for Ribbs for his hous,"[41] and a contract in 1743 for a barn to be erected in Ipswich specifies "four princ[i]ples Each side [of the roof] and three Ribs Each Side and a Rige poole."[42]

COLLAR

The collar is that member introduced into the triangular roof frame to resist compression arising from the downward pull of gravity upon the rafters and a consequent tendency for them to sag at the mid point where not stabilized, as they are at the top and bottom (figure 49). The normal method of framing is with the mortise and tenon (figure 54). The use of a tie joint for the collar in a conventional roof frame (as at the Gedney house in Salem, figure 55) is exceptional, and can perhaps best be explained as an unreasoned harking back to earlier English practice when, in the absence of a tie beam, the collar functioned as a tie resisting extension. The technical proof of this historic framing logic is nowhere better illustrated than in the roof of the late seventeenth-century Peak house in Medfield, where the gable end collars connecting rafters housed in the end ties are mortised and tenoned while the collars of the intermediate rafters, birdmouthed over the plates, are secured with a tie joint (figure 151). This logic is formalized in the early nineteenth century by Peter Nicholson, who writes that "the collar-beam may either be in a state of compression or extension, according as the principles are with or without tie-beams."[43]

Rearing of the house frame was preceded by the selection of the appropriate timbers and their felling. John Evelyn reported in 1662 that "The Time of the *Year* for this destructive *Work* is not usually till about the end of *April*," but he readily admitted that "the Opinions and Practice of Men have been very different" concerning the best time to fell timber. Much of his counsel is based

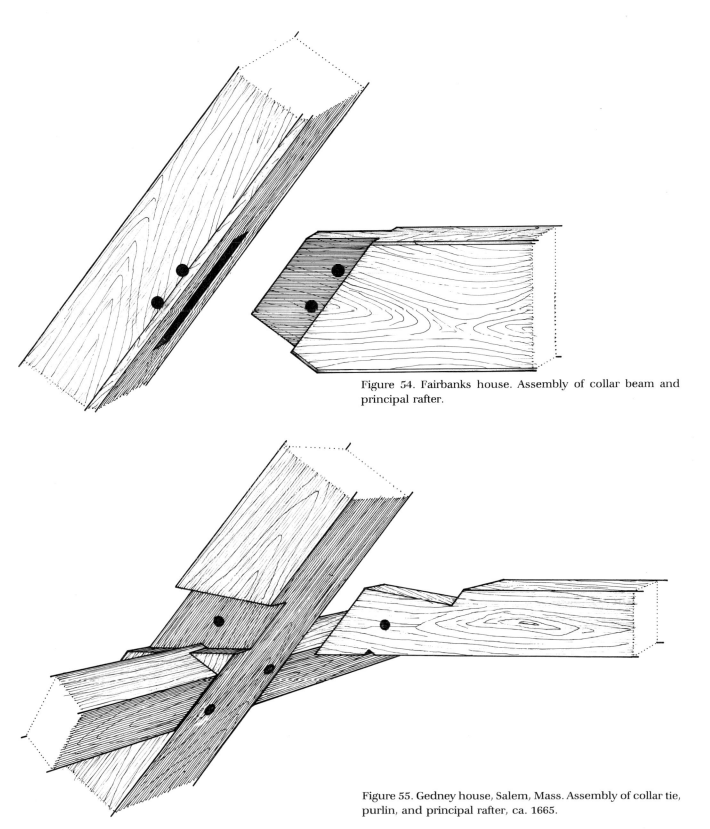

Figure 54. Fairbanks house. Assembly of collar beam and principal rafter.

Figure 55. Gedney house, Salem, Mass. Assembly of collar tie, purlin, and principal rafter, ca. 1665.

Assembly and Rearing of the House Frame

on presumed scientific theory with respect to the growing habits of trees. Thus, "the wild *Oak*, and many other Sorts, *fell'd* over-late, and when the *Sap* begins to grow proud . . . [will] be very subject to the *Worm*; whereas, being cut about *Mid-Winter*, it neither *casts*, *rifts*, nor *twines*; because the cold of the *Winter* does both dry and consolidate." Evelyn's *"old Rules"* on the other hand carry the flavor of those more remote periods in time during which they were formulated. "Fell in the *Decrease*, or four Days after *Conjunction* of the two great *Luminaries*; some [say in] the last Quarter of it," he advocates, or even on the last day of the Winter solstice "that *Timber* will prove *immortal*."[44]

Statistical figures reveal that the seventeenth-century builders at Massachusetts Bay were governed in the main by the more "scientific" recommendations for felling. Grants for timber in Cambridge from 1646 to 1687 disclose at once that the major activity was spread over the months between November and May, with heaviest concentrations in January, February, and March.

While Evelyn has fairly extended remarks on the subject of seasoning, and advises, in fact, that the builder, once his timber is felled, should not "by any Means put it to Use for three or four *Months* after,"[45] it is clear that the larger structural units were normally dressed and put into the frame almost at once. This is well attested by the common appearance of checks and splits in the timbers which occurred very early in the life of the building as the green lumber began to dry in situ (figure 78).

Fabrication of the frame did not invariably take place on the site of eventual erection. Rather, the individual members were cut and hewn where most convenient for the carpenters. Robert Taft of Braintree, housewright, for example, agreed in 1679 to erect a house in Boston for John Bateman and "to pay for the transportation. of the sd. fframe . . . from Brantery the place where it is to bee framed to Boston."[46] In support of off-site preparation of the frame one can point to the universal trait of marking all of the major units at

Figure 56. Boardman house, Saugus, Mass. Detail of collar beams and principal rafters, showing raising numerals, ca. 1687. *Photo, William W. Owens, Jr., 1973.*

their intersecting joints for ease of identification in assembly once the individual sticks had been carted to the place of erection. The practice is of almost incalculable age, and the various devices employed by early carpenters, both in England and on the Continent, make a study in themselves. For seventeenth-century Massachusetts Bay the use of Roman numerals was the standard preference. Often squat in proportion and usually incised rather deeply, these figures can be found in plain view in the roof structure on the exposed surfaces of rafters and collars (figure 56). Elsewhere, however, they are apt to be covered by trim or have been cut on a concealed inner face of the joint.

Without pictures or written description we cannot tell how every single detail of assembly

and rearing of the house frame was managed in the seventeenth century, and whether indeed there may not have been a number of alternate methods, depending upon technical circumstance. Analysis of structure indicates the logic and progressive order of framing and sometimes reveals how individual details were engineered. The absence of explicit information, however, raises two crucial questions: to what extent were component sections of the frame reared as prefabricated units, and to what degree did the builders recognize and utilize the factor of elastic movement within the frame before all the joints were finally secured with pins? By examining three individual structures we may provide some answers at least, although our explanations depend ultimately upon the not always determin-

able logic of technical procedure which characterizes seventeenth-century thinking rather than ours of a later generation.

In the Fairbanks house in Dedham, ca. 1637—

our first case study (figure 57)—one assumes that the two bents consisting of chimney posts and binding beams on either side of the chimney were reared as prefabricated units (figure 60A). It is a well-established fact that later nineteenth-

Figure 57. Fairbanks house, Dedham, Mass., ca. 1637, with eighteenth-century additions. *Photo, Wilfred A. French, ca. 1880.*

Assembly and Rearing of the House Frame

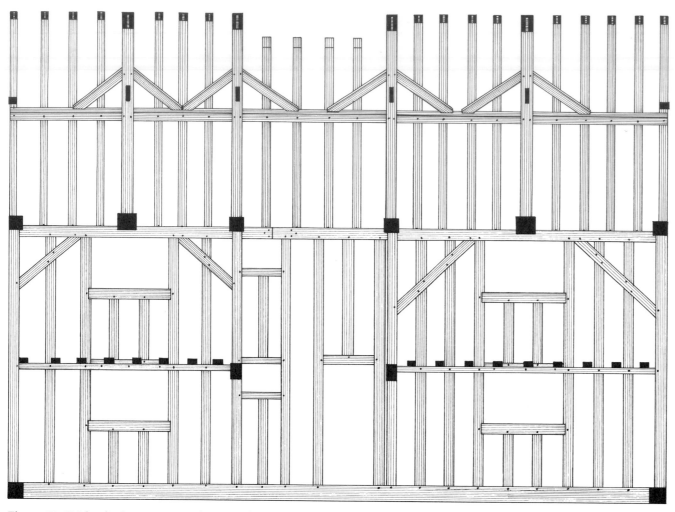

Figure 58. Fairbanks house. Front elevation (looking south), longitudinal section showing framing. (Plates and principal purlins as first constructed probably projected far enough to receive an additional set of common rafters which supported the oversailing roof ends.)

0   5   10   Feet

Figure 59. Fairbanks house. End elevation (looking west), transverse section showing framing.

century builders, in framing and rearing barns, almost invariably erected the bents which define the bays of the carcass in this manner, as illustrated by a photograph of a barn-raising in Ontario, Canada, no later than 1914 (figure 61). The final bent of the end bay is shown rising into position with the aid of no fewer than a dozen pike poles. The bent as framed consists of corner posts and binding beams at the first- and second-story levels, on the latter of which are spaced two clerestory posts connected by two shorter rails. The side girts, which are to connect this bay in rearing to the already standing portions of the

carcass, have been framed into the upright posts and are being held aloft, their tenons ready to enter the mortises of the corner posts rising to meet them.

Photographs of a barn-raising in Granby, Connecticut, in 1902 furnish further valuable information.[47] The barn is not a large one and, admittedly, there are structural conditions that are not at all peculiar to the seventeenth century; for example, the four (rather than two) posts of the bent in rearing are capped with a transverse member which functions presumably as a tie beam although it does not ride over a plate. Instead, that unit which might otherwise be thought of as a plate, and has gains for rafter feet, is in sections, one of which has been fastened already to the bent and is rising with it (figure 62). Nevertheless, here again is unequivocal evidence for the erec-

tion of prefabricated elements at a late date, and it can be seen that the men are surrounded by the timbers of the next bent, which are resting upon the foundation ready to be raised into place.

The gable end walls of the much earlier Fairbanks frame, lacking girt or bearer, did not constitute a bent in the technical sense of the word and could not have been reared as an entity. The four corner posts, therefore, would almost certainly have been erected next, a stick at a time, and connected to the standing chimney posts with their respective bearers (figure 60B). The individual studs of two-story length could then have been inserted in the frame in both the front and rear walls and pinned to the bearers one at a time, with the possible exception of those studs which in helping to frame doors and windows may have risen as prefabricated units (figure 60C).

The second-story braces would have been inserted next and were pinned from the outside. At this point the builders were faced with one of the major technical problems of the raising, that of hoisting the plates from the ground to their position atop the walls (figure 60D). The units themselves, each of which in the Fairbanks frame consists of two continuous lengths of timber, scarfed near the midpoint, were perhaps lifted up in sections, but mechanical aids may well have been brought into play. At a later date and in connection with a more ambitious building, the town of Boxford voted fifteen shillings in 1701 "for the geer and Ropes to Raies the meting houes," and further "that goodman foster should have five shiling for cariing the Roopes and bluckes whom a gaien."[48] The reference here is unquestionably to a block and tacklc, which may imply the necessity of poles erected just outside the frame to give the pullies sufficient height.

With the front and rear walls of the Fairbanks house erect and partially stabilized, the builders must then have proceeded to fit into the mortises of the sills at the gable ends the two-story studs reaching from sill to tie beam. In the west gable end wall there is an original door frame which would have been inserted at this time, as well as the presumptive yoke between the central pair of studs which received the end of the summer beam, similar to that which is visible at the Whipple and Austin Lord houses in Ipswich (figure 51). Several persons standing at foundation level could each have held one if not two studs steady, while other members of the raising crew capped the entire range and corner posts with the end ties which had been hoisted up to the top of the frame (figure 60E). The second-story studs of the chimney bay and the chimney ties would have been engineered in the same way.

The jointing of plate and post with the tie beam was one of the most ingenious assemblies of the

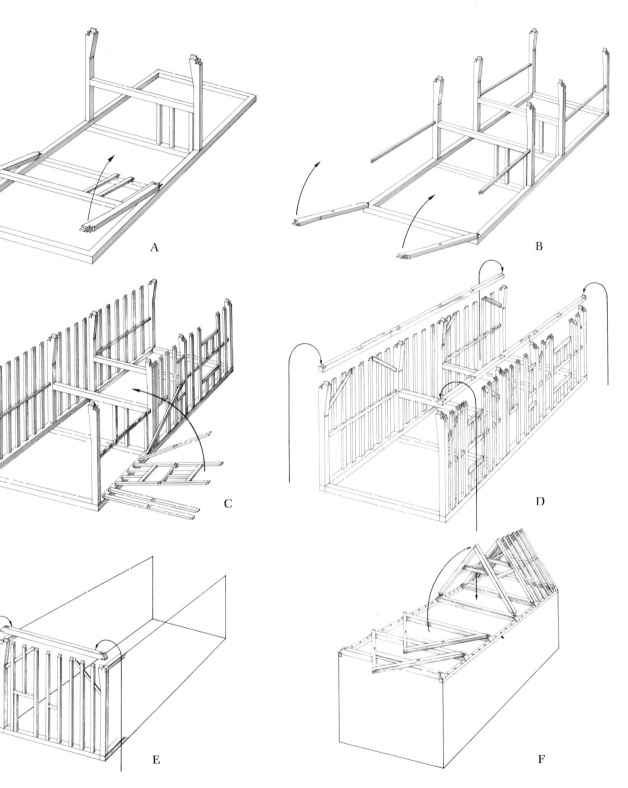

Figure 60. Fairbanks house. Conjectural raising sequence: A. first phase, B. second phase, C. third phase, D. fourth phase, E. fifth phase, F. sixth phase.

Assembly and Rearing of the House Frame

entire frame. The post head was cut and fitted with a tenon for the plate (with the pins driven from the outside), the plate and tie were united with a dovetail joint, and the tie was mortised to the post head by means of the teazle tenon (figure 53). The choice of the half dovetail joint, found for example in the Gedney and Boardman houses, in Salem and Saugus respectively, or the full dovetail, which occurs here at the Fairbanks house, may have been governed by the width of the individual units or other reasons altogether.

Once the tie beams were in place the remaining members of the Fairbanks house carcass could readily have been installed individually. The character of the joints, in other words, can be explained as a desire on the part of the builders to make the process of assembly as simple as possible. The summer beam of the hall, for example, could have been maneuvered into place with its far end balanced on the yoke and pushed out through the end wall far enough to allow the raising crew to bring it forward and seat the tusk tenon with unusual upper lip securely in its housing in the chimney girt (figure 63). The floor joists of the first story, having tusk tenons where they join the summer beam, simply rest on the bearer at the other end, and, like the summer, could have slid into place. In the second story the joists are furnished at their junction with the summer tie with tusk tenons and are seated in the end and chimney ties by means of a cog or open housing into which they could easily be dropped in process of construction (figure 64). Similar evidence, in fact, can be found in all surviving houses built by the first generation at Massachusetts Bay (where not concealed) and even in later examples where the tusk tenon continues to be used as a conservative feature, for example, the Browne house in Watertown, built between 1694 and 1701.

The appearance of the open cog in the earliest years of settlement at Massachusetts Bay raises technical questions. In particular we must ask whether the adoption and rapid spread of this uncomplicated joint in place of the tusk tenon were for reasons of rearing efficiency, economy,

Figure 61. Barn-raising in Ontario, Canada, 1914 or earlier. (Above)

Figure 62. Barn-raising in Granby, Conn. *Photo, George and Alvah Howes, 1902.* (Below)

The Framed Houses of Massachusetts Bay

structural stability, or all three. In terms of earlier English developments it can be shown that the tusk tenon, referred to also as a bare-faced soffit-tenon with diminished haunch, succeeded the joist joint that consisted of a bare-faced soffit-tenon only (figure 65).[49] Despite the fact that numerous floors in sixteenth-century English houses still survive with joists supported by bare-faced soffit-tenons, it is apparent nevertheless that the tusk or beveled shoulder is an improvement in that the tenon is strengthened at just the point at which it is most vulnerable to fracture through sheer downward stress. This evolutionary step forward in floor framing had been taken in the sixteenth century, well before the first settlers arrived in New England, although at least one archaic survival of the earlier system has been found in the Jonathan Cogswell house in Essex, Massachusetts, built probably in the early 1730s, where a seventeenth-century summer beam containing mortises for bare-faced soffit-tenons has been reused in the framing of the ground floor (figure 66).

The newer principle was formally recognized by Joseph Moxon writing about 1680. The tusk, he explains, is "A Bevel shoulder, made to strengthen the Tennant of [the] Joyst, which is let into the Girder,"[50] and the term apparently survived among New England builders. Edward Shaw, carpenter and architect, born in Hampton, New Hampshire, in 1784, defines the tusk, as had Moxon much earlier, as "The beveling shoulder above the tenon in binding joists." Elsewhere he indicates that the purpose was to "obtain more strength in the tenon."[51] Archaic survivals of this joint with its distinctive bevel or tusk continued to occur in special load-bearing situations, for example, in Boston as late as 1825-1826, where employed in the heavily framed floors of the brick and masonry North and South Market Stores which form part of the Faneuil Hall Markets.

It has been argued that the bevel or haunch owes its special character to theoretical knowledge, acquired during the sixteenth century, of compression and tension areas in a piece of timber used in construction. Within the context of a

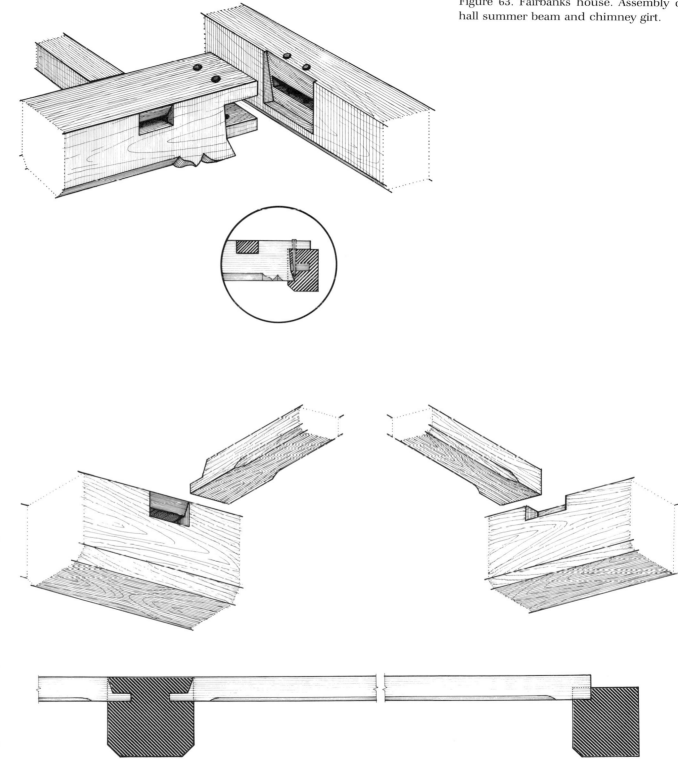

Figure 63. Fairbanks house. Assembly of hall summer beam and chimney girt.

Figure 64. Fairbanks house. Housing of chamber floor joists in end and summer tie beams.

Assembly and Rearing of the House Frame

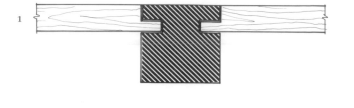

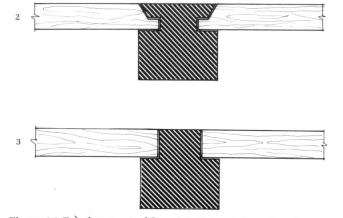

Figure 65. Development of floor joist joint: 1. bare-faced soffit-tenon, English, sixteenth century and earlier, 2. tusk tenon, English and American, mid-sixteenth to mid-seventeenth century, 3. butt cog, American and English, mid-seventeenth century onwards.

Figure 66. Jonathan Cogswell house, Essex, Mass. Detail of reused summer beam in cellar from an earlier, seventeenth-century house, showing open mortises for original joists. *Photo, William W. Owens, Jr., 1974.*

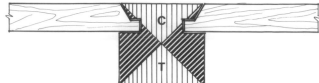

Figure 67. Diagramatic relationship of tusk tenon to vital compression and tension areas of a load-bearing timber.

diagramatic representation, the tusk tenon could thus be seen as an effort on the part of the builders to avoid cutting any more than absolutely necessary into vital compression wood (figure 67).[52] The point is well taken with respect to the jointing of principal floor framing members. For the smaller, common floor joists a different line of reasoning is in order, which leads directly to the question first posed. If we assume that the early carpenters were aware of the fact that their major bearing timbers were sufficiently overengineered to withstand what amounted to a negligible weakening of vital compression wood, and indeed, that the summer beam was not the crucial member but rather the joists themselves, with a more serious threat of sheer strain, then we can no longer argue for an evolution of joist joints from poor to satisfactory to debased (figure 65). Instead, the open cogs that received the joist at each end become, after the middle of the seventeenth century, the ultimate refinement in a progressive sequence designed to minimize the danger of fracture through sheer downward stress. And if this is the case, the system employed in the second story of the Fairbanks house can be interpreted perhaps as an intermediary stage, with the sophisticated builder recognizing a different technical situation at each end of the joist: where it enters the summer beam, which reaches over open space and is thus possessed of a greater bending moment, he continues somewhat cautiously to house his tusk-tenoned joist in noncompression areas of the wood which will weaken the timber as little as possible; at the other end, however, the beam is supported from the ground all along its length by posts and studs, and the carpenter here could employ an open

cog, which also simplified the process of erection (figure 64). Surely this practical advantage made for technical improvement, in addition to which the cog is demonstrably a less expensive joint.

The appearance of the cog joint at once in the earliest surviving framed houses at Massachusetts Bay, representing the experience of immigrant carpenters from a number of English counties, would argue for ongoing perpetuation of existing building traits rather than immediate invention. Whatever the source of its origin, however, the open cog became throughout the latter part of the seventeenth century the almost universally standard method for housing *both* ends of the joists in the timber-framed houses of New England, the earliest known example being found in the Gedney house in Salem, ca. 1665. It has remained the principal joist joint in all but exceptional cases from that time to the present, during a period in which carpentry has been transformed from a craft into a science.

While the carcass of the Fairbanks house with the tie beams in place represents a single boxlike unit, these ties nevertheless are properly a part of the roof and are mortised to receive the feet of the principal rafters. The framing of the roof was in all likelihood facilitated by the laying of boards across the ties and joists to form a temporary platform. At a somewhat later date at least the frame in process of erection was utilized in this fashion. In 1773 a large company of people was collected in Wilton, New Hampshire, to raise a meetinghouse. They had reared "the Body of it, the Beams and Joists, and on these had laid a large quantity of Boards for the more convenient standing," when a beam underneath this platform "broke at the Mortise in the middle, by which upwards of 50 Persons fell to the bottom of the House," with several deaths and serious injuries.[53]

The tie beams at the Fairbanks house are numbered from east to west, and the principal rafters, bridle-jointed at the apex (figure 68), with their connecting collars, must have gone up in this direction also, because all pins except those of the east gable end have been driven from the east (the

Figure 68. Fairbanks house. Bridled joints at apex of principal and common rafters.

numbering system of the rafters themselves is unaccountably scrambled). In other words, the individual roof frames would have been pinned together on top of the carcass, overlying one another, and the wall of the east gable would have been erected and pinned from the inside (figure 60F). A daring and unique feature, encountered in no other seventeenth-century structure at Massachusetts Bay, is the way in which the purlins are clasped or supported at either gable end by means of a notched stud tenoned into the tie and inclining slightly toward the slope of the roof, in an effort, presumably, to furnish some of the force of a strut. There are no principal rafters at the gable ends, their place being taken by common rafters which ride over the ends of the purlins (figure 69).

With the east gable end erect and the purlins in place, the first roof frame, consisting of principals and collar, was ready to erect over the summer tie of the east chamber. In suggesting, however, that the individual roof frames were thus prefabricated, one should note in passing the pronounced unswept camber of the collar tenons (figure 70), the purpose of which could easily have been that of facilitating separate entry if the collar was supported and the paired rafters eased down to receive the tenons. In any event, when the tenons of the rafter feet dropped into the mortises in the upper surface of the tie it was necessary to hold the structural members in a vertical position, and this implied that the purlins in turn must have some up-and-down play in their corresponding mortises to permit the delicate negotiation. Thus one notes with interest that all mortises for purlins in the principal rafters have been made longer by at least three quarters of an inch than the tenons which occupy them (figure 70). Then, with all the roof frames in place, the west gable end was erected and also pinned from the inside. The common rafters would have followed next and were pinned to the purlins from the outside and pegged at the apex. The union here is also with a bridle joint (figure 68), and the common rafter feet are housed in the plate with a joint, the fundamental purpose of

Figure 69. Fairbanks house. Detail in attic of eastern gable end wall with portions of original wattle and daub infill. *Photo, William W. Owens, Jr., 1974.*

Figure 70. Fairbanks house. Detail of principal rafter, collar, and principal purlins. *Photo, William W. Owens, Jr., 1974.*

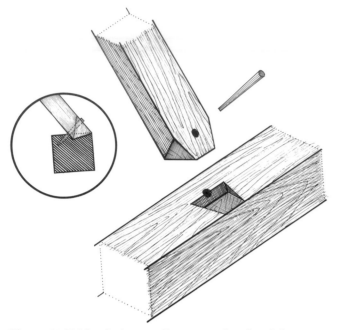

Figure 71. Fairbanks house. Common rafter foot joint.

Figure 72. Fairbanks house. Detail of wind braces in the roof frame.

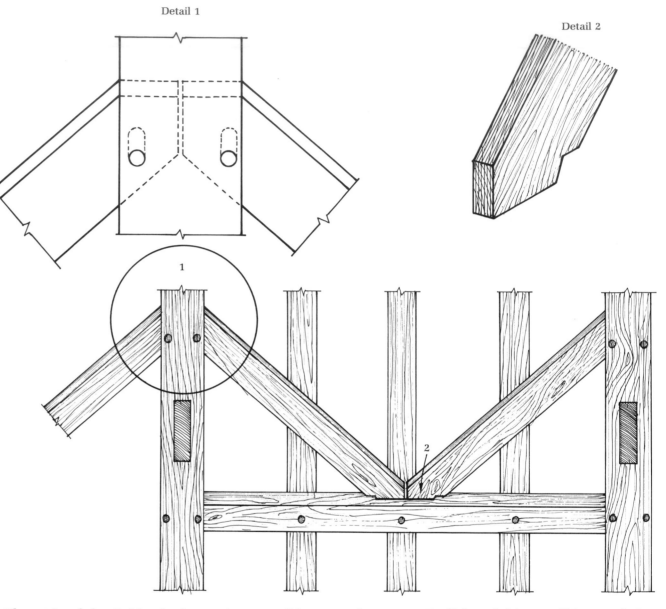

Detail 1

Detail 2

which was to resist with greater assurance the danger of outward thrust implied in an unusually heavy load placed upon the roof (figure 71). Found also in the Samuel Pickman house in Salem, it is a joint which does not as yet appear to have been common to any degree in the houses of East Anglia. Finally, at the Fairbanks house came the introduction of wind braces, the tenons for which were designed to be inserted after the frame was erect and were then pinned (at the top only) from the outside (figure 72). The slightly convex wind braces, designed to prevent longitudinal movement of the roof, are as much an architectural feature as a structural necessity, harking back to earlier, more highly visible English roof forms. It is interesting also that those pins which secure the common rafters to the principals have been given a geometric heading where they project through into the attic at eye level, a nicety which by comparison with English work of the period would be considered archaic (figure 73).

The attic of the Fairbanks house is accessible only by ladder. In the lower entry there are two chamfered joists laid in a flatwise position and one presumably later unchamfered floor joist of smaller scantling laid depthwise. These joists support the floor of the second-story entry, and that joist closest to the chimney serves also to define the present later stairwell. They are not housed in the frame of the building but simply rest on top of the east and west chimney girts. Further, the joists have tenons at one end, sug-

gesting reuse. In light of this condition and the fact that the entry is so shallow in depth, allowing only a very narrow and cramped space for the later stairs, it is quite possible that here is the only physical evidence at Massachusetts Bay of a stairless arrangement in which, for a time at least, the second story as well as the attic was reached by ladder only.

Somewhat larger in scale and more complex in its framing is the Boardman house in Saugus, ca.

Figure 73. Fairbanks house. Detail of wind braces and principal purlin. *Photo, William W. Owens, Jr., 1974.*

the foot posts, to guide the tennon into the mortice as the framed side rises serenely in the air." When the master workman was sure that all was in order, and after a preliminary round of drinks, he gave out the order "Pick 'er up." The frame was lifted as high as men could lift by hand, when hand spikes and pike poles were brought into use, and thus raised further until the tenons sank home in the mortises, and the whole side reached a perpendicular position. It was then securely fastened by temporary braces and stays. The second side went up as did the first, after which "they next proceeded with ends, and middle timbers of the frame, in the same manner as with the sides." Mr. Somers confirms other traditional reports that it fell to the lot of the apprentices or in any event younger persons of light weight and agility "to mount to the corners and guide the tennons into the mortices and pin them together."[55]

One can readily visualize the process which Mr. Somers describes whereby the principal posts at the corners and along the front and rear sides of the building were laid out on the ground and united by the intermediary girts at the first-story level. The corresponding studs would have been tenoned into the girts and placed in position for rearing, as there is no way that they could subsequently have been inserted between the sill and girt once the frame was erect. Since the building was a large one, Mr. Somers continued, it would require upwards of fifty men to raise it, a figure that tallies with the account of raising the Wilton, New Hampshire, meetinghouse in 1773. Earlier, in 1677, the Reverend William Hubbard writes of an Indian raid on the town of Hatfield in the Connecticut River Valley at a moment when "a considerable Number of the Inhabitants of that small Village were employed in raising the Frame of an House," noting that several "were shot down from the Top of the House . . . and

1687, our second case study in assembly and rearing (figure 74). Here, as was customary in a number of seventeenth-century structures with a framed overhang along the front, the first-story front wall was capped with a plate over which the projecting transverse girts were cantilevered, ruling out almost certainly any possibility of assembly in a lateral direction in terms of prefabricated bents (figure 77A). This poses at once the question as to whether prefabrication of the front and rear walls, for which there is later nineteenth-

century descriptive evidence,[54] played any part in the process. The Reverend A. N. Somers of Lancaster, New Hampshire, about 1900 recalled from his youth that in the rearing of a large building this technique was sometimes employed. "First the two sides of the structure were put together on the sills and underpinnings and securely pinned in the joints," he writes, and when all was in readiness, the master workman directed the raising crew to their places. "The oldest and most trusty men were assigned to the task of tending

Figure 74. Boardman house, Saugus, Mass., ca. 1687, with lean-to added before 1696.

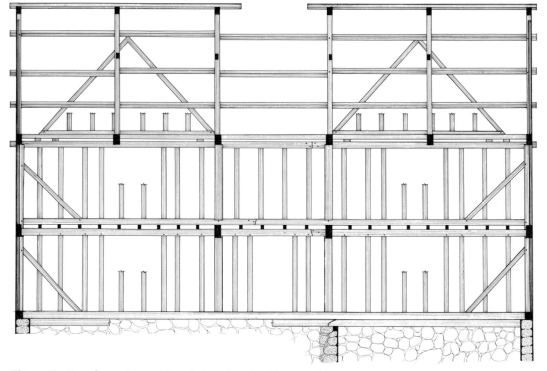

Figure 75. Boardman house. Front elevation (looking south), longitudinal section showing framing. (Location of original window sills undetermined.)

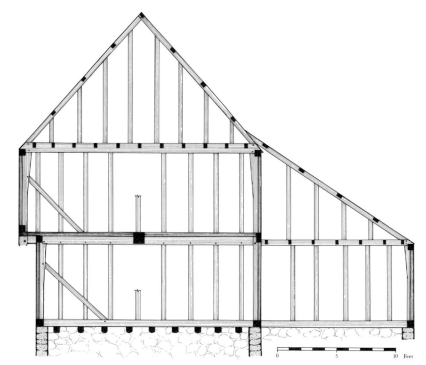

Figure 76. Boardman house. End elevation (looking west), transverse section showing framing. (Location of original window sills and form of pendants of overhang undetermined.)

sundry were carried away captive, to the Number of twenty or more."[56]

Thus by the nineteenth century whole walls were being framed on the ground and erected primarily by manpower alone. Whether this was also a common practice in the seventeenth century is less certain (figure 77C). The alternative would have meant rearing the front and rear walls a stick at a time or with partially prefabricated units. The critical point at issue is the elastic flexibility of the various frame members in the process of assembly. Once two-story posts, for example, have been erected as single sticks and their tenons have sunk home into the mortises in the sill, is there enough "play" before pinning to allow these units to part slightly and receive the tenons of that section of horizontal girding at the first-story level which is to unite them and cap a range of single-story studs at the same time? And what of the highly complicated problem of framing the longitudinal summer beams into the transverse girts? If these large transverse units could not spring apart sufficiently to permit the insertion of the summers individually, then we can only argue for the cumbersome process of pinning the tusk tenons of the summers into their respective transverse girts on the ground, creating a pair of H frames. The girts, thus connected, could have been elevated at the front end and supported, perhaps with blocks, over the corresponding teazle tenons atop the first-story posts, and then raised at the rear for the tenons to enter the mortises in the posts while engaging at the same time the first-story studs of the end walls (figure 77B).

If the problem was solved in this way, the rear wall once erected would have been temporarily freestanding and would have required props. Shallow gains or "scotches" will occasionally be found in the exterior surface of story posts a few feet below the level of the plate, though none have been discovered yet at the Boardman house, where original oak clapboards still conceal much of the outer surface of the rear wall frame. These "scotches" were not gains in which to catch the tips of pike poles in the rearing of prefabricated

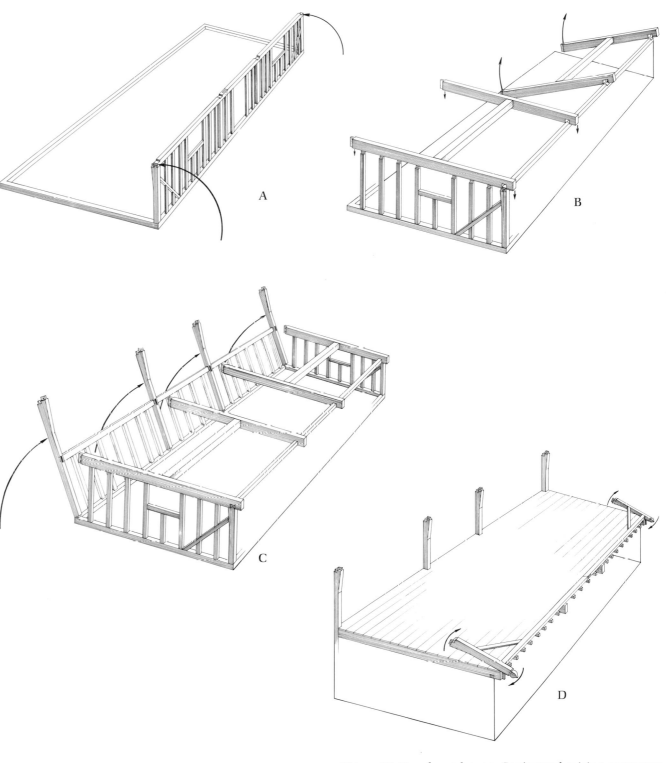

Figure 77. Boardman house. Conjectural raising sequence: A. first phase, B. second phase, C. third phase, D. fourth phase.

Figure 78. Todd house, Salem Mass., late seventeenth century. Demolished 1957. Detail of transverse summer beam at point of junction with rear story post. *Photo, William W. Owens, Jr., 1974.*

units (for one important reason because they were too shallow for a secure hold in so unwieldy a process). Rather, they were designed for situations in which the wall frames had to be momentarily propped up until they could be permanently restrained from falling outwards by the superimposition of the tie beams—or as in this case, until the transverse girts were in place.[57] The tenons of the transverse chimney girts at the Boardman house are squared off quite tightly in their mortises, which suggests that they had entered the rear posts pretty much in a horizontal position.

For houses with overhanging second stories along the front and transverse rather than longitudinal summer beams we find a different situation. The summer and indeed the chimney girts could easily have been engineered into place as single sticks once the front and rear walls had been erected and connected at the ends with transverse end girts. This is almost certainly what took place when the late seventeenth-century Todd house in Salem was erected. The rear tenon of the transverse summer was sufficiently beveled at the top and bottom to have permitted the necessary play which must have occurred once it was lodged in the mortise in the rear post and the front end of the stick had to be raised just enough to clear the plate and top of the teazle tenon in the front wall (figure 78).

The framing of the overhanging second-story front wall at the Boardman house would have followed, and with the first-story summers and butt-cogged joists in place, boards could once

again have been laid for temporary flooring to facilitate this next operation. There are only twenty extant houses with framed overhanging second stories from the first century of settlement at Massachusetts Bay, though an additional twenty-six examples are known from the record. Of this total of forty-six, twenty-six represent framed overhangs along the front or sides only and twenty at both front and sides. It is startling to learn, however, that while we still have twelve representatives of the framed overhang along the front and five at the side or end only with both groups closely related in framing technique, there are no more than three surviving houses with framed overhangs at both front and sides.

The framed, as distinguished from the hewn, overhang could be engineered in different ways. The most common method when it occurs just at the front was to suspend the second-story corner posts on the stoutly tenoned ends of the projecting end girts and these posts in turn received the tenoned ends of the jettied front girt. This construction allowed the lower ends of the posts to project downward for several inches or more and to be carved in ornamental fashion (figures 79 and 166). For the end overhang it is the front and rear rather than the end girts which are cantilevered out to carry the second-story corner posts on their end tenons. The unit which we call colloquially an overhanging girt is that which the English consistently refer to as a bressummer. The term does not seem to have been carried to New England for it never appears in the documents, at least at Massachusetts Bay, nor in the language of construction which has survived. The reason may well be that the first generation of builders seldom employed the overhang, with the result that at its "revival" later in the century the second and third generation American carpenters had no first-hand knowledge of the word.

The corner posts of the overhanging second story were presumably negotiated into place individually by the raising crew working from that upper level of the carcass. The posts would have been elevated and then lowered gingerly until the mortise in each post hooked over the

projecting tenon of the transverse member. At the Boardman house the overhanging girt is in two sections, scarfed, and could easily have been let into the mortises of the posts in two operations. Where the overhanging girt was of a single length, however, one must hypothesize a procedure in which the corner posts and overhanging girt were assembled and pinned together on the second story of the carcass and then negotiated into place as a prefabricated unit (figure 77D). It is a difficult maneuver to imagine, and was aided only by the fact that the jettied front girt was further supported by the cantilevered ends of transverse chimney girts and occasionally, as for example at the Paul Revere house in Boston, ca. 1680, Parson Capen house in Topsfield of 1683, and Hooper-Hathaway house in Salem, by the cantilevered ends of transverse summer beams as well. Ladders would have been of real assistance at this and other points, and in 1662 one Salem carpenter reported that he could not raise the frame of a house he had agreed to build because ladders had not been provided.[58]

The second-story chimney posts at the Boardman house were then seated *upon* the overhanging girt over its intersection with the transverse girts below (figure 80). In only one known example, the White-Ellery house in Gloucester, erected ca. 1710, are both the second-story corner and chimney posts hung upon the tenons of the projecting end and chimney girts with the jettied girt framed between these posts in sections, and here the problem of rearing the frame of the second-story overhanging front wall would have required considerable ingenuity (figure 81). Without more explicit evidence we cannot be dogmatic. The joints and the demonstrable logic of assembly would have dictated the order or sequence of framing. The individual ways in which the successive tasks were engineered would have varied according to tradition and personal experience and the degree to which raw manpower and mechanical aids were balanced against one another.

Once assembled and in place the overhang presented no major structural difficulty. The amount of projection was slight—seldom more

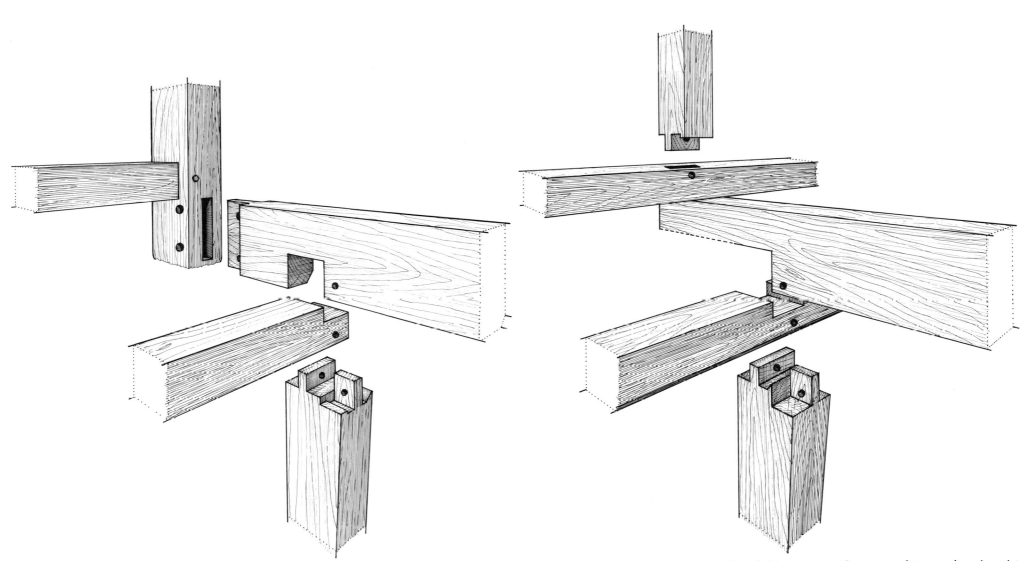

Figure 79. Boardman house. Assembly of corner post, first-story plate, overhanging girt, end girt, and second-story corner post.

Figure 80. Boardman house. Assembly of chimney post, first-story plate, overhanging girt, chimney girt, and second-story chimney post.

than two feet—and the size of the supporting units answerable to the loads which they had to sustain over open space. In at least one case, however, that of the end overhang of the south parlor ell which was added to the Turner house in Salem probably before 1680, the span was more than twenty feet. And here is revealed one of the rarer seventeenth-century instances of insufficient skill in engineering which caused the overhanging girt to sag badly in the middle during the intervening years. This is all the more surprising when one considers that the builder, John

Turner, was one of the wealthiest men in seventeenth-century Essex County and erected one of its most ambitious houses.[59] The basic construction is typical, with second-story posts, connected by the jettied girt, hung upon the end tenons of the cantilevered front and rear girts of the ell. There are both common joists and two oversize joists housed in one of two transverse summer beams and projected out over the first-story end girt. The two larger joists, spaced at intervals of one-third the width of the ell, are tied into the summer with a half dovetail but are

halved *over* the overhanging girt at that end and thus provide no support whatsoever. Further, for reasons hard to understand, the joists in the two outer bays created by the oversize joists come to within an inch or two of the overhanging girt and simply stop, again furnishing no support. Those in the central bay, however, are tied to the summer with a half dovetail (and a spike as well) and are housed in the overhanging girt with a tusk tenon joint (figure 82). All of which did little or nothing to solve the real problem, which was the full weight of the brick-filled second-story end

Assembly and Rearing of the House Frame

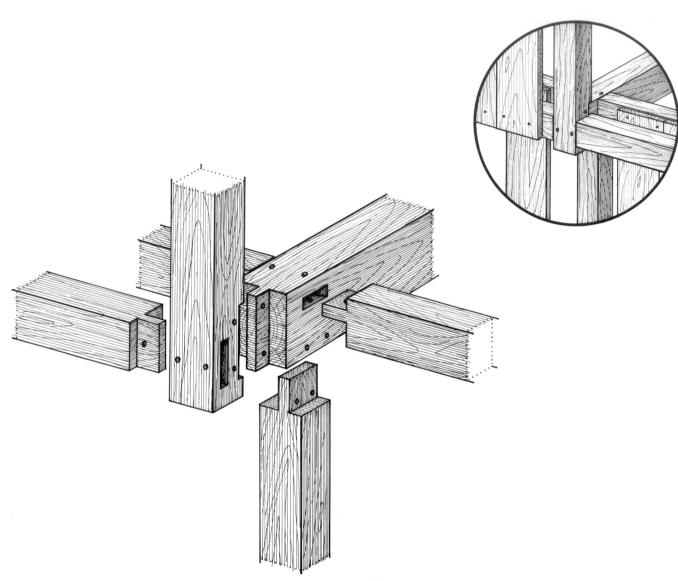

second-story girt. This we find at the Boardman house and at the Appleton-Taylor-Mansfield house, ca. 1680, both in Saugus, though in the latter example the joists project on the hall side of the house only. The parlor is equipped with a transverse summer, a lingering expression, perhaps, of the earlier English habit of hitting up the superior end of the house.

The assembly and rearing of the overhanging second story which extended along both front and sides could have proceeded from either direction, judging at least from the Ward house in Salem, erected after 1684, in which the jettied front and side girts, supported on the cantilevered ends of the lower-story transverse girts and summers and joists, carried the second-story corner posts in turn (figure 83). While at least four houses having a second-story overhang at front and sides framed in the time-honored English manner with the use of a dragon beam survived into recent historic time, two in Ipswich and two in Boston, only one has been carefully recorded, the Sun Tavern in Boston, destroyed in 1912 (figure 52).

Exceptional evidence for the framing of an overhang on front, side, and rear walls of a domestic building exists at the late seventeenth-century Ross Tavern in Ipswich. Originally of one-room plan, two and one-half stories high with an end chimney bay, the house was furnished not only with a transverse summer beam on posts, projecting at both the front and rear to support the overhanging second story, but also with a second summer beam or bridging agent, housed in the transverse summer beam at right angles to it and projecting over an end post to help support the overhang at the side. In that bay formed by the chimney girt and transverse summer beam there are joists running between summer and girt and a unique secondary set halved over them at right angles (figure 84). The overhang itself is composed of three lengths of molded girt, mitered at the intersections. They are supported on the projecting ends of the chimney girt, transverse summer beam, and bridging agent, and the second-story corner posts above were fur-

Figure 81. White-Ellery house, Gloucester, Mass. Assembly of first- and second-story chimney posts, chimney girt, first-story "plate," and overhanging girt, with detail showing vertical planking, ca. 1710.

wall superincumbent upon the twenty-one-foot girt hanging out over open space. Total collapse has been prevented only by the boxing in of the overhang early in the eighteenth century and, more recently, when the overhang was reopened in the restoration of 1909 and the same adverse forces were once again unleashed, by the introduction in 1972 of auxiliary support.

When the summer beam is longitudinal the joists will also be cantilevered over the plate of the ground-story wall in traditional English fashion and thus help to support the overhanging

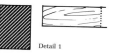

Detail 1

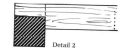

Detail 2

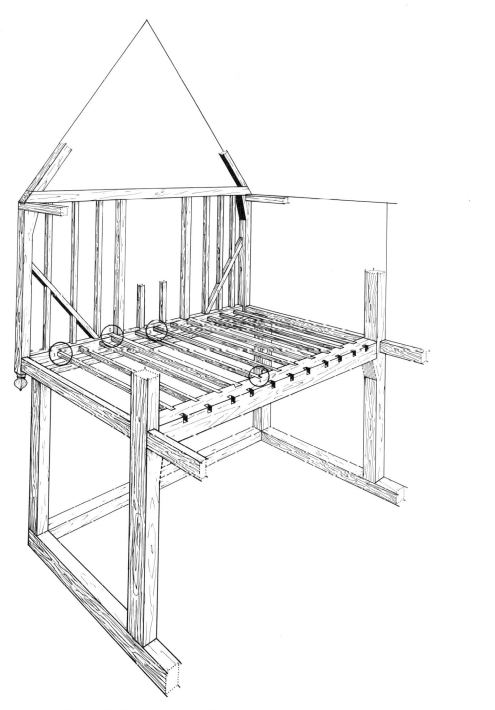

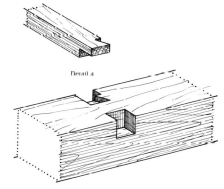

Detail 3

Detail 4

Figure 82. Turner house, Salem, Mass. Frame of south parlor wing, added probably before 1680.

Figure 83. Ward house, Salem, Mass. Detail of first-story front and end overhangs, after 1684.

Figure 84. Ross Tavern, Ipswich, Mass. Floor framing, second story, late seventeenth century. (Frame dismantled and re-erected on a new site.) *Photo, Frank O. Branzetti, 1940.*

nished with a continual right-angle tenon which bound the miter joint (figure 85).

In the rearing of the Boardman house, when both front and rear walls were erect and connected, and the second-story studs and braces and window sills were in place, the plates would have been hoisted into position. Like the plates of the Fairbanks house, those at the Boardman house consist of two continuous lengths of timber scarfed together. By the seventeenth century in East Anglia, the joint used almost universally for this purpose was the bladed scarf (figure 86).[60] It is a well-designed joint with small susceptibility to twisting or winding or to lateral stress, the forces to which the plate is most subject. At the Fairbanks house the pins holding one blade of the scarf in the front plate are driven from one di-

rection while those holding the other are driven from the opposite direction. The same condition is found in the front plate at the Boardman house, and the rear plate as well with the pattern reversed. The scarfs themselves as a general rule are unaligned, perhaps for defense against the event of subsidence or upheaval of the frame at one side or another, in which case a pair of aligned scarfs might constitute an even breaking point. The rear plate scarf at the Fairbanks house is just a few inches west of the west chimney post and the front scarf a foot or more from the east chimney post. At the Boardman house the front scarf is in the chimney bay also, a foot or more from the west chimney post, while that at the rear is in the east chamber, three feet beyond the east chimney post. The Pierce house in Dorchester, ca. 1650, is one of the only examples in which the

scarfs are more or less exactly in line (again in the chamber, just to the east of the chimney post).

The availability in the New World of long straight pieces of timber has greatly reduced the incidence of this interesting classification of carpenters' joints. As for Massachusetts Bay, we have only occasional examples of the bladed plate scarf and rare survivals of such common English scarfs as the bridled scarf with concealed table and squint butt or slanted cheek. This we find in the first-story wall plate and overhanging girt of the Boardman house (figure 87). The squint butt that was uppermost "could not subside without the lower, while the tongue, or 'bit' of the bridle prevented the lower butt from subsiding."[61] The joint was thus well adapted to the load-bearing purposes for which it was designed, as seen here as part of the overhang assembly. The less sophisticated bridled scarf, lacking either concealed table or squint butt, in the plates of the Porter-Bradstreet house and the Darling-Prince house,

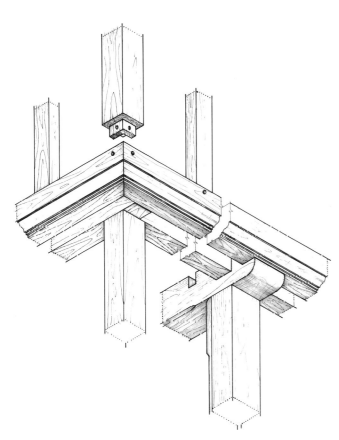

Figure 85. Ross Tavern. Detail of overhanging second story, rear and end walls, with assembly of second-story corner post.

both in Danvers and both dating to about 1700, has not been found elsewhere (figure 88).

The tie beams followed next in the rearing of the Boardman house, and here we encounter a further complexity in framing. The end and chimney ties are entirely normal. The summer ties, however, project beyond the face of the front wall plate and helped support a pair of façade gables which disappeared many years ago and for which we have now only the structural evidence. Referred to simply as a "gable end" in the contemporary documents, at least three different

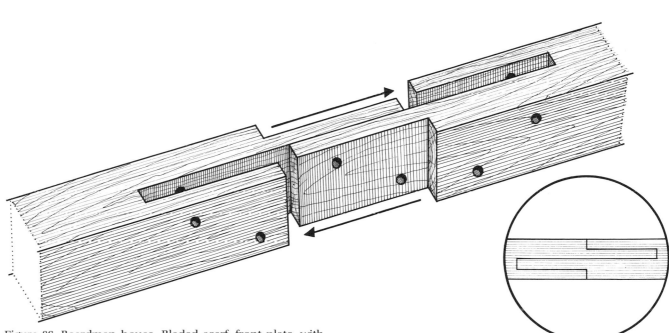
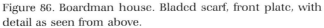

Figure 86. Boardman house. Bladed scarf, front plate, with detail as seen from above.

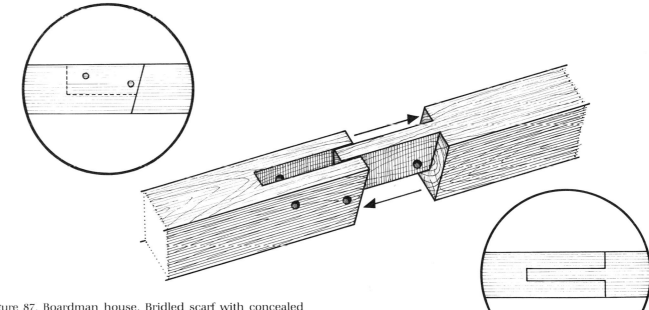

Figure 87. Boardman house. Bridled scarf with concealed shelf, first-story plate, with details.

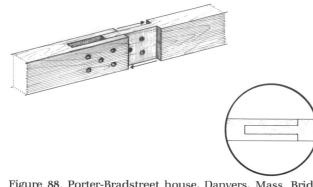

Figure 88. Porter-Bradstreet house, Danvers, Mass. Bridled scarf, rear plate, with detail as seen from above, probably ca. 1700.

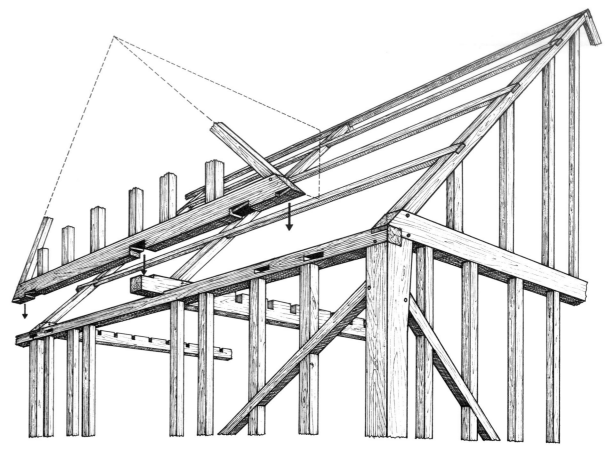

Figure 89. Boardman house. Roof frame with assembly of façade gable.

schemes have been noted at Massachusetts Bay for the framing of this feature, of which that at the Boardman house is matched only by roughly similar evidence at the Pierce house in Dorchester. The projecting ends of the Boardman summer ties helped support an outer or secondary tie beam at right angles, which in turn received the feet of the rafters and studs that formed the face of the gable (figure 89). The structural clues might have been even less capable of interpretation had it not been for the fortuitous survival of both secondary or gable ties, more or less in the same location in the frame but completely reused in connection with a later cornice. Missing entirely are the units that filled the mortises in the face of the wall plate and were clearly designed to assist in catching up the outer tie. Such "fashion pieces" exist in the seventeenth-century house called Curd Hall at Little Coggeshall, Essex, and were present also at the Pierce house (figure 124),

where, however, the outer unit was supported on the tenoned ends of projecting joists as well as the summer tie beam. This situation finds further English precedent in the building known as Bay Tree Farmhouse, Stisted, Essex, dating probably to ca. 1625.[62]

Another system altogether for carrying the façade gable in such a way that it overhung the second story is implied in photographs of the Old Feather Store of 1680 in Boston (figure 39). Here we may suggest that both the end and intermediary ties projected in order to receive a single length of timber on which the gables were erected. The simplest structural system, however, is that for which evidence exists in the form of rafter feet mortises in the wall plates of the Gedney and Ward houses, both in Salem, the Blake house in Dorchester (figure 126), and in the original portion of the Turner house in Salem, ca. 1668. Here the gable itself is preserved within the attic of the house by the addition of the higher studded parlor ell. Other façade gables surviving until the turn of the twentieth century are well attested by photographs and drawings, but it is abundantly clear that either through the dictates of fashion or because of the problem of keeping the valleys properly flashed, or for reasons of changing domestic use, they were unsparingly removed during the course of the eighteenth and nineteenth centuries. At the Turner house, where all exterior gables had been shorn from the house well before the middle of the nineteenth century, the one remaining concealed example in the attic is not tied into the frame of the roof, and the gable side purlins and common rafters simply butt against the horizontal boarding of the front slope (figure 90). Something of the sort may have happened at the Boardman house as well, where no structural evidence exists to show that the gables were tied into the roof frame. One assumes, therefore, that whether the gable was to be erected upon the front plate of the carcass or upon a projecting unit, its framing followed the erection of the roof proper, so that if tied only into the boarding that feature would already be in place.

Only at the Gedney house in Salem and at the Peak house in Medfield is there evidence for valley rafters that would have facilitated the union of long-vanished façade gables with the front slope of the roof. The evidence at the Gedney house takes the form of pinning in the common rafters to which the valley rafters were secured. Happily a portion of one of these survives in the house in a reused position, showing it to have been of relatively slim scantling, three inches or more by one and three quarters inches, laid flatwise. At the Peak house, wide planklike valley rafters are pinned to the rafters, again in a flatwise position (figure 151). Original valley rafters of the projecting two-story porch at the Appleton-Taylor-Mansfield house in Saugus also remain in place, although the porch itself (now restored) disappeared many years ago.

In most of these examples we are dealing with roofs of principal and common rafters. The

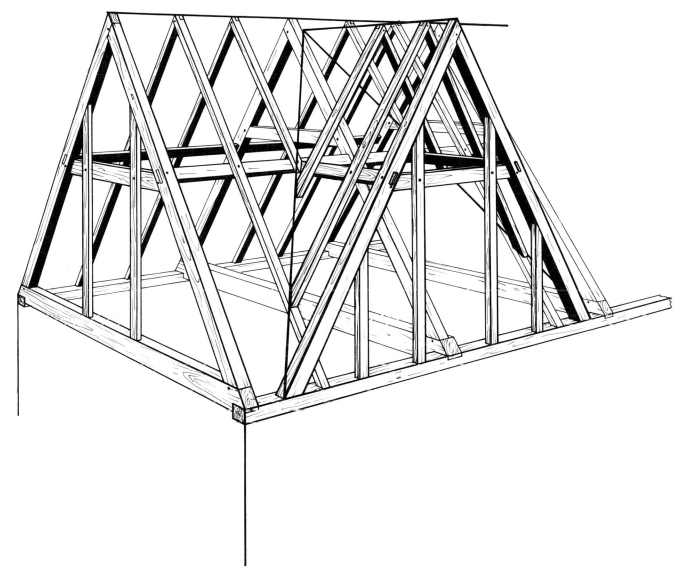

Figure 90. Turner house, Salem, Mass. Detail of frame of façade gable, ca. 1668.

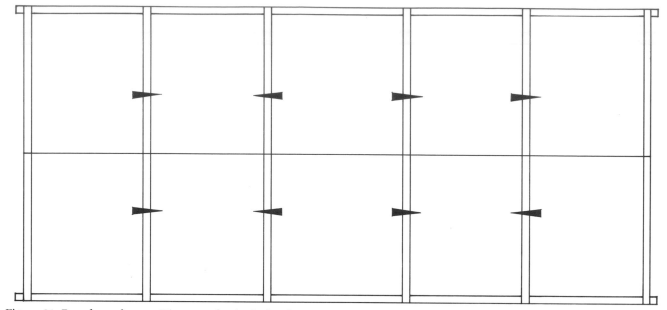

Figure 91. Boardman house. Diagram of principal rafters as seen from above showing directional pattern of pins securing the collar beams.

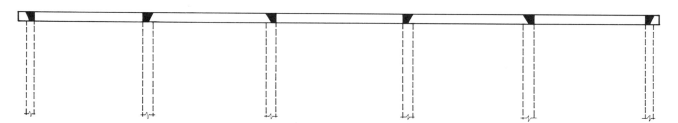

Figure 92. Boardman house. Diagram of tie beams and front plate showing the pattern of half dovetail joints.

Figure 93. Gedney house, Salem, Mass., ca. 1665, with later modifications. *Photo, 1886.*

Boardman and Ward houses, however, represent a different system altogether, consisting of principal rafters and common purlins or ribs (figure 89). The widespread adoption of the ribbed roof at Massachusetts Bay by the end of the seventeenth century is owing probably to a combination of circumstances: early abandonment of thatch and tile and universal adoption of shingles (native materials factor), realization, once they had been selected, that shingles were essentially light-weight and did not require the heavily framed principal and common rafter system (structural factor), and, finally, recognition that less timber was required and the assembly and rearing process was thereby greatly simplified (economy factor).

Once the pairs of principal rafters with their

collars had been erected, the carpenters need be concerned only with the temporary staying of the individual pairs (and perhaps all pairs), while the common purlins or ribs, including the ridge purlin, could be laid in the open trenches waiting to receive them on the outer surface of the principals. They were then pinned from the outside. It was necessary in the rearing of such a roof to take pains that the end gables, with their studs, were properly engineered. That principal rafters in a ribbed roof could easily have been erected with their collars a stick at a time, however, can be argued at the Boardman house, where, according to the numbering of the principals, erection proceeded from east to west. The pinning of the collars to these same principals is sufficiently erratic to suggest that the units went together individually with the pins driven into the erect trusses from whichever side was handiest for the carpenters at the moment (figure 91). While there is no discernible order in the functional pattern of pinning collars to the principal rafters at the Boardman house *in a context which was to remain visible*, there is on the other hand a rhyming alternation to the pattern with which the *invisible* half dovetails of the tie beams are disposed (figure

The Framed Houses of Massachusetts Bay

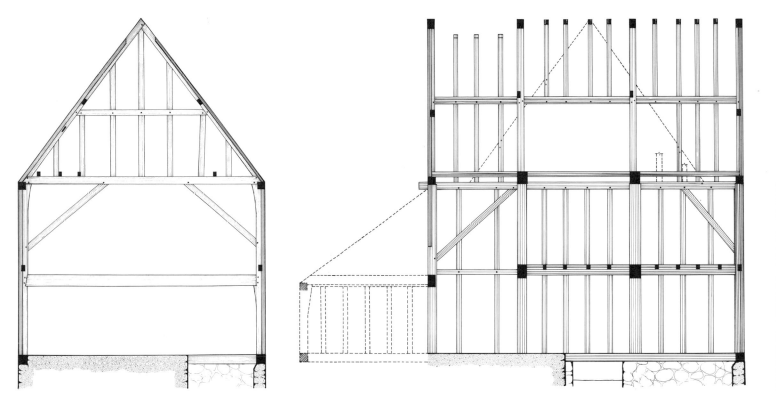

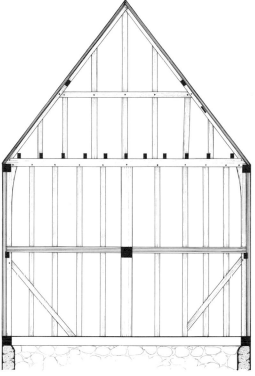

Figure 94. Gedney house. Front elevation (looking east), longitudinal section showing framing. (Center)

Figure 95A. Gedney house. Transverse section at right of chimney showing framing. (Left)
Figure 95B. End elevation (looking south), transverse section showing framing. Original sill missing. (Right)

92). Depending upon the amount of projection of the plate at each end, the pattern of the two outer dovetails can be said to have been fixed by structural necessity. Did the builders rationalize a structurally practical reason for the pattern of the intermediary half dovetails, or did this represent a purely poetic gesture? We can say only that English students have noted parallel situations in much earlier buildings there, and that seventeenth-century carpenters at Massachusetts Bay were by no means consistent in the matter, there being examples easily found which fail this aesthetic test.

Our third and final case study in assembly and rearing techniques, the Gedney house in Salem, ca. 1665 (figure 93), involves a full consideration of the bay assembly method. Commonly used among descendants of the first English settlers in raising late nineteenth-century barns in New England, it could be argued that it may also have been the familiar method in use at an earlier date for those many straightforward house frames that lack the structural complexities described in either of the two foregoing case studies.

We can postulate here a raising sequence in which the various story posts would have been laid out on the ground, connected with their corresponding transverse girts or binding beams, and reared a bent at a time (figure 96). The corner posts in the left-hand gable end, together with the prick post, which has no other function than that of supporting the secondary summer beam housed in it, may well have been erected manually. With the raising of the principal bent of the hall, consisting of story posts with summer or binding beam, the horizontal bridging agent had to enter the binding beam as it rose, and here we find an additional advantage for the tusk tenon. At that moment when the housing of the rising bent is about to receive the tusk tenon of the bridging agent with its spur (having maximum capacity to pick up the load from the bottom with a minimum of cutting into vital areas of the timber), the incline cut in the mortise to receive the tusk would facilitate the coupling of the two elements.

Assembly and Rearing of the House Frame

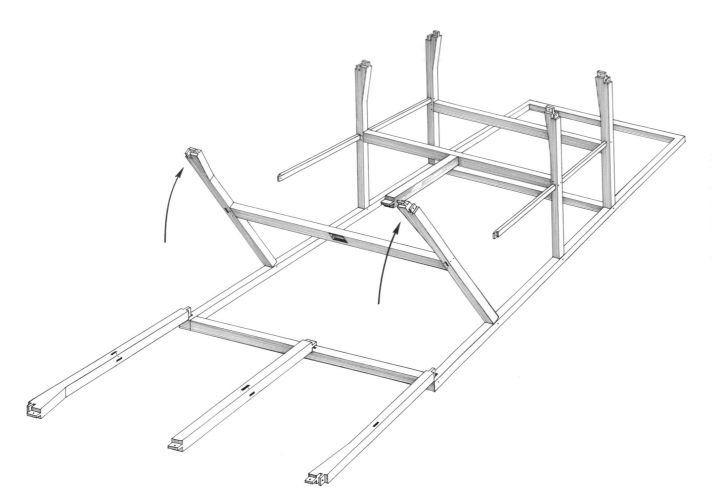

Figure 96. Gedney house. Conjectural raising sequence, second phase.

The principal argument for the development of the tusk tenon joint in terms of insuring structural stability, however, remains unchanged. The cutting away of compression timber for common floor joists in the heavily dimensioned summer itself would have weakened that timber in only negligible degrees. The cutting of a pair of large open cogs in the summer or binding beam to receive the ends of the respective bridging agents on either side would have represented a much more significant assault on the beam at the very midpoint where it is most vulnerable to bending (figure 97). Whatever the conscious theorizing of the carpenters at the time, it is unarguable that they had to avoid a dangerous weakening of vital compression and tension timber here in fashioning the joints. The joint at the Gedney house has in fact failed, owing to the paring away of the

lower surface of the summer by later generations, presumably to gain more headroom (figure 98). Complete collapse was prevented only because of the subsequent introduction of a partition along the line of the beam.

With the frame of the carcass erect, the two-story studs and other secondary members of the frame could have been engineered manually. While the English evidence reveals for the most part that the bearers were simply pinned onto the studs, the evidence here, as at the Fairbanks house, Dedham, and in the letter of Samuel Symonds, written in 1638, indicates that the studs were trenched to receive the bearer (figure 99). No English parallel has as yet been found, but further research there will probably yield examples and determine that this relatively recent innovation in the support of floors had led to the development of more than a single system of jointing.

The lap-face dovetail joint which ties the collar to the principal rafter of the two intermediate roof frames at the Gedney house is, as we have mentioned earlier, a puzzle (figure 55). Our purpose has been to show that the different timbers of the house frame were united with the joints traditionally considered appropriate for their functions. Being in compression the normal joint for the collar is the mortise and tenon (figure 54). Lacking any other logical explanation, the dovetail here can perhaps best be explained in terms of throwback to an earlier period when the principal rafters were in extension.

The principal rafter feet are of particular interest, especially if compared with those added at the north end of the house about 1700, when the parlor lean-to was raised to a full two stories. The earlier carpenters cut the tenons of their rafter feet to sweep back and avoid weakening the thin wall of timber at the beveled end of the tie beam where outward thrusts are at their maximum. The later carpenters have failed to do this, and the straight-cut tenon leaves that much less vital timber in place (figure 100). Paradoxically, however, the original carpenters have neglected to provide any joint whatsoever for the feet of their common rafters, preferring rather to let

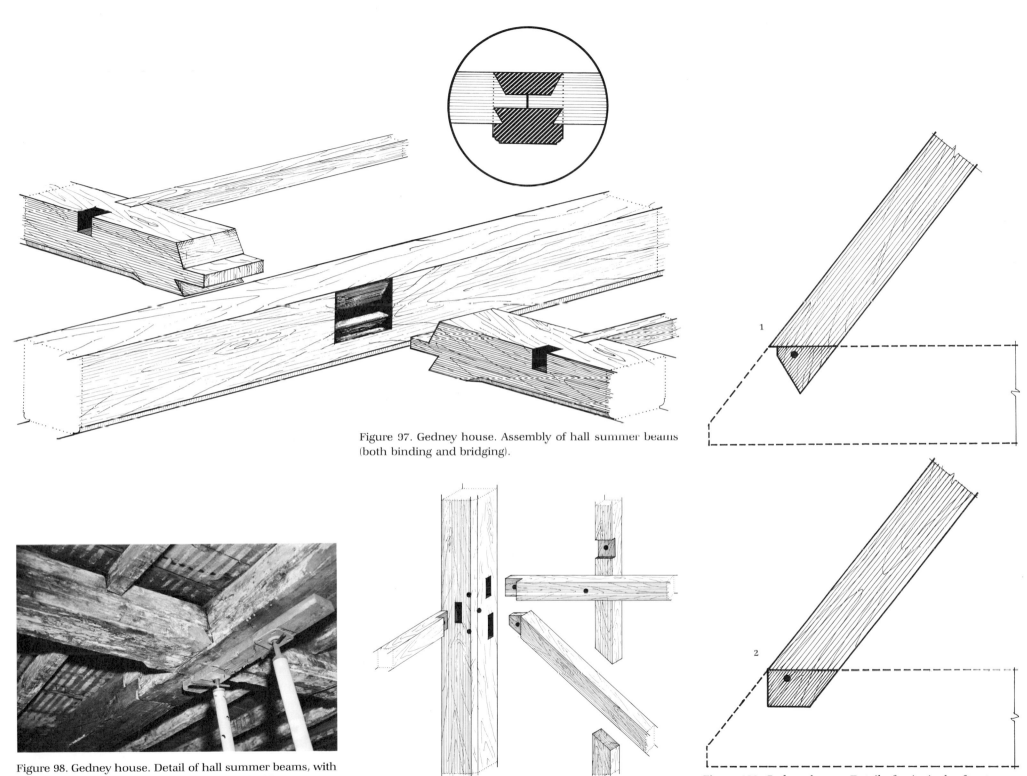

Figure 97. Gedney house. Assembly of hall summer beams (both binding and bridging).

Figure 98. Gedney house. Detail of hall summer beams, with auxiliary support introduced upon removal of later interior partition. (Rear portion of binding beam a modern replacement.) *Photo, Peter Zaharis, 1963.*

Figure 99. Gedney house. Assembly of corner post, front and end bearers, wall brace, and stud.

Figure 100. Gedney house. Detail of principal rafter tenons housed in tie beams of 1. original house, ca. 1665, and 2. later enlargement, ca. 1700.

Assembly and Rearing of the House Frame

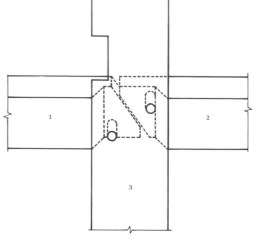

Figure 102. Gedney house. Details of principal purlin, collar tie, and principal and common rafters.

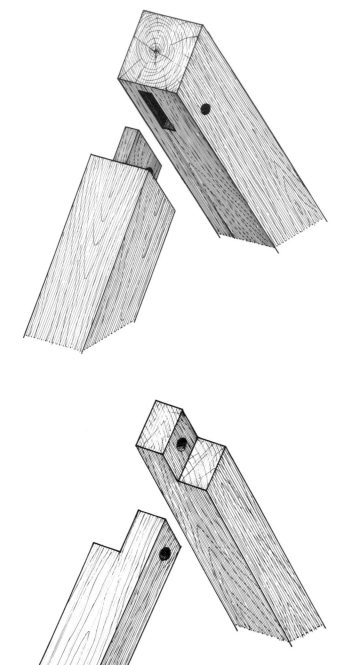

Figure 101. Gedney house. Bridled and half-lapped joints at apex of principal and common rafters.

them simply butt on the upper face of the plate. Consequently, they are secured only at their apex by a half-lap joint (figure 101), and where pinned to the purlins. The purlins, incidentally, are ingeniously fashioned to secure maximum purchase in the joint (figure 102).

The seventeenth-century lean-to at the Fairbanks house in Dedham, added to the rear wall of the original house, is undoubtedly the earliest extant lean-to at Massachusetts Bay (figure 32). Its outer wall consisted of two single-story corner posts and two intermediary posts spaced equidistant from each other, all having a pronounced jowl or flare at the top. There are massive cham-

fered studs which were apparently exposed in the room and convey both in terms of size and character an impression of considerable age. The wall is capped with a plate which probably received the feet of the rafters of the lean-to roof, though the originals have long since disappeared. Resistance to the thrust of this roof is managed somewhat unusually: there are a series of ceiling joists of two varieties, four that measure roughly six by three and a quarter inches and nine (three to a bay) of smaller scantling. The larger units occur at regular intervals and coincide with the posts of the rear lean-to wall, where they were joined to the teazle tenon (figure 103). The ends of these joists are let into a trench atop the plate which is but slightly splayed to form a dovetail, and the only real security from thrust at this point, therefore, is the tenon of the post. At the opposite end, however, where the principal joists were let into the rear wall of the original house, they have been furnished with a vertical half-dovetail which was intended, apparently, to assume the function of withstanding any thrusts transmitted to the rear plate from the roof. Since this joint had to be engineered in connection with a pre-existing structure, the builders ingeniously designed an enlarged mortise into which the dovetail could be inserted and dropped, locking the joist in place (figure 104). These mortises occur on the rear face of the corner posts, east chimney post, and a stud of the rear wall of the original house. Failure to utilize the west chimney post is owing entirely to the fact that the chimney bay is off center, and the principal joists of the lean-to are spaced with careful regard to symmetry. That joist which is tenoned into a stud is further supported by a shaped corbel or bracket.

The floor joists of smaller scantling perform no other function than that of furnishing support for the floor boards of the lean-to attic overhead. At the outer end of the lean-to they rest upon the rear plate, and where joined to the rear wall of the original house at the west end, each of the joists is simply corbeled onto the head of a shaped bracket which has been spiked to the wall, a system which originally may have been employed in toto.

The original lean-to roof rafters added to the Boardman house in Saugus almost certainly before 1696 were simply laid over the existing roof boarding just above the rear plate, and as a consequence have caused a break in the rear roof line which is considered a distinctive indication of the added lean-to (figure 76). Among much earlier buildings, however, original construction might include a lean-to affixed to the house as a subsidiary mass. Both the Narbonne house, ca. 1672, and the Gedney house, in Salem, appear to have had such original appendages, though little is known of their exact character. For the lean-to which forms a fully integral part of the house structure, on the other hand, the rafters are no

longer an added feature but an inherent part of the frame. Here the tie beams are projected over the rear plate for two or three feet to support rafters which now cover both the main house and the lean-to without a break in the rear roof line (figure 105). It is assumed that the rearing of the integral lean-to will have proceeded according to a logical pattern predetermined by the front portion of the carcass. And it is interesting that the White-Ellery house in Gloucester, of integral lean-to construction, has, like the added lean-to of the Fairbanks house, a system of principal and common joists which form the frame of the ceiling. The common joists are fitted into the outer face of the rear girt of the main carcass with barefaced tenons, and the principal joists, measuring six inches deep, five and a half inches wide, enter the story posts of the main house where they are diminished by one-half or more of their width, providing in effect a vertical bare-faced tenon. The common joists rest on the back plate of the lean-to, while the principal joists ride over the post head and plate and receive the feet of the rear roof rafters.

One of the most ambitious integral lean-to houses, though built originally about 1680–1687 on a half-house plan, is the Norden house in Marblehead. The roof is exceptionally high and wide in its span, providing for long collars and six purlins plus a ridge purlin, all of which permit a deep and commodious lean-to kitchen framed with proper summer beams at right angles to the rear plate and girt, as opposed to the enlarged "joists" normally found. The rafter system employed at the White-Ellery house is by far the most common, and implies that the rafters of the rear roof slope, supported more or less at their midpoint by the cantilevered tie beams, are all of one length (figure 105). A single exception is found at the Cooper-Frost-Austin house in Cambridge, ca. 1689. Here the lean-to rafters continue to be of two separate lengths. The upper are footed upon a purlin which is clasped by the ends of the cantilevered tie beams, and the lower set covering the lean-to itself are tenoned into the beveled ends of the ties (figure 106). The irresist-

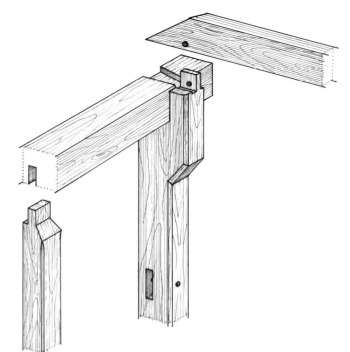

Figure 103. Fairbanks house, Dedham, Mass. Assembly of post head, "tie beam," plate, and stud, with mortise in post for falling brace, rear wall of lean-to at northeast corner, probably before 1668.

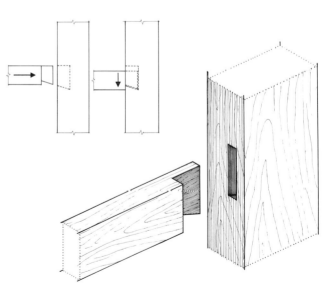

Figure 104. Fairbanks house. Detail of interlocking tenon of lean-to "tie beam," mortised into rear chimney post of original house.

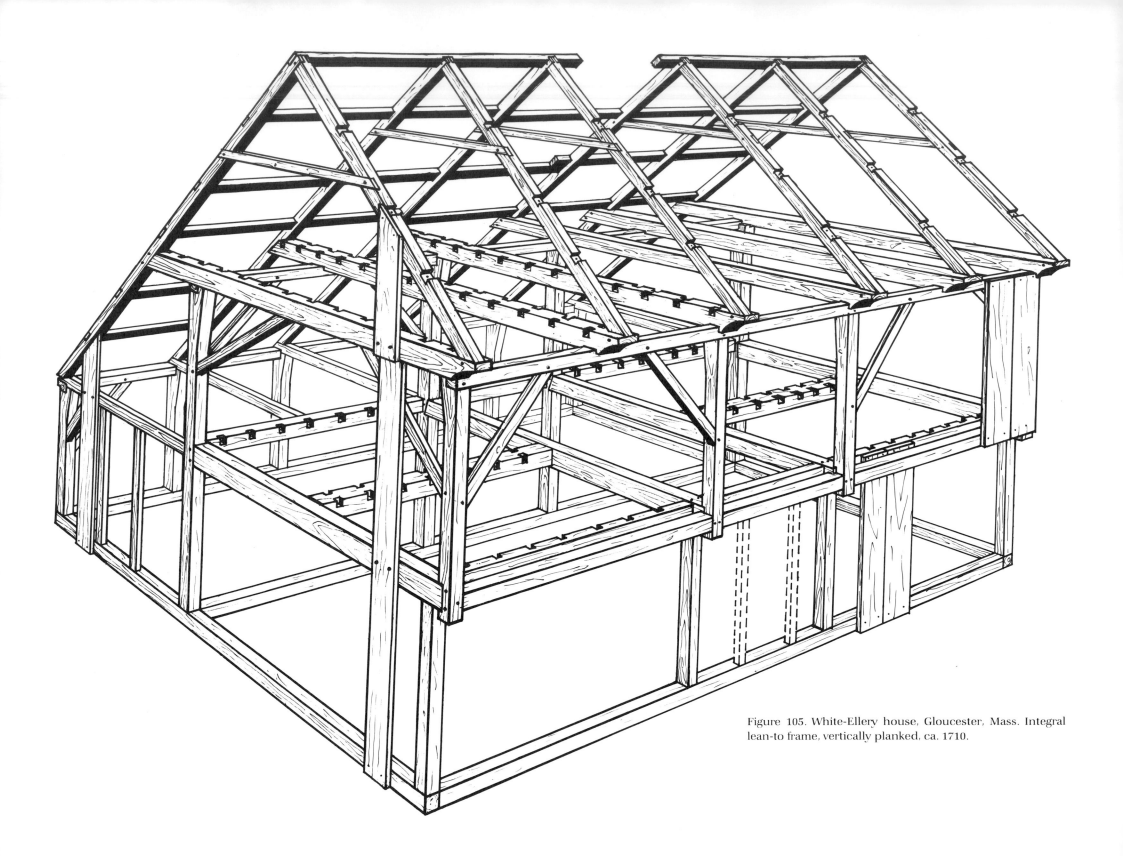

Figure 105. White-Ellery house, Gloucester, Mass. Integral lean-to frame, vertically planked, ca. 1710.

ible urge to suggest here a transitional stage in the evolution of the integral lean-to should be suppressed in light of its appearance in this isolated example some ten years after the single length rafter system is known to have become fully developed. In any event, the integral lean-to which makes use of the cantilevered tie beam would appear to be an innovational feature in the American experience. Taken in conjunction with planning considerations, this construction may be seen as a logical response to the functional demands that service rooms be clustered at the rear of the house in a lateral file, the central one of which might take advantage of the all-important central stack of the chimney.

For the early story-and-a-half house form, we have no more than six or seven examples remaining in the Massachusetts Bay area (figure 107). Such "cottages" must have been much more common in the seventeenth century than the small number of survivors would suggest, especially in the early years when short-order housing was very much in demand. While the existing structures reveal very little new information about the methods of assembly and rearing, they do vary slightly among themselves in form. For the most part, these houses are framed according to a bay system consisting of posts and binding beams, so joined that the posts extend some three feet or more above the point of junction. Thus the chamber or loft contains a short section of upright wall, and, as seen in the Balch house in Beverly, could be furnished with façade gables which provided both light and some slight additional headroom (figure 108). The normal tie beam was impractical in such a situation and the rafters therefore spring directly from the plate. At the Balch house the principals are in line with the posts (figure 109), but at the Peak house in Medfield a series of principals are bird-mouthed over the plate at intervals of roughly five feet (figure 151).

At least two houses of single-story height have been noted which are exceptions to the method of framing walls just described. Of these, the Woodcock-Langley house in Hingham, con-

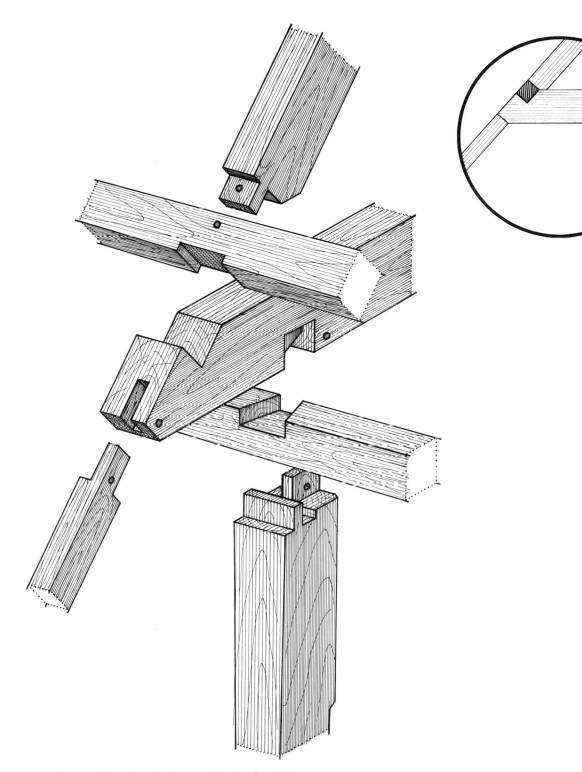

Figure 106. Cooper-Frost-Austin house, Cambridge, Mass. Assembly of post head, rear plate, chimney tie beam, purlin, and principal rafter, ca. 1689.

Assembly and Rearing of the House Frame

Figure 107. Peak house, Medfield, Mass., late seventeenth century.

Figure 109. Balch house. Detail of post head, rear plate, and principal rafter, earliest chamber. *Photo, William W. Owens, Jr., 1974.*

Figure 108. Balch house, Beverly, Mass. Earliest chamber, seventeenth century, restored. *Photo, William W. Owens, Jr., 1974.*

structed before 1687, is the earlier. The plan is a full two rooms in depth, an arrangement found in nearby Plymouth Colony and Rhode Island to the south, and the rafters which pitch from the tie beams atop the single-story posts cover a relatively wide span. In Essex during the period of 1570 to 1640, "a number of lobby-entrance houses are of only one storey and attics with the roof timbers rising from the wall-plate or only a little way above it." Such houses "perhaps mark the progress of the housing revolution to a slightly poorer class of yeoman than hitherto."[63] The statement must have distinct socioeconomic implications for New England as well. At least one central chimney or "lobby-entrance" story-and-a-half dwelling, however, the Cushing house in Hingham of 1679, was built by a prosperous yeoman, and it is in every respect an expensive house with elaborate joints and embellished quarter-round chamfers.

There were medieval single-storied cottages in Essex which, like the more commodious farmhouses, were converted during the great period of reconstruction in England during the sixteenth and early seventeenth centuries. Normally the hall was divided horizontally, a chimney stack was inserted, and dormer windows introduced to light the loft area. "Occasionally, a genuine upper storey (as distinct from attic bedrooms) may have been added,"[64] and a number of story-and-a-half houses at Massachusetts Bay have undergone just such a modification in the process of improvement. The original portion of the Balch house, for example, was raised to a full two stories in height, almost certainly before 1725, and the same transformation can be observed in the Cushing and Woodcock-Langley houses in Hingham, and the Austin Lord house in Ipswich. The three latter structures now present an impression of the typical two-and-one-half story house, though at the Austin Lord house the placement of the chimney stack forward of the roof ridge is a suspicious indication of internal alterations (figure 110).

While by no means numerous, there were at least two additional structural systems employed by the early builders at Massachusetts Bay which reflect the ample availability of pine in the New World. Both of these to one degree or another make use of traditional box framing methods, but both also are significantly different. Houses of plank frame appear in appreciable numbers in Plymouth Colony[65] and the earliest settled regions of Maine and New Hampshire, where examples of log construction can be found as well. For the plank frame, one should note the very occasional use of vertical plank in earlier English framing, for instance, the Cotheridge Parish Church bell tower in Worcestershire, of late fourteenth- or early fifteenth-century date. Precariously maintained links with such a tradition, however, are perhaps less important than recognizing that an abundance of pine and the early development of the sawmill in New England

Figure 110. Austin Lord house, Ipswich, Mass., before 1653, with later modifications. *Photo, George E. Noyes*, ca. 1925.

encouraged the widespread adoption of this distinctive form as a practical construction alternative. The term itself is contemporary, as we find in 1719 when the town of Manchester in building a new meetinghouse voted "that the hous shall be planket and not studed."[66]

For the squared log house it has been suggested that then-prevailing knowledge of late medieval log structures along the Scottish border which have not survived were carried to the New World by Cromwell's Scotch prisoners of war, imported to work in the water-powered sawmills that formed a major industry of the Piscataqua River.[67] The largest number of early log houses occurs in this region, and we can produce no more than two or three extant examples for Mas-

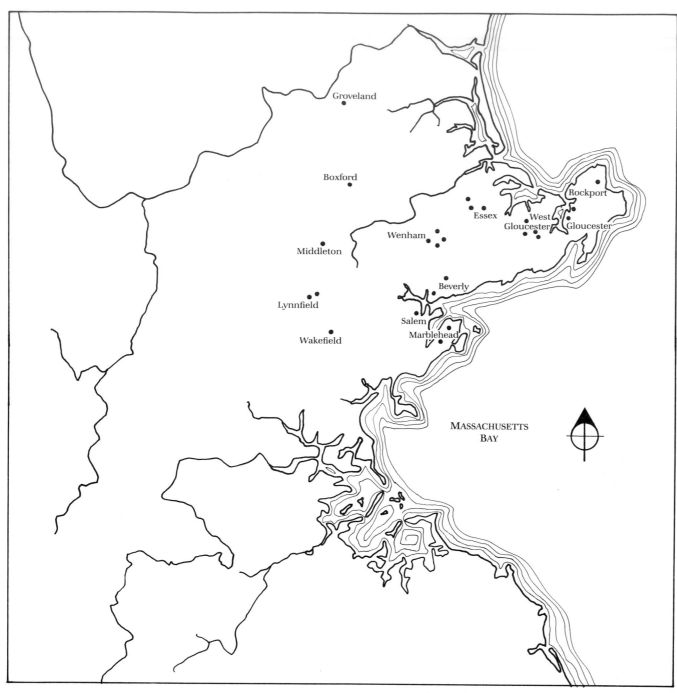

Figure 111. Massachusetts Bay, showing distribution of plank frame houses before 1725.

sachusetts Bay. These, not surprisingly, are at Cape Ann, which borders nearly on that area where the log house is commonly found.

The plank frame house, however, presents a more complex problem in terms of its geographical and chronological distribution throughout Massachusetts Bay, and is found more commonly. Owing again to the early prevalence of sawmilling in southern Maine and New Hampshire, it is not surprising that the highest concentration of plank frame houses occurs also in and around Cape Ann (figure 111). The smaller but nevertheless significant grouping in the Wenham area is of interest in that the buildings all date more or less within the same decade and reveal further, through the use of serpentine wall bracing, the hand of a unique personality or "school." For the remaining scattered examples, all north of Boston, we can only assume that purely individualistic reasons lie again at the root of selection of this less familiar form of construction. Among the known examples not one is earlier than the mid 1680s, and many are of the first quarter of the eighteenth century. We are dealing, then, with a period in which third- and fourth-generation American carpenters were working with building concepts assimilated over a period of time, presumably from southern Maine and New Hampshire to the north. It can thus be argued that the plank frame was a known structural variant in New England by the late seventeenth century, though obviously the majority of carpenters in all parts of the area clung to the traditional English method of framing walls with stud and nogging.

All of this ignores the economics involved, which may have been a determining factor in many cases. The characteristic framed house with a full complement of joints was surely more costly in terms of time and expense than the plank frame house, in which the joints are reduced to an absolute minimum. Further, the number of individual frame members (materials factor) is reduced as well, and we are left with a consideration of the cost of the sawn planks themselves. Many of the planks used at Massachusetts Bay may have been imported from the sawmills in southern Maine and New Hampshire,[68] and a transportation charge would thus have been reflected in the client's cost. On the other hand, in those locations where we find heaviest concentration of late seventeenth-century plank frames, there were by then local sawmills. Liberty for a sawmill had been granted by the town of Gloucester as early as 1652,[69] and Wenham had similarly authorized John Porter and James Friend in 1691 "to stop a brooke in the Common . . . so they maye have the priviledg of the watter to set up a Sawe mill."[70] One of the earliest plank frame houses at Massachusetts Bay was the Story house in Essex, ca. 1684, with studs and joists as well as the planks all sawmill sawn. Here, too, as early as 1656 the town had voted that a sawmill be built on Chebacco River, and liberty to cut timber had been granted, provided that the inhabitants be charged no more than 4 percent.[71] Both Seth Story for whom the house was built and his father, William Story, were carpenters, living near Chebacco River, and when Seth drew his will in 1724 he was then part owner of a sawmill there.[72]

The plank frame house presented few problems in terms of erection. The carcass will have been reared according to any one of the methods we have described and the planks then raised manually into a vertical position and secured to the braced frame (figures 105 and 81). This involved drilling holes and pinning the planks to the first-story girts and spiking them to the sill. In the White-Ellery house in Gloucester, several of the planks are pinned *and* spiked. Normally the planking preceded the crowning members of the carcass, for the planks are not spiked at the top but let into two inch grooves in the bottom of the plates and end ties. At the late seventeenth-century George Giddings house in Essex the front plate has been molded, and at the Story and White-Ellery houses the end ties project sufficiently beyond the groove to create a slight overhang at the gable end (figures 112 and 113). As seen at the Story and Goldsmith-Pickering houses (the latter in Wenham, ca. 1700), the grooving is

Figure 112. Story house, Essex, Mass, ca. 1684. Demolished 1957. Vertical planking stripped of clapboards. *Photo, Peter Zaharis, 1957.*

Assembly and Rearing of the House Frame

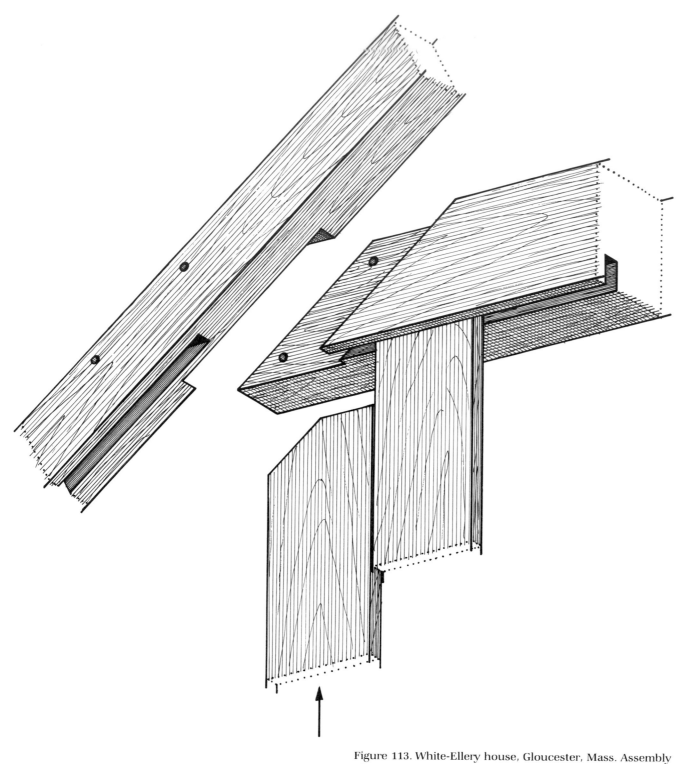

Figure 113. White-Ellery house, Gloucester, Mass. Assembly of principal rear rafter and end tie beam, showing rabbet for vertical planking in that portion of the rafter not included in the projecting gable end, ca. 1710.

The Framed Houses of Massachusetts Bay

discontinued in those portions of the plate and ties where a window was to be inserted, and the space itself was determined by omitting a requisite amount of planking (figure 114). The wall between the upper and lower window openings in the Story house is composed of shorter lengths of vertical plank, while the same areas in the George Giddings house and the Captain Thomas Fiske house in Wenham, ca. 1698, are pieced out with horizontal lengths.

In most cases there were at least two studs in each wall that was to receive a window, located one on either side of the opening. They were intended obviously to provide some support for the window frame and perhaps also additional support at the point at which the planking was discontinued. The planks were seldom less than two inches thick and were customarily square edged, butting without any joint. The planked wall, once erect, was then, in terms of finish, clapboarded on the outside and lathed and plastered on its inner surface (figures 114 and 211).

There are no more than three known examples of log construction at Massachusetts Bay, two of which are as yet entirely undated and may be later than our period. While the house built of squared logs was not invariably erected for defensive purposes, this was often an important motive. As the seventeenth century wore on and the Indians became more fully aware of what they were losing, New England entered upon a fear-gripping era of intensified border warfare, extending well into the eighteenth century. In 1676, during King Philip's War, a "Military Committee" was authorized "to Vew and Consider the Severall townes," and to propose "what may bee adviseable, In order to the Security of the people . . . In this time of trouble." We met at Andover, their report began, "Where wee found 12 Substantial Garrisons well fitted," and at nearby Newbury they recorded: "we finde Severall of the remoat houses fortified."[73]

Concerning these houses built from the start with both dwelling and defense in mind, Governor Thomas Hutchinson, writing during the mid-eighteenth century, reports that "in every frontier

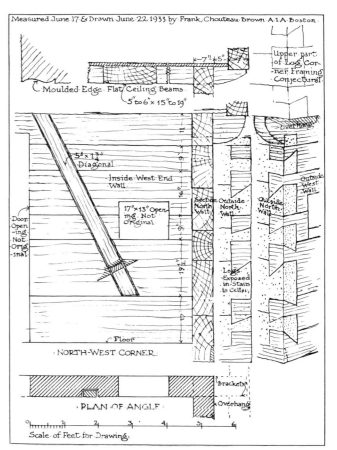

Measured June 17 & Drawn June 22 1933 by Frank, Chouteau Brown, A.I.A. Boston.

Figure 114. Goldsmith-Pickering house, Wenham, Mass. Detail of end tie beam and brace, showing mortise for window stud, rabbet for vertical planking, and original lath and plaster, ca. 1700. (Stud and portion of planking removed for later window opening.) *Photo (during restoration), Peter Zaharis, 1963.* (Upper Left)

Figure 115. Witch house (so-called), Rockport, Mass. Details of log wall construction, ca. 1700. (Above)

settlement there were more or less garrison houses, some with a flankart at two opposite angles, others at each corner of the house . . . [and] others, which were smaller, built with square timber, one piece laid horizontally upon another, and loop holes in every side of the house."[74] One of the best surviving examples of the latter is the John Gilman Garrison house in Exeter, New Hampshire, ca. 1700. The second story overhangs the first and the walls consist of interlocking mill-sawn logs, dovetailed at the corners and pierced at the outset with abnormally small windows. The Gilman Garrison is unique among those that have survived for preserving evidence that the original front entrance was furnished with a portcullis type door. The oaken pulley by which this door could be raised and lowered remains embedded in the structure of the second story.

Not all of the squared log structures that have survived in Maine and New Hampshire were built fundamentally as "forts," however, and this would seem to be the case with a log house erected at Springfield in the Connecticut River Valley in 1677. The contract specifics a building twenty-four feet long by eighteen feet wide with a stone or brick chimney, "the Loggs or Timber to be full 6 Inches thick when sawne," and set on end, but with no reference to any purely defensive features.[75] Such was the case also, apparently, with the principal remaining example of the type at Massachusetts Bay, the so-called Witch house at Rockport, ca. 1700. No firing ports have as yet been discovered here, and we must conclude provisionally that the house employs the structural techniques of the true garrison house with defense, perhaps, only secondarily in mind.

The logs selected for the construction of the outer walls of the Witch house were of tamarack, seven inches thick by nine to nineteen and a half

Assembly and Rearing of the House Frame

Figure 116. Witch house (so-called). Hall, showing close-set girders supporting second story. *Photo, Arthur C. Haskell, ca. 1933.*

inches high, and were fitted, in the lower story at least, with a precision which is nowhere better illustrated than in the close-fitting of the joints and in the dovetailing of the logs at the corners (figure 115). In the second story, unexplainably, the chinks between the individual units are quite wide in places. The framing of the first-floor ceiling, which cantilevered out to support the overhang, consists of hard pine girders approximately five by seventeen inches, spaced about thirty inches apart, laid flat and molded at the edges with a delicate cyma curve (figure 116). This heavy construction was obviously designed to bear the weight of log walls in the second story. The second floor ceilings are constructed in the usual manner with summers supporting floor joists. The chimney, end, and front girts project also to help support the overhang. The assembly and rearing here would presumably have proceeded a stick at a time.

CHAPTER VI

English Regional Derivations and Evolutionary Trends

THE FIRST IMMIGRANT carpenters at Massachusetts Bay transferred from England to America habits of construction peculiar to their own region. Thus we may expect to find here at the beginning, more clearly, perhaps, than at any other moment in the seventeenth century, the most explicit links with English precedent. The range and diversity of regional types, in fact, must have been quite startling at the first. We are concerned, however, with what remains, and the association of specific carpenters with individual buildings, though not in terms of singular creative traits. The earliest builders, in constructing their house frames, were governed by broadly collective rather than narrowly personal schematic concepts. We seek to discern in the houses themselves the regional differences that indicate whether the personalities involved came from East Anglia or the more westerly parts of England, and beyond that, somewhat hesitantly, their individual counties of origin.

It is not beside the point to consider the pattern of origins for the earliest inhabitants of Massachusetts Bay as a whole. Dedham, on the South Shore, for example, in which the Fairbanks house is located, is characteristic of many communities whose first townsmen were drawn from a wide range of English localities. For those men admitted during 1636 and 1637, there are representatives from the City of London, Suffolk, Norfolk, Essex, Bedfordshire, Hertfordshire, Buckinghamshire, and Yorkshire, from which came Jonathan Fairbanks himself. North Shore Newbury, on the other hand, which claims the Coffin house, presented an alternate pattern of settlement. When Ipswich became overcrowded with inhabitants in the beginning years, "some of them presently swarmed out into another place, a little further eastward." Mr. Parker, the minister, "choosing . . . to accompany some of his countrymen that came out of Wiltshire in England, to that new place . . . removed with them thither, and called it Newberry."[1]

For this community, then, we can expect to find a concentration of neighbors, relatively speaking, which would have included their artisans. Thus for at least four carpenters and a joiner resident here during the 1640s and 1650s when the Coffin house was built, three have been traced to points of origin in Hampshire and Wiltshire: John Emery, carpenter, who came to New England from Romsey, Hampshire, in 1635, aged thirty-four; Hugh March, joiner, from Nether Wallop or Tytherley in Hampshire, who arrived in 1638, aged about twenty, servant to Stephen Kent; and Henry Jacques, carpenter, from Stanton or Rodbourne in Wiltshire, born about 1619.[2]

In Dedham, whose settlers were drawn from a wider range, we also find that its earliest builders, by coincidence, were neighbors in old England. Thomas Fisher, from Winston in Suffolk, apparently middle-aged, was admitted a townsman in July 1637 and "undertooke the Meetinghouse," but died on August 10, 1638, before it was finished. John Roper, who called himself carpenter when he left England at the age of twenty-six in 1637, came from New Buckenham, Norfolk, close to the southern border of the county, and having landed at Boston on June 8, 1637, is mentioned for the first time in the Dedham records on August 11.[3] There was also present among the Dedham company as early as August 1636 one John Kingsbury who came from Boxford in Suffolk where he had been baptized in 1595. Although we have no record of his craft, the inventory of his estate in 1660 includes an impressive array of carpenters' tools as well as a "mason trowell," "lathing hammer," and "one thatchers needle and rake."[4]

Here then, in this early period, we have record in Dedham of two or three builders from the northern sector of East Anglia, including Suffolk, which sent the largest number of settlers to New England, and in Newbury three contemporaries

Figure 117. Swan Green Farmhouse, Cratfield, Suffolk, Eng. Rear elevation (looking southwest), longitudinal section showing framing of original house (at right), ca. 1600, and parlor addition with new chimney, ca. 1625 or later.

about 1625 or later. The high-pitched roof of this addition contains two sets of purlins from the upper of which the wind braces rise (figure 117). Fully comparable in size and position to those of the Fairbanks house built little more than a decade later, and located within a twenty-five mile radius of Winston and New Buckenham, these braces in the roof frame of Swan Green Farmhouse represent a regional peculiarity which can be found to extend southward into northern Essex, where a similar condition exists in the roof of Lyons Hall, Braintree, a substantial clothier's house of about 1600. Boxford, we recall, from which John Kingsbury emigrated, is less than twenty miles from Braintree.

The modular relationship of the individual units of the roof of the Fairbanks house—the dimensional ratio, for example, of principal to common rafters—is also consonant with East Anglian work of the early seventeenth century. The common rafters, however, are secured to the purlins with a single pin, a practice not always to be found in the earlier buildings of East Anglia. Yet once again late English examples, including a cottage at Tinker's Green, Finchingfield, in northern Essex, and a seventeenth-century house and barn at Hall Farm on the Weston-Shadingfield border in Suffolk, have just such pinning of their common rafters. Those of the roof frame of the latter house (which employs reused material) reveal an erratic pattern with only some of the rafters pinned. One might argue that the practice was a recent innovation in seventeenth-century East Anglian work, and was carried by its carpenters to New England, where a continuing degree of ambivalence is to be encountered among the houses of clear-cut East Anglian derivation, some examples being found with their common rafters pinned and others not.

There are additional parallels which help to place the Fairbanks house in an East Anglian context. The studs, for example, rise in a single length for a full two stories and are trenched in the front and rear walls for thin bearers which support the ends of the floor joists of the chamber floor (figure 58). The concept of two-story studs derives pre-

who came from English counties farther to the west. To what extent are regional characteristics reflected in the extant houses in each of the two towns which may with no undue stretch of the imagination be ascribed to these artisans or their direct influence? The Fairbanks house, ca. 1637, can be readily identified with East Anglia in all major respects of both profile and detail, except that the wind braces in the roof, of perceptible convex profile, *rise* from the purlins to the principal rafters, speaking in visual terms, rather than fall below them, which is the common practice throughout England as a whole and East Anglia as well. English precedent for an otherwise seemingly contradictory treatment can be found, however, in that northern sector of East Anglia from which Dedham's earliest carpenters were drawn. An unequivocal example is the now restored sixteenth-century structure called Swan Green Farmhouse at Cratfield in Suffolk, to which a one-room, two-and-a-half-story addition was made

sumably from a somwhat earlier period during which floors were being inserted into formerly open halls, the bearer being fastened to the existing studs to help perform the function of support. By the opening years of the seventeenth century, this structural expedient appears to have been taken over, to some extent at least, as an integral framing device. Seventeenth-century precedents can be found for this peculiarity in the north of East Anglia, for example, in the story-and-a-half cottage at Tinker's Green and in Hunston, Suffolk, in connection with a porch containing stairs, added probably in 1619 to a house of earlier date.

The pattern of wall braces in the chamber story of the Fairbanks house, which rise from the principal posts to the plates and tie beams, is noteworthy (figure 58). The most superficial comparison of English postmedieval houses discloses that the practice is common in the western counties and is by no means typical of East Anglia, where the braces normally fall from the principal posts to girts and sill. The Suffolk-Norfolk area, however, particularly in its seventeenth-century phases, has not received as much study as Essex, and recent investigation has revealed an increasing number of late regional prototypes for what was thought to be an uncharacteristic building trait. A striking example is Mill Cottage at Wetheringsett, Suffolk, for which a date about 1600 could be argued. This small house of two-room, central-chimney plan is constructed with both two-story studs and rising wall braces that are trenched into the studs (figure 118).

The seventeenth-century postmedieval house in England has only very recently become an object of intensive study. And insistently it is the seventeenth rather than the sixteenth-century smaller English farmhouse which has the most immediate relevance for developments in New England. Indeed, we may well ask whether the flatwise positioning of floor joists found in the Fairbanks house is indicative of conservative thinking on the part of its carpenters when compared with dated examples in Essex, where by the early seventeenth century the depthwise positioning of joists appears to be fairly widespread,

or whether it may be yet another indication of regionalism. Flatwise positioning of joists is the rule rather than the exception for modest houses well into the seventeenth century in Suffolk, and its appearance at the Fairbanks house may thus have more regional than evolutionary significance.

For Newbury, and the Coffin house of about 1654 in particular, we discover a sharp break with East Anglian influence. The characteristic post-medieval English roof frame that makes use of principal and common rafters, especially prevalent in the eastern counties, is replaced here with a system of principal rafters, ridge piece, and common purlins (figure 119). The salient feature is the purlin itself, for which the principal rafters have been trenched and not mortised. The ridge piece, in fact, continues to lie also in a trench throughout the seventeenth century and does not evolve, at least in domestic work, into the form of a proper ridge pole until the eighteenth century (figure 120).

Among postmedieval English carpenters, the principal and common rafter roof system was pre-eminent, with any substantive differences between representative examples in the east and west most generally occurring in the dimensional ratio of scantlings, for individual timbers are apt to be heavier as one moves from the east to the west of England, period for period. There are other distinctive roof framing traits in the more westerly English counties, derived ultimately from cruck construction, so common to the region.[5] Cruck building is of considerable antiquity and involves the use of single lengths of inclined or curved timbers, rising often from ground level and meeting at an apex. The lower portions serve in one sense as the posts and the upper ends function as the rafters of the roof. The purlins characteristically lie in a trench at the rear of the cruck "blades," as these continuous units are called (figure 121). The westerly counties, then, are clearly the area in which to search for American prototypes, although so far it has proved impossible to find an explicit precedent for the Coffin house roof frame. The links are there,

Figure 118. Mill Cottage, Wetheringsett, Suffolk, Eng. Chamber, showing wall framing, ca. 1600 *Photo, Dennis H. Evans, 1971.*

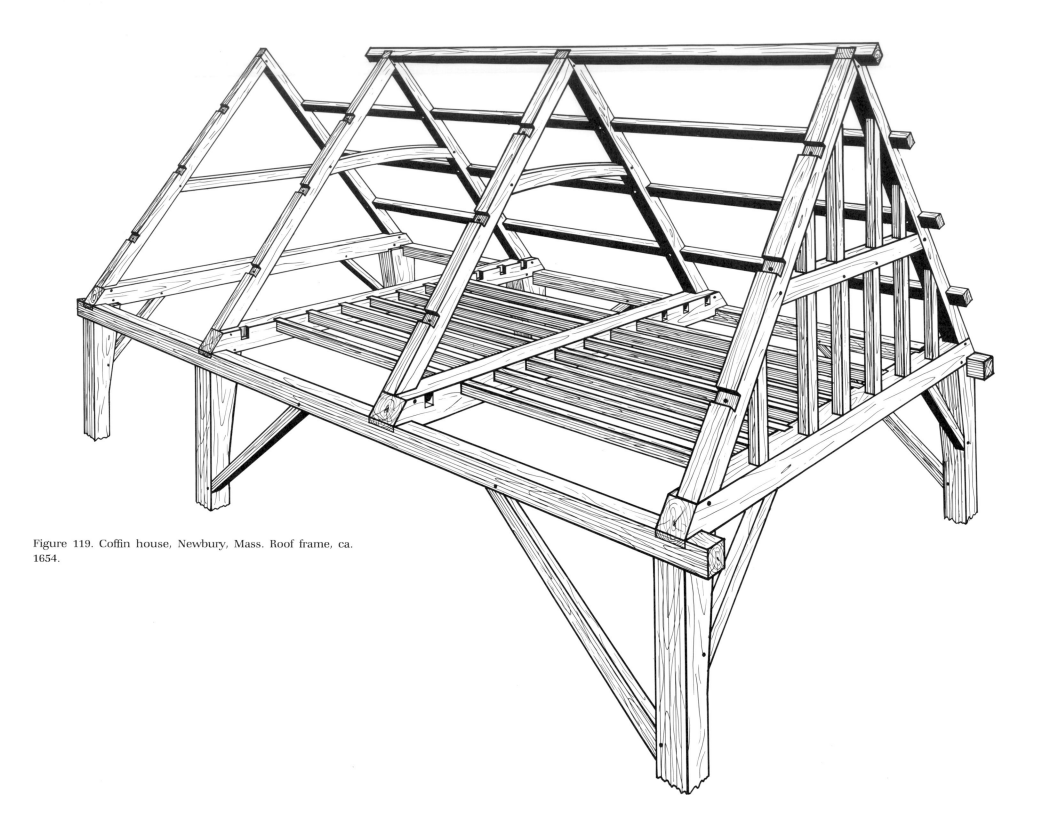

Figure 119. Coffin house, Newbury, Mass. Roof frame, ca. 1654.

however. In the center of Rodbourne, Wiltshire, for instance, the vicinity from which Henry Jacques of Newbury set out for the New World, there is a brick barn, probably no earlier than the late seventeenth century, with two large purlins and a smaller ridge purlin which are housed in trenches on the rear face of the principal rafters. These horizontal members support a series of closely spaced common rafters riding from plate to ridge piece. The purlins at least present affinities with the roof of the Coffin house, although the common purlin in New England is clearly designed in terms of its slender scantling and relatively close spacing to receive roof boarding and shingles, not thatch, tile, or stone, the common roofing materials in England at the period.

In all likelihood the Coffin house roof combines derivation from such obviously related roofs as those found in Wiltshire with the New World innovation of boarding. And if such features in New England as underboarding for roofs and walls, plank frames, clapboards and shingles, and wall sheathing do indeed imply immediate and widespread innovation, then we launch directly from speculation about English origins into a discussion of uniquely American developments. Boards and shingles respectively strengthened and lightened the roof, and the carpenters seem to have responded almost at once by diminishing the size of the individual structural components. While the principal and common rafter roof was by far the more universal in England at the time of the Great Migration, the roof frame of principal rafters and common purlins, or ribs, had established itself firmly as the preferred system at Massachusetts Bay by the end of the seventeenth century. Among a total of some 135 frames erected before 1725 where the original roof scheme of one or the other variety is known, twenty-six only consist of principal and common rafters, and all of these with but five or six exceptions are before 1685 in date. The balance, 109 examples, are of the common purlin variety, of which number only thirteen are clearly before 1685.

With respect to the slender quality of many of the late seventeenth-century principal rafter and

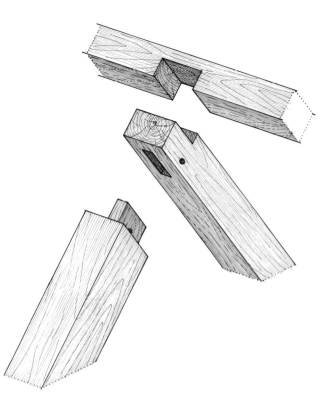

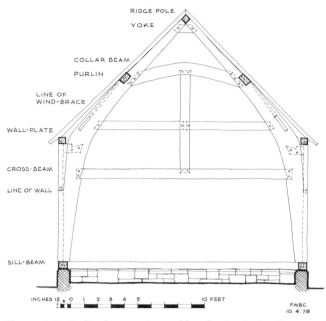

Figure 120. Coffin house. Assembly of principal rafters and ridge purlin. (Left)
Figure 121. Woolstaston Hall, Leebotwood, Shropshire, Eng. Transverse section of frame showing medieval cruck construction. (Above)

common purlin roofs at Massachusetts Bay, it is apparent that our carpenters went one step further in the direction of experimentation in reducing the scantling of the purlin in particular to a point rather delicately commensurate with the load. That they were successful in this experiment is amply attested by the number of roof frames which have survived in relatively sound condition from the seventeenth century. However, in enough cases to form a significant sampling, including the Boardman house in Saugus, ca. 1687, and the even later Captain Matthew Perkins house in Ipswich, erected between 1701 and 1709, common purlins have snapped during the course of their later history. The implication is that in the slenderizing tendencies which accompanied the widespread adoption of a roof framing system congenial to lighter weight-bearing loads, the purlins had become reduced in dimension to a barely adequate level. As long as New England carpenters, particularly in rural areas, framed their dwelling houses in the long-established traditions of English-derived carpentry, they never

Figure 122. Captain Matthew Perkins house, Ipswich, Mass. Detail of roof frame and east gable end of attic with remnants of original lath and plaster finish, 1701–1709. *Photo, Peter Zaharis, 1955.*

Figure 123. Eliakim Morse house, Medfield, Mass. Detail of roof frame, ca. 1750. *Photo, Richard Merrill, 1969.*

again so pushed their luck (figure 122). Beginning with the second quarter of the eighteenth century and continuing well into the nineteenth, there is a marked return to more amply dimensioned roof timbers, even to the extent of a "revival" of the principal and common rafter roof system, or closely related derivatives. The characteristic later eighteenth-century roof frame, in other words, whether pitched, gambrel, or hipped, is apt to be more heavily framed, with more substantially dimensioned timbers, than its earlier counterpart (figure 123).

Among those other mid-century houses dotted about the perimeter of Massachusetts Bay for which an almost certain probability of construction by English-born carpenters can be assumed, we also find evidence of regionalism, with a somewhat higher incidence of East Anglian forms and influence. In Dorchester, which claims the contemporary Pierce, Blake, and Capen houses

(the latter now relocated in Milton), all dating to the middle of the century, there were two or three carpenters of varying backgrounds who may well have been involved in their construction. The first of these, John Whipple, came to Massachusetts Bay about 1632. His origin is unknown, although John Whipple of Ipswich, who arrived also during the first wave of migration, came from Bocking in Essex. Furthermore, Dorchester's John Whipple was little more than fifteen years of age at the time of arrival, and he may well have served his carpenter's apprenticeship in the New World. In any event, he was a grantee of land in 1638 near Stoughton's mill on the Neponset River (not far from the Pierce house), and remained there until 1658, when he removed to Providence, Rhode Island.[6] Whipple was resident here, therefore, and presumably active at his trade during the period in which the Pierce house was built, about 1650. Its falling braces and

roof of slender principal and common rafter construction, with common rafters pinned to the purlins, are in all respects typical of East Anglia. In addition, one set of principal rafter feet are bird-mouthed over the front and rear plates and thus do not align themselves vertically with the posts and tie beams (figure 124). The consequent disparity between the equally spaced bays of the roof and the functionally spaced bays of the carcass is a feature found recurrently as a regional variant in Suffolk and Norfolk, and occurs in northern Essex as well in that portion of the much earlier Paycocke's House in Coggeshall which was erected about 1500 (figure 125). The Capen house, erected probably before 1658, is similar in all respects to the Pierce house and may well have been built by the same carpenter(s).

The Blake house, ca. 1650, on the other hand, reveals another personality altogether, in addi-

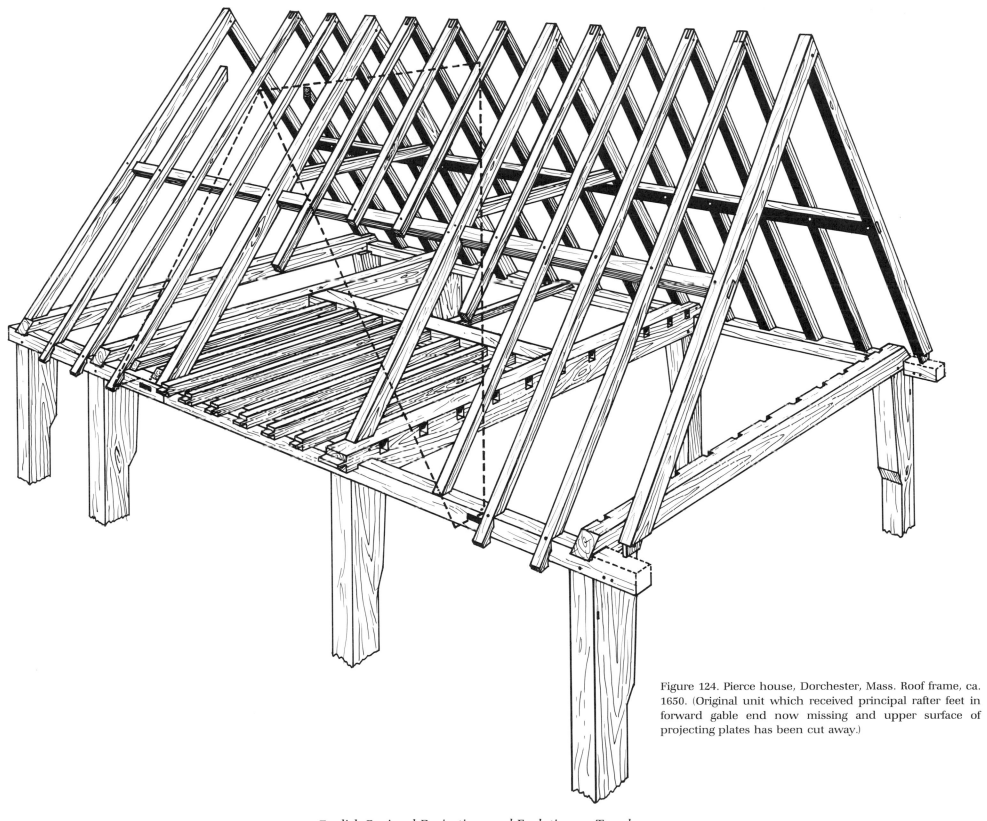

Figure 124. Pierce house, Dorchester, Mass. Roof frame, ca. 1650. (Original unit which received principal rafter feet in forward gable end now missing and upper surface of projecting plates has been cut away.)

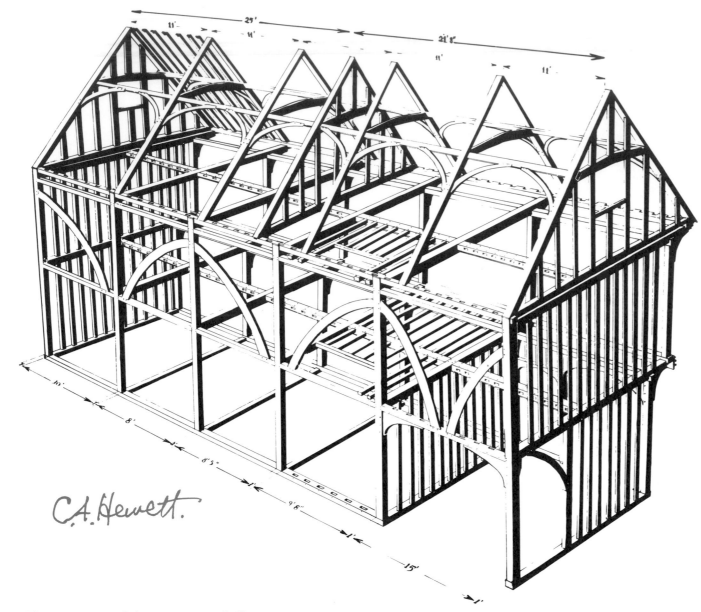

C.A. Hewett.

Figure 125. Paycocke's House, Coggeshall, Essex, Eng. Frame of that portion built ca. 1500.

tion to which its roof frame contains one set of characteristics unmatched in seventeenth-century work at Massachusetts Bay: there are no intermediary principal rafters between the end gable rafters and those which limit the central chimney bay (figure 126), while the common rafters are tenoned into the principal purlins (without pins) rather than riding over them. The heavily dimensioned roof framing as a whole suggests

a west of England derivation, especially if one argues that later East Anglian carpenters never so squandered timber in their roof frames (figures 127 and 128). Moreover, the top plates at the Blake house are furnished with squint butt bridled scarfs, uncharacteristic for this position in the frame of modest seventeenth-century East Anglian houses but not at all uncommon for seventeenth-century top plates in the more westerly counties. And in the use of four vertically aligned pins to secure the tenons of the chimney girts, the builder has clearly allied himself with con-

struction habits of the latter region, two pins, as seen in the same situation at the Gedney house, ca. 1665, being more typical for East Anglia by the second quarter of the seventeenth century (figures 129 and 130). It is not surprising, then, to find that there were at least two other carpenters in Dorchester during the period who were not East Anglian: Job Lane of Great Misenden, Buckinghamshire, born about 1620,[7] and Roger Billing from Taunton in Somersetshire, born in 1618, who appears to have lived in the vicinity of the Blake house.[8]

In attempting to associate the construction of the Blake house or any other, with known carpenters in the area, however, we should note the ever-present possibility of workmen coming in from outside the community. There seems to have been considerable mobility among seventeenth-century carpenters in New England. For Dorchester itself we have an early instance, when John Scobell, a Boston carpenter, brought suit in 1640 against John Holland, who had become indebted to the plaintiff "for carpentry worke done by the plt. . . . at his house in Dorchester."[9] Job Lane, restless as were so many of the early settlers, migrated from Dorchester to Malden, where he contracted to build the meetinghouse in 1658, to Billerica about 1667, where he lived for several years, and to Malden again in 1686, where he died in 1697. During that period he undertook building assignments in Boston, Charlestown, and as far afield as New London, Connecticut.[10] Lane's contemporary, the carpenter John Elderkin, who arrived at Lynn in 1637 at the age of about twenty-one, has been traced to Boston, Dedham, Reading, and Providence, Rhode Island, moving finally to New London and Norwich, Connecticut.

It is easy to see how regional differences carried to Massachusetts Bay by the earliest English carpenters became diffused and even scrambled to some extent in the thinking of their second- and third-generation successors or remained focalized. Evidence can readily be found for the perpetuation of distinctive English regional traits, especially in areas where there were concentrations of builders from a single locality. The classic

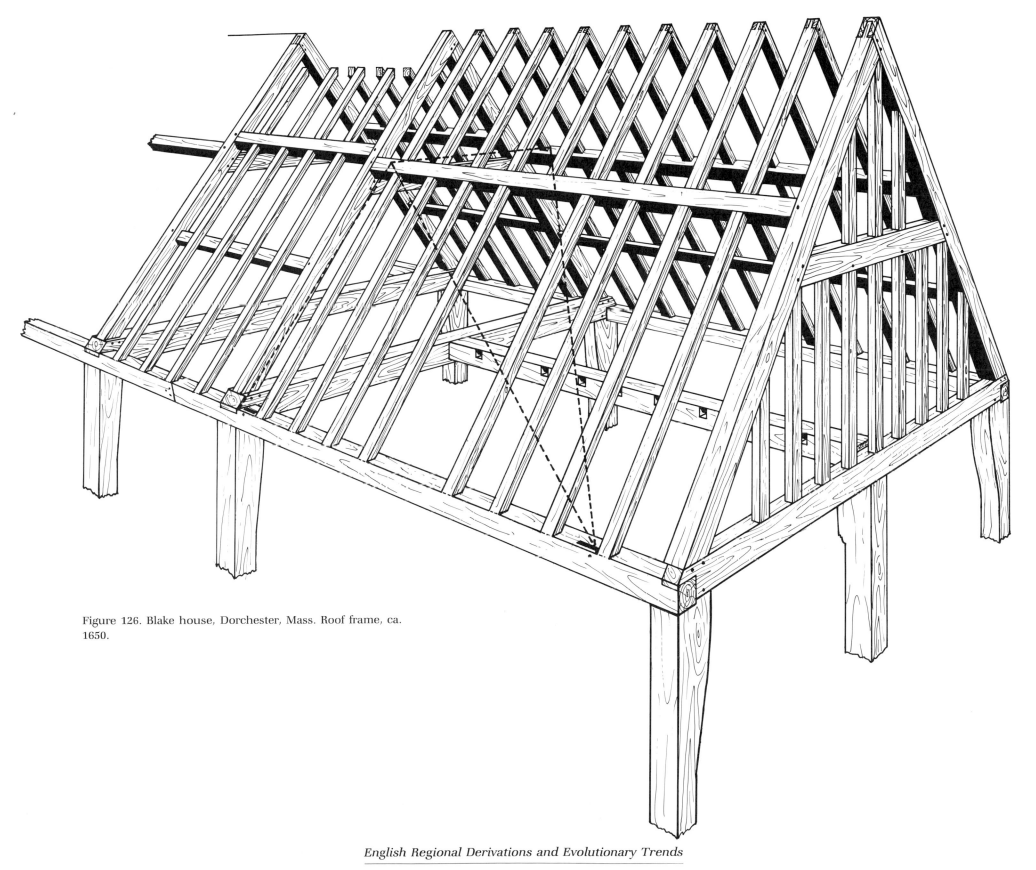

Figure 126. Blake house, Dorchester, Mass. Roof frame, ca. 1650.

Figure 127. Blake house. Detail of roof frame. *Photo, Richard Merrill, 1967.*

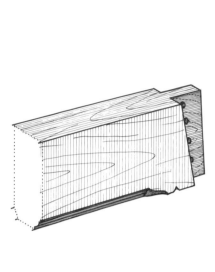

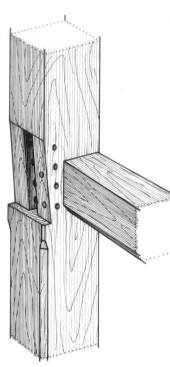

Figure 129. Blake house, Dorchester, Mass. Assembly of chimney girt, chimney post, and rear girt, ca. 1650.

Figure 128. Ivy House, Little Dunmow, Essex, Eng. Detail of roof frame, early seventeenth century. *Photo, Dennis H. Evans, 1968.*

Figure 130. Gedney house, Salem, Mass. Assembly of chimney girt and chimney post with mortise for bearer, ca. 1665.

case in this respect is Hingham on the South Shore. Settled in 1633, its peopling was almost entirely from the parent community of Hingham in Norfolk. No other town at Massachusetts Bay can claim such close-knit homogeneity among its first inhabitants. Although no buildings of the first generation have survived, there are at least four, possibly five, houses from the last quarter of the seventeenth century, at least one of which, the Andrews House (the Old Ordinary, so-called), built between 1685 and 1690, preserves the Suffolk-Norfolk tradition of a framing system in which the bays of the roof, evenly spaced, do not align with the uneven bays of the carcass (figure 131).

For the North Shore, the bulk of the earlier houses date also to the last three decades of the seventeenth century and the opening years of the eighteenth century. Many of these buildings reveal a stylistic affinity, especially in the prevalence of the transverse ground-story summer beam supported on posts ornamented with carved shoulders (figure 132). Of ninety examples of this transverse, as opposed to the more common longitudinal, positioning of the summer beam noted at Massachusetts Bay, fifty-eight are located in Salem or its derivative communities, while an additional seventeen examples are to be found in Essex County towns just above Salem (figure 133). The carving of the shoulder can be quite simple or can rise to such levels of elaboration as that found in the Samuel Pickman house in Salem, built before 1681 (figure 134).

Is this narrowly confined regional expression at Massachusetts Bay something which represents a distinctive local development at the hands of second- and third-generation American carpenters, with roots, of course, in a well-established English tradition of carved embellishment? Or does it perpetuate traits imported from a particular area in England by immigrant carpenters? And if the latter is the case, where should we look for parallels? While Salem grew steadily in the seventeenth century, many of her first settlers shared a common west-of-England background. Francis Higginson, for example, writes that the

Figure 131. Andrews house (The Old Ordinary), Hingham, Mass. Detail of principal rafter foot, plate (with molded coverboard), post, and tie beam, earliest chamber, 1685–1690. *Photo, William W. Owens, Jr., 1973.*

Figure 132. Stanley-Lake house, Topsfield, Mass. Detail of first-story summer beam and supporting post, original house, ca. 1680–1690. *Photo, Richard Merrill, 1967.*

Lyon's Whelp, which arrived at Salem in mid-July 1629, brought "above forty planters, specially from Dorchester and other places thereabouts," and men from Dorset and Somerset can be identified among those who arrived in the *Abigail* at Salem in 1628 with Endicott himself.[11] Further, of the Old Planters, so-called, who came to Salem from Cape Ann in the autumn of 1626 and thus preceded Endicott's settlement, the majority were from the western part of England.[12]

Salem's earliest builders would bear out this pattern of derivation. Among twenty known carpenters who arrived at Salem before 1650 and either remained there or settled in nearby communities, nine have been traced to their point of origin. Of these, six came from the counties of Lancashire, Yorkshire, Warwickshire, and Dorset; a seventh, Nathaniel Pickman, aged twenty-four at his arrival in 1639 from Bristol, lived until 1685 and may conceivably have been vigorous enough

in his later years to have been involved in the construction of the house built for his son, Samuel Pickman, about this time (figure 134).

If we are correct in our association of the transverse summer beam with west-of-England building practices, one reason at least may be found in the recognized lag of the west behind the southeastern counties. Acceptance of the internal chimney stack, for example, moved from east to west, this feature having become part of an integral building pattern in East Anglia before the end of the sixteenth century. Even in the somewhat retarded county of Suffolk, houses will be found early in the seventeenth century with an integral chimney stack in the midst, for example in Chevington, where in a very simple three-bay vernacular building on Weathercock Hill the original chimney bears the date of 1605. In a majority of these central-chimney structures in East Anglia, the ground-floor summer beam is apt to run

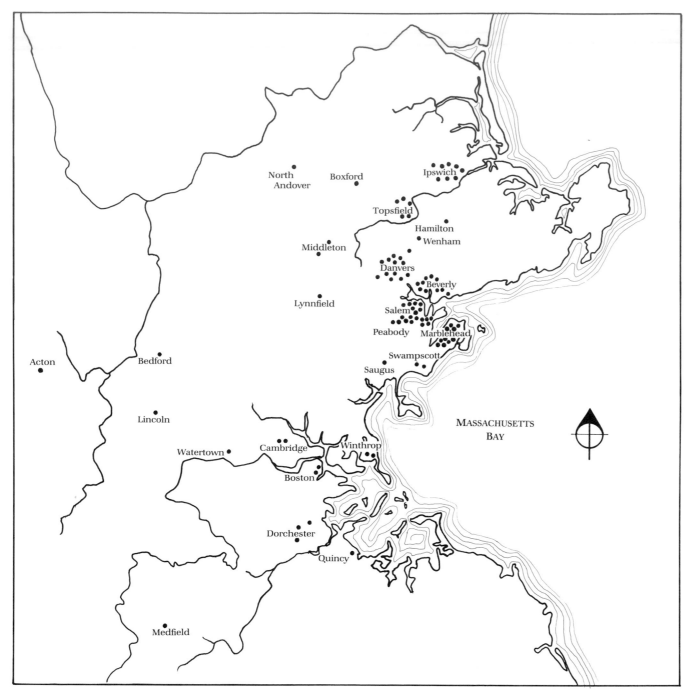

Figure 133. Massachusetts Bay, showing distribution of transverse summer beams before 1725.

in a longitudinal direction from end to chimney girt, a habit in positioning established by the opening of the seventeenth century. The derivation, presumably, is from an earlier expedient hit upon in the process of inserting a chimney stack and flooring over the previously open hall. The easiest way to accomplish this, as we have seen, was to lodge one end of the newly inserted summer beam in the end girt and the other in the masonry of the chimney stack.

In the west of England this development took place more slowly in the simpler rural houses. At Coalbrookdale in Shropshire, for example, the changeover is illustrated in a modest timber-framed structure known as Boring Mill Cottage. Erected in 1636, as a contemporary date carved in the tie beam of a front gable attests, the house underwent "modernization" almost at once. The changes included the insertion of a timber-framed chimney stack and the plastering of the hitherto half-timbered exterior, with a new date of 1642 incised in the plaster.

Here, then, as late as 1636 one finds the traditional transverse positioning of the summer beam in a house without a chimney. Even in the absence of more widespread data, we may suggest that this retarded thinking left its mark on the builders from the western counties of England who migrated to the New World and tended to perpetuate such bits of conservatism in houses built after the middle of the century for which integral chimney stacks had been planned from the outset.

As the spiritual sons and grandsons of the immigrant carpenters at Massachusetts Bay pushed beyond the borders of the first towns and ultimately into the western parts of the state, they carried with them some at least of the specifically local English framing traits we have described. Thus, if the rising wind brace that appears in Dedham at the Fairbanks house does indeed represent a narrowly circumscribed regional peculiarity, imported by carpenters from the northern sector of East Anglia, then one notes with interest its peripatetic persistence. Examples occur in such obvious localities as Medfield, just west of and originally a part of Dedham, where we find it in the roof frame of the Eliakim Morse house of about 1750 (figure 123), and even further afield in the roof of the Sheldon-Hawks house in Deerfield, built during the second quarter of the eighteenth century.

Closely associated with the question of regional derivations is the consideration of chronological relationships between the early seventeenth-century vernacular houses of England and those erected at Massachusetts Bay by the first immigrant carpenters, and continuing developments in building technology in the New World. The subject is hampered by a lack of quantitative data for the first two or three decades of settlement, for the larger groupings of extant houses occur after 1660. Roughly speaking the numbers swell proportionately with each passing decade. Geographic distribution, on the other hand, is erratic. Heaviest concentrations are to be found in Ipswich and the closely related Salem-Danvers-Beverly area. Essex County, in other words, heads the list by far, numerically speaking, but even here there is seldom a sufficent density of structures to permit hard and fast rules about evolutionary trends.

Contrary to some popular thinking, there is very limited indication of provincial lag in the oldest timber-framed houses that survive in the communities surrounding Boston. This fact is of striking importance in any consideration of time and distance comparisons among buildings dating from the 1620s and 1630s in England, those erected during the mid-seventeenth century at Massachusetts Bay, and those constructed later in the century throughout Massachusetts as a whole. The overall absence of provincial lag is by no means to be wondered at when we recognize that the earliest carpenters were predominantly younger men who would have brought with them ideas current at the time of their leave-taking for a comparable level of building. Despite the continuing juxtaposition of conservative with progressive traits in any given structure throughout the century, the fact remains that these build-

Figure 134. Samuel Pickman house, Salem, Mass. Detail of summer tie beam and supporting post, earliest chamber, before 1681. *Photo, William W. Owens, Jr., 1974.*

ings by and large march briskly in the front ranks with similar vernacular houses being built by contemporary carpenters at home in England. The few backward-looking traits that appear on rare occasions in the New World at the very outset are abandoned almost at once by our young immigrant carpenters, and there is no further evidence of their use, even though the same practices in England will be found to linger in isolated pockets beyond the middle of the seventeenth century.

Native developments at Massachusetts Bay—no matter how affected by local conditions—should at all times be seen and studied in direct relation to the levels of English technology at the same moment. We must measure each of our earliest surviving buildings against what the carpenters involved had been doing at home before their departure in the 1630s. The vital period is roughly the first half of the seventeenth century in En-

gland, and we look particularly to the 1620s and 1630s, for it is just then that our young immigrant carpenters will have emerged from their apprenticeships in the Old World. We may expect to find some conservatism, of course, for "Old fashioned workmen," as native New England carpenter-architect Asher Benjamin wrote at a much later date, will "leave their old path with great reluctance."[13] Builders of more mature years, however, were in a distinct minority at the beginning.

For a more thoroughly sensitive understanding of the problem it is necessary to recall that carpentry, as it had evolved through medieval and postmedieval phases in Europe, embodied elements of artisanship (particularly those involved in the working up of the individual frame members), technology (the ingenuity with which these members were fitted together to withstand both tension and pressure and thus produce a stable structure), and aesthetics (the elaboration of the frame members and their further arrangement, within the limits imposed by technology, to create a satisfying appearance). There were continual evolutionary forces that affected all of these factors, though in differing degrees. Elements of artisanship, which included the hewing out and sawing of timbers and their dressing for use, despite the introduction of the sawmill during this period, altered far less during the last two or three centuries before the industrial revolution than did the technological aspects. Throughout the sixteenth and seventeenth centuries there are striking and continual changes in the fabrication of the house frame. The disappearance of the crown post from the roof, for example, with its structural consequences, the acceptance of smaller scantlings and wider spacing of individual frame members (whether related to style or diminishing timber supplies), and above all, the refinements in carpentry joints and changes in the positioning of timbers directed toward greater mechanical efficiency—all are readily apparent phenomena which occur during this period.

At the heart of the problem lies the mobility of the carpenter, the degree to which he traveled

Figure 135. Shell Manor, Himbleton, Worcestershire, Eng. Detail of wall, solar wing, ca. 1450, with late sixteenth-century painted detail. *Photo (during restoration), F. W. B. Charles, 1960.*

around meeting other carpenters, working on projects other than those in his own locality, and thus acquiring new technical knowledge. The ultimate in mobility, of course, for some of these men was their migration to the New World, where cross-fertilization of ideas must have continued. It can be assumed as a matter of course that a carpenter from Essex, shall we say, must have found himself often enough in one small community or another sharing a building monopoly with a carpenter from Devon or Wiltshire.

Looking at the more salient features of the house frame to determine chronological relationships, we begin with the exterior wall members, which played such an important visual role in the overall effect of the Elizabethan framed house. In the characteristic sixteenth-century half-timbered structure, for example, the studs were massive in size and in many English areas as late as the opening years of the seventeenth century

were still spaced at intervals of little more than their own width. Such close studding was primarily for purposes of display. The rear walls of the house, for example, often contained a less lavish show of timber, and at the late sixteenth-century Shell Manor, Himbleton, and Rectory Farm, Tibberton, both in Worcestershire, widely spaced studs were visually supplemented with close-set intermediaries *painted* on the plaster (figure 135).

Close spacing of the studs survives into the seventeenth century at Lower Dairy Farm, Little Horkesley, Essex, where the contemporary date, 1601, is carved on the bressumer of the south wing (figure 136). It is not at all surprising to find even later examples of close studding in the somewhat more conservative western counties. At Stoke Prior in Bromsgrove, Worcestershire, for example, a small two-bay farmhouse with a contemporary date of 1631 carved in the gable end tie beam reveals a pattern of studs measuring seven and a half inches in width and again spaced at little more than their own width, between fourteen and sixteen inches on centers (figure 137).

During the early years of the seventeenth century, however, with style changes and with the full impact of timber depletion more widely felt in England, the studs tended to become smaller and more widely spaced, a process which is graphically illustrated in early and later portions of a house at Newport, Essex (figure 19). Wider intervals can be observed also in the small house of two-room, central-chimney plan, with added lean-to, in Colne Engaine, Essex, erected in 1620. Here the studs, about five inches in width, are now spaced at fifteen and a half to seventeen inches on centers.

The English carpenter thus moved in the opening decades of the seventeenth century toward a wider spacing of the studs in his house frame, a process which was in full swing by the time the first settlers arrived in New England. The average interval found in the earliest houses at Massachusetts Bay had progressed to as much as twenty-one and three quarters inches. A random sampling discloses that, with the single exception of the original portion of the Whipple house in Ips-

Figure 136. Lower Dairy Farm, Little Horkesley, Essex, Eng., 1601. *Photo, Richard Cheek, 1975.*

Figure 137. Tanhouse Farm, Bromsgrove, Worcestershire, Eng., 1631, with later additions. *Photo, Martin Charles, 1973.*

Figure 138. Fairbanks house, Dedham, Mass. Detail of studs trenched for wall brace, hall chamber, ca. 1637, revealed upon removal of later wall boards. *Photo, Richard Cheek, 1972.*

Figure 139. Fairbanks house. Detail of plate, trenched stud, and wall brace.

Figure 140. Fairbanks house. Detail of hall summer beam and joists and original molded wall finish. *Photo, William W. Owens, Jr., 1974.*

Figure 141. Blake house, Dorchester, Mass. Detail of prick post, summer beam, end tie beam, and joists, hall chamber, ca. 1650.

wich, ca. 1655, where the interval is one of the widest on record, the average spacing continues after the middle of the century to increase slightly and stabilizes in the range of twenty-three to twenty-five inches. A Marlborough building contract of 1661 specifies as well that the studs shall stand at such a distance "that A foure foote and A halfe Claboard may reach three studs" (that is, the studs were to be spaced approximately twenty-four inches on centers).[14] Narrower spacings which crop up from time to time and occasional examples of wall studs with a width of five inches or more are recessive. Those of the Fairbanks house in Dedham, being six and a half inches, are among the widest on record (figure 138). Elsewhere the stud, even as early as about 1650 (Pierce house, Dorchester), is no more than four inches wide, and this—or an even narrower width—is typical for the balance of the period.

In the earlier postmedieval English house frame, the wall brace, often curved, functioned as a secondary element, while the studs were primary (see figure 11). Late wall braces, usually straight, are generally of the same scantling as the studs and, having become primary wall members, completely divide them in two.[15] Wall bracing with studs thus interrupted has been found as early as 1575 in the dated structure known as Rook Hall, Cressing, Essex.[16] Still another East Anglian example has been noted in a house on the High Street in Maldon, Essex, of about 1680. In this structure the interrupted studs are nailed or spiked to the braces, a practice found consistently in later seventeenth-century Massachusetts houses.[17] The Fairbanks house in Dedham and the Austin Lord house in Ipswich, erected before 1653, are the only conservative examples presently known in which thin braces are "slotted into" the intervening studs in the continuing tradition of sixteenth-century English work (figures 138 and 139). The studs of the original portion of the Pierce house in Dorchester, built just a few years later than the Fairbanks house, are completely interrupted by the braces, which for the most part descend from the posts in the tradition of Essex construction. This progressive trait in wall framing occurs, then, in fully developed form at Massachusetts Bay by the middle of the century and is invariable thereafter (figure 99).

The wind brace, whether rising from purlin to principal rafter or falling below the purlin, is a feature which tends to characterize mid-seventeenth-century construction, despite its archaic persistence inland as late as the nineteenth century. It is found but seldom along the coast during the late seventeenth century, a development which coincides with the observation of English students that wind bracing in the roof was "on the way out" in Essex, at least, during the period 1600 to 1650.[18]

The floor joists reveal striking evidence of evolutionary development, one of the most conservative expressions being the flatwise positioning at the Fairbanks house (figure 140). There is, in fact, but one other example of the flatwise treatment at Massachusetts Bay, which occurs in those joists in the frame of the ground floor of the Giddings-Burnham house in Ipswich, ca. 1680, where they are thought to have been salvaged from an earlier building. The mechanically more efficient depthwise positioning of floor joists had appeared in Essex by the mid-sixteenth century, as seen, for example, in a house dated 1565 at 52-54 Church Street, Coggeshall. The practice occurs also in the house known as Merrivale, Abbey Foregate, Shrewsbury, dated 1601 (now destroyed), and at Tanhouse Farm of 1631, Stoke Prior, Bromsgrove, Worcestershire, indicating that this change had taken place early in the seventeenth century in the west of England among buildings of modest size. For the young carpenters who made up the bulk of the working forces at Massachusetts Bay, it was clearly the preferred system.

Similarly, the earliest builders in New England relied consistently upon the tusk tenon, which was then the currently accepted means of housing floor joists (figure 141). No more than a single archaic survival of the earlier bare-faced soffit-tenon is known at Massachusetts Bay. Indeed, the open cog which appears as early as about 1637 at the Fairbanks house in a special context,

Figure 142. Austin Lord house, Ipswich, Mass. Detail of summer tie beam and joists, revealed by lifting attic floor board, probably after 1705. *Photo, Peter Zaharis, 1955.*

was thoroughly accepted by the mid-1660s, and is thereafter the commonest joint for the housing of *both* ends of the floor joist (figure 142). Later use of the tusk tenon (as, for example, at the Browne house in Watertown, built between 1694 and 1701) is conservative. The butt-cogged joist joint apparently developed simultaneously in old and New England, and the lingering persistence of the tusk tenon in Essex has been noted there as well.[19]

There is striking evolutionary development in the spacing of the floor joists. A few dated English examples in comparison with a more comprehensive sampling of intervals recorded at Massachusetts Bay reveal how quickly the measurement increased during the opening decades of the seventeenth century, thereafter stabilizing in the range of twenty to twenty-four inches.[20] The noticeably wider spacing which appears in the Appleton-Taylor-Mansfield house in Saugus, ca.

1680, in advance of the general trend, occurs in an ambitious dwelling built by a member of a leading mercantile family, and can thus be seen as a pace setter. With respect to the evolution of floor joist joints, we have shown a beginning rejection of the tusk tenon in favor of the butt-cogged in the 1660s. Here is additional evidence that the dynamics of floor framing, which plays such a vital role, visual as well as structural, in the support of solid weight over one's head, received conscious attention during the first century of settlement, and that continuing experimentation in the economy of joist spacing proved satisfactory in its results.

The tie joint, having undergone a long course of development at the hands of English carpenters,[21] had achieved noticeable refinement by 1623, when the Granary in the Cressing Temple complex in Essex was erected. Here the teazle tenon is moved to one side of the root of the dovetail, in which position it does not detract from the strength of the central fibers of the tail. The common location in English work before the opening of the seventeenth century had been on axis with the tail, and the tie joints at the Fairbanks house in Dedham represent at least one conservative expression of this earlier practice (figure 53). Normally, however, at Massachusetts Bay, one finds the up-to-date positioning of the teazle tenon to one side of the dovetail (figure 143).

Recessive also is the method by which the chimney girts or binding beams of the Fairbanks house are framed into the flush surface of the upright posts of the chimney bay. The strength of the girt is thereby reduced to that of its vertical tenon (figure 144). The mortise and tenon joint with sunken housing which involved the entire depth of the horizontal unit in load bearing was by now fully accepted in English construction and appears as early as about 1650 in the Blake house at Dorchester (figure 129).

The characteristic seventeenth-century bladed scarf, associated with the top plate, is fully developed in the Granary of 1623 in the Cressing Temple complex and is furnished with a set of two

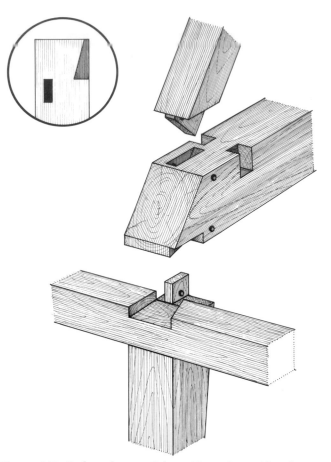

Figure 143. Gedney house, Salem, Mass. Assembly of post head, plate, tie beam, and principal rafter, with detail of underside of dovetail joint, ca. 1665.

pegs for each blade and a large peg in the center (figure 145).[22] It has been suggested[23] that the absence of the larger center pin in the Fairbanks scarf, similar in other respects, is a progressive trait in light of contemporary English work which increasingly omits this refinement as the century wears on (figure 146). Yet the larger center pin was used in late scarfs at the Parson Capen house in Topsfield, the Cooper-Frost-Austin house, Cambridge, ca. 1689, and in the otherwise completely up-to-date frame of the Blanchard-Wellington house in Medford, ca. 1720.

Are these three examples merely to be dismissed as archaic survivals? In further comparison with contemporary English work, the sets of three pegs for each blade of the Fairbanks

scarf would seem outspokenly archaic (figure 146). Characteristic later seventeenth-century scarfs in Essex, like those in the 1623 Granary, have just two pegs at each end, and this indeed is the case with most bladed scarfs found between 1650 and 1725 at Massachusetts Bay. It has also been suggested that the abbreviated form of the top-plate scarfs at the Boardman house in Saugus (figure 86) might imply that shortened examples were introduced in the late seventeenth century,[24] but there seems to have been a somewhat higher incidence of increased length for this rare classification of joints as time went on.[25]

Early in the seventeenth century the overhang tended to disappear in the more modest farmhouses of England and the walls henceforward were built straight up. Whether or not this development can be laid to diminishing timber supplies or to reasons purely stylistic, it is closely echoed in New England. Among the limited number of extant early houses at Massachusetts Bay there are no examples of an overhanging second story until after the mid 1660s, and not until 1663 in urban Boston did certain inhabitants begin to complain "of hurt done and further danger by the lownes of Jetties over the towne land [that is, streets]."[26] Here we encounter a marked departure from late seventeenth-century English practices that may be described as uniquely a product of the New World experience. The first generation of young carpenters, trained in England, were now passing into old age. With the sharp fall-off in immigration at mid-century, expertise and judgment in building affairs fell increasingly into the hands of the second and third generation, the first full-fledged Americans, most of whom had no first-hand knowledge of their ultimate homeland. There continued to be a steady trickle of building artisans from England throughout the seventeenth and eighteenth centuries, and in them we may surely see one means at least by which new ideas affecting technology and style were introduced from time to time. Of greater significance, however, was the increasing influx of venturesome businessmen who, in company with a fast-rising native New England mercantile

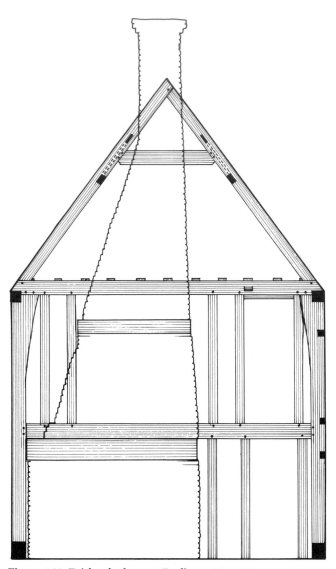

Figure 144. Fairbanks house, Dedham, Mass. Transverse section at chimney bay showing framing, ca. 1637.

aristocracy, were to be major contributors to a broadened and enriched economy for the colonies.

With the rigors of first settlement behind them, and in a climate fully favorable to growth and development, the older and more mature core communities along the coast began to experience a period of growing prosperity. In architectural terms alone, it may be no exaggeration to refer to the final three decades of the seventeenth century as a Golden Age—with clear evolutionary implications for the house frame itself. During the

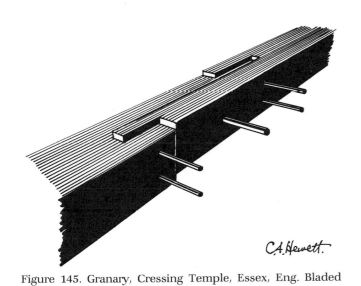

Figure 145. Granary, Cressing Temple, Essex, Eng. Bladed scarf, front plate, 1623.

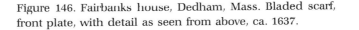

Figure 146. Fairbanks house, Dedham, Mass. Bladed scarf, front plate, with detail as seen from above, ca. 1637.

1670s and 1680s and well into the 1690s, the homes of the more prominent clergy, mercantile leaders, and substantial artisans and yeoman farmers blossomed forth with boldly projecting overhangs, façade gables, and decorative finish. The Whipple house in Ipswich and the Turner house in Salem are striking illustrations of this architectural coming-of-age. In each case we find a leading member of the community building at first a house of practical proportions with little or no special pretense of elaboration—John Whipple, Sr., about 1655 and John Turner about 1668. In both cases additions were projected early in the last quarter of the century. John Turner had erected, probably just before 1680, the great parlor wing to the south of his hall, of higher stud than the original house and furnished with façade gables and an overhang (figure 38); and John Whipple's son had, before 1683, similarly enlarged the house he inherited with a spacious parlor and chamber above, finished with crossed summer beams and a finely carved overhang of the hewn variety in both stories of the gable end (figure 36).

The evidence is everywhere available and of an exciting richness. It is not entirely easy, on the other hand, to explain why this understandable outpouring in response to material prosperity should have taken quite the form that it did. The first generation of English settlers, once landed in a heavily wooded area, did not return to the lavish building habits of their parents and grandparents. Rather, they continued to use timber sparingly in construction and even to impose a strict system of rationing. Why, then, in the closing decades of the seventeenth century did their grandsons return to so conspicuous a feature of the Elizabethan house as the overhang? Here, at least, was one immediate opportunity for decorous ostentation, and surely the form itself had by no means had time to fade entirely from memory. It was still, in fact, an inherent part of the English postmedieval building tradition. As such, it was closely associated with the façade gable, which had an early and continuous history of use, and the projecting two-story porch, which appeared before the middle of the century in the dwellings of the more affluent.

The end of this brief three- or four-decade period is also of evolutionary significance. While the overhang persists in its hewn, rather than framed, form in the more substantial houses, we find just after 1700 a marked decline in the late-seventeenth-century flowering of postmedieval architectural forms. One of the latest appearances of façade gables occurs in the Lewis Hunt house in Salem, ca. 1698 (figure 147), and of the framed overhang in the White-Ellery house, Gloucester, ca. 1710. The most important reason, of course, for the sudden disappearance of the framed overhang and the façade gable, both of which were, for the most part, nonfunctional indices of material well-being or status, was the ultimate impact of the Renaissance as new ideas in style began to filter down to a vernacular level and were enthusiastically accepted by a new and more formally oriented generation. Not only were "old-fashioned" façade gables given up, they were also consistently, throughout the eighteenth and nineteenth centuries, shorn from the buildings which they had adorned. Changing social usages probably had a lot to do

Figure 147. Lewis Hunt house, Salem, Mass., ca. 1698. Demolished 1863.

Figure 148. George Hart house, Ipswich, Mass. Detail of carved corner post, ca. 1698. (Frame dismantled and re-erected in the National Museum of History and Technology, Washington, D.C.) *Photo, Peter Zaharis, 1963.*

with the matter. The façade gable does not normally add a single square foot of floor space to the attic, and in many cases the original carpenters did not alleviate the inconvenience of having to duck under low purlins to gain access to whatever additional headroom was afforded. The major purpose of the façade gable, other than appearance, seems to have been that of admitting light. Garrets were commonly occupied in the seventeenth century, but by the nineteenth century this space was given over primarily to storage in more modest structures and therefore needed less and less light. Later occupants of seventeenth-century houses were presumably quick to sense the economic wisdom of eliminat-

ing an obsolete feature which presented constant problems in maintenance.

The hewn overhang is in a different category. Structurally speaking, the form is not a function of framing. Rather, the wall posts are cut to allow a projection of the second story by a few inches (figure 148). The result can scarcely be called an overhang, but more accurately an articulation of the several stories of the house. This characteristic American form, with discernible roots in English practice,[27] gradually disappeared at Massachusetts Bay during the first quarter of the eighteenth century, but lingered commonly in Connecticut throughout the eighteenth and into the nineteenth century. It does not evolve from the framed overhang and appears at Massachusetts Bay as early as the 1670s and 1680s in a number of documented structures. Thereafter its use seems to have been a matter of choice (figure 149).

As for the integral rear lean-to and its evolutionary significance, the earliest known example is the Whipple-Matthews house in Hamilton, erected between 1680 and 1683 (figure 34). While houses continued occasionally to be built on a two-room, central-chimney plan with subsequently added lean-to, the integral lean-to house increased rapidly in popularity and became an eighteenth-century commonplace. It had some effect also on the pitch of the roof. In certain of the earlier houses this could be as much as fifty-four degrees (Fairbanks house, Dedham), though forty-five to fifty degrees was a more normal range for the average house of the seventeenth and early eighteenth centuries. The form of the integral lean-to reduced this figure still further in many instances, for example at the Parson Barnard house in North Andover, ca. 1715, where the pitch of the front slope is forty-two degrees and the rear roof thirty-five degrees (figure 150). The front slope could also be affected slightly in pitch, as at the Barnard house, by the projection forward of the tie beams and introduction of a false plate, often in the interest of providing a cove cornice, examples of which do not appear before the 1690s (figure 149).

Finally, the distinctive roof frame composed entirely of relatively closely spaced rafters of principal rafter dimensions which appears late in the seventeenth century and is not uncommon thereafter in the hinterland of the Massachusetts Bay Colony, especially in those communities which make up the outer perimeter of Middlesex County, seems to be without an exact English prototype. The earliest known example is the late-seventeenth-century Peak house in Medfield, a community settled originally from Dedham in Suffolk County and adjoining Middlesex County.

The roof is constructed without purlins and is dependent therefore upon the horizontal boarding for whatever lateral stability exists. There is sophistication, nevertheless, as we have seen earlier, in the recognition of differing structural problems posed by rafters footed in the end ties (the collars of which are in compression and are tenoned to the rafters) and those which are bird-mouthed over the plates (the collars of which are in tension and are tied to the rafters with dovetail tenons) (figure 151). The excessive high pitch here is not easily explained, nor is the apparent engineering logic for heavy loading. In contrast, the prevailing roof frame along the coast, that of principal rafters and common purlins, which gradually

Figure 149. Pillsbury house, Newburyport, Mass., traditionally ca. 1700, with later additions. Partially destroyed by fire in 1889.

English Regional Derivations and Evolutionary Trends

Figure 150. Parson Barnard house, North Andover, Mass., ca. 1715. *Photo, William W. Owens, Jr., 1976.*

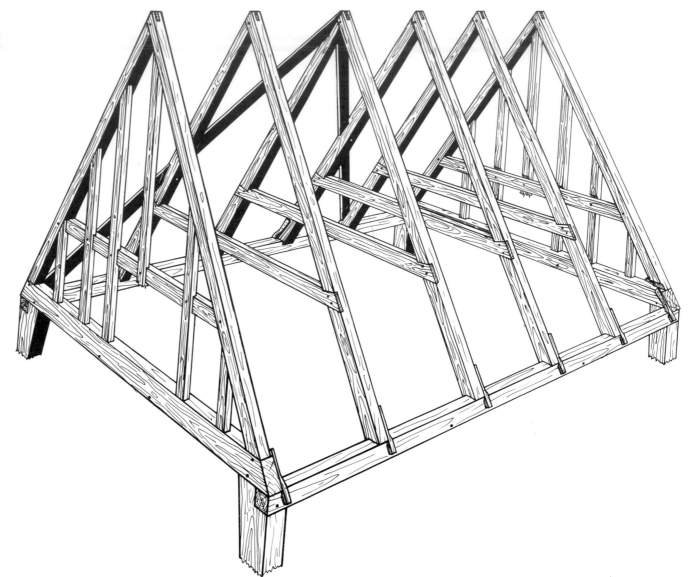

Figure 151. Peak house, Medfield, Mass. Rear view of roof frame, late seventeenth century.

supplants the principal and common rafter roof, is demonstrably related to the lighter weight covering of wooden shingles. The Peak house retains much of its original roof boarding and betrays no hint of preparations for thatch. It is conceivable, nevertheless, that these heavily framed roofs of a later period must be explained in technomorphic terms and owe something of their genesis to the use of thatch, which lingered in outlying areas beyond the middle of the seven-

teenth century, especially in the towns west of Boston.

In summary, then, we have traced those aspects of evolution in framing which can be readily discerned among the houses surviving from the first century of settlement at Massachusetts Bay. Special attention has been focused on the mid-century phase, which limits to a large degree the exclusive activity of English-born carpenters and their apprentices. Here we find a complex of forms and technological features that reflect on-going transitional developments in contemporary English carpentry. The more recessive features occur largely during the earliest years and either disappear or alter significantly during the second half of the seventeenth century. The most re-tarded forms, in fact, are to be found in but a sin-gle dwelling, the Fairbanks house in Dedham, whose carpenter(s) migrated to America from the more northerly portions of East Anglia, where conservative traditions lingered.

Certainly the dimensional factor will weigh heavily in any assessment of the postmedieval character of our earliest houses at Massachusetts Bay. If we accept a late sixteenth- early seven-teenth-century English chronology for technolog-ical changes associated with the evolution from medieval to Renaissance carpentry techniques, and acknowledge as well the reduction in size of such structural elements as the stud in English buildings at this period, then we readily find rela-tionships between the smaller framed houses of old and New England during the reign of the Stuarts and later. Above all, the virtually unique floor joist mortises of the reused summer beam in the Cogswell house in Essex, designed for bare faced soffit-tenons, the characteristic six-teenth-century wattle and daub wall fill and the flatwise floor joists of the Fairbanks house, and the massive collar beams of the Coffin and Blake houses (figure 152) hint strongly that among some at least of the long-vanished dwellings of our first settlers, built during this richly interesting transitional period in English vernacular archi-tecture, we might have found even more startling evidence of backward-looking postmedieval fea-tures, transported to the New World by a distinct minority of conservative carpenters, to flower here for only a brief moment in time.

Figure 152. Coffin house, Newbury, Mass. Detail of roof frame, ca. 1654. (Raised rafters at upper left cover later addi-tion.) *Photo, Richard Merrill, 1959.*

English Regional Derivations and Evolutionary Trends

CHAPTER VII

The Chimney

ONCE THE FRAME of the house was erect, three important tasks remained: building a chimney and infilling the walls; enclosing the roof and walls with suitable cover; and introducing stairs, interior partitions, and finish trim. Construction of the chimney involved arrangements no more sophisticated than preparing the hard surface of the ground immediately below sill level to receive the foundation of the stack. What appears so often on superficial examination to represent a chimney foundation in the cellar is actually a retaining wall of stone which contains the solid unexcavated earth (figure 31). The arched chimney foundation was not introduced until the last quarter of the seventeenth century. The contract that Jonathan Corwin executed in 1675 with Daniel Andrews for the masonry work of his house on Essex Street in Salem implied a chimney foundation in the traditional manner. Almost immediately, however, the contract was altered and Andrews agreed instead that there was to be a cellar "under the whole house and the Stack of Chymnyes to Come from the Bottome of the Celler,"[1] suggesting an arch. The arched chimney foundation for the stack that serves the south parlor of the Turner house in Salem, added probably before 1680, represents the earliest surviving example at Massachusetts

Bay and measures ten feet, six inches wide in its overall dimensions. The arch, however, did not supplant the more conventional ground-level foundation until the turn of the century, and then only in urban and progressive rural situations. The Boston mason John Goodwin, for example, agreed with the selectmen of that city on November 24, 1701, in finishing the house of the Latin schoolmaster, "to turn an Arch in Said Celler and to build a good Stack of brick Chimneys,"[2] and in September 1706, John Marshall, mason, who was at work on the cellar and foundation of Edmund Quincy's house in Braintree, recorded that from the third to the seventh he had spent "every day at mr quinceys about the arch."[3] This masonry feature, six feet high, five feet, five inches wide, and four feet deep, remains today in the front left-hand cellar of the Quincy homestead in what is now Quincy.

The chimney stack was invariably of brick and maintained a solid core, except for the openings and flues, from the foundation to the chimney top. Stone chimneys can be found rarely and almost entirely in those timber-framed houses erected after 1700 in Middlesex County. Assuming these stone chimneys west of Boston have earlier antecedents, it is more than likely that a traditional preference for the material can be

argued among settlers from English counties where stone was commonly used. This would be particularly true of Sudbury, a number of whose early builders emigrated from Hampshire and surrounding counties.

Dimensions of the brick, used far more commonly at Massachusetts Bay, reveal little if any evolutionary change before the second quarter of the eighteenth century. Those at the Fairbanks house in Dedham, ca. 1637, measure nine and one-half to ten inches in length, four and one-half inches in width, and two and one-half inches in height. These figures do not vary much from those prescribed by law in England in 1625 as nine inches by four and one-half inches by three inches,[4] nor from those of statute or common bricks, defined three-quarters of a century later as nine inches by four and one-half inches by two and one-quarter inches.[5]

During the course of the seventeenth century there were occasional efforts to regulate brick size in New England. In 1679, for example, the Court at Massachusetts Bay decreed that "the size of bricks be nine inches long, two and one quarter inches thicke, and fower and a halfe inches broad."[6] Such regulatory references are almost entirely absent from the local town records which are often quite specific about other aspects of brick manufacture. Minor variations in size are probably best explained by English author William Leybourn, who writes in 1668, when specifying the inside dimensions of brick molds as nine inches by four and one-half inches by two and one-quarter inches, that "you shall seldome find them to hold out so, for the drying and burning will abate something in the thickness, but little in the breadth; and in the length inconsiderable."[7]

It has been continuously repeated that seventeenth-century bricks were brought as ballast in the early ships. Arrangements were indeed made in 1629 for the importation of "10 thousand of bricks" from England, one item among many in a memorandum of articles which would be essential at the colonists' first coming ashore.[8] This record, however, is exceptional. At Salem during the same year, Francis Higginson wrote that "At this instant we are setting a brick-kiln on work, to make bricks and tiles for the building of our houses,"[9] and it is abundantly clear that the earliest settlers sought out suitable sources of clay and commenced at once the manufacture of brick.

The making of brick, like the erection of the house frame, was no task for the rank amateur. In Boston, for example, Jasper Rawlins, brickmaker, was granted the use of a rood of upland in 1644 "for the making of Brickes,"[10] and in Dedham as early as 1640, John Kingsbury, John Hayward, and John Bacheler, or any two of them, were "deputed to search for Bricke earth and provide a place necessary to burne bricke upon." Their decisions, the record continues, must satisfy "the Brickemaker Thomas Eames."[11] Later, in 1663, John Littlefield of the same town was granted liberty "to take so much clay as may be sufficient for the makinge a clampe of Brick for to supply the Towne" and sufficient wood to burn it, provided "he shall supply the Inhabitants of the Towne with marcantable brick the next sumer not exseedinge 25s a 1000 so farr as a clamp will supply them."[12] Edward Johnson included brickmakers among his list of those artisans who by 1650 were "orderly turn'd to their trades,"[13] and there were

by then several in Salem,[14] and two or three in Ipswich.[15]

Moreover, the court order in 1679 regulating size implies that the activities of brickburners were not left to chance. Clay to make bricks, the legislators declared, "shallbe digged before the 1st of November, and turned over in the moneth of February and March ensuing, a moneth before it is wrought," and no one was to "temper their bricks with salt water or brackish." All molds for making brick, they continued, were to be of the size specified, "and well shod with iron." A later amendment to this order in 1684 provided that "every toune (where bricks shall be made or sold) shall annually choose two or more able men . . . to veiw, divide, and cull all bricks from time to time that shall be exposed to sale."[16] Surely it may be argued that there were aspects of this craft, stacking and firing for instance, sufficiently recondite to have placed uniformly successful operations beyond reach of any but the most clever amateurs or craftsmen with related skills.

Well before the end of the seventeenth century, Medford had become a center for the manufacture of brick, and in 1697 one Joseph Squire of that town billed Mr. John Pratt of Boston for 1500 of "hard bricks" at £1-10-0 per thousand, and for 1100 of "Samin bricks" at thirteen shillings per thousand.[17] The descriptive adjective "Samin" may refer to the salmon color, although Richard Neve defines *Samel, or Sandal-bricks* in 1703 as those "which lie out most in a Kiln, or Clamp, where the Solt-peter is not digested for want of Heat, and these are very soft, and will soon moulder to dirt."[18] Such light-colored or pink bricks were used commonly for wall fill at Massachusetts Bay, and will indeed disintegrate if left exposed to the elements. In fact, they may occasionally have been naturally produced, for the law required in 1684 that any "parcell of bricks" to be merchantable must include at least three quarters of "hard and through nealed ware, and not sunne [dried] bricks."[19] Not all bricks intended for wall fill, however, were of this character. Regular hard-fired bricks were used as well,

and these will sometimes be found to contain examples from the kiln which by reason of shape or overfiring were unsuitable for use in other situations.

Locally manufactured bricks were thus available from the outset and were used consistently. The nonmasonry timber-framed chimney was common only at the beginning. Both the Rix-Davys contract of 1640[20] and Deputy-Governor Symonds in 1638 specified wooden chimneys,[21] and the Salem meetinghouse in 1639 was to have "One Catted Chimney of 12 foote longe and 4 foote in height above the top of the buildinge. The back whereof is to be of brick or stone."[22] The latter provision represented some improvement at least over the chimney entirely of timber. Winthrop writes in March 1631 of a wooden chimney in Boston which took fire, "the splinters being not clayed at the top," and burned the house to the ground.[23] Elsewhere Increase Mather speaks of a "katted or wooden chimney" in Duxbury, Plymouth Colony, in 1653,[24] and there is mention of building a catted chimney in a tenant farmhouse in Peabody as late as 1656.[25]

The form in New England, however, seems to have been quite rapidly abandoned because of the hazards in a cold climate, and no physical evidence whatsoever has survived. Early timber-framed chimneys, on the other hand, are still to be found in England, one such having been constructed in 1642 when the somewhat earlier house known as Boring Mill Cottage in Coalbrookdale, Shropshire, was "modernized." The lower portion of the frame, with heavily beaded units, enclosed two fireplaces back-to-back measuring nearly eight feet in width. Davys, for whatever reason, had been instructed to frame the chimney of the house he was to build in Boston "without dawbing," and in the timber stack at the Old Medicine House at Wrinehill in Staffordshire, erected probably in the early seventeenth century, daubing was applied to a network of closely woven sticks fixed within the major units of construction (figure 153).

In plan the characteristic early brick chimney, referred to often as a stack of chimneys (the latter

Figure 153. Old Medicine House (so-called), Wrinehill, Staffordshire, Eng. Interior detail of timber-framed chimney stack, ca. 1600. *Photo, Malcolm Jennings, 1970.*

Figure 154. Cooper-Frost-Austin house, Cambridge, Mass. Detail of hall fireplace, ca. 1689. *Photo, J. David Bohl, 1977.*

Figure 155. Swett-Ilsley house, Newbury, Mass. Detail of hall fireplace, ca. 1739 or earlier. *Photo, Arthur C. Haskell, 1932.*

word being synonymous with fireplace in the seventeenth century), was apt to be about seven feet in width and could measure as much as ten or more feet in depth at the base in a house of central-chimney plan. An end chimney, on the other hand, might be no more than three and a half to four feet wide, allowing for only a single fireplace on the ground floor. The hall fireplace measured seven to nine feet on the average in width of opening, and the parlor fireplace six to eight feet. The depth was never more than three and a half feet, and the height of the opening to the bottom of the lintel was between four and five feet. Despite the fact that one is apt to find the rear cor-

ners of the workaday hall fireplace squared off, both hall and parlor openings could be enhanced in purely decorative terms by having their rear corners rounded and by the insertion of a panel of brickwork laid up in herringbone fashion at the center of the rear wall beneath the smoke panel (figures 33 and 154). The hall fireplace was consistently wider, owing primarily to the presence of an oven, and the fireplace in the Swett-Ilsley house in Newbury, one of the widest on record measuring ten feet, three inches and dating to a period of alterations in the second quarter of the eighteenth century, contains an oven in the rear wall at each end (figure 155). The hall fireplace reached its most exaggerated width during the early decades of the eighteenth century, a particularly striking evolutionary development when compared with earlier measurements. As seen at the Swett-Ilsley house and in the later portions of the Abbot house in Andover and the Story house in Essex, the two latter added about 1725 or later, and measuring respectively nine feet, six inches and ten feet, we recognize a brief climax. This was followed by a dramatic reduction in the size of the cooking fireplace when, during the second quarter of the eighteenth century, the oven was removed from the opening altogether.

Bake ovens were not invariable in the earliest years, although by the later decades of the seventeenth century at Massachusetts Bay the oven in the hall fireplace had become a commonplace fixture. The location of the opening was usually set diagonally in the front corner, which caused the belly to bulge somewhat from the surface of the stack in the cellar stairwell (figure 27). There are some exceptions, as for example in the hall fireplace of the Parson Capen house in Topsfield of 1683. Here the oven opening is in the rear corner, which was clearly the case also with that house in Ipswich mentioned in a court deposition of 1668 where the "oven on the outside and backside" projected beyond the surface of the rear wall, unlike the rear oven at the Capen house which is contained within the frame.[26] There would seem to be no other immediate reason than choice for the placement of the oven at one end of the fireplace or the other.

The oven lacked a flue of its own at this period, and the smoke from a fire built within to heat it would have vented into the flue of the fireplace itself. This location of the oven, inconvenient though necessary because of the smoke-venting arrangements, the unsplayed side walls, and the straight-rising rear wall of the fireplace, which together with the cavernous size of the opening contributed to heat loss, typify the functional inefficiency of a feature which had but recently been introduced as an "improvement" in the postmedieval vernacular house. The ensuing history of the chimney is concerned with a succession of evolutionary modifications designed to prevent heat loss and direct the warmth of the

Figure 156. Cooper-Frost-Austin house, Cambridge, Mass. Detail of hall fireplace and rear wall, ca. 1689. *Photo, J. David Bohl, 1977.*

The Chimney

fire more effectively into the room. Until well into the eighteenth century the only technical refinement was the shallow recessed smoke panel in the center of the rear wall of the fireplace opening which the builders must have thought would facilitate a draft in conveying the smoke upwards (figure 155). Least functional of all were the arrangements for suspending pots over the fire. Slender poles were embedded thwartwise in the throat of the chimney while still green and across them was laid a green lug pole from which chains and pothooks were hung. At least one set of stone lug pole supports has been found in Middlesex County, in addition to which there are occasional references to iron bars,[27] and these were surely some improvement over wooden poles which could, of course, burn through if not carefully watched.

The massive lintel was also of wood, continuing an English tradition, and this, too, burned through on occasion. A significant number, however, have come down to the present day, at least one or two of which have been found to have the slanting rear surface lathed and plastered with clay as a fire resistant measure. A still further structural refinement of the lintel occurs at the point of its support within the stack. The lintel ends are not seated directly on the brick piers but upon thin slabs of softwood, about two inches thick, which extend back into the chimney (figure 156). While in one or two instances the sleepers, as they are called, are unexplainably of slate or stone (for example, at the Parson Barnard house, North Andover, ca. 1715), it is assumed nevertheless that the builders relied on this expedient as a means of assuring some elasticity in movement if the heavy oak lintel, installed green, should warp or twist. The lintel's position was otherwise stabilized by the superincumbent weight of the masonry wall of the chimney resting upon it.

In some cases the stack was set back several inches behind the rear surface of the chimney girt and this normally allowed the brickwork above the lintel of the first-story fireplace to be formed into a quarter-round cove. The upper course of bricks was wedged against the rear of the chimney girt, and the surface of the cove could then, if desired, be given a finish coat of plaster (figure 156). The purpose of this construction, no examples of which have been found before the last quarter of the seventeenth century, was the support of the hearth of the chamber fireplace overhead. In both stories the hearth, consisting normally of seven- or eight-inch square hard-fired brick tile, seldom extended more than two rows, or under eighteen inches, into the room. The use of decorative ceramic tiles to embellish the surface of the brick piers on either side of the fireplace is an eighteenth-century refinement. Only one unusually early exception has been found in the substantial house built in Salem for the merchant Jonathan Corwin in 1675, where Daniel Andrews, the mason, was instructed "to sett the Jamms of the 2 Chamber Chimneys, and of the Eastermost roome below with Dutch tyles."[28]

The throat of the fireplace is almost invariably parged with clay and the flues are aligned one beside another with those serving the second story on the outside of the stack (figure 117). The chamber fireplace seldom exceeded five and a half feet in width (an opening of four to five feet being typical). While more shallow than those of the ground floor, averaging two feet or less in depth in order to accommodate the ground-story flues, they were between three and a half and four feet high and finished also with wooden lintels on sleepers. The Fairbanks house in Dedham was furnished with only one chamber fireplace (figure 24). Similar omissions of one or the other chamber fireplace occur, often at the west or warmer end of the house, and at the early eighteenth-century Old Garrison, so-called, in Chelmsford, of central-chimney plan, there were no fireplaces at all on the second floor. Only very rarely will a fireplace opening be found in the attic, that specified in the Jonathan Corwin contract of 1675 being the earliest on record.[29]

Clay was the only "mortar" in which the bricks of the chimney stack were laid, to the level of the roof at least, and the efficacy of this material is abundantly proved by the soundness and plumb condition of a substantial number of early chimneys. The chimney stack above the roof ridge, on the other hand, required a more weather resistant mortar. Lime is mentioned as early as 1638 when Captain Robert Sedgwick agreed "to find one hoggshead of lyme" with which Samuel Cole promised to mend "the backe of the chimney of the leantoo and the rough cast of the outsyde of the new house" that Cole was selling to Sedgwick.[30] This lime was presumably imported, and imported lime was also probably meant when the building committee for the Salem meetinghouse specified in 1673 that the underpinning of that building be pointed with white lime.[31]

Despite optimistic reports on the availability of limestone at Massachusetts Bay from the first writers, proper lime was not readily available during the early years, and its scarcity created real problems. Governor Winthrop wrote in 1631 that "having erected a building of stone at Mistick [Medford], there came so violent a storm of rain, for twenty-four hours, from the N.E. and S.E. as (it being not finished, and laid with clay for want of lime) two sides of it were washed down to the ground."[32] In 1663 the English visitor John Josselyn also noted the absence of stone that would "run to lime, of which they have great want."[33] Not until late in the century were extensive beds of limestone discovered at Newbury.[34] In the meantime the colonists resorted to a substitute, as we learn from Edward Johnson who reports about 1650 that "the country affords no Lime, but what is burnt of Oyster-shels."[35] As late as 1696 the town of Lynn voted to fine anyone who might "cause to be Caryed any Clamshells out of The Town Nor any Lime that shall be Made of any Clam shells."[36] The presence of minute bits of shell in the plaster and mortar of the earliest houses, however, does not necessarily mean that the lime content was derived from burning calcareous shells. Unless that process can be proved by scientific analysis, we must assume that the particles may represent shells which were crushed and thrown into the mortar as aggregate or filler, or were perhaps present in the sand used for the same purpose.[37]

The chimney top which straddled the roof ridge was characteristically as much as five or six feet high, at least five feet wide, and normally quite shallow, measuring between two and a half and three feet in depth (figure 34), very much in contrast to the somewhat lower, square stacks of the later eighteenth century. When a lean-to was added at the rear of the house with a fireplace of its own, the flue was attached to the rear of the existing stack (figure 157). A separate rear flue, however, does not necessarily imply an addition. The present lean-to fireplace at the Narbonne house in Salem, ca. 1672, appears to be contemporary with the main stack, and its flue projects at one side at the rear. By the beginning of the eighteenth century, with the rapid adoption of the integral lean-to, the separate flue for the lean-to kitchen fireplace, an integumental part of the main stack, often continues to have the appearance of being added, though sometimes, as at the Parson Barnard house in North Andover, it is carefully centered at the rear (figure 159).

While perfectly plain chimney stacks were common, embellished tops were also popular, though in at least three instances—the "Rebecca Nurse" house in Danvers, erected probably after 1700, and the French-Andrews house, ca. 1718, and Capen house, both in Topsfield—decorated chimney tops have, in the course of restoration, replaced undecorated predecessors solely on the basis of conjecture. The embellished stack in New England is derived from the soaring, highly elaborate chimney tops of Elizabethan England, with handsome and varied arrangements of flues continuing to appear in even the simple vernacular houses of the early seventeenth century (figure 160). The majority of original stacks at Massachusetts Bay, unaltered above the ridge, are modest in their decoration, although a certain amount of diversity exists. The commonest form is the pilaster, of which there are three distinct variations: the single pilaster on the face of the stack, two (rarely three) individual pilasters spaced evenly on the face of the stack (figure 161), and the superimposition of one narrow pilaster upon another, broader one (figure 162). The most highly

Figure 157. Boardman house, Saugus, Mass. Rear view, showing appended flue for lean-to fireplace, original house, ca. 1687, with lean-to added before 1696. *Photo, Wilfred A. French, ca. 1880.*

Figure 158. Parson Barnard house, North Andover, Mass. Front elevation of chimney, ca. 1715. *Photo, William W. Owens, Jr., 1976.*

Figure 159. Parson Barnard house. Rear elevation of chimney. *Photo, William W. Owens, Jr., 1976.*

The Chimney

123

Figure 160. House on Weathercock Hill, Chevington, Suffolk, Eng. Detail of chimney, 1605. *Photo, Dennis H. Evans, 1969.*

Figure 161. Cooper-Frost-Austin house, Cambridge, Mass. Detail of chimney, ca. 1689. *Photo, J. David Bohl, 1977.*

Figure 162. Capt. Matthew Perkins house, Ipswich, Mass., 1701—1709. *Photo, Arthur C. Haskell, 1936.*

decorated chimney top at Massachusetts Bay, at the Parson Barnard house in North Andover, is of this variety. Here the superimposed pilasters are girdled with projecting belt courses, and the narrow ends of the stack are pilastered as well (figure 158). Somewhat less common is the paneled chimney top, the shallow panel being almost invariably arched. Both single and paired arched panels have been noted (figure 163), and the form seems to be confined to the later decades of our period, certainly in the rural communities.

English examples will often reveal a bold projection of the crowning courses, and the practice may well have been followed at Massachu-

setts Bay. It is probably significant that the very few examples of a heavily projecting cornice known are to be found in nineteenth-century photographs when the chimney stack was still in relatively sound condition (figure 26). We are much better informed on the finish of the early stack as it emerges from the roof, where almost invariably will be found a single projecting drip course along the front and rear surfaces just above the roof slope, and on the sides just above the ridge (figure 162). The derivation again is from English practice, and the ostensible purpose was to prevent moisture from finding its way down the face of the stack and under the roof covering.

The Framed Houses of Massachusetts Bay

As for the reputed secret staircase in the brick stack of the original, first-built portion of the Turner house in Salem, ca. 1668, no really logical reason has been advanced, and regrettably the original chimney does not survive. There was no awareness of the staircase when Mrs. Henry Upton purchased the property in 1883 and a decision was made to take down the great central stack. The workmen began at the roof, writes Miss Caroline Emmerton who later restored the house, and had not proceeded very far when the dramatic discovery was made. "Mr. Upton walked down the secret staircase . . . [and] came out in the dining room closet. Then the work of demolition continued." The chimney was replaced with a small spindly stack, which in turn gave way to the present construction at the time of the restoration that began in the spring of 1909. Thus our knowledge of the details of this "secret staircase" must depend utterly upon Miss Emmerton's sanguine account of her efforts to have the ancient chimney recreated accurately, and upon her statement that when the work was completed Mr. Upton, then still living, was invited to see the finished product and declared that "it was just as he remembered it."[38] The present reproduction, however, is a curious affair at best, and only increases our regret that the original did not survive.

Figure 163. Poore Tavern, Newbury, Mass., probably ca. 1700, with later additions. Demolished 1890.

CHAPTER VIII

Exterior Finish

THE HOUSE FRAME could be simple and boxlike, or its mass could be more complex, the profile of the individual surfaces broken with oversailing upper stories. The consequent play of light and shade and the juxtaposition of forms creates, for our modern eyes at least, much of the visual appeal of a seventeenth-century house. The structure was otherwise sparsely ornamented. Among the more modest efforts to embellish the outer surface of the house frame we may single out the door frame at the Fairbanks house, ca. 1637, which was found during repairs in 1972 to have been boldly chamfered with the intersecting joints carefully mitered (figure 164). A characteristic postmedieval English treatment thus survives here in one of our earliest and most conservative houses. Similar evidence was found during repairs to the Whipple house in Ipswich in 1953–1954, but not restored, and at the Hooper-Hathaway house in Salem, ca. 1682.[1] The surface of the header of the Fairbanks house doorway appears to have been weathered for an interval of about two inches just above the chamfer, suggesting that the exterior covering stopped at this point.

Common in the second half of the century was the carved pendant drop that ornamented the overhang and that also derives clearly from postmedieval English practice. When part of the house frame, the drop was invariably fashioned from the lower ends of second-story overhanging posts that were allowed to project downward some twelve inches or more. Despite its popularity, only two examples have survived at Massachusetts Bay, one set dating to about 1700 at the Stanley-Lake house in Topsfield (figure 165), and the other at the late seventeenth-century Brown house in Hamilton (figure 166). All others are twentieth-century replacements, determined on the basis of explicit evidence (as at the Paul Revere house in Boston, ca. 1680) or on the basis of conjecture.

Another form of exterior decoration carved out of the frame itself, most examples of which are to be found in northern Essex County, is the embellishment of the first-story post head where it meets the overhang, either framed or hewn. Those examples at the late seventeenth-century William Howard and George Hart houses in Ipswich, and in the even later Davis-Freeman house, traditionally dated ca. 1709, in the western part of Gloucester, are characteristic of the simplest variety (figure 167). They are, in fact, little more than a shallow bracket carved from the post at the first-story level of hewn overhang houses. Far more ambitious are the richly carved post heads at the

Knowlton house, ca. 1700, in Ipswich. Here and elsewhere there is conscious coming to grips with the vulnerability of the house frame to the penetration of rain and snow. The remainder of the post below the bracket has been cut into to receive the underboarding of the wall, and there is a groove on either side of the post head to receive the skived ends of the clapboards as well (figure 168).

The projecting timber ends that help to support the overhang may also be decorated. The refinement ranges from a simple rounding off of the blunt end of the oversailing units, as we find at the late seventeenth-century Ross Tavern in Ipswich (figure 85), to more complex profiles, as at the Hooper-Hathaway house in Salem where the projecting girt and summer ends have been given a cyma profile and ornamented further with a delicately scalloped fillet (figure 169). There is also the exterior molded girt, found either in the overhang at the side only, as in the later half of the Whipple house in Ipswich, added before 1683, or at the front and sides, as seen in the Ross Tavern in Ipswich (figure 170) and in the later Captain Matthew Perkins house built between 1701 and 1709 in the same community. In nearly every case the profile is that of a cyma curve, terminating at times in a chamfer at each end,

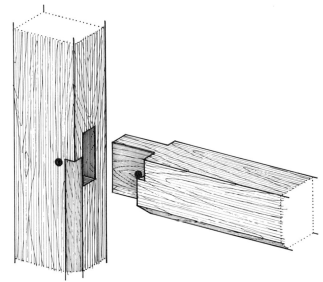

Figure 164. Fairbanks house, Dedham, Mass. Elevation of front wall, chimney bay, showing entrance and window, with detail of chamfered door frame, ca. 1637. (Chamfer stops are conjectural.)

here by the end of the century a distinctively elegant regional school. With respect to such details as the molded exterior girts, for example, virtually all surviving examples known from the period are to be found in Ipswich and the closely related communities of Essex, Hamilton, and Wenham.

With the frame of the house raised and embellished and the chimney stack constructed, it was essential in the New England climate that the entire structure be covered as rapidly as possible. The enclosure of the walls, in fact, preceded the infilling of the frame. Before turning, however, to the more technical aspects of wall and roof covering, it is important to review the traditions and immediate background of the immigrant English builders and their initial experiences in the New World. These experiences produced changes in established concepts relating to the finish of the house frame that have innovational significance.

There is perhaps no more readily discernible contrast between the simpler seventeenth-century houses of old and New England, when comparable in other ways, than the clapboarded walls and shingled roofs. This was certainly true during the seventeenth century and remains true

and at the Whipple house, where the overhang is hewn rather than framed, the molded end girt is further enriched with simple carved brackets in the posts. The late seventeenth-century George Giddings house in Essex is unique in having its front plate molded in a generous quarter-round profile (figure 171).

These little bursts of decorative exuberance are confined almost entirely to the last quarter of the seventeenth century. At the same time, and within the context of New England's first architectural coming of age, we recognize not a few examples, even among the more ambitious houses,

in which no effort was made to decorate the exposed portions of the frame. Ipswich remains the exception, at least in terms of surviving material. Although no longer the seat, as it had been in the beginning years, of such leaders of the colony as Saltonstall, Dudley, Bradstreet, and the younger John Winthrop, the town nevertheless continued to number among its inhabitants several persons of substance, including the Appletons, Whipples, Stanifords, and the unidentified client who commissioned the Ross Tavern. The patronage of these and other aspiring families provided unusual opportunities for local builders, creating

Figure 165. Stanley-Lake house, Topsfield, Mass. Detail of pendant at overhang of first addition to original house, ca. 1700. *Photo, Richard Merrill, 1967.*

Figure 166. Brown house, Hamilton, Mass. Detail of pendant at end overhang, ca. 1680–1700. *Photo, William W. Owens, Jr., 1975.*

Figure 167. Davis-Freeman house, West Gloucester, Mass. Detail of carved corner post at overhang, traditionally ca. 1709. *Photo, William Sumner Appleton, 1919.*

Figure 168. Knowlton house, Ipswich, Mass. Detail of carved chimney post at overhang, ca. 1700. *Photo (during restoration), Peter Zaharis, 1962.*

today, even among the weather-boarded houses of Essex, for instance, where the relatively modern English cladding often varies from early American examples in the width of that portion of the board that is exposed to the weather (figure 172). The fundamental reason for the shift away from traditional finish materials at Massachusetts Bay can be found in conditions imposed by nature which led to an adaptation of local resources. Whatever the similarities in physical environment between the Old World and the new, the first English settlers were forced at once to adjust to significant variations in the climate. John Winthrop records on October 30, 1631, what was apparently his company's first experience at Massachusetts Bay with severe autumn weather. "The governor," he notes impersonally, "having erected a building of stone at Mistick [Medford], there came so violent a storm of rain, for twenty-four hours, from the N. E. and S. E. as (it being not finished, and laid with clay for want of lime) two sides of it were washed down to the ground; and much harm was done to other houses by that storm."[2] Earlier still, in nearby Plymouth Colony, the Pilgrims in 1621 had their first encounter with the full rigors of a wintry New England gale: "Sunday the 4. of *February*, was very wett and rainie, with the greatest gusts of winde that ever we had since wee came forth . . . and it caused much daubing of our houses to fall downe."[3]

In most of the areas in England from which the first settlers were drawn there were lingering early seventeenth-century examples of half-timbering, and it can be argued from the Plymouth statement that similar conditions may have also existed here at the first. Yet we find early and frequent mention of some form of board covering for houses, and one reference at least in 1638 to roughcast or plaster, which had become widely popular as an exterior wall finish in England during the late sixteenth and early seventeenth centuries. Governor Winthrop referred in 1632 to "a small house near the wear at Watertown" which was "made all of clapboards,"[4] and a "litle Claboard howse" was sold by William Aspinwall of Boston in 1636.[5] In that same year one Ezekiel

Figure 169. Hooper-Hathaway house, Salem, Mass. Detail of overhang, ca. 1682. *Photo (before restoration), Frank Cousins, ca. 1908.*

Holliman of Dedham was fined because "he hath covered his house with Clapboard" contrary to an order designed to conserve the initial supplies. Two years later in 1638, apparently in the face of overwhelming logic, the Dedham community voted that "the Clapboarding of houses [be] set at liberty unto all men from this tyme forward."[6] It was during 1638 also that Deputy Governor Symonds wrote to John Winthrop, Jr., about the house to be built for him in Ipswich, thinking it best "to have the walls without to be all clapboarded besides the clay walls," and he added, incidentally, "I desire to have the sparrs [rafters] reach downe pritty deep at the eves to preserve the walls the better from the wether,"[7] a valuable insight into what must have been widespread innovational patterns of thought. The weather again was clearly a principal factor in the minds of Boston's city fathers when they ordered in 1642, in connection with a salt peterhouse to be erected in the prison yard, that it be "set upon posts 7 foot high above ground, with a covering of

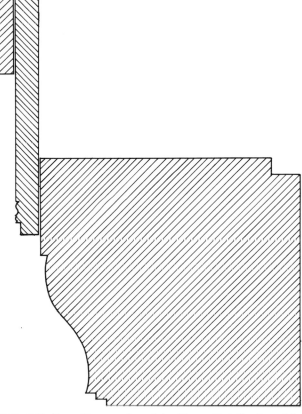

Figure 170. Ross Tavern, Ipswich, Mass. Detail of molded overhanging girt with molded sheathing and dentil course, late seventeenth century.

thatch, and the wall claboarded tight from the injury of rayne and Snow."[8]

The immigrant builders were thoroughly familiar with clapboarding, although when the Englishman at home had finally turned to some form of covering for the hitherto exposed house frame it was not the clapboard. During the late sixteenth and seventeenth centuries in East Anglia "the walls of newly-erected houses and many older ones were completely covered with lath and plaster. It was then that patterned and moulded plaster work or *pargetting* was fashionable." Not until the eighteenth and early nineteenth centuries were "many old timbered houses as well as those newly constructed [in Essex] . . . covered with weatherboarding, espe-

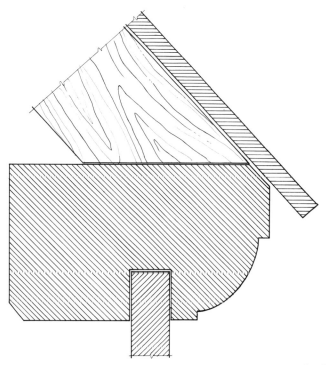

Figure 171. George Giddings house, Essex, Mass. Detail of principal rafter, roof boarding, and molded front plate with rabbet for vertical planking, late seventeenth century.

cially in eastern and southern parts of the county."[9]

Weather-boarding of dwelling houses in East Anglia has thus been considered a late development, and the question of how early the practice came into general use is consequently of little serious interest to the student of English vernacular buildings. For the American student, on the other hand, inasmuch as clapboarding occurs at the outset, the issue has a fundamental importance. Indeed, one English authority, in discussing briefly the buildings of seventeenth-century New England, remarks that "weather-boarding was the commonest finish, and this suggests that weather boarding goes back to the seventeenth century (rather than the eighteenth) in Essex."[10] Actually, of course, it goes back a good deal further in England. This was demonstrated during the excavations in 1960–1961 at Weoley Castle in Birmingham, where thirteenth-century horizontal weather-boarding, varying in width from six

Figure 172. Crown Inn, Loughton, Essex, Eng., ca. 1600 (?).

exposed while the "Stables" and "Barnes" are weather-boarded (figure 173).

One can argue, therefore, that the first settlers at Massachusetts Bay, faced with an immediate problem in a new and more severe climate, turned readily in light of abundant timber reserves to a form of protective covering which they knew, at least in connection with their outbuildings. Certain it is that the common practice of plastering or roughcasting, with which the first generation were by then thoroughly familiar, would have been expensive in the New World, where at the outset proper lime had to be imported.

A representative number of seventeenth-century clapboards have been preserved in cases where later additions are attached to an older structure. At the Fairbanks house in Dedham cedar clapboards, dating presumably to about 1637 and measuring forty-five (the more typical dimension) to fifty-eight inches in length, are still in place on the rear wall of the original dwelling in the lean-to attic. The individual clapboards taper in thickness and are shaved or skived at their ends as well for the purpose of overlap. The pattern of application is irregular. At the Pierce house in Dorchester, ca. 1650, however, the overlapping ends of each layer come together in a single vertical file (figure 46). The material here is also cedar and the average length is forty-three to forty-eight inches with an exposure to weather of three and a quarter to three and three-quarters inches. The width of exposure at the Fairbanks house ranges between three and four inches, and these consistent figures are less than the average exposure of five inches or more found when the clapboards are of oak. Length was controlled to a large extent by the spacing of studs. The nailing sequence, on the other hand, was more flexible. One normally finds the joints staggered and thus ostensibly more weather resistant than they would be when vertically aligned. At the Boardman house in Saugus, ca. 1687, for example, the original oak clapboards of the rear wall are forty-nine to fifty-three inches long, and each layer is fastened in a regularly repeating pattern to alter-

inches to ten inches and in thickness from one inch to one quarter of an inch, was found in connection with a framed out-kitchen of oak. Herein lies one possible explanation for the easily demonstrated absence of exterior boarding on the much later timber-framed houses of sixteenth- and seventeenth-century East Anglia and elsewhere in England: if this detached kitchen dependency discovered in Warwickshire is in any way typical, then perhaps the use of weather-boarding, when it occurred, was more generally confined to outbuildings. There are barns in the same area "of seventeenth-century or early eighteenth-century date where both vertical and horizontal weather-boarding are used, and they may represent a continuance of tradition."[11] In other English counties as well, barns were clapboarded long before houses received any such covering,[12] as we learn, for example, from a sketch made in 1715 of Clitterhouse Farm, Hendon, Middlesex, in which an earlier appearing house has its frame

Figure 173. Clitterhouse Farm, Hendon, Middlesex, Eng.

nate studs (figure 174). Other surviving seven-teenth-century clapboards do not vary signifi-cantly in character and dimensions. Despite the presence of beaded clapboards used for interior wall sheathing at the Fairbanks house in Dedham and beaded clapboards laid with an exposure to weather of eight to eight and a half inches on an outer wall of the lean-to, protected by the addi-tion of the eastern ell (figures 235 and 175)—both of which if original could date to the middle of the seventeenth century—this variety of exte-rior covering was not commonly in use at Massa-chusetts Bay until the second quarter of the eigh-teenth century. The clapboard fragment with molded edge reportedly discovered during the course of restoration and now reproduced at the Paul Revere house in Boston is unique.

The clapboards at the Boardman house are preserved in both the upper and lower stories and reveal on the average a greater exposure to weather at the top than at the bottom. The same condition has been noted in later, eighteenth-century houses and more than one explanation has been advanced. It is perhaps barely conceiv-able that the early New England carpenters were sufficiently aware of visual refinements to have widened the exposure toward the top of the building in order (as one occasionally hears) to compensate at a distance for the interval ob-

Figure 175. Fairbanks house, Dedham, Mass. Detail of side wall of lean-to uncovered during repairs, showing end of projecting plate and beaded clapboarding, before 1668 (?). *Photo, Richard Cheek, 1975.*

Figure 174. Boardman house, Saugus, Mass. Detail of rear wall with original clapboards, ca. 1687. *Photo, Richard Merrill, 1954.*

Exterior Finish

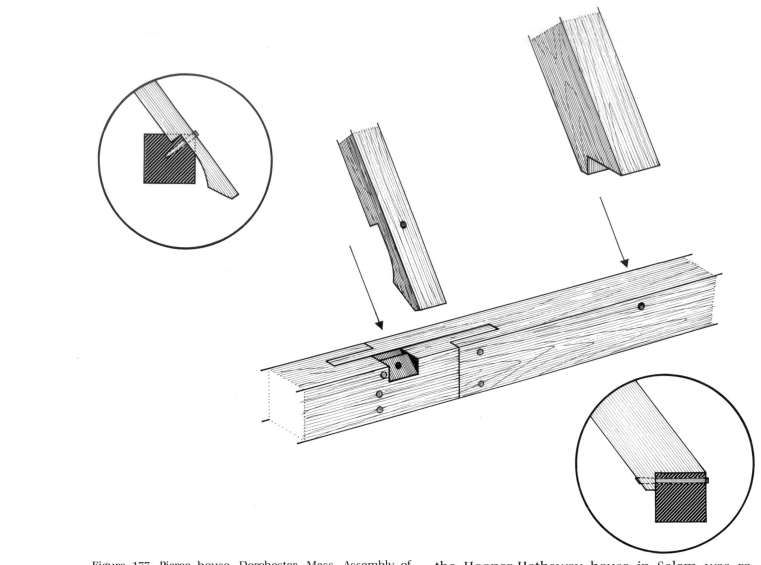

Figure 177. Pierce house, Dorchester, Mass. Assembly of plate (with bladed scarf), principal rafter (bird-mouthed), and common rafter (with molded feet), ca. 1650.

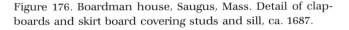

Figure 176. Boardman house, Saugus, Mass. Detail of clapboards and skirt board covering studs and sill, ca. 1687.

served at eye level. It is far more likely, however, that the purpose was purely practical. The lower portions of the frame were more vulnerable to the weather, and a closer spacing of clapboards here may well have been thought advantageous. Surely the builders gave the matter some consideration, for the sill at the Boardman house is covered by a stout skirt board, thirteen and one-half inches high and skived at the top to receive the butt end of the lowermost row of clapboards (figure 176), and an even wider example was discovered when

the Hooper-Hathaway house in Salem was restored.

At the top of the wall there seems to have been no finish whatsoever, at least at the rear of the house. Although the projecting feet of the common rafters at the Pierce house in Dorchester have been nicely molded in a continuing postmedieval English tradition (figure 177), the clapboards at eaves level simply leave off halfway up the plate. Consequently, the joint formed by the roof boards and the top of the plate is unprotected. Later generations of New England carpenters would correct this situation by boxing both the front and rear cornices. The evidence at the

Pierce house, however, which is repeated at both the Fairbanks and Boardman houses (figure 174) and elsewhere, suggests that the seventeenth-century builders were not immediately concerned with security of this joint over and beyond the partial protection afforded by the downward slanting ends of the roof boards, which extended little more than a few inches. A driving, upward-swirling snowstorm could have created particular problems here, and at the front of the house as well, where we have virtually no idea how the clapboards were stopped (if at all). Nor do we know how the junction of roof boarding and front plate was flashed until the very end of the century, when we begin to find a plaster cove cornice here.

The cove cornice was formed by projecting the tie beams beyond the front plate and fashioning a quarter-round profile at the ends to receive the lath for the plaster (figure 178). At the Whittemore-Smith house in Lincoln, erected after 1693, the outer plate is covered in part by a board which has been decorated along its lower edge with a delicate cyma curve and which extends sufficiently below the bottom of the plate to serve as a backstop for the upper edge of the plaster cove. A superimposed cyma cornice molding that is interrupted by the projecting feet of the common rafters may or may not be a part of the original construction. At the Benaiah Titcomb house in Newburyport, built probably after 1700, the plaster cove was stopped at the base by a bold reverse cyma molding of wood which received in a groove along its lower surface not only the upper edge of the topmost course of clapboards but also the tenons of the side rails of the chamber windows (figure 179). At the Hovey-Boardman house in Ipswich, ca. 1710—1720, a single beaded board, several inches wide, covering a portion of the plate, received a wooden member against which the cove was stopped at its base, and in this case the board was skived at bottom to receive the thin edge of the topmost row of clapboards (figure 180).

The popularity of these cove cornices, which provided some oversailing protection for the

Figure 178. Joseph Blaney house, Swampscott, Mass., ca. 1700. Demolished 1914.

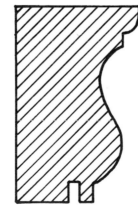

Figure 179. Benaiah Titcomb house, Newburyport, Mass. Detail of molded base of plaster cove cornice with rabbet for clapboards, probably after 1700. (Frame dismantled and re-erected in Essex, Mass.)

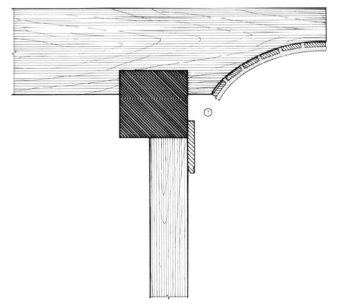

Figure 180. Hovey-Boardman house, Ipswich, Mass. Detail of plaster cove cornice, with one missing element, ca. 1700–1720.

Figure 181. Gedney house, Salem, Mass. Frame of hall chamber showing exterior sheathing, ca. 1665. *Photo, William W. Owens, Jr., 1974.*

more widespread before 1700 than we have realized (figure 186). As early as 1649 the selectmen of Dorchester directed that the walls of a house there should be "borded,"[13] and in 1660 a Boston deed mentions a "frame erected . . . and boarded nere round and the Rooffe with severall boards."[14] These references are by no means as explicit as that found in a 1679 building contract in Boston. According to its terms, James Townsend, housewright, was only "to inclose and cover the sides and Roofe with Clapboards and shingles," but the client, John Williams, changed his mind as the work progressed. One of the workmen deposed that having been employed at the house in July of 1679 Mr. Williams "would not let me go forward with my worke, because hee would have it boarded under the Clapboards."[15]

The earliest known example of underboarding can be found at the Gedney house in Salem, ca. 1665. The inch-thick horizontal boards, skived or bevel-lapped at top and bottom, are eighteen and a half inches wide on the average and enclose the frame entirely (figure 181). Surely it can be argued that the more severe climatic conditions, which led the early builders to wrestle almost at once with the problem of an effective form of weather repellent, kept them continually on the alert for further improvements. And as additional insulation seemed desirable, there were abundant native materials to satisfy the need. Occasionally when clapboards are removed from a house of the colonial period it will be discovered that the underboarding has been exposed to the weather for an appreciable length of time before receiving any outer covering. The reason was probably economy. In one or two important instances, however, the underboarding was intended as the final finish. In the south parlor wing of the Turner house in Salem, added to the original structure probably before 1680, the thirteen- to seventeen-inch wide horizontal boards found beneath later clapboards at the time of restoration in 1909 were handsomely molded at their overlapping edges and had clearly been exposed to the weather as well (figure 182). The same condition was found on the eastern end of the Cooper-Frost-Austin

walls below and furnished a distinctly decorative touch as well, is confined largely to the first quarter of the eighteenth century. No examples earlier than the 1690s are known, and only three unrestored examples remain in Massachusetts: the Rea-Putnam-Fowler house in Danvers, ca. 1700; the Whittemore-Smith house in Lincoln; and the Parker-Orne house in Marblehead, ca. 1711.

Riven lengths of clapboard nailed directly to the studs were butted at right angles where they met at the four corners of the house. Corner boards did not come into use until the eighteenth century. Underboarding the frame with wide horizontal pine boards, which had also become commonplace in the eighteenth century, was

house in Cambridge, ca. 1689, during the course of restoration and repairs in 1912.[16] Lacking any parallel in smaller English houses of the period, one can suggest again an innovational significance for this treatment, whether the boards are perfectly plain or decorated.

The rapidly accepted popularity in East Anglia in the sixteenth and early seventeenth centuries of plaster or roughcast as a wall covering has been explained not only as a stylistic measure but also, in part, as a means of concealing the increasingly lackluster quality of the house frame, owing to the limited availability after 1600 of top-quality building trees. Because of the scarcity of lime, the use of plaster or roughcast in New England seems to have been limited to urban areas almost entirely. Examples in Salem and Boston are known, but none for the country—until the eighteenth century. Furthermore, while as early as 1638 Samuel Cole had agreed to mend "the rough cast of the outsyde" of a new house in Boston, the practice did not become common until later in the century, and then apparently for practical reasons.[17] Boston, being almost entirely a city of wooden buildings during much of the seventeenth century, was subject to the ravage of periodic fires. Major conflagrations occurred in 1653, 1676, 1679, 1683, 1690, and 1691. The fire of 1679 began about midnight of August 8 and "continued till near noon the next day; the most woeful desolation that Boston ever saw; eighty odd dwelling-houses and seventy odd warehouses, with several vessels and their lading consumed to ashes."[18] The General Court, "having a sence of the great ruines in Boston by fire, and hazard still of the same, by reason of the joyning and neereness of their buildings," was determined that the rebuilding should not be without some method. On October 15, 1679, within just a few weeks of the disaster, they ordered "that henceforth no dwelling house in Boston shalbe errected and sett up except of stone or bricke, and covered with slate or tyle." This legislation, understandably, with its promise of higher replacement costs, raised among the sufferers an immediate outcry, and the law was suspended for three

Figure 182. Turner house, Salem, Mass. Detail of exterior overlapping molded sheathing of parlor wing (concealed by later clapboards), probably before 1680. *Photo (during repairs), David McLaren Hart, 1972.*

years.[19]

The amendment does not suggest roughcast as a practical compromise, but its obvious fire resistant qualities seem to have recommended it to a number of those living in the burned-out area. The antiquarian, Dr. Jeremy Belknap, writes in 1795 that "The houses and warehouses near the town-dock, which were rebuilt after the great fire of 1679, were either constructed with brick, or plastered on the out side with a strong cement, intermixed with gravel and glass, and slated on the top. Several of these plastered houses," he adds, "are yet remaining in Ann[North]-street, in their original form."[20] By the end of the century there are frequent references in the public records, such as the license in 1700 permitting Edward Brattle "to erect a dwelling house of timber

upon his land . . . in Boston, provided he slate or tile the roof and rough cast the sides."[21]

The only seventeenth-century roughcast house which survived in Boston long enough to be photographed was the Old Feather Store (figure 39). Erected immediately after the fire of 1679 in Dock Square near the head of North Street, its roughcast was keyed to large riven laths nailed to the cedar underboarding.[22] The covering was described as "a strong, and, as time has proved, durable cement, in which was observable coarse gravel and broken glass, the latter consisting of fragments of dark-colored junk bottles."[23] These were "broken into pieces of about half an inch diameter, the sharp corners of which penetrate the cement in such a manner, that this great lapse of years has had no perceptible effect upon them."[24]

In the peak of the principal gable the date 1680 was impressed into the roughcast cement in Arabic figures, "together with various ornamental devices"[25] which show up well in photographs and drawings. Directly above the date panel there was a heart, with an inverted heart just below it. There were single diamonds in the second story, one on either side of the windows in the side elevation and one between each of the end windows and corners of the building in front. One early writer speaks of "diamonds and flowers-de-luce,"[26] by which he probably means the hearts. No fleurs-de-lis can be seen in the views, though one such example existed in Salem in the Sun Tavern, built after 1664 (figure 183). There were also "ornamental squares" which followed the rake of the roof in the gables and ran along the rear corner of the building and between the windows of both second and third stories as a decorative enframement.

There was an ornamental bracket tenoned into the underside of the projecting end tie at the Old Feather Store (figure 39), and there are at least two examples elsewhere of brackets, both somewhat less complex in profile. The first, of pine, was attached to the overhanging gable end of the Andrews house in Hingham, built between 1685 and 1690, and has been protected through the

Figure 183. Sun Tavern, Salem, Mass., after 1664. Demolished ca. 1824. Detail of ornament in rough-cast finish of exterior wall. *Photo, J. David Bohl, 1978.*

years by a later addition (figure 184). The second outlasted the rigors of more than two hundred New England winters and remained exposed in the west gable end of the Parson Capen house in Topsfield of 1683 when that structure was restored in 1913 (figure 185). It served as a model for the present brackets of the first-story overhang at the front of the house, structural evidence for which was discovered during the course of restoration. These nicely molded brackets were a familiar ornament of the more pretentious homes of minister, merchant, and prosperous yeoman, with ample precedent in contemporary English work. They first appear (although the brackets themselves no longer exist) in the overhanging gable ends of the mid-century Pierce and Capen houses in Dorchester, where the front and rear

plates oversail the posts by as much as seventeen inches and are mortised for the tenons of the brackets.

The Old Feather Store was finished with a dentil course in the gable end facing Market Square, and important evidence for a similar treatment was discovered beneath later clapboards at the Ross Tavern in Ipswich. The original underboarding stopped an inch or so above the uppermost fillet of the molded overhanging girts in both stories and its lower edge was molded. A few inches higher there was a molded dentil course nailed to the underboarding, fragments of which were recovered during the course of restoration, and the marks of which are outlined by an early, perhaps original, coat of red paint covering the exposed trim of the house (figures 170 and 186).

Figure 184. Andrews house (The Old Ordinary), Hingham, Mass. Detail of bracket at gable overhang, 1685 – 1690. *Photo, William W. Owens, Jr., 1973.*

Figure 185. Parson Capen house, Topsfield, Mass. Detail of west gable end with original bracket, 1683. (Restored chimney and fenestration conjectural.)

The Framed Houses of Massachusetts Bay

The late seventeenth-century William Howard house in Ipswich was also found to have its original underboarding molded at the overhang of the second story a few inches below the point at which the clapboards were applied, and two other Ipswich houses, the Manning house, built probably during 1692–1693, and the later half of the Whipple house, added before 1683, reveal unmistakably in the molded girts of the overhanging second stories that original underboarding stopped an inch or two above the uppermost fillet, creating an elaborate profile. At the Whipple house, in fact, photographs taken before the restoration in 1898 show clearly the molded edge of the underboarding (fig. 187).

In addition to the drops carved out of the lower ends of the posts of overhanging second stories, there were also ornamental drops attached to the frame. Although the original context is no longer known, two drops or pendants survive with a Newbury history. Both were designed to be tenoned and pinned into the frame, and one continues a familiar English tradition in having its center carved out to form an open pattern (figures 188 and 189). In addition to the applied brackets at the Capen house in Topsfield, evidence was found as well for drops tenoned into the frame of the first-story and gable end overhangs, and these were restored in 1913 (figure 185).

The exterior covering of the house was fixed in place before the infilling of the frame. Infilling itself perpetuates in the New World an English building tradition extending over many centuries. Its function was that of closing in the open spaces of the house frame, and until the seventeenth century the fill usually remained exposed as part of the wall structure. Force of habit seems to be responsible for continuity of the practice in New England until well into the eighteenth century, even though the colonists had begun to cover their house frames almost at once. If the early New England builders rationalized any functional reason (insulation, for example, or

Figure 186. Ross Tavern, Ipswich, Mass. Detail of sheathed gable end wall with clapboards removed, showing original (horizontal) and later attic window openings and paint evidence for dentil course at overhang, late seventeenth century. (Open gains in molded end girt received the upper ends of studs which later boxed in the overhang.) *Photo, Daniel S. Wendel, ca. 1940.*

Figure 187. Whipple house, Ipswich, Mass., ca. 1655 and before 1683, with later modifications. *Photo (before restoration), Wilfred A. French, 1880–1895.*

Figure 188. Newbury, Mass. (?). Pendant of overhang, seventeenth century. *Photo, Richard Merrill, 1960.*

Figure 189. Newbury, Mass. (?). Pendant of overhang, seventeenth century. *Photo, Richard Merrill, 1960.*

even, as we have been told by the romanticists in connection with brick infill, protection against the musketry of hostile Indians), no contemporary reference to it has been found. The infilling of the gable end walls of the attic at the Blake house in Dorchester, ca. 1650 (figure 190), the Coffin house in Newbury, ca. 1654, and the original portion of the Turner house in Salem, ca. 1668, whether of brick and clay or clay and chopped straw alone, may well have been intended as insulation. This supposition is strongly corroborated by the filled gable end at the Corwin house in Salem, where the original 1675 mason's contract called for an attic fireplace.

During the early decades of the seventeenth century wattle and daub as the long-preferred English method of infilling the panels of the frame were giving way to brick. This trend is echoed at Massachusetts Bay, where we have no more than one or two conservative examples of wattle and daub wall fill. At the Fairbanks house in Dedham the time-honored English custom persists of using slim wattles of riven oak, approximately one-inch square in cross section (figure 191). The horizontal sticks are sprung into shallow grooves in the sides of the studs, and are laced with the vertical, free-standing pieces but are not fastened to them with hemp or willow bark as one often finds in the mother country during the late sixteenth and early seventeenth centuries. Moreover, as seen in two adjacent panels of the front wall, the horizontal wattles alternate, being on the outer surface in the first panel and the inner in the second. The first panel contains the pressure marks of a board against which the clay has been forced (figure 192), implying that the daub was applied from within, and such is surely the case with the second panel. Here, then, is early evidence, whether the board was used as a temporary backstop or constituted an early form of permanent siding, for what was to become the invariable practice in New England of inserting the wall fill from within, in contrast to the earlier English habit of daubing over the wattle from within and without.

Only one other example of wattle and daub is

known at Massachusetts Bay where, in the Giddings-Burnham house in Ipswich, ca. 1680, single horizontal lengths of wattle are sprung into notches in the studs (figure 193). Here the builder, a carpenter by profession, was in his sixties and one suspects a lingering of tradition. Far more common, if not universal, was the infilling of the frame with brick and clay or, rarely, as at the Wilson-Appleton house in Ipswich, erected after 1672, and the Gedney house in Salem, with clay and chopped straw alone. Where original underboarding remains, or there are original clapboards nailed directly to the frame, it is readily observable from the way in which the clay daub, in flowing around the bricks, has taken the im-

Figure 190. Blake house, Dorchester, Mass. Detail of roof and gable end daubed with clay and chopped straw, ca. 1650. *Photo, Richard Merrill, 1967.*

Figure 191. Fairbanks house, Dedham, Mass. Detail of wattle and daub wall fill, west gable end, ca. 1637. *Photo, William W. Owens, Jr., 1974.*

Figure 192. Fairbanks house. Detail of wattle and daub wall fill, front wall. *Photo (during repairs), Richard Cheek, 1972.*

Figure 193. Giddings-Burnham house, Ipswich, Mass. Detail of wattle and daub wall fill, ca. 1680, revealed by vertical cut in exterior clapboarded wall. *Photo (during alterations), David McLaren Hart, 1977.*

print of the boarding or clapboards that the outer covering was applied first and the infill then laid into the frame against it (figure 174). No case is known at Massachusetts Bay of finish bricks laid into the frame in herringbone pattern for reasons of visual display as one finds in England. Furthermore, for those areas of the frame where the fill might be exposed within, for example on top of the plate, the bricks were either plastered over (as at the Boardman house in Saugus) or covered with board trim (figure 256).

Wall fill of brick and clay continues to be uniformly popular until into the eighteenth century at Massachusetts Bay. Only very rarely will the frame be filled with any other material, for example, a tight packing of eel grass. Several early examples are known on the South Shore, two in Quincy, the Baxter and Bass houses (figure 194), and at least four in nearby Dorchester.[27] The rationale here was almost certainly insulation.

There was conscious concern for fire resistant roofing materials in the seventeenth century, as seen for example in the legislation of 1679 prohibiting the use of anything other than slate and tile. If the Old Feather Store, built immediately after the Boston fire of that year, was roofed with slate or tile at the beginning, as the law specified, such was not the case in its later years when photographs show a much weathered covering of wooden shingles (figure 39). Indeed, when the English textile manufacturer Henry Wansey visited Boston in 1794 he noted that many of the buildings were "weather boarded at the side, and all of them roofed with shingles."[28] Concurrent with the early and widespread use of roof shingles at Massachusetts Bay, however, other traditional English roofing materials were also in vogue.

Thatch was a common sight at the first and to a lesser degree throughout the seventeenth century. The articles of agreement between Samuel Cole and Captain Sedgwick in 1638 for finishing a house frame "next M. Greenesmith's" in Boston tell us that the captain was to "pay for the thatching of the said house, and lend the Said Samuel Cole a lighter to fetch the thatch for the same."[29]

This is but one of many such early references. The official records mention in 1649, but do not name, "a towne within this jurisdiction," whose inhabitants "at their first siting downe, did generally agree to set a part a certeine parcell of land, to the value of about 20 acres, lying between the salt marsh and the low water marke, for the use of the whole towne, to be improved for thatching houses," and somewhat earlier in 1630 thatchers appear among a list of workmen whose wages were subject to regulation.[30]

The abandonment of thatch (fairly rapidly at first and thereafter more gradually, especially in the country) can be credited largely to the dangers of fire. In 1631 Winthrop records that "the chimney of Mr. Sharp's house in Boston took fire, (tho splinters being not clayed at the top,) and taking the thatch burnt it down."[31] Thomas Dudley, commenting on this same disaster, adds tersely,

> For the prevention whereof in our new town
> [Cambridge], intended this summer to be
> builded, we have ordered that no man there
> shall build his chimney with wood, nor cover his
> house with thatch; which was readily assented
> unto, for that divers other houses have been
> burned since our arrival, (the fire always begin-
> ning in the wooden chimneys,) and some En-
> glish wigwams, which have taken fire in the roofs
> covered with thatch or boughs.[32]

Efforts at legislation do not seem to have made an end of the matter, however. Winthrop writes on February 1, 1634, of the house of Mr. Cradock at Marblehead, "burnt down about midnight," the occupants being preserved "by a tailor, who sate up that night at work . . . and, hearing a noise, looked out and saw the house on fire above the oven in the thatch."[33] A few years later, in 1639, two real estate transactions in Dorchester specified that altogether new houses were to be thatched. In one of these, husbandman William Robinson promised to "thatch the said house and all other housing" that might be built upon the premises during a term of seven years.[34]

Thatch probably became an unfamiliar sight in Boston within a relatively short time except, perhaps, for the simplest houses. Winthrop writes in 1646 of one Captain Cromwell who with "all his men had much money, and great store of plate and jewels of great value," but who, nevertheless, "took up his lodging in a poor thatched house."[35] Elsewhere its occasional use clearly persisted until the end of the seventeenth century and even a bit later in isolated pockets. It may ultimately develop, in fact, that thatch lingered somewhat longer as a roof covering for barns than it did for houses. A lease in the town of Malden in 1672 provides that the lessor was "to shingle the fore-side [of the roof]" of the farmhouse, while the barn on the other hand was to have its thatch renewed,[36] and in Ipswich as late as 1700 the estate accounts of Captain Symon Stacy include an item for "Thatching one Syd of the barn."[37]

There is no physical evidence at Massachusetts Bay for the use of thatch, with the possible exception of the Fairbanks house at Dedham where the present roof covering conceals a section of thin stavelike strips of oak, six to eight inches in width, fixed to the rafters at intervals of about half their width (figure 195). These might just as well have been designed to receive shingles, nor do they correspond readily to the English method of support for thatch, which was closely spaced withes or poles. They might, on the other hand, be described as lathlike, in which case one notes with interest that a contract in 1677 for framing and boarding a barn on Hog Island in Ipswich stipulated that the carpenters were "to get laths and lath the roof for thatching."[38]

We have only the documents to tell us of other traditional English forms of roof covering soon superseded by native materials, adapting to both the climate and economic realities of the new settlements at Massachusetts Bay. Higginson had remarked in 1629 that they were then setting up a brick kiln in Salem "to make bricks and tiles for the building of our houses,"[39] and in the capital city itself by 1650 some of the buildings were "fairly set forth with Brick, Tile, Stone and Slate."[40] Later, in 1678, Increase Mather records a bolt of lightning which "broke into the next

Figure 194. Baxter house, Quincy, Mass., probably early eighteenth century. Demolished 1960. Detail of eel grass wall fill and fragments of original clapboards. *Photo, Everett Tatreau, 1959.*

Figure 195. Fairbanks house, Dedham, Mass. Detail of roof frame and covering, ca. 1637. *Photo, William W. Owens, Jr., 1974.*

house to the colledge" in Cambridge and "tore away and shattered into pieces a considerable quantity of the tyle on the roof."[41] Tile was surely utilized in urban situations, but not extensively because of the higher costs, and it was phased out largely before the end of the seventeenth century. Slate, on the other hand, seems to have increased in popularity in the more densely settled communities. William Wood boasted in 1634 that among the country's natural resources there were "quarries of Slate, out of which they get covering for houses,"[42] and as early as 1650 Slate Island (so-called) in Boston Harbor was granted to one William Torrey, provided "that it be free for any man to make use of the Slatt."[43] Like tile it was apparently favored by the well-to-do (Sewall tells us in 1708 that "Mr. Dudley had been at great Charge to Slate his House Roofe and Sides"[44]) and by this period begins to be advertised. Mr. Jarvis Ballard, for example, in the columns of *The Boston News-Letter,* offered on October 13/20, 1718, "A Parcell of Slate, ready Hol'd and Cut, fit to be Laid on Houses."

While thatched roofs were relatively common during the earliest years at Massachusetts Bay, and other roofing materials appear occasionally as well, there are many more references to the boarded and shingled roof. As early as January 7, 1633, the town of Cambridge ordered that all houses built there "shalbee Co[vered with] slate or board and not with thach."[45] A nontraditional roof finish was under consideration, therefore, from the beginning. Samuel Symonds wrote a few years later, in 1638, that he wanted his farmhouse in Ipswich to be "covered [that is, roofed] with very good oake-hart inch bord,"[46] and in that same year it was agreed by contract that the meetinghouse in Salem was to be "covered with inch and halfe planck and inch board upon that to meete close."[47] The William Rix contract for a small house to be built in Boston in 1640 specified that both walls and roof were to be clapboarded,[48] and in Dorchester, as late as 1674, Ensign Richard Hale was "empowered to see that the Scholehous be repaiered either by Clobording or shingleing the Roofe."[49]

These reports of boarding or clapboarding of roofs as a final finish are rare. Shingles are another matter. As early as 1649 the selectmen of Dorchester directed that the house which had belonged to Mr. Tilley have "the Rooffe shingled,"[50] and Josselyn reports in 1663 that the colonists used white cedar to "make shingles to cover their houses with instead of tyle, it will never warp."[51] Like the clapboard, shingles can be found in England (though more commonly at an earlier period) and are defined by Moxon, writing about 1680, as "Small pieces of Wood used to cover Houses with, instead of Tiles or Slates."[52] While the English settlers in America cannot be credited with the invention of the wooden shingle, their early and widespread exploitation of local timber resources for this purpose can nevertheless be seen to have innovational significance.

Few if any seventeenth-century roof shingles have survived at Massachusetts Bay. We gain only a partial impression of their size and shape from such documents as the order in 1688 for repairing the meetinghouse in Salem, which specified that the workmen "shall Shingle the whole Roofe . . . with good Short Seader Shingle of halfe an Inch Thick on the butt End and Joynted or Edged."[53] The term "short" occurs again in a Boxford building contract of 1726 where the roof covering is defined as "white pine Shingels: Short shingels."[54] Further, a contract of 1681 between Robert Swan and John Whittier of Haverhill for a dwelling to be erected by Whittier provides that the roof be "covred with bords and short shingles."[55] Size was regulated at least by 1695 when it was ordered "That all shingles exposed to sale, shall . . . bear eighteen or fifteen inches in length, and not under three and half inches in breadth . . . [nor] under full half an inch thick, and [be] well shaved."[56] These dimensions seem slightly longer than one might have expected, and may account for the specification of "short" shingles. If original, the shingles found on the roof of the earliest portion of the George Hart house in Ipswich could date to the closing years of the seventeenth century and are longer than the superimposed mid-eighteenth-century shingles of the roof valley which concealed them through the years (figure 196). In any event, size seems to have become an increasing matter of statutory concern by the first quarter of the eighteenth century, at least in Boston, and the *Boston News-Letter* for March 23/30, 1713, would imply a no-nonsense attitude: "On Wednesday last, while the General Court was sitting here, a Bonefire was made in King-Street below the Town-House, of a parcel of Shingles, (upwards of Eight thousand out of Ten thousand,) found defective by the Surveyors both as to length and breadth prescribed by the Law, which Shingles were rather Chips than Shingles." For the future, they moralized, "both makers and sellers of Shingles had best conform to the Law and prevent any more such Bonefires."

Shingles were also used commonly at a later period in New England as a covering for walls, but scarcely if at all at Massachusetts Bay during the seventeenth century. The only documentary reference, in fact, that of the Dutch visitor Jasper Danckaerts from New York, who reported in 1680 in his native language that the houses in Boston "are made of thin, small cedar shingles, nailed against frames, and then filled in with brick and other stuff,"[57] may be cited as a likely example of the perils of translation.

The roof frame was tightly boarded to create support for the shingles. In Billerica, for example, in 1667, when the town ordered the construction of a stone house for fortification, it was specified that the roof be "covered with bords, chamfered [feathered] and after shingled."[58] Here again we encounter innovation in traditional building habits stimulated by a colonial timber economy. Both English tile and thatch were fixed to a more or less open system of support, with the result that one sees the underside of the covering in the attic. No seventeenth-century house survives at Massachusetts Bay, on the other hand, without roof boarding, and an early if not original date for these boards is often affirmed by the cuts for long vanished façade gables.

The character of the frame determines the positioning of the boards. Roofs composed of princi-

pal and common rafters employ horizontal boarding. For the far more common roof frame of principal rafters and common purlins or ribs, the covering is applied vertically. The boards themselves, whether vertical or horizontal, were extended a few inches at the gable ends to provide protection for the walls. This required some further support from the frame, and in common purlin roofs the purlins in their trenches projected far enough beyond the end rafters to perform this function (figure 75). The projecting roof end is firmly rooted in English building traditions, and it afforded the Tudor carpenter an opportunity for embellishment with decorated

Figure 196. George Hart house, Ipswich, Mass. Detail of roof valley at junction of house erected ca. 1698 with mid-eighteenth-century addition (at right), showing early, perhaps original, shingles covered by later valley shingles. *Photo, Peter Zaharis, 1963.*

Figure 197. Downing-Bradstreet house, Salem, Mass., seventeenth century. Demolished 1758.

tionable views of the Downing-Bradstreet and Corwin houses in Salem, executed in 1819 by Samuel Bartol, include pinnacles at the apex of the gable ends (figure 197), comparable with contemporary English examples, and the Reverend William Bentley, describing in 1793 the ambitious home of Philip English in Salem, ca. 1690, tells us that there were "ornaments rising two feet" upon the peaks of the roof.[60] The *Boston News-Letter* for July 14/21, 1707, reports a bolt of lightning which struck "upon the Pinnacle on the Gable end" of the home of Mr. Creese of Boston, apothecary, but we know little about the precise shape and character of these long-vanished features, conjectural examples of which were mounted on the gables of the Appleton-Taylor-Mansfield house in Saugus, ca. 1680, when it was restored by Wallace Nutting in 1915 (figure 272).

Similarly, no original roof gutters have survived from the seventeenth century, and the houses themselves reveal no recognizable structural evidence of their presence. As early as 1697, however, there were gutters on the "foreside" and "backside" of the house James Townsend, housewright, contracted to build for John Williams of Boston.[61] Later, in 1714, in the same city where it had been found "by long Experience, that the Common usage of Conveying Watter by Troughs, or Gutters from the Eves of Houses . . . So as to drop the Same into Such parts of the Streets or High wayes, where the Inhabitants and others do usually pass and repass hath been a great annoyance, espeshally in Stormy wether and dark nights," it was ordered that all gutters must be furnished with "drop-gutters or Trunks, Close to their respective Houses . . . So as to deliver or Cast the Same, not exceeding four feet distant above the Surface of the Earth."[62] Somewhat earlier, and in one of the smaller communities, the estate accounts of George Mountjoy of Braintree, mariner, include an item of payment in 1699 "for Spouts round" the deceased's house.[63] These references are meager, however, and are rendered somewhat more complex by the fact that the term gutter could have more than a single meaning in the seventeenth century. Richard Neve in

barge boards. The few early photographs of houses in New England with their original roof ends intact reveal nothing but straight-cut barge boards, and these indeed may have been later replacements. Only a single example of a decorated barge board in Massachusetts survives outside the Bay area where at the Old Indian House of about 1700 in Deerfield a much weathered scalloped barge board with an overlay of dentils was salvaged when the house was demolished in 1848.[59]

Final details of roof finish include such ornamental touches as the pinnacle and the more purely functional gutter at cornice level to facilitate the discharge of water. The somewhat ques-

1703 defines gutters primarily as the "*Vallies* in the Roofs" between gables which join at right angles, and then goes on to describe their more conventional function at eaves level.[64] John Norman of Manchester, house carpenter, was instructed in 1658 to "shingle the gutters" of the porch he had contracted to add to the home of Dr. George Emery in Salem,[65] and at least one example of a heavily shingled valley or "gutter" has survived, though in a somewhat later context. When not many years before 1752[66] George Hart of Ipswich built a new dwelling, adding to it at the rear for a kitchen the frame of an older, seventeenth-century house, creating thereby a T-shaped structure, the resulting vallies of the roof were shingled (figure 196). Such rare physical evidence, however, only serves to remind us that the exterior trim of the earliest houses in New England has consistently been the element most vunerable to loss through decay and replacement.

Concurrent with the infilling of the frame and boarding and/or clapboarding of the walls was the fashioning of door and window openings. Successive style changes in a feature as prominent as the front entrance have greatly restricted our knowledge of its original placement and dimensions. In at least four structures—the Fairbanks house in Dedham, the earliest half of the Whipple house in Ipswich, the Story house in Essex, ca. 1684, and the Browne house in Watertown, built between 1694 and 1701—the front doors were pushed to the far left of the entry or chimney bay (as one faces the house). The Fairbanks and Browne house doorways were framed up separately, with the left-hand jamb fixed tightly against the chimney post (figure 164), while at the Whipple and Story houses the chimney posts themselves formed the left jamb of the door frame. For the balance of our evidence—fewer than a dozen examples—the entrance is located more or less in the center of the chimney bay. The width of opening ranges quite consistently between thirty-two and thirty-seven inches. Not until late in the period, as at the Boardman house in Saugus, does the width jump to as much as forty-two inches, implying here and in such other progressive houses as the Parson Barnard house in North Andover, ca. 1715, that the entrance has by now been furnished with a vertically divided door. At the Barnard house, in fact, where the interval is also forty-two inches, pintle holes for hinges supporting the individual halves or leaves were found in each of the door posts. At the White-Ellery house in Gloucester, erected ca. 1710, of integral lean-to construction, an exterior rear door in the gable end measures forty-four inches in width, suggesting that the double door was by then appropriate for secondary entrances as well. In the matter of height we find a practical correlation with headroom, which is seldom more than six feet. In one particular case, that of the Story house in Essex, the height of the opening was only five feet, two inches, a striking reminder that the average stature in the seventeenth century was markedly different from ours of the twentieth.

We have no more than two or three examples of the doors themselves, the most complete of which, the original door of the Old Indian House in Deerfield, ca. 1700, is outside the Massachusetts Bay area (figure 198). This example, however, compares well with two fragmentary remnants of doors which have survived at the Turner house in Salem and at the Robert Peaslee house in Haverhill, a brick structure built between 1707 and 1714. In all three cases the outer vertical boards, an inch or more in thickness, are battened on the reverse with shorter lengths laid horizontally. These layers or laminations are fastened together with nails, the well-fashioned heads of which form an exterior diamond pattern which could be subtly reinforced through the presence of lines scored in the surface of the wood, connecting the individual nailheads. The doors were hung with long strap hinges upon pintles driven into the door posts at the top and bottom and opened inwards. The posts or other frame members were furnished with a rabbet to receive the door.

Like the doorway, the window in the earliest houses is often an inherent part of the frame. Patterns of fenestration reveal a relatively high de-

Figure 198. Ensign John Sheldon house (Old Indian House), Deerfield, Mass., ca. 1700. Demolished 1848. Detail of front door showing original knocker/latch, decorative patterns of nailheads, and perforation made during Indian raid of 1704 which reveals horizontal boarding of the interior surface. *Photo, Anne du Mont, 1978.*

Figure 199. Plymouth Colony, Mass. (?). Window frame, seventeenth or early eighteenth century.

gree of uniformity, amounting almost to a formula for the placement of windows, although few elements of the seventeenth-century house are more puzzling. With not many exceptions original structure and finish have been obliterated by later replacements. Thus we have little more than a composite picture with facts gathered in fragmentary form from many different locations.

Among the more modest English houses which antedated the migrations to the New World in the 1630s and 1640s the refinement of glazing was of relatively recent origin. As late as about 1600 the traditional opening in the wall into which had been set stout oak mullions without glazing persisted in the house called Raven's Farm in Woodham Walter, Essex, its only refinement a solid draw-shutter which could be pulled across the opening to keep out the cold and rain (figure 15). By the third and fourth decades of the seventeenth century, however, the rank and file of settlers at Massachusetts Bay were apparently in step with trends at home and accustomed to glazing for their windows. In 1629, Francis Higginson reminds his friends in England to be sure to "furnish yourselves with . . . glass for windows,"[67] and William Wood advises prospective planters in 1634 that "Glasse ought not to be forgotten of any that desire to benefit themselves, or the Countrey: if it be well leaded, and carefully pack't up, I know no commodity better for portage or sayle."[68] Indeed the London port books include numerous entries for window glass consigned to cargoes of ships sent from London to Governor Winthrop during the years 1634 – 1636 for the settlement at Massachusetts Bay.[69]

Were there, on the other hand, more primitive arrangements at the very first? The letter written in 1621 by Edward Winslow of Plymouth Colony urging newcomers from England to "Bring paper and linseed oil for your windows," may be dismissed as pure makeshift.[70] Nor can we easily visualize what Samuel Symonds had in mind when he advised John Winthrop, Jr., in 1638 that the windows in his farmhouse to be built in Ipswich should "all have current shutting draw-windowes."[71] About the year 1670 lightning "beat

down the shutter of the window" of a house in Roxbury,[72] and there are other references to shutters throughout the century. As yet, however, no evidence of provision for shutters in the conventional sense has appeared among the houses themselves. Virtually unique is an upright rectangular window frame attributed to Plymouth Colony.[73] Into the upper half has been let a small panel of fixed leaded glass while the balance of the frame has been fitted with unglazed bars of wood. A solid shutter covers this barred section and is designed to ride up and down in grooves with the aid of a string or thong which comes through a hole at the center of the frame. When the shutter is fully raised, light and air are admitted through the lower section but the glazed sash at the top is covered (figure 199).

The majority of the first framed houses at Massachusetts Bay were seemingly glazed from the outset and, indeed, Edward Johnson estimates as much as £18,000 for the "*charges expended by this poore People . . .* [for] Nayles, Glasse and other Iron-worke for their meeting-houses, and other dwelling houses, before they could raise any meanes in the Country to purchase them."[74] Glaziers appear among the early building artisans, and as time went along it is more than likely that, as with other builders, the strict limits of the craft became increasingly blurred, particularly in rural areas. In Ipswich, for example, in 1691 John Browne, glazier, was paid "for Running of bulletts or shott."[75]

Many of the early leaded window sash are apt to show picturesquely the irregular insertion of small pieces of glass set also in lead (figure 200A). These may represent a thrifty glazier making use of broken pieces, for window glass in New England continued to be imported until well into the eighteenth century, but it is equally likely that we are dealing with windows which have been broken at one time or another and mended. In the estate of Thomas Webb of Boston, for instance, in 1713, there is an item "for Ledding and mending the Windows."[76]

The Fairbanks house in Dedham reveals quite fully its original fenestration (figure 201-1). Thus we learn that the earliest builders were not accustomed to making window openings in the rear wall of the house. There are some exceptions toward the end of the seventeenth century, and the rear wall of an added or integral lean-to was almost invariably furnished with window openings. The Fairbanks house is virtually alone among surviving structures at Massachusetts Bay in having a west gable end wall without a window in either the first or second story, probably because there was an original appendage here, a situation not without English parallel. In both the east and west gable ends of the attic on the other hand, there are substantial remnants of four-part window openings. In character these openings follow English precedent in every respect, including the fixing of glass in place in rabbets or grooves in both the headers and sills.

The hall and parlor of the Fairbanks house, and their chambers, were furnished with wide horizontal banks of windows, and the entry in both stories was furnished with smaller windows of fixed glass having a mullion in the center. All of these windows are vertically aligned. The facade of the Fairbanks house thereby illustrates in all but the existence of a window in the entry of the ground story a typical scheme for fenestration. At the end of the house the usual arrangement was a single bank of openings in each story vertically aligned. The contract for building a parsonage in Marlborough in 1661, a house clearly of two-room, central-chimney plan, calls for "foure windows, on the foreside, and two windowes at the west end." Above the cornice level there were to be "two Gables on the foreside of ten foote wide . . . with two small windows on the foreside of the Gables."[77] Here, then, there were to be windows in the front wall of both of the principal rooms and their chambers, presumably matched in size, and smaller windows in the gables directly above. Two windows also vertically aligned, one assumes, were located in the west gable end wall. The lack of any fenestration for the wall opposite is reminiscent of the situation at the Fairbanks house, while the absence of windows in the rear wall is typical.

Figure 200A. Perkins house, Lynnfield, Mass. Casement window sash, exterior surface, ca. 1700. *Photo, Richard Merrill, 1960.*

Figure 200B. Buffum house, Salem, Mass., probably seventeenth century. Demolished. Casement window sash, detail of interior surface (with later board reinforcement along upper rail). *Photo, J. David Bohl, 1978.*

Characteristic also is the contract for a parsonage in Beverly in 1657, again a house of central-chimney plan "with a portch of eight foote square and Jetted over one foote ech way," in which it is specified that there will be four windows below and four above and "one in the stodie."[78] The one window in the study was probably located in the second story of the porch, directly above the front entrance. No windows are mentioned in the gable end of the house and the attic here was presumably without illumination. As late as 1702 when the house for the Latin schoolmaster in

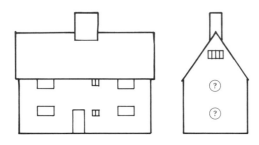
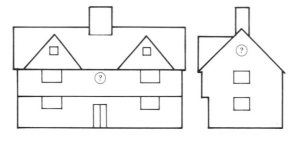

1

2

3

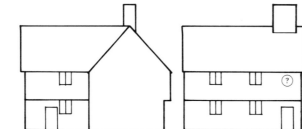
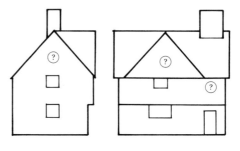

4

5

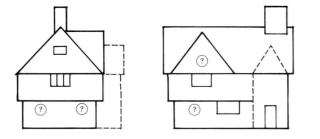
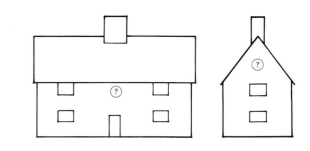

6

7

8

Figure 201. Patterns of fenestration (with indeterminate features indicated by a question mark): 1. Fairbanks house, Dedham, Mass., front and right-hand elevations, ca. 1637; 2. Boardman house, Saugus, Mass., front and right-hand elevations, ca. 1687; 3. Whipple-Matthews house, Hamilton, Mass., front and right-hand elevations, 1680–1683; 4. Paul Revere house, Boston, Mass., front, left-hand, and rear elevations (with angles corrected), ca. 1680; 5. Hooper-Hathaway house, Salem, Mass., front and left-hand elevations, ca. 1682; 6. Ross Tavern, Ipswich, Mass., front and left-hand elevations, late seventeenth century; 7. Browne house, Watertown, Mass., front and right-hand elevations, 1694–1701; 8. George Giddings house, Essex, Mass., front and right-hand elevations, late seventeenth century.

The Framed Houses of Massachusetts Bay

Boston was erected, there were again "two windows in each Roome one in the front and the other at the end," with no reference to illumination in the attic,[79] though it is possible, of course, that smaller attic windows and the small window found typically over the front entrance lighting the second-story entry may have been considered at times too trivial to mention (figure 202).

Normally the window studs in the first and second stories are in vertical alignment. Where the interval between pin holes for studs ranges between fifty-five and sixty-five inches, one can assume the former presence of a three-light window opening. An interval of thirty-five to forty-five or even fifty inches, on the other hand, will suggest a two-light opening (figure 201-5). A measurement of forty-four or forty-five inches is the most common in the latter category, which becomes prevalent in houses erected after 1700. Houses of plank frame construction or houses which have been underboarded before receiving clapboards usually preserve better evidence of fenestration than the framed wall by itself, especially when the studs have been moved about or removed altogether. At the Story house in Essex, openings cut in the planking for three-light windows are perfectly aligned above and below in the front and end walls.

The Whipple-Matthews house in Hamilton, built between 1680 and 1683, was found to have a relatively narrow bank of four-light window openings with transoms in both stories of the front and end walls, at least at the right, and a three-light window opening without transom in the west attic gable end (figure 203). There are additional examples of "transum windowes," as they are described in a Sudbury meetinghouse contract of 1652,[80] and others may be inferred from the documents. In the 1679 John Williams house contract in Boston, for example, the carpenter, James Townsend, was "to make and place four great casement frames in the front of said building, [and] two cleer storey windows in the gables,"[81] and in 1659 Ipswich carpenter William Averill agreed to make "too sto[o]le windows of 5 Lights a peece and t[w]o Claristory windows of 4

Lights a peece"[82] for Richard Jacob. English author Joseph Moxon, writing about 1680, defines the *"Cleer Story Window"* as "Windows that have no Transum in them."[83] If, as implied from the contracts, the transom window was not particularly rare, the physical evidence, on the other hand, is scanty indeed.

While corresponding window openings are normally of the same size, except for the attic story, there were irregular window arrangements in houses of the seventeenth century, most easily explained by the absence of classical canons, which accounted also for the placement a bit off center of the central chimney and front entrance. Lacking formal restraints, the builder and client could follow more purely functional inclinations

Figure 202. Converse house, Woburn, Mass., ca. 1700 (?), with later additions. Demolished 1876. Exterior view, showing original second-story window opening above front entrance.

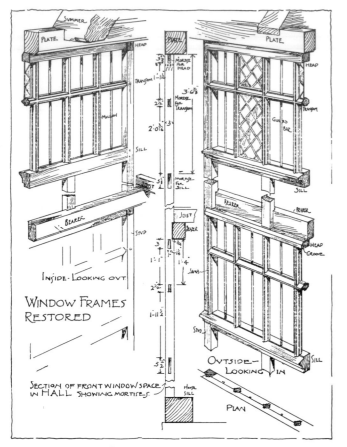

Figure 203. Whipple-Matthews house, Hamilton, Mass. Details of four-light window frame in hall and hall chamber, 1680–1683.

in the visual organization of the house front. The Hooper-Hathaway house in Salem, for example, was furnished with a three-light window opening in the principal room on the ground floor and a two-light opening immediately above it[84] (figure 201-5). The same evidence was found in the end wall of the Captain Thomas Fiske house in Wenham, ca. 1698.[85]

Such irregularities could be brought about also by the exigencies of the framing scheme. Where posts have been introduced for the support of transverse summer beams, for example, windows could not be centered in the front wall. Such is the case at the Ross Tavern in Ipswich, where stud and mortise evidence disclosed a three-light opening of seventy inches to the right of center in the first story of the facade, and above it, but to the left, another three-light opening that was only fifty-nine and three-quarters inches wide. An interval of fifty-nine and a half inches was also found in the gable end wall of this same chamber, while above it in the attic the underboarding had been cut for a two-part window opening forty-four inches in width (figures 186 and 201-6). Here, too, occurred one of the rare examples of a chamber window in a rear wall, the opening being fifty-three and a half inches wide. Similarly, at the Gedney house in Salem, where there is a prick post in the end wall, aesthetic organization of the fenestration was clearly secondary to structural demands. A narrow window in the hall chamber was placed off center immediately to the right of the prick post (figure 264). Further, and reminiscent of the condition at the Fairbanks house, when James Townsend contracted to build a house in Boston for John Williams in 1679, there was no reference to windows in the end walls. One of the workmen testified later, however, that "that end of John Williams his house joining to mrs. Pugliss's could not bee filled because there could not bee boards put up to fill against by reason it stood so neer it."[86] This condition must have been common among houses in crowded urban areas, and one example at least has survived at the Paul Revere house in Boston, where the existence of the Matthew Barnard house,

built about the same time and within a few feet of the gable end, led the builders to install double casements in both stories in the rear wall to compensate for loss of illumination in the end wall (figure 201-4).

Disparity between window sizes as one moved from one story to another or the omission of a window were not the only irregularities in fenestration. Additional windows were inserted as desired. At the Browne house in Watertown a regular pattern of three-light window openings exists in the front and end walls of the first and second stories and in the rear wall of the second story as well. In addition, a small single window of fixed glass was introduced at one end of the house near the front southeast corner post (figure 201-7). Obviously, it had some clearly defined purpose in the client's mind.

In terms of construction, we can easily differentiate between two basic varieties of window, those which were an inherent part of the house frame and those which were constructed separately and applied to it. In the first case the studs, or occasionally a stud and an adjoining post, became the window jambs. Into these were tenoned a header and a sill, which received in turn the tenons of the stout mullions that divided the window into two or more "lights." Sometimes the header was absent, and the mullions were let into a major structural unit, or, as at the Fairbanks house, the headers in the first story were pinned to the bearers. The Fairbanks window frames, however, bear no signs of mullions or other support for glazing, and we are uncertain as to how these details were engineered (figure 58).

The window frames in the gable ends at the Fairbanks house consisted of four-light openings, the overall dimensions from inner face of stud to stud being three feet, nine and a quarter inches and the height from header to sill being a fraction over two feet. The individual lights were originally separated by nicely molded mullions tenoned into the header and sill, which in this case are grooved and rebated to receive the fixed leaded glass (figure 204A and B). There is no such refinement on the studs that form the jambs, however,

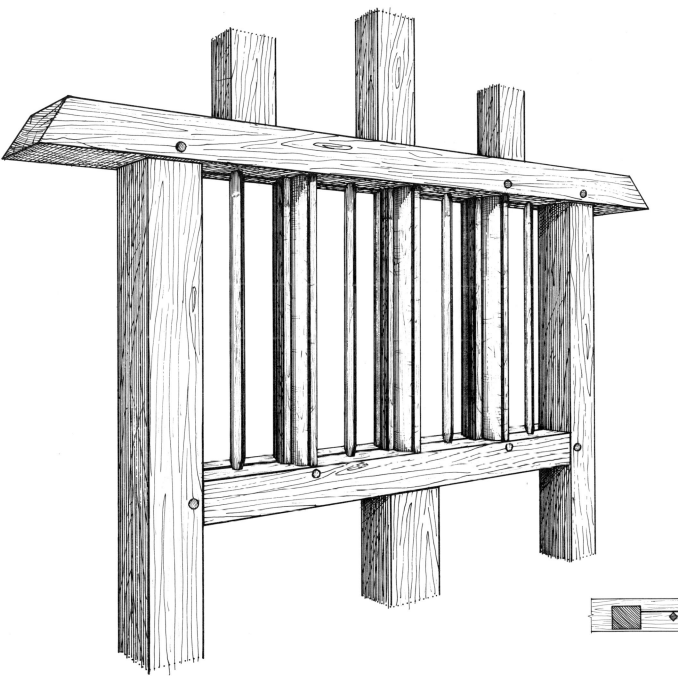

Figure 204A. Fairbanks house, Dedham, Mass. Interior view of four-light window opening, west attic gable end, ca. 1637.

Cross-section showing header

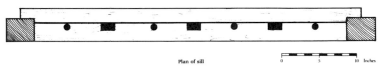

Plan of sill

0   5   10   Inches

Figure 204B. Fairbanks house. Four-light window opening, west attic gable end, plan of sill and cross section showing header.

Figure 205. Browne house, Watertown, Mass. Detail of three-light window opening found upon opening the north wall of earliest chamber, 1694–1701. (Molded mullion at the right has been fully exposed; that at the left remains partially covered.) *Photo (during restoration), F. P. Lemont, 1919.*

outer surface for fixed glass (figure 164). This example and the exceptional window opening in the entry between the first and second stories at the Coffin house in Newbury (which apparently illuminated the stairwell) represent all that we know at present about admitting light into the entry in the first story.

At the Browne house the window header, molded mullions, and sill were rabbeted for glass fixed in the two outer lights of the three-part opening, while the wall studs that form the jambs on either side were not so rabbeted and probably received a strip of wood no longer present that would have performed this service. The inner rabbets of the two mullions received a casement that filled the central opening (figure 205). At the Paul Revere house in Boston the window in the rear wall of the main room was furnished with two casements that came together at the center without the refinement of a mullion. Where any traces of a sill have survived, the careful shaping of this feature reveals that the builders seem to have kept in mind the advice of the English writer Joseph Moxon, who in his treatise on house carpentry about 1680 tells us that "the Rabbets on the Ground-sell [of the window frame] is bevell'd downwards, that Rain or Snow, *etc.* may the freelier fall off it."[87]

Our knowledge of the transom is derived primarily from the example at the Whipple-Matthews house in Hamilton (figure 203), and a single mutilated fragment of a stud or jamb from the Collins-Lord house on High Street in Ipswich. Built probably in the last quarter of the seventeenth century, the stud mortises along the south front of the house indicated an opening some sixty-one inches wide. The single jamb suggests that the height of the window as finished was at least fifty inches. There was a square pintle hole for a casement hinge, and above it a mortise for a transom bar. The transom area was rabbeted for fixed glass, and one or two nails that had been driven into the rabbet on an angle to hold the glass remained in place.

The second variety of window frame was constructed separately and applied to the studs, or

and one assumes that some trim existed here against which the leaded glass could be stopped, or that the glass was simply allowed to butt against the stud itself with nails toed in to hold the glazing in an upright position.

The window frames in the upper and lower entries at the Fairbanks house are two feet wide and eighteen and a half inches high and both made use of the east chimney post and the next adjoining stud for their jambs. The sills were framed into the upright members and the header in the second story was the plate. A single mullion divided each opening into two narrow lights, and there were holes bored in the headers and sills for a single vertical stay bar in the individual lights. The one remaining sill is rabbeted on the

in some cases the planking of the house or even the underboarding. This method of window construction has not been considered common during the seventeenth century. The characteristic physical evidence of the applied window frame, however, is by no means limited, beginning in mid-century at the Gedney house in Salem, where the original studs uniformly fail to reveal any trace of integral window frames. This house was underboarded, and once the requisite openings had been cut out the window frames must have been nailed through the boarding into the studs. Such was the case in the attic of the Ross Tavern in Ipswich, where the studs in the gable end are not mortised but gained for the header and sill or stool of the original two-part window. The top and bottom horns of this applied frame were secured to the gains with two nails (figure 186). Elsewhere in the same structure proper mortises were found in the chamber wall studs into which the original window stools were framed. In the gable end wall the pintle holes on which the hinged casement sash had been hung remained, one in each of the outer openings of a three-part window.

At the Story house in Essex, of planked frame construction, the planking on either side of the window openings in the front and end walls had been cut back or notched to allow the horns of applied window frames, fifty-two to fifty-four and a half inches wide by thirty and a half inches high, to be nailed directly to the underlying wall studs. In this case there seems to have been an additional supportive sill gained into the studs, immediately below the level of the applied sill.

One example, at least, of an early eighteenth-century applied frame was found in 1955, walled in by a later addition in a chamber of the Nathaniel Lord house in Ipswich. This frame, twenty-seven and a half inches wide by forty-three and a half inches high, was set between two studs of the second-story gable end, but not attached to them in any way. Instead, the underboarding alone was nailed to the rabbeted frame from the outside. There were pintle holes in the jambs for hinges, indicating a pair of casements below, and

a transom rabbeted for fixed glass with a single, horizontal stay bar (figure 206). The underside of the sill is grooved to take the upper thin edge of the exterior clapboards. Proper flashing of the joint between the frame of the window and the clapboards was essential, since the attached window frame projected from the surface of the house and was less protected from the elements. Similar evidence exists in a fragmentary window header from the Samuel Pickman House in Salem, erected before 1681.[88] Here the header was deeply rabbeted at one edge to receive the ends of the clapboards or underboarding. An applied frame that survived in place until 1919 in the west attic gable of the French-Andrews House in Topsfield, ca. 1718, was also nailed to the exterior underboarding from the outside through the horns at the corners of the frame. There were pintle holes on the left side only for a single swinging casement. The molded cap was equipped with a well and fitted down over the head of the frame (figure 207). As the eighteenth century wore on this method of window construction became the preferred system, and in an early frame from the Conant house in Townsend Harbor,[89] dating probably to a period early in the second quarter of the eighteenth century, the sill and jambs contain heavy spikes for fastening the frame. The spike, however, does not seem to have been used to any extent for this purpose before 1725.

Concerning the swinging casements themselves, the English form was carried to the New World with little or no modification beyond the widespread acceptance here of pine for the frame. Casements of iron, found so commonly in England, are mentioned from time to time—as, for example, in a Rowley inventory of 1648, "eight Casements of Iron"[90]—and a pile of iron casements of different sizes with leaded glass remained in the attic of the Boardman house in Saugus as late as about 1898.[91] The casement with pine frame was far more common, however, and can be found in all major window openings in the first and second stories at least in part, although the elaborate four-light transom window frames in the front and end walls of the Whipple-

Figure 206. Nathaniel Lord house, Ipswich, Mass. Demolished 1955. Casement window frame found in second-story end wall of first addition to original house, ca. 1725. (Reproduction glazing bar in transom replaces fragments of the original.) *Photo, J. David Bohl, 1978.*

Figure 207. French-Andrews house, Topsfield, Mass. Detail of attic window frame, ca. 1718. *Photo, William Sumner Appleton, 1919.*

Figure 208. Clough-Vernon house (Charter House), Boston, Mass., 1697–1698. Demolished 1931. Casement window sash, interior surface. *Photo, Richard Cheek, 1977.*

Matthews house in Hamilton were apparently entirely of fixed glass. A typical casement, from the Buffum house in Salem, of probable seventeenth-century date, measures twenty-nine inches high by twenty and a quarter inches in width and is fitted with three horizontal stay bars which stiffen and support the glass.[92] Narrow strips of lead are bent around these stay bars and are soldered to the lead "cames" or dividers which hold the individual diamond-shaped panes of glass, measuring characteristically some six inches in height by four and a half inches in width. The hardware, consisting of L-shaped strap hinges and a pivotal latch, is complete (figure 200B).

The first indications of style changes that would affect the construction of windows occur at the turn of the eighteenth century in the urban centers. A casement with wooden muntins or glazing bars and oblong panes of glass from the brick end wall of the otherwise timber-framed Clough-Vernon or Charter house in Boston, 1697–1698,[93] reflects the ambivalence that must have existed in many minds at this time of transition (figure 208). In a somewhat higher socioeconomic bracket, Thomas Banister, a Boston merchant, wrote a year or two later on April 29, 1701, to Thomas Blettsoe, a supplier of merchandise in London, that "tho Sash windows are the newest Fashion I dont so well fancy them as casements." He had seen in Boston "some curious clear glass if I mistake not it is called crown glass. it seems to me to be such as that put before the Diall plate of Clocks. Mr. Eliakim Hutchinson hath glazed the front of his house with it and it looks exceeding well. I have a great mind to have one room or two glazed with that glass." Having noted that he had "other glass Enough for the back side of Said house," he ordered some two hundred feet of the new variety, "not very larg about 6 Inches wide and 8 inches long each square seems to be a very good Size for I purpose to set them in lead and not in wooden frames and to have Iron casements." The windows themselves were to be of a generous size: "four foot broad and six feet long from outside to outside."

Later in the same letter he adds, "having pro-
ceeded thus far I gave my Letter to my son [who had just come "from Colledge"] to Coppy who found fault with my directions about the above mentioned glass which caused a dispute and a resolution to alter the above orders. we now resolve for sash windows." Ambivalence again is borne out by Banister's statement that "I have seen some set in wood and some in Lead. I matter not which way it is done. if it be sett in wood the putty must be very good. if in Lead said Lead must be very thick and extraordinarily well cimmented or by reason of the violence of our storms it will not hold." He directed further that "the glass be all made and set in the Frames ready to put up. . . . One maine reason why I would have it sent ready fitted," he explains, "is that few if any of our workmen know how to doo it."[94] Within just a few years, however, up and down sash windows must have been a far more common sight in Boston. Samuel Sewall, in 1714, records "a great Flash of Lightening" which "Ript off the Clap-boards" of Colonel Vetch's house and "lifted up the Sash window, [and] broke one of the squares." Sewall indicates that the house was apparently undergoing modernization, "though the Work of Transformation be not finished."[95]

The popularity of these changes in fenestration did not take long to reach the country. In 1726 Benjamin Porter of Boxford, joiner, contracted to make an addition to the tenant farmhouse of David Peabody, yeoman, in the same town, and agreed "To make and put up: six windows . . . above and below: three to: a: Rome . . . and all the windows to be of the bigness as they are generaly made now to housing newly built here abouts in the neighbourhood."[96] From this time forward the Boston newspapers regularly distinguish between rectangular and diamond panes of glass and also between qualities, for example, "Newcastle *Glass*"[97] and "*Crown and common Sheet Glass in Crates, and Boxes of* 6 and 4" and "*Diamond cut Common Glass.*"[98] London and Bristol glass and lead were advertised throughout the next two decades and as late as 1752 the Boston papers continued to offer "Dimond" panes and "Bar-Lead."[99] Colonel Timothy
Pickering of Salem recalls that in 1751 the windows of his childhood home, the mid-seventeenth-century Pickering house, "were [newly] glazed with small panes, some diamond-shaped, and the others small oblongs. These were all set in leaden strips, formed thin, with grooves (by a machine made for the purpose) for the reception of the glass."[100] The Reverend William Bentley writes of seeing leaded windows of diamond-shaped glass still in place in older Salem houses in 1794 and 1796,[101] although they must have become an increasing curiosity during the opening years of the nineteenth century, when there was so much rebuilding of earlier structures. The few ancient houses that had escaped more or less unaltered until that time were then given new windows, wallpaper, and fashionable mantels and doorcases. Even when casements were retained, as we find in photographs from about 1860 of the Old Feather Store in Boston and of the Lewis Hunt house in Salem, ca. 1698 (figures 39 and 147), it is only in the attic story. In both cases the casements have square panes set in wooden muntins, and may well represent replacements of original leaded sash.

Only two or three examples of leaded glass survived until the turn of the twentieth century. The first of these is the Keith house in Easton (just outside the Massachusetts Bay area), erected probably in the second quarter of the eighteenth century. The addition of a shed has preserved an original window consisting of two square leaded glass sash which were fixed in an up-and-down position[102] (figure 209). The only known late-surviving example at Massachusetts Bay was in the Cutler house at Woburn, drawn and published by Edwin Whitefield before its destruction late in the nineteenth century and identified by him as "the only old house in which a genuine old-fashioned diamond paned window is still to be seen"[103] (figure 210).

One final consideration is raised by the Easton example, the leaded glass of which is neither fixed in the frame in the traditional manner nor in casements. Rather, it is set in more or less square sash designed for an up-and-down win-

The Framed Houses of Massachusetts Bay

dow frame. The upper sash, though an entity unto itself, was permanently fixed in its rabbet. Only the lower sash could move freely up and down, and there were no pulleys and weights. There is enough evidence in the form of stud locations and consequent control of window openings to suggest that a significant number of otherwise "seventeenth-century" framed houses during the early eighteenth century were incorporating this newer, vertical window concept. The point is of interest if for no other reason than that so many of the leaded glass windows which have survived in public and private collections reveal clearly that they were designed *not* as casements, though commonly so designated, but as sash for up-and-down frames. Many of the more or less square sash we see without hinges but with clear indications on two sides of having been protected by the rabbet of an up-and-down frame may well be retarded survivals from the second quarter of the eighteenth century. In any event, it is a matter of no small interest that while at least five leaded glass window sash of the rectangular fixed (or sliding) variety as well as casements survived in the attic loft of New England's oldest framed dwelling, the Fairbanks house in Dedham, where they had been stored, not a single one fits the extensive window evidence revealed in the fabric of the house as first built. These sash, then, take on even greater significance as mute witnesses of successive changes in fenestration extending perhaps until the middle of the eighteenth century or even later, but preserving in this conservative rural hamlet the characteristic glazing of the seventeenth century, consisting for the most part of diamond-shaped panes of glass set in lead.

Figure 210. Cutler house, Woburn, Mass., ca. 1700 (?). Demolished 1896.

CHAPTER IX

Interior Finish

IF THE EXPOSED exterior members of the house frame were often thought a suitable field for carved embellishment in a continuing medieval and postmedieval English tradition, this was equally the case with the interior exposed surfaces of the frame. Almost totally lacking, on the other hand, was the English penchant, still current in the mid-seventeenth century in conservative situations, for cutting and arranging the individual frame members in decorative patterns (figure 137). One of the few exceptions at Massachusetts Bay can be found in the Wenham area where, at the very end of the seventeenth century, a single individual or school made use of the S-curve in fashioning wall braces. These occur entirely in connection with houses of plank frame construction, and as seen at the Captain Thomas Fiske house in Wenham, ca. 1698, are outlined against the plaster wall surface, adding immeasurably to the decorative quality of the room (figure 211).

Elsewhere the embellishment of the frame was confined to the carved and incised decoration of the individual units. The commonest of these was the chamfer and the most elaborate was the molded post head. There were at least three distinctive types of chamfer, with their variations. The simplest, universal form was the plain cham-

fer, whereby the sharp right-angle edge of a major structural unit, including posts, was rendered oblique with the aid of a drawknife (figure 212-1). The same treatment occurs commonly with floor joists as well in sixteenth-century England. For Massachusetts Bay the only known full-blown example is at the Fairbanks house in Dedham, ca. 1637 (figure 213), though one often finds on close examination that the otherwise sharp edges of the exposed floor joists have been perceptibly softened by a miniscule chamfer little more than an eighth or three sixteenths of an inch in width (figure 214).

Less common was the quarter-round chamfer, which because of its greater elaboration was naturally a more expensive decoration. For that reason it was not only found mainly in the more pretentious houses (though it seems to have been favored by many individuals who thought they could afford it) but also confined to a principal frame member, almost invariably the summer beam, while other units in the same room were given plain chamfers. Variations of this form occur at the Coffin and Swett-Ilsley houses in Newbury, ca. 1654 and ca. 1670, respectively, and the Blake house in Dorchester, ca. 1650, in which the quarter-round chamfers have an additional fillet (figures 212-2 and 214).

Much more rare was the interior chamfer of cyma profile, of which an almost comprehensive catalogue includes the Capen house in Dorchester, erected probably before 1658, the Cooper-Frost-Austin house in Cambridge, ca. 1689, and the later half of the Whipple house in Ipswich, added before 1683 (figure 212-5 and -4). Known also in only two or three examples at Massachusetts Bay is the diminutive cyma molding executed at the edge of and parallel with the surface of the beams of the Haskell house in West Gloucester, erected probably early in the eighteenth century, and the Witch house, so-called, in nearby Rockport, ca. 1700 (figure 115).

In the case of all chamfers, plain or decorated, it was customary to arrest the molding at each end with a "stop" before it ran into an intersecting timber. While a large variety of chamfer stops have been noted for the medieval and postmedieval periods in England,[1] the range is much more restricted for Massachusetts Bay (figure 212). There are, in fact, only a handful of profiles, the plainest of which is the taper stop (figure 215). More elaborate is the lamb's tongue stop, sometimes augmented with an incised diamond-shaped cut or pip just beyond the head of the stop, the earliest example of which can be found at the Fairbanks house in Dedham. When the

Figure 211. Capt. Thomas Fiske house (Claflin-Richards house, so-called), Wenham, Mass. Left-hand room, ca. 1698. *Photo, J. David Bohl, 1978.*

quarter-round profile is employed, the lamb's tongue stop is normally separated from the chamfer by a flat band or collar. For the quarter-round chamfers with additional fillet at the Coffin, Swett-Ilsley, and Blake houses, it is possible to suggest an origin for the carpenters in the south central counties of England. Similarly in Hingham, the presence unique to this community of incised V-shaped lines in the collar of the lamb's tongue stop may well be taken as the signature of a carpenter or local school (figure 212-6).

There is evolutionary significance as well in the decoration of the interior house frame. The chamfer with its stop, having become a hallmark of seventeenth-century work, begins to give way late in the period to the quirked bead (figure 215). Appearing no earlier that the late 1690s, this profile became common during the first quarter of the eighteenth century, and lingered thereafter among conservative builders. At the Parker Tavern in Reading, ca. 1725, clear evidence remains in the attic stairwell for the way in which the quirked bead was fashioned with an incising tool and knife.

Nor is the quirked bead the only indication of a late date with respect to the molded house frame. Quarter-round and cyma chamfers disappear al-

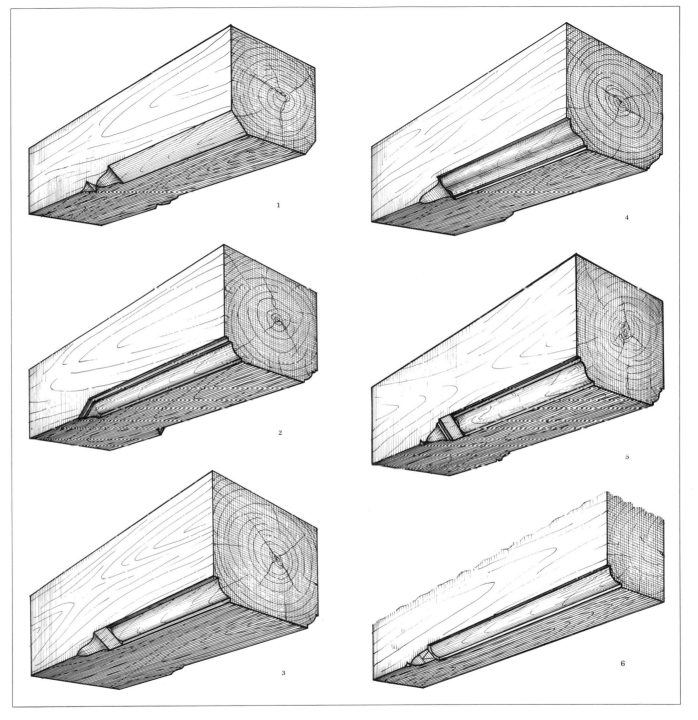

Figure 212. Details of chamfers and chamfer stops: 1. Fairbanks house, Dedham, Mass., hall summer tie beam, ca. 1637; 2. Coffin house, Newbury, Mass., summer tie beam, earliest chamber, ca. 1654; 3. Whipple house, Ipswich, Mass., hall summer beam, ca. 1655; 4. Whipple house, Ipswich, Mass., parlor summer beam, before 1683; 5. Cooper-Frost-Austin house, Cambridge, Mass., hall summer beam, ca. 1689; 6. Cushing house, Hingham, Mass., original collar beam, right-hand chamber, 1679.

Figure 213. Fairbanks house, Dedham, Mass. Detail of summer tie beam and joists, hall chamber, ca. 1637. *Photo, Richard Merrill, 1968.*

together soon after 1700, and the plain chamfers of the first quarter of the eighteenth century tend to be thin and anemic. They are finished usually with little more than an inelaborate taper stop, almost as though the builders were losing interest (figure 215). As the earliest expression of Renaissance vernacular forms, in particular the casing of the house frame, appeared in the urban centers and began to spread, the quirked bead and puny chamfer were restricted increasingly to the work of conservative builders and to less ambitious houses. The exposed and decorated frame was already a thing of the past in the more forward-looking houses of the early eighteenth century. Moreover, in such interesting transitional examples as the Parson Barnard house in North Andover, ca. 1715, any sense of "decline" present in the quirked beading and thin chamfers was quite offset by the impact of juxtaposing within the same rooms a rich display of applied finish trim that foreshadowed the upcoming academic styles. Such expressions will scarcely have been labeled as "transitional" by their creators, yet here is that understandably human looking forward and backward at the same time which so often gives to any watershed moment in the study of art history its salient interest.

The molding of the post head tends to be confined to houses with transverse summer beams supported by posts, and hence geographically to the Salem-Beverly-Peabody-Danvers area and towns to the north in Essex County. There are exceptions, for example at the Blake house in Dorchester, where one finds an unusual situation with prick posts supporting longitudinal summer beams in both stories. Here the flare of the post head is robustly decorated (figure 141), and having been fashioned at an early date and undoubtedly by first-generation carpenters, reveals that the practice was soon rooted at Massachusetts Bay. Elaborate examples of the molded post head on the North Shore can be found at the Samuel Pickman house in Salem, built before 1681 (figure 134), and the Balch house in Beverly, of undetermined seventeenth-century date (figure 216). The treatment, on the other hand, can be relatively

Figure 214. Blake house, Dorchester, Mass. Detail of parlor summer beam and joists, ca. 1650. *Photo, Richard Merrill, 1967.*

Figure 215. Parson Barnard house, North Andover, Mass. Detail of summer tie beam and supporting post, parlor chamber, ca. 1715. *Photo, William W. Owens, Jr., 1974.*

Figure 216. Balch house, Beverly, Mass. Detail of hall summer beam and supporting post, seventeenth century. *Photo, William W. Owens, Jr., 1974.*

simple, even in such ambitious structures as the Corwin house in Salem, ca. 1675 (figure 217).

Of the various forms of finish trim which render the house frame habitable and attractive, the floor was at once the least glamorous and most necessary. Chamber floor boards of the sixteenth- and early seventeenth-century English house were at times considered, along with the glazing, as furnishings or movables, and thus not secured to the frame.[2] By the time of which we write the concept seems to have been pretty well superseded and the rare seventeenth-century references to loose floor boards at Massachusetts Bay seem to refer rather to an unfinished or perhaps even a shiftless condition.[3] By 1680 the urban English carpenter at least was given explicit directions for securing the floor boards to the frame.[4] It is Moxon's London treatise, in fact, that furnishes an explanation for a situation which has often led the architectural investigator astray,

namely, the even way in which lengths of floor boards have been pieced out when necessary. Intelligent reasons have been sought: the regular line of cut has been said to suggest the former existence of a partition, for instance, or even a stairwell. Yet Moxon tells us that "if the [floor] Boards are not long enough to reach athwart the whole Room, the ends may all lye in a straight Line, that the straight ends of other Boards laid against them may make the truer Joint, and this they call a *Beaking Joint.*"[5]

Native pine was rapidly adopted and became the almost invariable material for flooring. By and large the second story and attic floorboards have demonstrated a high survival rate, testifying to the suitability of softwood in these situations. The

Interior Finish

Figure 217. Corwin house, Salem, Mass. Detail of parlor summer beam and supporting post, ca. 1675. *Photo, Peter Zaharis, 1964.*

the floor joists were connected by oak pins like the rounds of a ladder and fitted into holes well towards the bottom of the floor joists. . . . On top of these pins were placed oak boards and on top of these, that is, filling the space between these oak boards and the under side of the floor boards, was a filling of clay and chopped straw.[6]

It became apparent in another case, when the Story house in Essex, ca. 1684, was being demolished, that the wall plaster of the original chamber had been applied to the planking of the frame from plate to girt before the floors were laid. This would imply the loose laying of boards as a platform basis for operations, while in the late seventeenth-century Ross Tavern in Ipswich, the girts were finished along their upper inner surface with a rabbet to receive the edges of the floorboards (figure 170). This refinement, which occurs in earlier English work, has not been noted elsewhere at Massachusetts Bay.

Few elements in the seventeenth-century house were as starkly functional as the staircase. At the vernacular level the builders generally allotted for their entries no more space than was necessary for circulation from one room to another. In New England, where the entry and stairs were usually combined, this left only a minimum of space for the principal staircase, which was crowded up against the chimney. Composed at times entirely of narrow winders and steep in pitch, the average stairs in the earliest houses of New England could boast only indifferent success in achieving vertical ascent within the least possible amount of space. Fully enclosed, they were further robbed of any advantages that natural light might have thrown upon the problem. Not until the final quarter of the seventeenth century, for the rural house at least, did this feature take its first hesitating steps in a significant evolution which would culminate in the broad, ornamental staircases of the eighteenth century and the graceful circular flights of the Federal period.

We cannot begin to know how large a proportion of the first houses were furnished with a

Figure 218. Gedney house, Salem, Mass. Detail of original stairwell sheathing, ca. 1665, with later stairs and paneled door to cellar. *Photo, William W. Owens, Jr., 1974.*

roughly inch-thick boards were consistently laid in single layers, ranging in average width of individual boards from fifteen to twenty inches, with their whitewashed undersides (occasionally lathed and plastered between the joists) forming the ceilings in the rooms and chambers below. Half-lap joints have been found, though a simple butt joint seems to have been acceptable, and on more than one occasion evidence in the court records turns upon what was seen and heard through cracks in the floor. The normally more heavy wear and tear in the ground story has reduced the amount of original flooring there. In one instance at least, insulation seems to have been intended for the west parlor of the Parson Capen house in Topsfield, 1683, when it was found that

staircase, and how many made shift with the more primitive arrangement of a ladder. As late as 1685 there is reference to a constable mounting a ladder to get to the chamber of one John Williams's house in Marblehead.[7] While this condition was probably not uncommon, especially in the very simple cottages built before and during the middle of the seventeenth century, it is significant that those houses which have come down to us from the second half of the seventeenth century invariably include provisions for a staircase. The Fairbanks house stands alone among the extant buildings in preserving some structural evidence that there may originally have been no stairs from the first to the second story, as there never have been from the second story to the attic.

The staircase has always been vulnerable to renewal because of the concentrated wear it receives and for reasons purely stylistic. As a focal point upon entering the house, it was very apt to be up-dated—or simply rebuilt to render it more commodious. The number of original examples, therefore, is severely limited. Among the earliest houses, the staircase from the first to the second floor, whether composed partially or altogether of winders, is invariably a single straight run, enclosed. While the present stairs at the Gedney house in Salem, ca. 1665, are of later date, the original enclosing wall has survived, composed of unmolded vertical boards. The stairs were entered at the right, and the single post in which the treads were housed is tenoned into the joist overhead and furnished with pintle holes for hinges, revealing that the staircase was further

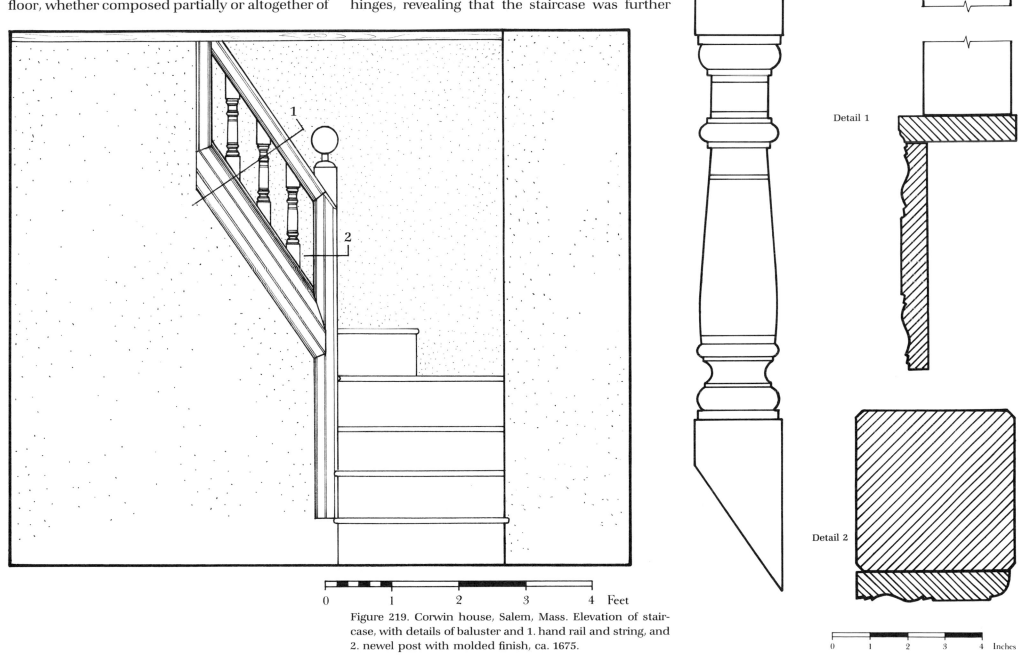

Figure 219. Corwin house, Salem, Mass. Elevation of staircase, with details of baluster and 1. hand rail and string, and 2. newel post with molded finish, ca. 1675.

Interior Finish

163

Figure 220. Parson Capen house, Topsfield, Mass. Detail of staircase, 1683. *Photo, William W. Owens, Jr., 1974.*

Figure 221. Benaiah Titcomb house, Newburyport, Mass. Detail of staircase, probably after 1700. *Photo, George E. Noyes, before 1911.*

shut off with a door (figure 218). Similar evidence for a door closing off an enclosed staircase has been found at the Paine-Dodge house in Ipswich, built after 1700, but this late example is conservative. Elsewhere the long process of elaboration had already begun.

The first steps away from an enclosed staircase in the house of central-chimney plan had assuredly been taken in Boston in houses no longer extant. Yet the earliest authentic example of stair balusters is not until about 1675 at the Corwin house in Salem. Entered from the right, the single run of stairs ascends steeply with three pie-shaped winders at the bottom. Despite the high style and fine quality of this ambitious house built for a successful merchant near the center of town, the exchange of an enclosing wall for an open balustrade is nevertheless hesitant. The open space itself is abbreviated and is sufficient

only for three short stubby turned balusters. Both the closed string and railing, however, are broadly molded and the newel post has been finished with a continuation of the same molding, an unexpected refinement (figure 219).

This example was followed soon by a similar staircase in the house built in Topsfield by the town's minister, the Reverend Joseph Capen, in 1683. The single flight of stairs is once again entered from the right with three winders at the bottom. The sense of spaciousness is somewhat increased over that of the Corwin house, and the four turned balusters are slimmer and longer. Curiously, however, the newel with its shaped finial, supported on a slim square stock, has not been correspondingly increased in height, with the result that the descending rail of the balustrade is awkwardly housed in the finial itself (figure 220).

From these tentative beginnings, the development of the balustrade moved slowly at first, even in the finer houses of the period. At the Benaiah Titcomb house in Newburyport, built probably after 1700, the staircase is also conspicuous for its short stubby balusters—if anything, less academic in profile than those of either the Corwin or Capen houses. Yet this staircase is at least more open in its proportions and is furnished with three unusually wide winders at the foot of a single flight which is entered from the left. While there is no important advancement in form present in this example, executed in the opening years of the eighteenth century, there is additional elaboration in the half balusters applied at the upper end of the balustrade and to the newel, the edges of which have been nicely chamfered and stopped. Further, the railing is heavily molded on both sides, a symmetrical arrangement which foreshadows later developments inasmuch as the railing continues to be molded on the outer side only during the early period. The most interesting and by no means common feature, however, is the sheathing with broad applied moldings, which create the impression of sunken wainscot paneling so familiar in the seventeenth-century English house (figure 221).

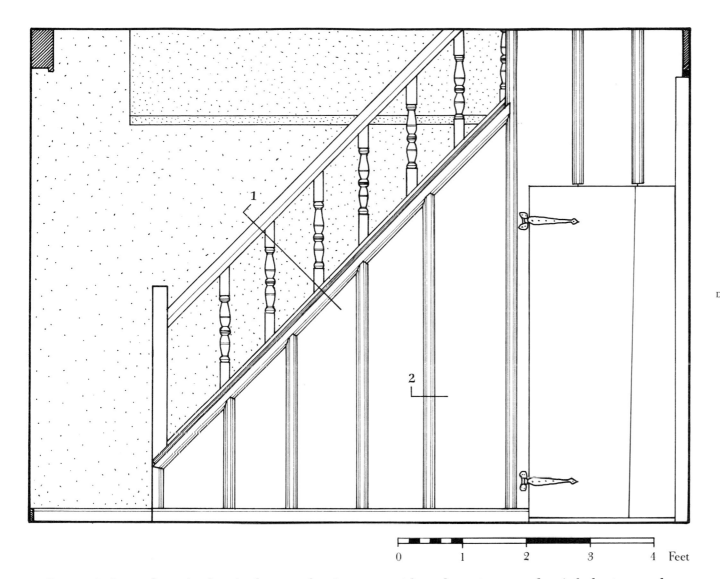

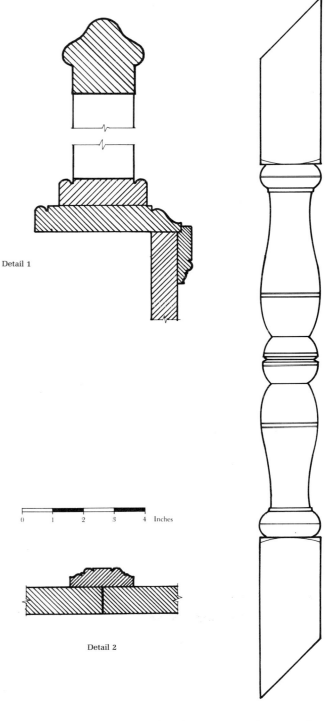

Detail 1

Detail 2

0 1 2 3 4 Feet

0 1 2 3 4 Inches

One variation at least in the single run of stairs with open balustrade can be found in the Captain Matthew Perkins house in Ipswich, built between 1701 and 1709, which in other respects is similar to that in the Benaiah Titcomb house. Here the molded strips applied to the sheathing are vertical only and thus provide for a less complex pattern of "paneling." The newel is unchamfered and the railing simply molded, again on both sides. The customary winders at the bottom, however, have been omitted, and instead one begins the ascent within the stairwell itself. The balustrade is brought down to within a few inches of the floor, and being that much longer

provides adequate space for six balusters and one half baluster, at least, at the upper end (figure 222). In both the Titcomb and Perkins houses the sheathing has been furnished with doors giving access to the cellar stairs. For the earlier years these stairs, located under the run from first to second story, are normally entered from the adjoining room through a door in the fireplace wall.

By far the most developed staircases are those of the early eighteenth-century Parson Barnard house in North Andover and the White-Ellery house in Gloucester (figures 223 and 224), both of them structures erected by influential minis-

Figure 222. Capt. Matthew Perkins house, Ipswich, Mass. Elevation of staircase, with details of baluster and 1. hand rail and string, and 2. batten of sheathing, 1701–1709.

Interior Finish

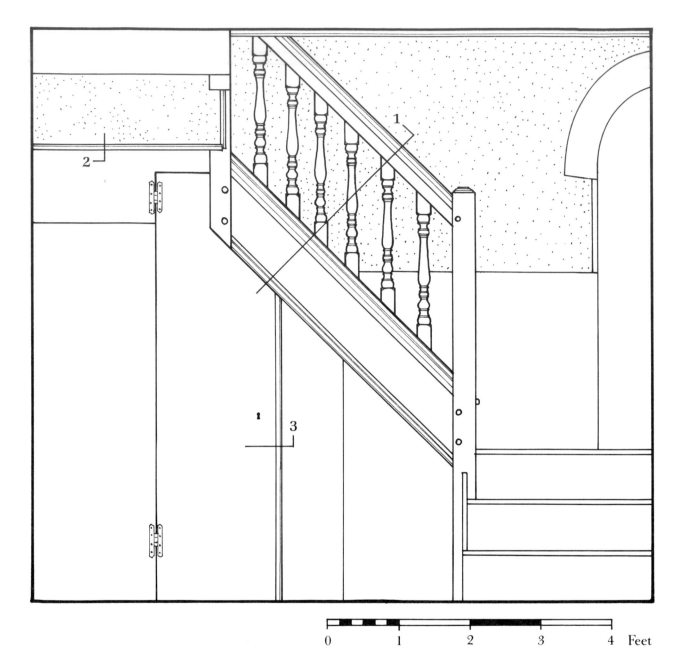

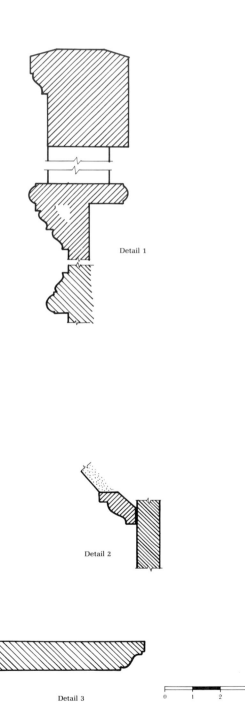

Detail 1

Detail 2

Detail 3

0   1   2   3   4   Feet

0   1   2   3   4   Inches

Figure 223. Parson Barnard house, North Andover, Mass. Elevation of staircase, with details of baluster and 1. hand rail and string, 2. trim which stops plaster on soffit of upper run of stairs, and 3. molding of door to closet under stairs, ca. 1715.

ters who occupied an important position in the community. While the balusters are housed in a closed string instead of resting on the individual stair treads, as will later be the case, there is a step forward in purely stylistic terms in the vase-shaped profile of the balusters, which are much less stubby than their predecessors, greater in number, and more regularly spaced. Even more significant, however, is the fact that the form is now that of the triple run staircase punctuated with landings, rendering the ascent that less steep. While these examples just after 1700 are the earliest surviving representatives of a new sophistication, acceptance of the form itself had apparently occurred somewhat earlier in the urban setting. The Matthew Barnard house in Boston's North Square, ca. 1680, seems to have been furnished with a staircase of triple run,[8] and, importantly, the Appleton-Taylor-Mansfield house in Saugus, ca. 1680, and nearby Boardman house, ca. 1687, reveal structurally that they were designed originally for staircases which must have been of triple run (and such has been restored at the Appleton-Taylor-Mansfield House). In both cases, distinct connections with the metropolitan area can be argued in terms of the backgrounds of the men for whom these forward-looking houses were built. No other rural examples of the triple run staircase are known until after 1700. Nor, while undoubtedly present in Boston, do we have examples of the twisted Baroque baluster popular in English buildings of the later seventeenth century, and found also in the Wentworth house in nearby Portsmouth, New Hampshire, ca. 1700.[9] The early and interesting staircase of three individual runs with twisted balusters and vine carving in the Norden house in Marblehead, built between 1680 and 1687, is a relatively modern intrusion and problematical in terms of provenance.

The stairs from the second floor to the attic were either closed or open, and were almost invariably situated over the main staircase. While normally composed of a single run which gave access to one end of the attic or the other, there are a number of attic staircases that begin their

Figure 224. White-Ellery house, Gloucester, Mass. Detail of staircase, ca. 1710. *Photo, William W. Owens, Jr., 1974.*

Figure 225. Boardman house, Saugus, Mass. Detail of attic staircase, ca. 1687. *Photo, William W. Owens, Jr., 1973.*

ascent in the center of the upper entry and are furnished with a landing against the chimney from which the stairs divide and rise on either side. This arrangement, of obviously greater convenience, is found as early as about 1687 in the relatively ambitious Boardman house in Saugus, and thereafter in more modest structures (figure 225). In one case at least, the Caldwell house in Ipswich, erected probably after 1709, the first run is almost ladderlike in its steepness (figure 226).

Cellars were occasionally entered through trap doors in the ground floor, and such seems to have been the original condition in the eastern end of the Parson Capen house in Topsfield as

late as 1683. More commonly, however, the cellars were reached by stairs located underneath the main file of stairs in front of the chimney. Only in a very few cases have stairs to the cellar survived, and among these a significant number are of the triangular log variety. Henry Thoreau took note of this fact as early as 1859, when the old Hunt house in Concord, built probably in the last quarter of the seventeenth century, was demolished. On March 14 he recorded that he "saw E. Hosmer take up the cellar stairs. They are of white oak . . . sawed diagonally. These lie flat on their broadest sides on the slanting earth, resting near each end on a horse, which is a white

Figure 226. Caldwell house, Ipswich, Mass. Detail of attic staircase, probably after 1709. *Photo, Peter Zaharis, 1955.*

oak stick with the bark on, hewed on the upper side and sunk in the earth, and they are fastened to this by two pins of wood."[10] Among the better preserved examples, still in situ, at least in part, are those in the cellar stairwell in front of the chimney stack at the Boardman house in Saugus (figure 31). Like the stairs of the Hunt house, they are bedded in the slanting earth. The form itself was in use for stairs above the ground level before the end of the sixteenth century in English vernacular houses,[11] at which time it begins to be replaced by the framed staircase (except in very rural areas). In only a few instances, for example the Narbonne house in Salem, ca. 1672, the Burnham house in Essex, ca. 1685-1695, and the later Hovey-Boardman house in Ipswich, ca. 1710-1720, are the cellar stairs of stone.

The house frame, covering, chimney, floors, and stairs were essential components without which the house would have failed in its fundamental purpose. Wall finish, on the other hand, was to some extent optional, and raised almost at once a philosophical question concerning worldly superfluities. Robert Cushman, for one, wrote of the nearby Plymouth settlement in 1620 that "our purpose is to build for the present such houses as, if need be, we may with little grief set afire and run away by the light. Our riches shall not be in pomp but in strength."[12] Winthrop's biographers have not failed to discover in the personality of the governor at Massachusetts Bay—a man older than most of the immigrant colonists —austerity and an aversion to frivolity, traits that explain the sharp exchange that took place between him and his deputy governor. It is Winthrop himself who reports the incident in 1632, noting that he had criticized Thomas Dudley for bestowing "such cost about wainscotting and adorning his house, in the beginning of a plantation, both in regard of the necessity of public charges, and for example, etc., [and] his answer now was, that it was for the warmth of his house, and the charge was little, being but clapboards nailed to the wall in the form of wainscot."[13] The distinction which Dudley

introduced between insulation and adornment surfaces again in 1652 when one Goodman Whittredge of Ipswich was directed to repair a house which he rented, "as much as was needful for warmth and as two men should judge; but if he laid out more than was needful, for ornament, he was to bear the cost himself."[14]

Surely there was a stark simplicity in many seventeenth-century interiors, or an omission of finish trim altogether, related, perhaps, more often to reasons of economy or specific domestic functions than philosophical considerations. Despite the fact that some of our finest finish trim of the seventeenth century will be found in the second-story chambers, for example, those at the Boardman house in Saugus, each with a fireplace and furnished, according to an inventory of 1696, with expensive bedsteads, tables, chests, and chairs,[15] there are also quite different situations. The Fairbanks house in Dedham presents another picture, one which can be matched elsewhere during the colonial period and, indeed, well into the nineteenth century. Here the hall chamber at the left was never furnished with a fireplace. An inventory of 1668 enumerates contents for this room that hardly suggest a polite usage or the need for elaborate trim: "many small tooles for turning and other the like worke," sheeps' wool, "Cotton woole," linen and cotton yarn, tubs, keelers, sieves and "small Lumber" (odds and ends), scales and weights, and "Hops in a bag."[16]

The Boardman and Fairbanks inventories represent a seeming correlation with the physical evidence. For rural Suffolk County, between 1675 and 1725, there are a total of fifty-three room-by-room inventories on file, eight of which have one chamber or another that lacks any indication of a fireplace and is given over primarily to storage of food stuffs and provisions. However, there are twenty-nine rooms that include bedding as well as storage, indicating some occupancy at least, which also reveal an absence of fireplace tools. These statistics may have more social than architectural significance, and the corroborative physical evidence is meager. Successive changes in the name of efficiency and fashion have obliterated in all too many cases the ephemeral finish trim of the seventeenth century, and only a fraction of the inventories can be associated with specific surviving houses.

In other parts of the house, simplicity or omission of finish trim is readily understandable. The attic, including the lean-to attic, was almost invariably left unfinished, despite the fact that these areas were often occupied. While the mason's contract for the Corwin house in Salem in 1675 specifies a fireplace in the attic, the Captain Matthew Perkins house in Ipswich contains the only unrestored example that has been identified. In addition to the fireplace in a recess finished with simple trim, the gable end was roughly plastered as well. The roof construction, however, remained exposed (figures 227 and 122).

Equally interesting as a phenomenon are those important rooms in the house left unfinished for reasons of expediency or expense. Known examples are confined almost entirely to chambers and are few in number. They are of startling significance, however, in light of the time span during which the condition was allowed to persist, especially when combined with trim of the highest order. An outstanding example is the Boardman house in Saugus, the hall chamber of which contains the most ambitious trim in the entire structure and yet remained partially unfinished through each successive generation of Boardman family occupancy. The frame was nicely chamfered and the fireplace wall sheathed with fine molded boards, but the three outer walls as late as 1914 had never been plastered and the rear wall with its brick and clay fill, and with one stud curiously aslant, preserves this condition today. The entire surface had been whitewashed occasionally and finally (in the nineteenth century) painted green (figure 228).

A later example existed in the more modest dwelling in Saugus built by a grandson of the first Willian Boardman, probably in the 1740s. The house in nearly every aspect of form and finish looked backward, in addition to which the farming families who lived there through the years never got around to finishing the left-hand cham-

ber. Again the studs and wall fill were bare of any other cover than a coat of whitewash (figure 229), and there was no fireplace.

In most houses of the seventeenth century, however, we recognize an early and consistent desire to clothe the frame, to some degree at least, with surface trim. The normal procedure, both upstairs and down, was an application of plaster on riven lath to the three outer walls of a room and the introduction of vertical board sheathing for the inner, fireplace wall. Original plaster walls of puddled clay and chopped straw have on rare occasions survived to the present day and were characteristically finished with a coat of whitewash or a thin skim coat of white plaster (figure 230). In many more cases they have been preserved behind later walls, particularly those introduced during the period of great rebuilding after the Revolution.

Figure 227. Capt. Matthew Perkins house, Ipswich, Mass. Detail of attic fireplace (later bricked in and plastered over), with traces of original plaster on side wall of recess, 1701–1709. *Photo, Peter Zaharis, 1955.*

Figure 228. Boardman house, Saugus, Mass. Detail of rear wall, hall chamber, ca. 1687. *Photo, J. David Bohl, 1978.*

forward-looking structures as the Parson Barnard house in North Andover and persists even later in conservative houses.

Plaster was also used for other minor details of finish. In the right-hand chamber of the Boardman house in Saugus, the brickwork above the mantel shelf was left exposed. Where the slant of the chimney at the back left a large, roughly triangular gap between the stack and the wall sheathing, a board was cut and fitted into the aperture and its surface roughened to receive a skim coat of plaster. And despite the unfinished condition of the walls in this same chamber, an even thicker skim coat of plaster was applied directly to the surface of one or two courses of brick which were laid on top of the plates here and in the left-hand chamber to close the gap between the top of the wall and underside of the attic floor boards (figure 256). More often, this gap was closed by means of a molded wooden coverboard, and at the late seventeenth-century George Giddings house in Essex and the Gedney house in Salem, the coverboard above the plate was lathed and plastered.

Later windows have obliterated all but the most fugitive evidence of finish trim around original openings in plaster walls. At the Paul Revere house in Boston, ca. 1680, the studs that form the jambs of an original casement frame preserved in the rear wall by a later addition were covered with a strip of molded finish trim rebated at its outer edge to receive the sash and projecting beyond the inner face of the stud to act as a stop for the plaster of the wall. Less sophisticated conditions as revealed in the three-light opening at the Browne house in Watertown involve the application of a strip of wood (now missing) to the frame against which the plaster of the wall was stopped, leaving the rest of the stud exposed (figure 205). The complete casement frame with transom, dating probably to about 1725, from the Nathaniel Lord house in Ipswich is another rare example that preserves at the outer edge of the frame small fragments of vertical trim. These reveal the presence of a rabbet which presumably received the ends of hori-

The laths, whether applied directly to the studs or to vertical planking, were apt to be of hard wood and were riven in single lengths (figures 114 and 233). Normal spacing was from one to three inches apart to allow the course clay and straw to secure a good purchase. In some examples lime plaster was used alone, as at the Browne house in Watertown, erected between 1694 and 1701, where the plaster was applied directly to the surface of the stud and brick-filled wall without laths. Here the studs were nicked or roughened to secure the plaster (figure 231). In all cases the plaster wall finish came down to the floor or exposed sill without the refinement of a baseboard. This condition is still found in such ambitious

Figure 229. Boardman-Howard house, Saugus, Mass. Parlor chamber, ca. 1740–1750. (Frame dismantled and re-erected in Boxford, Mass.) *Photo, Richard Merrill, 1954.* (Left)

Figure 230. Coffin house, Newbury, Mass. Detail of summer tie beam and wall finish of clay and chopped straw with skim-coat of plaster or whitewash, earliest chamber, ca. 1654. *Photo, Richard Merrill, 1967.* (Above)

zontal sheathing boards rather than lath and plaster, owing to the absence of plaster burn marks.

Typically throughout the seventeenth century the front wall of the brick chimney stack as it appeared in the stairwell was exposed and sometimes whitewashed. Not until quite late do we find this surface finished in any other way. One of the earliest examples of an effort to conceal the brickwork is the Parson Barnard house in North Andover, where the chimney stack was plastered directly upon the brick and further embellished

with a painted decoration. A similar surface treatment of the earlier chimney stack in the stairwell of the Narbonne house in Salem dates also, in all likelihood, to the early eighteenth century.

Fireplace walls of lath and plaster, found commonly in the English seventeenth-century house, are quite rare at Massachusetts Bay during the same period. Nearly all examples, in fact, occur in Salem. For the Corwin house the mason, Daniel Andrews, agreed in 1675 "to Lath and plaister the partitions of the house with Clay and lime,"[17] while at the Narbonne house there is only the

Figure 231. Browne house, Watertown, Mass. Earliest chamber (rear wall at left), 1694–1701. *Photo (during restoration), F. P. Lemont, 1919.*

tered and molded trim flush with the plaster surface (figure 232). Behind the eighteenth-century paneled chimney breast was found the original fireplace opening, with a shaped and beaded enframement that covered the lintel and extended originally to cover the piers as well. All of this wooden trim was located in a recess no deeper than an inch or two, and the area directly above the fireplace, like the rest of the wall, was lathed and plastered (figure 233).

With the exception of the outer walls of the room, however, the readily available mill-sawn pine was used more commonly than any other material for interior finish at Massachusetts Bay. There is board finish, in fact, in the chamber of the Samuel Pickman house with the plastered fireplace wall. The interval between the end tie beam and the underside of the attic floor boards is closed with molded horizontal sheathing in single-board lengths. The individual molded boards are cut to fit around the floor joists and leave exposed the lower portions of the chamfered frame. Coverboards have been found more consistently than any other form of finish at the junction of frame members with the attic floor, and some form of creased molding is apt to be present during the seventeenth century (figure 131). During the first quarter of the eighteenth century the quirked bead, ranging in width from one half to three-quarters of an inch, becomes the more common adornment. All examples stop short of the exposed lower surface of the plate, with its almost invariable carved decoration, until the 1720s and later, when, in anticipation of newer style trends, the coverboard will occasionally extend to the very bottom of the unchamfered frame member. In the chamber of the Browne house in Watertown, the coverboard is joined at right angles by a molded board which extends flat-wise to the joist nearest to the plates, thus forming a rudimentary boxed cornice (figure 234). Nothing similar is known at Massachusetts Bay.

The vertical sheathing of the fireplace wall, usually molded, was normally related to the chamfered chimney girt with its supporting posts

mute testimony of lath nails and plaster burn marks discovered on the surface of the wall studs beneath later trim. The most interesting example, however, occurs in the principal chamber of the Samuel Pickman house in Salem with its four handsomely carved post heads. The laths were secured to thin vertical stavelike furring strips, five and a half inches wide and spaced more than a foot apart, which were face-lapped into the chimney girt. These strips served as a foundation for the elaborately mitered and molded trim of the doorways leading into the upper entry and the space behind the chimney, the trim so placed as to form a rebate for the doors. On either side of the fireplace were two small cupboards with mi-

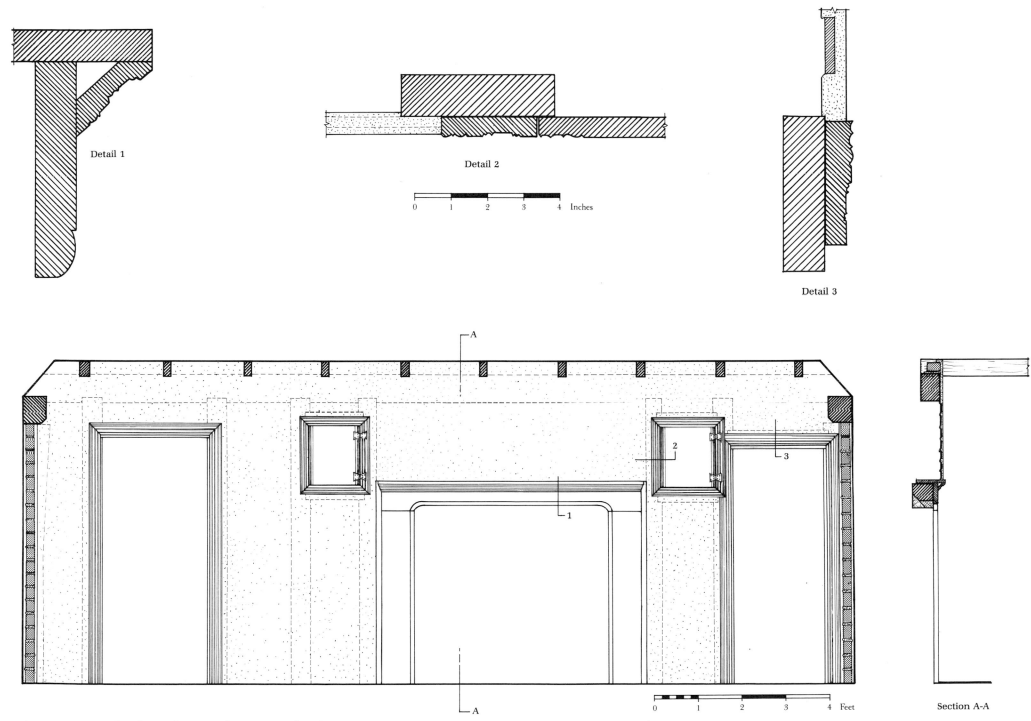

Detail 1

Detail 2

Detail 3

0 1 2 3 4 Inches

A

2

1

3

A

0 1 2 3 4 Feet

Section A-A

Figure 232. Samuel Pickman house, Salem, Mass. Elevation and partial section of fireplace wall in earliest chamber, with details of 1. mantel, 2. trim surrounding wall closets, and 3. trim surrounding door, before 1681.

Interior Finish

Figure 233. Samuel Pickman house. Detail of original fireplace trim, shown immediately following removal of eighteenth-century paneling in earliest chamber. *Photo, Peter Zaharis, 1969.*

out chamfers, suggesting that they were covered by the sheathing at the outset. Late examples are known in the Stanley Lake house in Topsfield, where along the fireplace wall of the lower room in the earliest portion of the building, dating to about 1680-1690, the vertical molded sheathing boards extend up to the underside of the chamber floorboards and are cut to fit around the joists. And at the Caldwell house in Ipswich the chimney girt in the lower left-hand room was found to have been chamfered and stopped but was quite clean, indicating that whatever the original intention its surface had been covered from the beginning.

Three basic varieties of molded wall sheathing occur throughout the seventeenth century within a roughly chronological framework. For the earliest years the physical evidence is meager, although happily amplified by the documentary record. In response to Governor Winthrop's rebuke, it will be recalled, Dudley replied that his wall sheathing was only "clapboards nailed to the wall in the form of wainscot,"[18] and in nearby Plymouth Colony a building contract of 1638 stipulated that a house, then unfinished, was to be "clap boarded within up to the [chamber] floore and a partition to be made of clap board through the middest."[19]

It is highly significant that three different examples of wall sheathing applied in overlapping clapboard fashion have survived at Massachusetts Bay's earliest framed structure, the Fairbanks house in Dedham. The molded horizontal sheathing of the left-hand room or hall and the chamfered overlapping sheathing within the present stairwell are thought to be contemporary or nearly contemporary with the period of original construction. Horizontal overlapping beaded siding in the upper entry may be somewhat later, though judgment is based solely on the fact that exterior beaded clapboarding has been considered eighteenth rather than seventeenth century in date (figure 235). This assumption may have to be revised.

The sheathing of the hall at the Fairbanks house is exceptional also in that it covered the

in such a way that the frame members formed an important part of the compostion. At the Gedney house in Salem the chimney girt of the right-hand room has been chamfered on the reverse side, not for purposes of decoration but to receive the upper edges of the sheathing boards, shaved on an incline for a snug fit. At the Boardman house in Saugus the upper ends of the boards were fastened to the girts with nails toed in. For the earlier years, however, the scanty evidence points to an alternate method of finish at this junction. In the left-hand room of the Ambrose Gale house in Marblehead, built probably about 1663, and in the earliest chamber of the Coffin house in Newbury, the chimney girts are crudely finished and with-

three outer walls of the room, a condition which occurs only rarely at Massachusetts Bay, and usually at a much later date. The sheathing here may well represent an actual example of the use of boarding for warmth, as Dudley had claimed, in advance of the soon to be developed preference for lath and plaster which must have been thought to possess superior advantages for insulation. Given the period and socioeconomic standing of Jonathan Fairbanks, for whom the house was built, the refinements are noteworthy. While the ends of the boards simply stop short of the chamfer of the exposed door posts in the west wall, there is, on the other hand, surprising sophistication in the molded collar which surrounds the summer beam at its junction with the sheathing, and in the molded casing of the front southwest corner post (figure 236).

The second variety of wall sheathing at Massachusetts Bay is mid-century in date, and might

Figure 234. Browne house, Watertown, Mass. Detail of summer tie beam, rear plate, and joist with molded trim, earliest chamber, 1694–1701. *Photo, J. David Bohl, 1977.*

Figure 235. Fairbanks house, Dedham, Mass. Details of horizontal wall sheathing, 1. stairwell, and 2. front wall of upper entry, ca. 1637 (?).

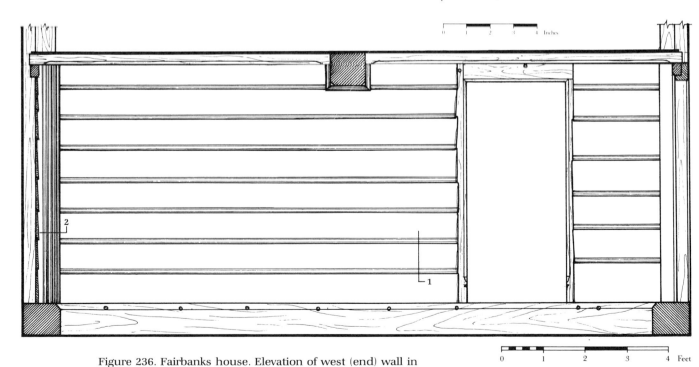

Detail 2

0   1   2   3   4   Inches

Figure 236. Fairbanks house. Elevation of west (end) wall in hall, with details of 1. molded sheathing, and 2. casing of corner post.

0   1   2   3   4   Feet

Detail 1

Interior Finish

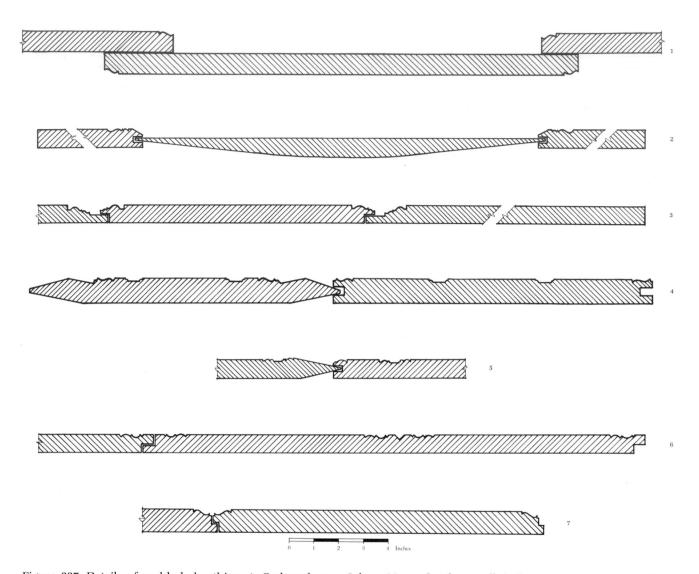

Figure 237. Details of molded sheathing: 1. Gedney house, Salem, Mass., fireplace wall, hall chamber, ca. 1665; 2. Blake house, Dorchester, Mass., fireplace wall, parlor chamber, ca. 1650; 3. Deane Winthrop house, Winthrop, Mass., fireplace wall, left-hand chamber, ca. 1638–1650; 4. Brown house, Hamilton, Mass., original location undetermined, probably 1662–1673; 5. Deane Winthrop house, Winthrop, Mass., fireplace wall, right-hand chamber, ca. 1638–1650; 6. Whipple house, Ipswich, Mass., fireplace wall, hall chamber, probably before 1683; 7. Paine-Dodge house, Ipswich, Mass., fireplace wall, right-hand chamber, after 1700.

also be classified as overlapping, although the boards are always vertical and do not take the form of the clapboard. As seen in the hall chamber at the Gedney house in Salem, a single board is overlapped at each side by contiguous boards having molded edges, an arrangement which occurs also in the contemporary Richard Jackson house of ca. 1664 in nearby Portsmouth, New Hampshire. The treatment is one again for which English precedent exists, and like clapboard sheathing seems to have been confined in popularity to a relatively brief time span, despite the existence of one or two late, lingering examples. Fragments of vertical wall sheathing, which may well be original, in the parlor chamber of the mid-seventeenth-century Blake house in Dorchester are similar in outward appearance, though joined with a tongue and groove (figure 237-1 and -2).

The third variety is by far the most common, in which case the sheathed wall presents a single continuous surface, broken only by the shallow profile of the creased moldings and the vertical joint at which the boards come together. The earlier jointing system tends to be that of the tongue and groove. The majority of later sheathed walls are half-lapped in terms of the jointing technique employed. If original, a few surviving vertical molded boards in the left-hand chamber of the Winthrop house in Winthrop, ca. 1638-1650, represent the earliest example of this detail, followed by the wall of vertical (though unmolded) sheathing in the right-hand parlor at the Gedney house in Salem, ca. 1665 (figures 237-3 and 238). By the last quarter of the seventeenth century the half-lap joint had become the undeniably preferred system.

While the underlying form of this latest variety of sheathing is relatively uncomplex, the decoration, on the other hand, lends a considerable if subtle sense of pattern to the surface of the wall. The moldings, in fact, seem to keep pace in their exuberance of detail with the maturation of other architectural embellishments during the late seventeenth century. Though seemingly alike, there is considerable individuality in the way the various profiles have been combined and a more self-

Figure 238. Gedney house, Salem, Mass. Detail of parlor fireplace wall sheathing, ca. 1665, shown following removal of eighteenth-century paneling. *Photo, William W. Owens, Jr., 1974.*

Figure 239. Whipple house, Ipswich, Mass. Detail of fireplace wall sheathing, hall chamber, probably before 1683. *Photo, William W. Owens, Jr., 1974.* (Right)

conscious aesthetic apparent in the presence now of creased moldings which do not necessarily coincide with the edges of the boards. Thus uniform, even symmetrical, intervals are registered in purely visual terms (figure 237-4). While one of the finest examples of this variety, including regularly spaced vertical moldings and applied molded trim surrounding the fireplace opening, occurs in the chamber of the earliest portion of the Whipple house in Ipswich where discovered underneath later lath and plaster during the restoration of 1898 (figure 239), it is likely that this sheathing represents an alteration, made perhaps when the high style parlor was added to the original house not long before 1683.

Interior Finish

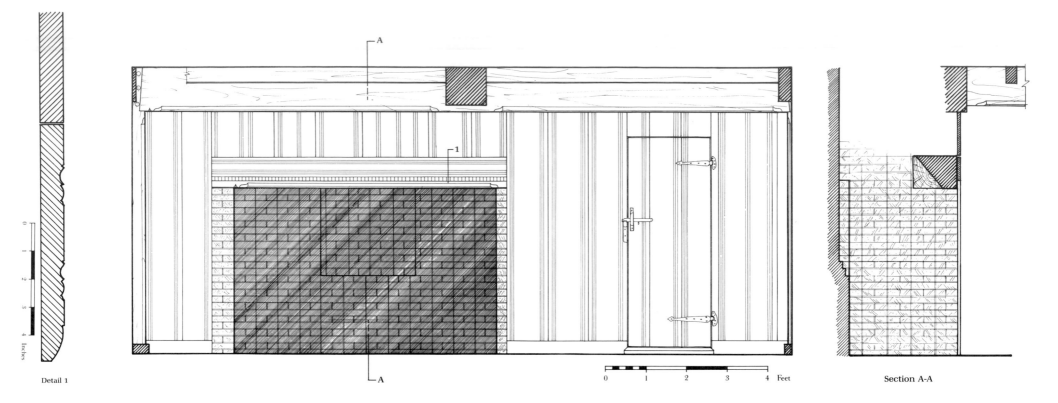

Detail 1   A   0   1   2   3   4   Feet   Section A-A

Figure 240. Cushing house, Hingham, Mass. Elevation and section of fireplace wall in left-hand room, with detail of lintel coverboard, 1679.

After 1700 and almost overnight the creased moldings disappear or give way to a simple bead or feather-edged joint, and ultimately, of course, to paneling. Perfectly plain, unmolded sheathing which can be found occasionally during the seventeenth century becomes more common now and the few creased moldings which do appear in this later period, for example in the sheathing of the staircase and right-hand chamber of the Paine-Dodge house in Ipswich, are thin and paltry (figure 237-7).

The vertical partition of molded pine boards can thus be seen to have become a rapidly accepted and widespread part of the New England architectural experience. Because it was so often associated with the fireplace, we must consider as well the relationship of the sheathed wall to the masonry.

The chimney stack was normally set back a few inches from the enclosing frame of the chimney bay, with the result that whether the vertical sheathing on either side of the fireplace was positioned at the rear of the chimney girt or at some

mid-point, or covered its front surface, it was necessary to close the gap between the wall and the brickwork of the chimney. This was usually accomplished by means of a vertical board which returned at right angles to the sheathing and butted against the outer edge of the exposed brick piers, creating a recess. If there was a plaster cove over the fireplace, the board was cut and fitted to take the angle of the cove (figure 156).

The lintel of the first-story fireplace seems to have been exposed throughout the seventeenth century as a general rule. There were exceptions, however, and at a rather early date. The lintel of the left-hand or parlor fireplace in the Parson Capen house in Topsfield, for example, was found to have been recessed an inch or so behind the face of the supporting brick piers, clearly to receive a horizontal coverboard, and examples are known elsewhere (figure 246). While a finely molded coverboard with incised lines to suggest denticulation was found in place behind later paneling at the Cushing house in Hingham of 1679, so arranged as to expose the chamfer and stop of the chimney lintel (figure 240), two of the most elaborate ground-story examples at Massachusetts Bay have been found reused in the wall construction of later eighteenth-century houses from which, obviously, a good deal of building material had been salvaged. The first of these is a lintel coverboard found in the Enoch Whiton house in Hingham, dating probably in its present form to the second quarter of the eighteenth century. The coverboard, thirteen inches high and ornamented with a single horizontal creased molding off center and a wide bead at the lower edge, shows the marks of long exposure, and bears a casually incised contemporary date of 1668.

The second example is more elaborate and again bears the marks of long exposure, with its edges worn smooth and its surface smoke-blackened and perforated with holes for pricket lamps. The board itself, now somewhat truncated, is nevertheless ninety-one inches long by eleven and a quarter inches high, and has been embellished with a horizontal creased molding, a beaded lower edge, and the same kind of compass decoration with punch marks that one finds on seventeenth-century chests and boxes (figure 241). This lintel coverboard was found in the wall of a now-demolished mid-eighteenth-century house at 28 East Street in Ipswich, standing on the site of a dwelling known to have been built by one John Knowlton between 1670 and 1689.[20] The denticulated board which now serves as a lintel cover in association with the wall of sheathing installed in the American Wing of the Metropolitan Museum of Art as part of a room from the late seventeenth-century Hart house in Ipswich was introduced into that house from another Ipswich dwelling altogether in 1902.[21] There are clear indications that the sheathing has been cut over to accommodate the coverboard, which may or may not have been an original part of the composition (figure 242).

Elsewhere, with the unusual exception of the Samuel Pickman house in Salem, little effort was made in even the very elaborate houses to conceal the brick piers of the fireplace or the face of

Figure 241. John Knowlton house (?), Ipswich, Mass. Detail of fireplace lintel coverboard with incised molding and scratch and punch decoration, 1670–1689. *Photo, J. David Bohl, 1978.*

the wooden lintel until very late in the seventeenth century. The Parson Barnard house in North Andover is among the pacesetters in providing a covering for both lintels and piers. The hall and parlor fireplaces are recessed and each is furnished with a plaster cove. In the hall on the left, the original unmolded vertical sheathing survives in part at the right of the fireplace, and here and in the parlor opposite, the plaster, while still wet, was stopped against some kind of board trim (now missing) which covered the entire surface of the masonry (figure 268).

The upper finish of the fireplace recess was accomplished in various ways. One solution was to close the aperture above the fireplace lintel with vertical molded boards which met the chimney girt. In the earliest chamber of the Andrews house in Hingham, built between 1685 and 1690, where original sheathing was discovered above the fireplace behind later lath and plaster, the boards are virtually erect. There is the additional refinement of a molded horizontal board which covers the lintel and against which the vertical overmantel boards are stopped. The brick piers are uncovered in the continuing tradition of the seventeenth century (figure 243). Evidence for a similar condition was found at the Old Garrison, so-called, in Chelmsford, early eighteenth century in date, where the boards tilted forward to meet some form of trim about midway of the undersurface of the chimney girt. Another system altogether occurs at the Boardman house in Saugus, where in the chambers a flat molded board is nailed to the underside of the chimney tie, far enough in from the front surface of that frame member to leave its chamfer exposed, but extending back to the stack and thus providing a roof or ceiling for the fireplace recess (figure 256). Neither builder nor client, apparently, was offended by the exposed brickwork above the fireplace. In the Boardman, Cooper-Frost-Austin, and Browne houses in Saugus, Cambridge, and Watertown, built more or less within a decade of each other, the brickwork of the chimney was recessed somewhat behind the fireplace lintel, which allowed that unit to be covered with not only a molded facing board but a mantel shelf as well. In each case the shelf projected forward over the facing board to receive a molded cornice board (figures 244 and 245).

A unique feature was discovered at the Parson Capen house in Topsfield in the form of an open panel of joiner's work, containing turned balusters, immediately to the right of the fireplace in the left-hand lower room. The wall itself, of unmolded vertical boards, appears to be later (figure 246). The grille, on the other hand, though not necessarily in situ, is characteristic of seventeenth-century work and may very well be contemporary with original construction. There was present in Topsfield at this period a joiner named Samuel Symonds who built the pulpit in the meetinghouse in 1684 and is known to have performed turner's work as well.[22] While the grille bears a superficial resemblance to the front panel of a livery cupboard, there are no indications that it had been associated with a piece of furniture, and the strong possibility remains that it formed part of the finish trim of this or another room in the Capen House.

Figure 242. Merrifield house (?), Ipswich, Mass. Detail of seventeenth-century wall sheathing as installed in period room from the Hart house, Ipswich, Mass., Metropolitan Museum of Art, New York City.

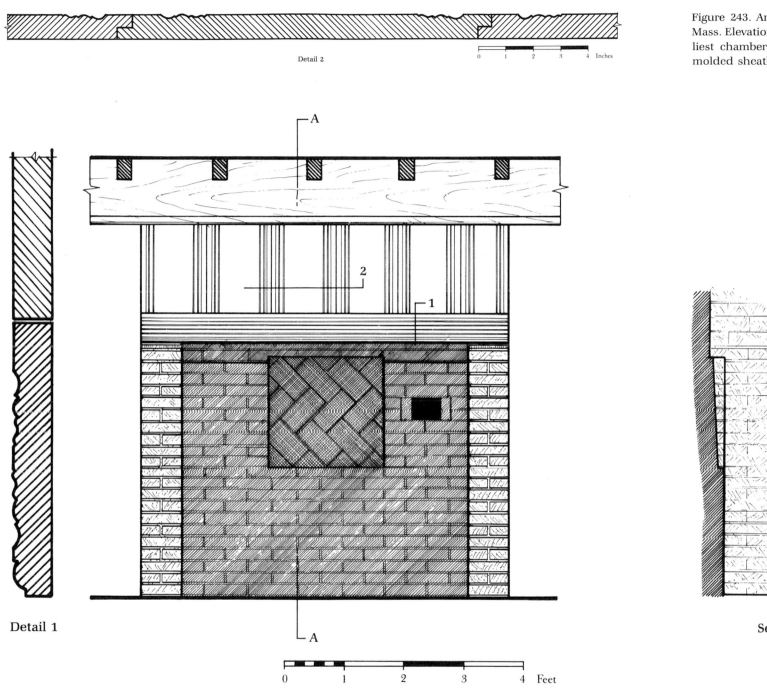

Detail 2

0 1 2 3 4 Inches

Detail 1

A

A

0 1 2 3 4 Feet

Figure 243. Andrews house (The Old Ordinary), Hingham, Mass. Elevation (in part) and section of fireplace wall in earliest chamber, with details of 1. lintel coverboard, and 2. molded sheathing, 1685–1690.

Section A-A

Interior Finish

Figure 244. Cooper-Frost-Austin house, Cambridge, Mass. Detail of fireplace wall, hall chamber, ca. 1689. *Photo, Richard Merrill, 1962.*

Figure 245. Browne house, Watertown, Mass. Detail of mantel, earliest chamber, 1694–1701. *Photo, J. David Bohl, 1977.*

Normally in the later period the vertical boards were half-lapped and this could on occasion facilitate the structural workings of the doors that were located in the partitions. In at least three of our earliest buildings, the Fairbanks house in Dedham, the Blake house in Dorchester, and the Whipple house in Ipswich, it is not surprising to find the persistence of more typically English structural forms, and there are very occasional conservative expressions, as for example at the French-Andrews house in Topsfield of about 1718. Here the interior doorways are formed of

doorposts framed into the chimney girts and tie beams (figure 247). Those at the Fairbanks house are chamfered and stopped (figure 248B), while the Blake and French-Andrews posts are finished with a molding at the outer edge. As the boarded partition increased in popularity, however, it became clear that the door could be made to operate within the context of the partition itself. As early as about 1665 we find in the parlor at the right of the entry at the Gedney house in Salem that original unmolded vertical sheathing, more than an inch thick, was furnished with a stout rebate against which the door was closed and secured with a turn button (figure 238).

More characteristically, however, the builder omitted the half-lap for those boards which

Figure 246. Parson Capen house, Topsfield, Mass. Parlor fire-place wall, 1683, with later alterations, shown immediately following removal of eighteenth-century paneling over fire-place. *Photo, William Sumner Appleton, 1913.*

formed the aperture of his doorway, and nailed to the outer surface of the sheathing a molded and mitered frame, projecting just far enough into the open to furnish the rebate against which the door was stopped. The door is thus nothing more than a part of the boarding of the sheathed wall, cut and battened with three molded battens, hinged and furnished with a latch (figure 265).

A number of wooden door latches consisting of latchbar, staple, catch or keeper, and latchstring have survived from the period (figure 239), but the metal latch appears early and is used consistently. In its commonest form, the so-called Suffolk variety, it consisted of two cusp plates and a grasp, fashioned from a single piece of metal, the cusps usually triangular or roughly floriate in

shape. The distinctive characteristic of the seventeenth-century Suffolk latch is the pierced hole within the upper cusp plate to receive the thumb piece (figure 249). Rare and unusually early remnants of a wrought iron Norfolk latch (that is, with grasp soldered to the shaped plate) survive on the chamber door leading into the upper entry at the Browne house in Watertown.

Figure 247. Whipple house, Ipswich, Mass. Detail of hall chamber door frame, upper entry, ca. 1655. *Photo, William W. Owens, Jr., 1974.*

Interior Finish

Figure 248A. Fairbanks house, Dedham, Mass. Door frame in west wall of hall, with detail of mitered junction of stud and header, ca. 1637. (Evidence for pin in right-hand stud concealed.)

Figure 248B. Fairbanks house. Elevation of post, chimney tie beam, principal rafter, and studs, showing chamfered door frame leading to parlor chamber.

The hinge was invariably of wrought iron, nailed to the door with the aid of leather washers. The most common variety, which as the century progressed was almost assuredly made by the local blacksmith, was the strap hinge, usually at least twelve inches long and designed either for a pintle or with its own integral shaped hinge plate (figures 251 and 250A). The flattened cusp at the end was normally pointed, in contrast to the later "bean-shaped" cusp of the eighteenth century, and some of these local hinges were quite decoratively fashioned (figures 250B and 251). Imported hardware, occasionally with a plated finish, can also be found, particularly the cock's head hinge, so-called, which was probably the item described in an Ipswich inventory of 1653 as "a payer of esses for doores" (figure 252). Butterfly hinges, referred to as "dove tails" in a Salem inventory of 1678, appear sometimes as well.[23] The earliest example of the H-hinge occurs at the Fairbanks house in Dedham and is perhaps before the middle of the century in date, with a degree of finesse which suggests an imported item (figure 254). The H-hinge (unless combined with a strap, see figures 244 and 253) is otherwise not found in the seventeenth century. Examples with floriate decoration become popular right after 1700 (figure 261), and tend to supplant other forms except in conservative rural situations where the locally made strap hinge persists.

The almost invariable use of lath and plaster for the three outer walls of the room gives way just before 1700 and increasingly during the first quarter of the eighteenth century to horizontal boarding, in all likelihood an economic triumph over whatever deeply rooted preferences had developed at Massachusetts Bay for the insulation of outer walls with lath and plaster. Material costs to one side, it can surely be argued that the labor involved in molding (or feathering) the edges of boards and jointing and securing them to the frame was almost certainly less than the time and expense of riving laths, nailing them, preparing plaster, and applying it.

Whether or not economically inspired, we find a mixture of conditions. At the Old Garrison, so-

Figure 249. Story house, Essex, Mass. Detail of Suffolk latch, ca. 1684. (Found on premises and shown here mounted on a reproduction seventeenth-century door.) *Photo, J. David Bohl, 1978.*

Figure 250A. Boardman house, Saugus, Mass. Detail of strap hinge of closet door, parlor chamber, ca. 1687. *Photo, J. David Bohl, 1978.*

Figure 250B. Boardman house. Detail of decorative hinge attached to nineteenth-century door leading to hall chamber. *Photo, J. David Bohl, 1978.*

Figure 251. Browne house, Watertown, Mass. Detail of decorative hinge on door leading to earliest chamber, 1694–1701. *Photo, J. David Bohl, 1977.*

Interior Finish

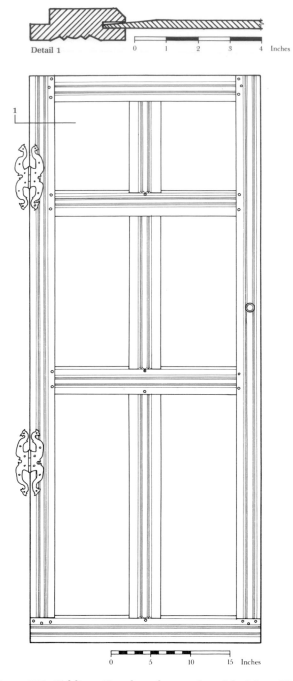

Detail 1

0 1 2 3 4 Inches

1

Figure 252. Giddings-Burnham house, Ipswich, Mass. Elevation of interior wainscot door, with detail of molding, probably before 1650.

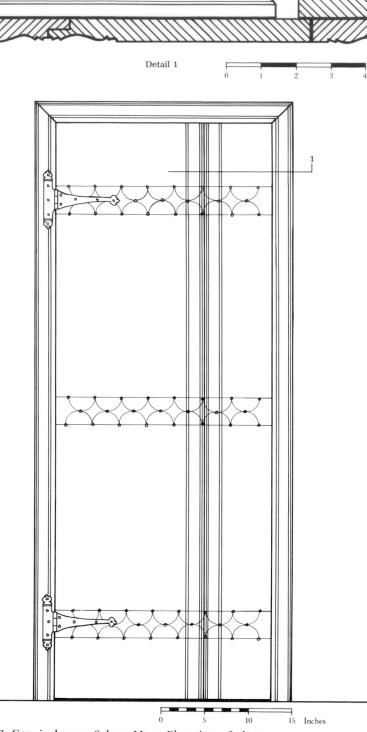

Detail 1

0 1 2 3 4 Inches

1

Figure 253. Corwin house, Salem, Mass. Elevation of closet door in parlor chamber, with detail of molding and trim surrounding doorway, ca. 1675.

Figure 254. Fairbanks house, Dedham, Mass. Detail of H-hinge on door leading to hall chamber, ca. 1637 (?). *Photo, William W. Owens, Jr., 1974.*

The Framed Houses of Massachusetts Bay

called, in Chelmsford, for example, the left-hand chamber walls are covered entirely with feather-edged boards, although there is a continuing use of plaster elsewhere in the same structure. At the Browne house in Watertown, of one-room plan with chimney bay and probably an outshot as originally built, the lower room was sheathed with horizontal boards, each molded at the edge where simply butted against the board below (figure 255). The three outer walls of the chamber above were plastered. At the Cooper-Frost-Austin house in Cambridge, on the other hand, conceived originally as a "half-house" with service rooms at the rear, the arrangement was reversed. Here the lower front room was lathed and plastered on the outer walls, with vertical board sheathing at the fireplace wall, while the rear wall of the principal chamber above (which has always been an inner partition) was sheathed with molded horizontal boards. At present the end and front walls are lathed and plastered, but whether originally so has not been determined.

The finely molded fireplace wall in the east chamber of the Boardman house in Saugus is characteristic of progressive trends and serves as an excellent introduction to the subject of evolutionary developments in style that eventually culminate in a wholly new psychology with respect to finishing the house frame (figure 256). The vertically molded sheathing is typical of late seventeenth-century work and yet includes a cornice with cyma profile which is normally associated with much later trim. By the opening of the eighteenth century there is a noticeable increase in molding profiles that foreshadow the Georgian style. These are combined with a still exposed house frame, chamfered or beaded, in a continuing postmedieval tradition, and other trim which is scarcely academic in character. Somewhat less canonical, for example, but clearly to be grouped with these transitional moldings is the exaggerated reverse cyma member which stopped the lower edge of the exterior plaster cove cornice of the Benaiah Titcomb house in Newburyport (figure 179).

Figure 255. Browne house, Watertown, Mass. Detail of horizontally sheathed rear wall in earliest lower room, 1694–1701. *Photo, J. David Bohl, 1977.*

It is the right-hand parlor chamber of the Parson Barnard house in North Andover, however, which preserves the most dramatic evidence of transition between two major style expressions at Massachusetts Bay (figures 257 and 258). Consistent with existing practices, the frame (for the most part) is exposed and beaded, and the three outer walls are lathed and plastered down to the floor, where there is a painted black band about four inches high at the point one would normally expect to find a baseboard. The focally important fireplace wall, on the other hand, represents a sharp break with seventeenth-century tradition. The board casing of the chimney tie and its supporting posts in this house built by a prominent

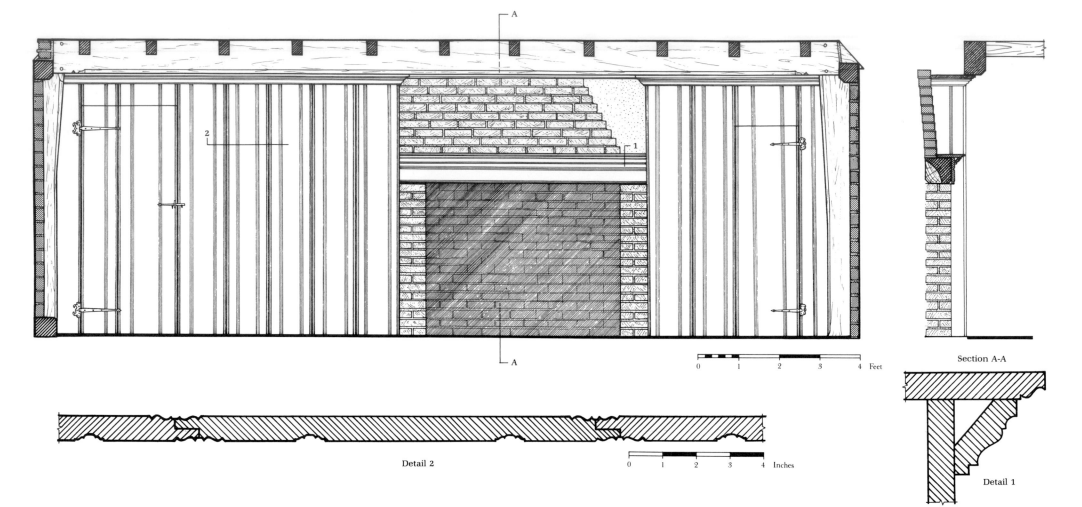

Section A-A

Detail 1

Detail 2

0 1 2 3 4 Feet

0 1 2 3 4 Inches

Figure 256. Boardman house, Saugus, Mass. Elevation and section of fireplace wall in hall chamber, with details of 1. mantel, and 2. molded sheathing, ca. 1687. (Surface only of brickwork above fireplace is shown in section.)

minister who had earlier lived in Boston is contemporary with construction, as is the plaster ceiling suspended from the joists. The bold bolection molding surrounding the fireplace is present also early in the eighteenth century in the less ambitious houses of Boston, and another fine, nonurban example survives at the Cushing-Robinson house in Hingham, ca. 1725, which here and elsewhere must be seen as looking forward to later stylistic innovations. Of equally striking importance, the plain unmolded vertical sheathing at the Parson Barnard house was conceived from the outset as a field for the application of raised moldings in simulation of paneling. The same condition existed in the parlor below, as investigation of the original wall has revealed. These moldings and the elaborate trim with

wooden cove directly above the fireplace are by no means unavowedly academic. The whole, however, represents an important stride toward the marked changes in style that occurred in the second quarter of the eighteenth century, heralded by a few provincial Renaissance mansions in Boston beginning as early as about 1690 with the construction of the Foster-Hutchinson house.

A more prosaic change during the early eighteenth century involved the replacement of vertical molded boards with feather-edged sheathing, the term "feather-edge" being defined by Moxon about 1680 as "Boards, or Planks, that have one edge thinner than another."[24] Concurrent with this development is the complete enclosure of the fireplace, including overmantel, lintel, and piers, with trim. All of these conditions can be found in the left-hand chamber of the Caldwell house in Ipswich, the doors of which are quite unusually hinged with interlocking staple eyes in the manner of a chest or box-lid (figure 259). In this example and in the left-hand chamber of the Cooper-Frost-Austin house in Cambridge, added to the original structure just after 1718, the doors are no longer battened, but are composed of stiles and rails enclosing two large panels. The edges of the panels are widely feathered, and the adjacent wall at the Cooper-Frost-Austin house is paneled in the same fashion, rather than vertically boarded, as is the wall of the Caldwell house chamber (figure 260).

Here, then, is the introduction at the very close of the period of our study of feather-edged paneling, preceded by the "proto-paneling" of the Parson Barnard house. Destined to become a hallmark of the mature eighteenth-century style, its appearance late in the first quarter of that century, combined still with a largely exposed post-medieval house frame, remains hesitant in some respects. In particular, the early paneling can almost always be differentiated from still later work by the excessive width of the feather, often at least two or three inches (figure 261). The exposure of the feather-edge as a part of the molding profile occurs but rarely in seventeenth-century sheathing, and then only in connection with the creased moldings typical of the period (figure 237-4 and -5). Not until after 1700 does it assume through interplay with a quarter-round bead fashioned in the edge of the adjoining board the form which will remain characteristic for the balance of the eighteenth century, both in board sheathing and fully developed paneling.

As for the source of these new ideas—including the bolection molding of the Parson Barnard house chamber, and indeed, the concept of paneling in place of sheathing—the most likely avenue of introduction in a period before carpenters' pattern books had begun to pour from the English press is the immigrant English builder. The Great Migration of the 1630s and 1640s had tapered off by 1650, and there are few statistics after

Figure 257. Parson Barnard house, North Andover, Mass. Parlor chamber, ca. 1715. *Photo, William W. Owens, Jr., 1974.*

this date for the rate of flow into Massachusetts Bay of trained English craftsmen. There are, however, some applications on file after 1671 for persons seeking permission to settle in Boston and pursue their calling, together with scattered port arrival records and inhabitants' bonds.[25] A number of English building artisans are identified among the newcomers, and of those turned away by the city fathers we may assume that some settled elsewhere in the Bay area. In addition to the interesting transitional trim at the Parson Barnard house in North Andover, for example, there is at least one further example of work presumably by the same hand at the Abbot House in nearby Andover, and the possibility of yet a third

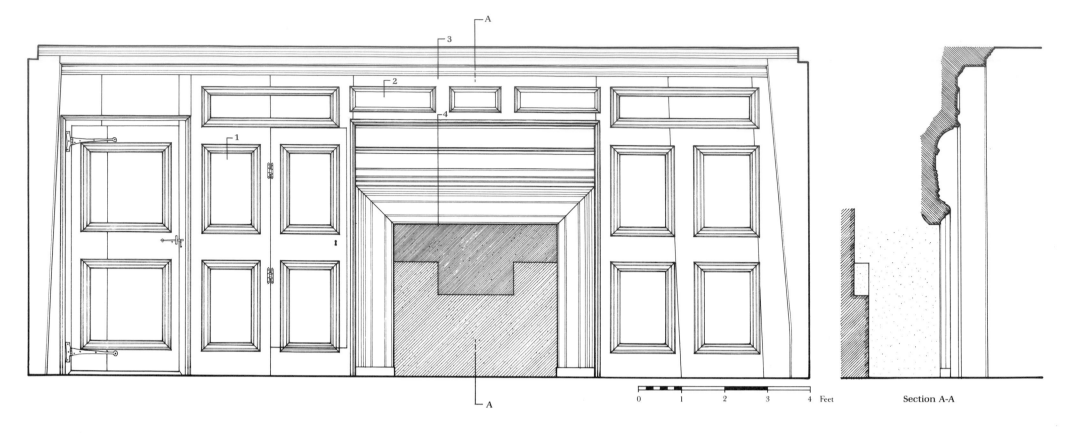

Figure 258. Parson Barnard house, North Andover, Mass. Elevation and section of fireplace wall in parlor chamber, with details of 1–2. moldings applied to wall sheathing, and 3–4. constituent elements of wooden finish trim extending from cornice to fireplace, ca. 1715.

instance at the Johnson house in North Andover, dating in all likelihood to the beginning of the second quarter of the eighteenth century. These related expressions suggest the presence in the community of a progressive artisan. Who was he and what was his background? The question may perhaps have more relevance for the student of later architectural phases at Massachusetts Bay, but cannot be ignored.

Beginning in the late seventeenth century the ceiling undergoes significant evolutionary change which affects the house frame structurally and subtly alters the composition of interior space. For the earlier years the concept of summer and joists exposed overhead with the underside of the floorboards forming the actual ceiling was apparently universal at Massachusetts Bay, in keeping with contemporary trends in English vernacular work. The only refinement, for which English precedent can also be found,[26] was the occasional lathing and plastering of the floorboards

between the joists, occurring as early as about 1655 at the Whipple house in Ipswich[27] (figures 44B and 36). The condition, found normally in the more expensive houses, is clearly specified in the contract drawn by Jonathan Corwin, the Salem merchant, with his mason, Daniel Andrews, in 1675. Surviving examples, or traces at least, can be found in the earliest portion of the Turner house in Salem, ca. 1668, and the ambitious Appleton-Taylor-Mansfield house in Saugus. Its presence in the Salem houses built for shipwright Eleazer Gedney (figure 98) and slaughterer Thomas Ives (the Narbonne house) is somewhat harder to explain, though considerations of upward social mobility may have some bearing on the matter. In Gedney's case we know that his first wife, for whom the house was built, was a sister of merchant John Turner.

It is, however, the parlor addition projected by John Turner, presumably before his death in 1680, which provides the earliest known and most dramatic evidence for progressive thinking

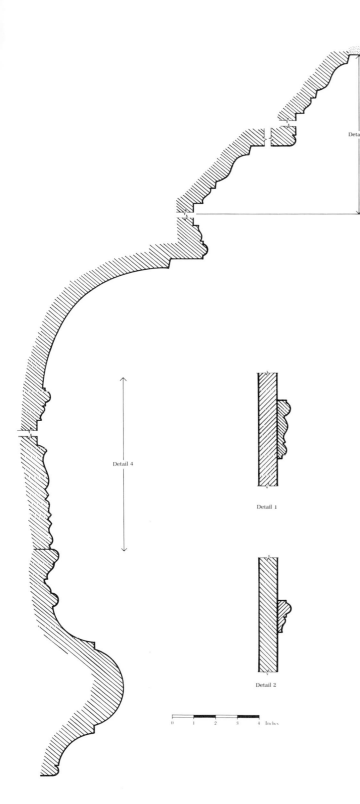

Detail 3

Detail 4

Detail 1

Detail 2

0 1 2 3 4 Inches

with respect to the finish of the ceiling and its role in determining spacial relationships. The ground-story ceiling height of the newly added ell is increased to as much as ninety inches. This is the first major break with what had heretofore been a typical module for the average seventeenth-century house, namely a height of between seventy-two and eighty-two inches measuring from the floor to the bottom of the summer beam in the lower story. While houses built during the first century of settlement at Massachusetts Bay can be found which reveal no difference in height between the stories, or a lesser headroom in the chambers, a majority of those recorded betray an increase of two or three inches in height in the upper story. The most common reason for this variation is that first-story summer beams are apt to be housed *in* the front and rear girts, while the second-story tie beams sit two or three inches higher *on* the plates. The appreciable increase in height of the lower rooms in pretentious structures, on the other hand, in the range of eight-two to ninety inches, is noteworthy during the last quarter of the seventeenth century, and these greater heights become standard during the first quarter of the eighteenth century in even very modest houses. For the more ambitious dwellings of merchant and minister a height approaching one hundred inches or more will be found—for example, in the later half of the Wilson-Appleton house in Ipswich, added before 1718, where the interval in the first story is ninety-eight inches and in the second 102 inches. The new parlor at the Turner house establishes a high-water mark for the earlier extant seventeenth-century examples. Taken as a whole, such increases in ceiling height mark the first conscious efforts to create formal proportions which will accompany the transition at a vernacular level from the postmedieval to the Renaissance.

The finish treatment of the ceiling serves as a confirmation of this trend. If, as supposed, John Turner's ell was projected before his death in 1680, it becomes the earliest known example at Massachusetts Bay of a plaster ceiling suspended

Figure 259. Caldwell house, Ipswich, Mass. Detail of fireplace wall, left-hand chamber, probably after 1709 (with later fireplace in original opening). *Photo, Peter Zaharis, 1955.*

Figure 260. Cooper-Frost-Austin house, Cambridge, Mass. Detail of fireplace wall, parlor chamber, after 1718. *Photo, Richard Merrill, 1962.*

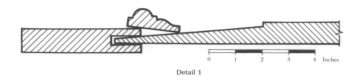

Detail 1

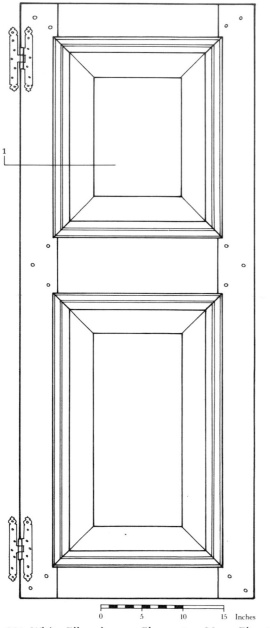

Figure 261. White-Ellery house, Gloucester, Mass. Elevation of two-panel door leading to right-hand room, with detail of applied molding, ca. 1710.

from joists, followed closely or perhaps paralleled by some evidence at least for a similar treatment at the Paul Revere house in Boston. In both cases the posts supporting the summer beams remained uncased. By the opening of the eighteenth century the concept of a plaster ceiling was spreading slowly in town and country alike. The ceilings in the lower rooms of the White-Ellery house in Gloucester and in both stories of the addition made by Samuel Appleton, Jr., to the earlier house erected by Shoreborn Wilson in Ipswich which he purchased in 1702 also seem to have been plastered originally.

No matter how simple the homes of the less affluent yeomen and artisans of the seventeenth century, there were prosperous men and women in New England who lived from the start surrounded by elegant possessions (figure 262). Much of this, to be sure, was concentrated in the urban centers of Massachusetts Bay, more particularly Boston and Salem, but one is reminded also of Edward Johnson's description of Ipswich about 1650: "The peopling of this Towne is by men of good ranke and quality, many of them having the yearly Revenue of large Lands in England before they came to this Wildernesse. . . . their Houses are many of them very faire built with pleasant Gardens and Orchards."[28]

Well before the end of the century there were houses of both complex and ambitious plan in Boston. Household inventories reveal that many of them were richly furnished and that color played an important role in the overall decorative scheme. Mr. Edmond Downes's "Brick House" in Boston boasted in 1669 a "Greene Chamber," a "Red Chamber," and a "Purple Chamber," and there was a "Green Chamber" in the handsomely furnished dwelling of the Boston merchant, Robert Gibbs, whose estate was appraised on February 1, 1675. These designations may have referred to a color scheme imposed by the fabric furnishings, but the Gibbs house contained a "Painted Chamber" as well.[29] A few years before, in 1672, one Lawrence Clenton of Ipswich about whom

very little is known, was credited with three and a half days' work at Mr. Baker's in painting a room,[30] and in 1695, Samuel Sewall records the visit of some friends to his home in Boston which had been newly repaired and enlarged, beginning in 1693: " 'tis the first time [Mr. Torrey] has been at our house with his new wife," he writes; "was much pleas'd with our painted shutters; in pleasancy said he thought he had been got into Paradise."[31]

In these isolated references to painted finish indoors in the seventeenth century, the medium may have been oil, but of this we cannot be certain. Nor do these documentary references reveal whether the woodwork was covered with plain colors or with painted decoration. Before turning, however, to the question of oil paints, we should consider the use of whitewash, both as a freshener for plaster and woodwork, and, when combined with colors, as a decorative agent. The employment of quicklime and water to whiten interior plaster walls and woodwork, references to which can be found in English documents of the sixteenth century,[32] extends well back into the seventeenth century in New England. As early as 1657 the town of Dedham voted to have its meetinghouse "lathed upon the studs and so dabed and whitted over workman like,"[33] and in 1676 there is an item of nine shillings "for whiteing the roome" among the accounts of repairs to the house of Freegrace Norton in Ipswich.[34] Whitewashing was performed in most instances by the mason. John Marshall of Braintree, for example, who called himself mason and bricklayer, recorded in his diary on May 16, 1697, that he "whited mrs Badcocks Room," and a month later, "I whitewashed at willards."[35] These and other references to whitewashing are sprinkled in among many entries having to do with his building of chimneys and plastering of walls. As an indication of how widespread was the use of whitewash in the seventeenth century—and indeed well into the nineteenth century—it may be said simply that there are few houses surviving from the first century of settlement at Massachusetts without some early trace of whitewash upon the frame, sheathing, and plaster walls, often in numerous layers.

Was it customary to whitewash both woodwork and plaster walls as soon as a house was finished, or to wait until these features had become sullied with smoke and dirt? In first-floor rooms, especially the hall or keeping-room, the great fireplace would presumably have deposited smoke stains on frame and woodwork within a short time. No example of a first-floor ceiling frame of the seventeenth century has been uncovered without some traces of whitewash being revealed. In the second story the fireplaces were smaller and probably used less frequently. While the chamber ceiling frames of a large proportion of surviving seventeenth-century houses are also apt to carry evidence of whitewash, it is significant, perhaps, that the east chamber of the Story house in Essex (before the overlay of later trim) had never been whitewashed. Moreover, occasional examples of houses built toward the end of our period, such as the Old Garrison, so-called, in Chelmsford, have revealed after the removal of later ceilings in the first story that the timbers overhead, while smoke-stained, had never been whitewashed. These structures, being of more recent date, were that much closer to the period when plaster ceilings and beam casings were apt to be applied to the previously exposed frames.

With so thoroughly widespread a use of whitewash—a use which extended at times to other portions of the house as well, the entry and closets, for example, and even the fireplace—it is not surprising to find the earliest appearance of color in this vehicle. Two varieties of expression can be distinguished, involving first the employment of color to accent structural members and to pick out moldings, and second, the creation of actual patterns. For the first of these, there is ample English precedent, for example at the late sixteenth century farmhouse called Raven's at Woodham Walter in Essex, where in the chamber area above the central hall the front plate and exposed studs were picked out in color, probably early in the seventeenth century. The vertical lines created by an application of color to the

Figure 262. Mrs. Elizabeth Freake of Boston with daughter Mary, ca. 1674.

studs can easily be distinguished from the diagonal lines created by the structural junction of stud and brace (figure 263). A similar example in red ochre has been noted in a cottage at Wick's Green, Earl Stonham, Suffolk. In both cases the color overlay forms an explicit denial of structural fact.

The custom of picking out structural members in color was also in vogue in Massachusetts at an early date. In the late seventeenth-century Todd house, in Salem, one of the chamfered summer beams of the first story was found to have had, above the first thick layer of whitewash, a thin coat of black, while the joists and underside of the floorboards that formed the ceiling overhead were whitewashed only. In another instance, that of the late seventeenth-century George Hart house in Ipswich, the summer beam, front, end, and chimney (but not rear) girts, together with

the front chimney post of the first-floor room, were found to have a wash of red vermilion applied to a thin coat of whitewash, while the rest of the frame was whitewashed only. The entire frame had received a second application of whitewash over the original coat at some later date, and in this case those members that before had been picked out in red were now painted with a thin coat of black. In both the early and later applications of color, the red and black, as revealed on the summer beam, extended up to within only an inch or so of the bottom of the intersecting joists, and this seems to have been the case also with the black paint on the summer beam of the Todd house in Salem.

The two most sophisticated examples that have come to light, however, represent a sequence of color combinations discovered at the Gedney and Turner houses in Salem. The Gedney house is the earlier, and here the frame of the hall chamber remained exposed until some time in the eighteenth century, when its members were cased and a ceiling of lath and plaster was hung from the joists. Before this occurred, however, a simple structural change had been made and a number of coats of whitewash and color had been added to the frame at various times.

The first finish, dating probably to the period of construction, is a wash of green in a thin, undetermined vehicle. This color covered the surface of all major frame units, including posts, end and chimney tie beams, plates, and summer beam. The green extends up no farther than the bottom of the joists on the summer beam and can be found also on the bottom of the joists, but *not* on the sides. It would seem likely that the sides of the joists were left at first in the natural wood color. Interestingly, at Mr. Gedney's death a few years later in 1683 there were in this same hall chamber "1 pair old green Curtains much stained."[36]

Between the first and second applications of color to the frame of the hall chamber in the Gedney house a structural change took place, at which time the summer beam was cut up into an inch or more, apparently to gain greater head-

Figure 263. Raven's Farm, Woodham Walter, Essex, Eng. Detail of wall framing in hall chamber, showing evidence for picking out the individual units in color, ca. 1600. *Photo, John E. Kimber, 1966.*

an even more vividly contrasting color scheme: the frame as a whole white, with the summer beam and its supporting posts accented in black (figure 264).

The final finish, dating perhaps to the early eighteenth century, was a thick, coarse, flaky whitewash tinted with yellow ochre which covers all of the frame except for the summer beam and its supporting posts. Where fragments remain in place, it can also be seen to have covered the lath and plaster ceiling between the joists (later removed). The summer beam and its posts were now overpainted a dark brick or sour red which extended over the entire surface. Thus in each of several stages of refinish for this room some form of color contrast existed, the last application being a uniform light yellow, with the summer beam and its supporting posts accented in red. Similar in every respect, the hall of the Turner house in Salem which was built about 1668 by the merchant John Turner, whose sister, Elizabeth, had married Eleazer Gedney in 1665, reveals two periods of decoration: the first a picking out of the principal frame members in red, and subsequently in a strong shade of gunmental gray, the vehicle for which is clearly whitewash.

Closely related to the accentuation of structural frame members by means of color was its use in picking out molded details. At the Haskell house in West Gloucester, for example, it was found that the corners of the exposed girts had been molded with a delicate cyma curve which bore traces of vermilion paint. Similarly, the early dentils over the fireplace now installed as part of the Hart Room in the Metropolitan Museum of Art are said to have had traces of alternating red and black paint.[37]

Other examples in an unrestored condition are known. One is a piece of wall sheathing from the Ross Tavern in Ipswich, found in a reused position when the house was dismantled in 1940. The board itself had never been painted, but the delicate creased molding which runs vertically along the surface was picked out with a light red brick color. A similar treatment was found on a scrap of reused seventeenth-century molded

room. A uniformly thin layer of whitewash which covers all the major structural units, including the joists, was added presumably at the same time the cut was made, not only to whiten the frame but also to cover the freshly exposed surface of the wood. As finished, the whitewashed surfaces of both the summer beam and its supporting posts were overpainted with a thin coat of black. Again the black extends up the sides of the summer beam only as far as the bottom of the joists which are framed into it. The rest of the summer beam above this point remains white. In this redecorated state, the room was thus given

sheathing facing into a wall of the mid-eigh-teenth-century house at 28 East Street in Ipswich. Here the surface had been whitewashed and the creased molding picked out in black.

It is a matter of real interest that all these examples of decoration are associated with houses built before 1700, and they are, for the most part, the earliest application of any finish to the surface of the woodwork. There is no reason, on the other hand, to assume that the second technique under discussion, namely, the creation of decorative patterns, appears any earlier than that date.[38] Of the half-dozen examples of "sponge painting" known, only one appears in a house that can be confidently dated before 1700—the Boardman house in Saugus—and here the decoration is almost certainly later. The Boardman house sponge painting, found on the molded sheathing of the upper entry, is an arrangement of black dots in an all-over pattern upon a ground of whitewash tinted yellow, and the dots, about one and a quarter inches in diameter, are spaced roughly three to four inches apart (figure 265). These dots give the impression of having been dabbed on with a spongelike agent, hence the name. In at least one other example, however, a different technique altogether is disclosed by the character of the dots themselves. The evidence is preserved on a single surviving board[39] that formed part of the whitewashed ceiling at the east end of the integral lean-to of the Joseph Blaney house in Swampscott, ca. 1700. The decoration of black spots here, which are about one inch in diameter and are spaced irregularly two inches or more on centers, was made with a brush that had simply been twirled in the fingers[40] (figure 266).

While circular dots were apparently the most popular device in these overall compositions, variations can be found. When the White-Ellery house in Gloucester was restored, the stripping away of a later ceiling in both ends of the integral lean-to revealed a pattern in black on whitewash, the freehand decoration here taking the form of what might be described as enlarged commas on both the ceiling and exposed joists (figure 267). At

Figure 264. Gedney house, Salem, Mass. Hall chamber.

the south end the decoration is of the spatter variety and extends also to the west wall where the whitewash and its painted design are applied directly to the original plaster. At the opposite end of the lean-to, on the north wall, fragmentary sections of plaster were found having a dark gray background with light-colored wavy lines. A color other than black occurs also at the Gedney house in Salem, where one of the more unusual variants of sponge painting has come to light. The heavy unmolded vertical sheathing of the right-hand room or parlor reveals that at some undetermined date, perhaps about 1700, a coat of whitewash was applied to this wall, together with an all-over freehand decoration in cocoa brown, looking like nothing so much as the tracks of some small three-toed animal. The practice in

Figure 265. Boardman house, Saugus, Mass. Upper entry, showing early eighteenth-century sponge painting. *Photo, Samuel Chamberlain, ca. 1936.*

Figure 266. Joseph Blaney house, Swampscott, Mass., ca. 1700. Demolished 1914. Detail of lean-to chamber floor board which formed ceiling of room below, decorated with sponge painting. *Photo, Richard Merrill, 1964.*

general seems to have continued to some extent at least throughout the eighteenth century. Later documentary references to sponge painting can be found, including a bill in 1741 from John Kneeland, mason, for "Colering and Spotting 2 Kitchens" at the Province house in Boston, official residence of the colonial governors of Massachusetts.[41] One of the latest examples dates from this same period and was found on the exposed ceiling frame of the hall, or left-hand room, of the Jason Russell house in Arlington, ca. 1740.

At a somewhat simpler level we should note here the survival in one or two instances of an overall surface application of color. Of uncertain (though perhaps early eighteenth-century) date is the treatment in the left-hand chamber of the Old Garrison, so-called, in Chelmsford, where the ex-

posed ceiling frame is covered with whitewash extending down to the upper edge of the chamfer ornamenting the girts and to the bottom of the bead of the casing that covers the plates. Below these points the frame and feather-edged sheathing of the room are covered with a coat of whitewash to which has been added yellow ochre. No less striking must have been the effect in the left-hand chamber of the Boardman house in Saugus, where the earliest application of whitewash to the molded vertical sheathing of the fireplace wall was colored a dark gunmetal gray. Again, by way of contrast, the exposed ceiling frame was uniformly white.

There are additional uses to which black paint could be put in architecture at the turn of the eighteenth century. These are relatively simple, and are confined almost entirely to the banding of fireplaces and plaster walls. One of the earliest examples in the former category was found on the original wall of the chamber in the Browne house in Watertown, where at a later period one would expect to find a baseboard (figure 231). The decoration of the fireplace is apt to take the form of a vertical band outlining the smoke panel and continuing horizontally at hearth level to the face of the jambs, and is normally painted upon a plaster lining applied directly to the masonry of the fireplace. A handsome and well-preserved example exists at the Parson Barnard house in North Andover. The vertical band here ornaments a smoke panel which is elaborately stepped back at the top in seven stages. The corners of the fireplace itself are pleasingly rounded and this segmental plan is echoed in the generous quarter-round profile of the painted decoration as the vertical and horizontal bands are joined (figure 268). Traces of banded decoration were also found in the original fireplaces in the chambers, and there is a painted black band approximately four inches high which runs around the walls of the west room, the northeast room in the lean-to, and both of the principal chambers at floor level. Painted directly upon the plaster (but not upon the sheathing of the fireplace walls), this banding is continued around the bottom surfaces of the wooden posts which are exposed and uncased in the rooms. Further, the same black banding can be found on the plastered surface of the chimney stack in the stairwell, following the outline of the risers and treads as they ascend to the second floor.

In contrast to plentiful traces of whitewash, we can point to no more than one or two examples of color in oil before 1700, and only a bare handful for the period 1700–1725. The documents, on the other hand, reveal that the practice was well established at least in the vicinity of Boston before 1700, at a time when the painter begins to emerge much more clearly as a professional person. Writing at the middle of the century Edward Johnson had boasted of New England's rapid material progress and the increased diversification of crafts, noting among others that "Carpenters, Joyners, Glaziers, [and] Painters, follow their trades only."[42] The first and only appearance by name, however, of any such figure in the Boston area before 1650 is Augustine Clement, who embarked from Southampton for New England in April 1635 in the *James* of London, listed as a painter, sometime of Reading in Berkshire.[43] Clement lived alternately in Dorchester and Boston, but we have no clues throughout the course of a long life as to how he may have exercised his craft. He did, however, train his only surviving son, Samuel Clement (1635–1678), for the same calling.

Other names appear before the end of the seventeenth century including that of Daniel George, who lived only four years after his arrival in Boston and died on July 18, 1684, aged twenty-nine. He is important, nevertheless, for the inventory of his estate, which reveals a highly sophisticated painter's stock in trade.[44]

Speculation as to just what these men of the seventeenth century may have painted in Boston and the surrounding towns is, of course, a tantalizing matter. An item appearing in an account rendered in November of 1657 in connection with the settlement of the estate of Captain Robert Keayne of Boston, "To the Painter for the scutcheons,"[45] indicates at least one of the tasks they

Figure 267. White-Ellery house, Gloucester, Mass. Lean-to kitchen with original painted decoration, ca. 1710. *Photo, Samuel Chamberlain, 1960.*

were expected to perform. Local New England painters may have been responsible as well for the "halfe headed bedsted with blew pillars" and the "livery Cupbord coloured blue" mentioned in an inventory of the contents of the King's Arms Tavern in Boston in 1651.[46] Somewhat more nearly related to architectural work, however, are the directions contained in a letter written by Samuel Newton from Barbados to Thomas Berry, mariner, of Boston in 1671. "God sending you safe to New England," he writes, "my order is that you receive into your custody the hull of the Catch; which I have building in Piscataquay. . . . And it is my order that you fit her Very well, and Set her forth handsomely with Carved work and very handsomely to Seile and Painte the greate Cabbin." Later in the same letter, he directs Berry to "take aboard what Loading I shall order you in Piscataquay, and then to carry her to Boston to fit

Interior Finish

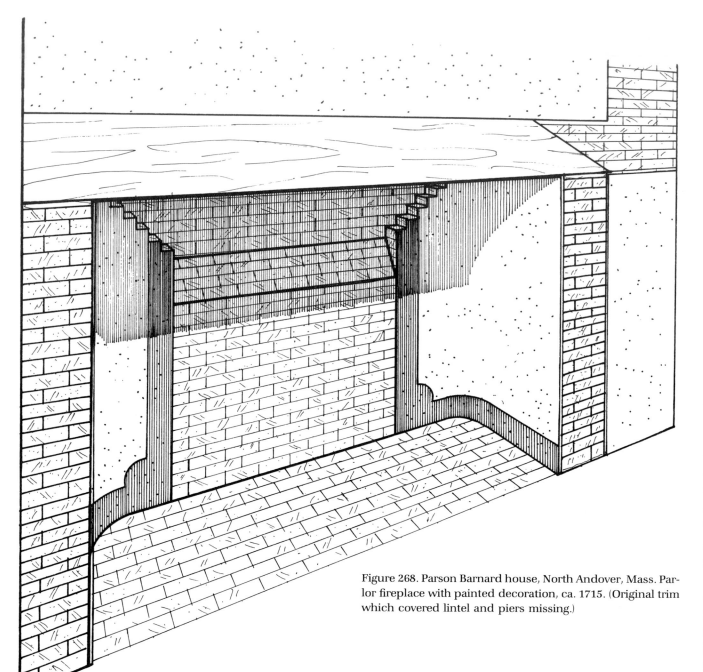

Figure 268. Parson Barnard house, North Andover, Mass. Parlor fireplace with painted decoration, ca. 1715. (Original trim which covered lintel and piers missing.)

her," which suggests that the painting was to be done there.[47]

Our first concise picture of architectural painting in late seventeenth- and early eighteenth-century Boston, however, can be found in the record of Thomas Child who was born and trained in England. He completed his apprenticeship and was admitted into the London Company of Painter Stainers in 1679, and is mentioned for the first time in America in 1685 when the name of "Thomas Child the Painter" occurs among a list of debtors to the estate of Mr. Samuel Smith of Boston.[48]

The earliest record of his professional activity is found in 1689 in "A memorandum of sure, honest, and well-disposed persons that Contributed their assistance for and towards erecting a Church for God's worship in Boston, according to the Constitution of the Church in England"—the predecessor of the present King's Chapel. Under a summary of costs, occurs the notation that "there was some other charge in painting the window frames by Tho. Child which demanded nothing for." His professional services were drawn upon again in 1698 when it was agreed at a meeting held on April 25 "That the window Shutters of the Church on the outside be painted by Thomas Child, as the Gates are."[49] A year earlier, on September 1, 1697, he had billed a "Mis Thomas" £2 for "priming 80 yards of flat worck" at "hur house," the first reference we have to any of his domestic work.[50]

Having been described as of Boston at the time of his marriage in 1688, and having lived briefly in Roxbury, Thomas Child acquired property in Boston in 1692 "joyning on the Creek, that leads from the Watermill," improved with two new brick buildings.[51] His purchases here can easily be identified with that small wedge of land bounded by the modern Hanover, Marshall, and Blackstone Streets, and facing south upon the mid-eighteenth-century Ebenezer Hancock house. Although there have been later encroachments in the widening of Hanover Street and in the conversion of the ancient Mill Creek to the modern Blackstone Street, and although the original buildings erected just before and during the occupancy of Thomas Child have given way to later construction, the area as a whole now has unusual significance. With its ancient street pattern and cluster of early buildings, it forms part of a small enclave which survives intact in a section of Boston whose historic topographical features were otherwise obliterated during 1963 and 1964 with the erection of the new Government Center.

Here Thomas Child lived and worked for the remainder of his life, and here his widow continued to carry on his painter's business; here, also, a nephew of hers, Edward Stanbridge, plied the same trade sometime between 1714 and 1725.[52] Of chief importance, however, is the almost miraculous survival on this site of two tangible relics of the Child business which have outlasted nearly three centuries of continual occupation and change. The first of these is the arms of the Painter Stainers' Company of London bearing the initials of Thomas and Katherine Child and the date 1697, soon altered to 1701 (figure 269). This device was attached to one of the new brick buildings which fronted on Hanover Street, and which remained standing into the nineteenth century, when it was described in a contemporary broadside as having been "of late years used as a hotel, and in front of which was an English coat of arms inwrought." The earlier building was removed in 1835 "to make way for the more modern Block which now occupies the spot, with the coat of arms replaced in front."[53] The building of 1835 is still standing and the arms remained plainly visible to passers-by until 1933 when cleaned of many coats of paint and sand and deposited in the Bostonian Society.

The second of the surviving artifacts is a stone paint mill which has never strayed from the site, and remains embedded in the foundation of the building erected in 1835 as one of the city's prominent landmarks under the name of the Boston Stone. A correspondent to the *New England Palladium* on March 26, 1822, furnishes an account of the site and its history:

Figure 269. Painter-stainers' coat of arms, bearing initials of Thomas and Katherine Child of Boston and the date 1701 (altered from 1697). *Photo, Barney Burstein, 1960.*

Figure 270. Paul Revere house, Boston, Mass. Detail of interior door with faint evidence of original painted decoration, ca. 1680. (The longer hinge is a twentieth-century reproduction.) *Photo, Richard Cheek, 1976.*

The second house in Marshal's lane, going from the northward, . . . was formerly occupied by a painter; and probably was built by him. . . . When the grandfather of the present occupant, purchased this house, the large square stone, now known as the *Boston Stone,* was in the yard. It is hollowed out in some measure, and . . . was probably used for grinding coarse paints. Being of no use in the yard, and the corner of the house where it now stands being greatly exposed to injury from the passage of carts and other carriages, it was removed to its present situation as a defence.

For the short span of Child's mature life, we have ample record of an active business career. On May 9, 1700, for example, Joseph Buckley of Boston noted payment to Thomas Child "for painting my howse[,] Territt and fences,"[54] and on October 30, 1702, the selectmen directed that "Mr. Thomas Child do the following work about the Latten Schoolmasters House vizt. finish the Gate and prime the fence, finish the Out side work of the house. And to prime the Inside worke of the Same."[55] In May of 1706 he billed one Captain John Miles for painting a hall and chamber "stone" color as well as painting casements and cornice.[56] Following his premature death at the age of forty-eight years on the following November 10, 1706, his widow carried on with the servants in the shop, and on February 25, 1707, rendered to the same Captain John Miles a statement which includes the earliest known reference in unequivocal terms to decorative painting on woodwork in New England: "To painting 26 yds. green Marble color" and "To 24 yds. Walnut colour."[57] While we have no exact knowledge of the style and character of these early Boston houses being painted toward the end of our period, it is clear at least that the concept of protecting—and enhancing—the exposed woodwork and finish trim was well established by the opening years of the eighteenth century.

At the same time the number of painters in Boston began to multiply. Withal, one wonders how these specialists were kept busy at their trade. One John Adams, painter, for example, who "Sayes that he with his Servant came from England with Captain Osborn" and arrived here the preceding December 7, was warned to depart the town on January 27, 1718. Was this designed as a measure of protection for the painters already established and for whom there was only a relatively sufficient amount of work? In any event, Adams then requested permission "for Occupeying his Trade here for 6 moneths ensuing," and this petition, too, was rejected on February 4.[58] Thus thwarted he moved to Marblehead, where he lived and worked as a painter until his death in 1732, having apparently become involved in a business way in the mid 1720s with one James Pearson of Marblehead, "Chairmaker and Painter."[59]

It is disappointing that only a few and only very simple examples of painted woodwork from the period under study survive. The beaded frame of the Clough(?)-How house in Vernon Place, built probably between 1697 and 1700, had a thin red paint or stain as its first coat of finish, applied perhaps at the very outset, and a gunmetal gray occurs in the entry of the Parson Barnard house in North Andover about 1715. The one really important exception, however, is a painted interior door found in a reused position at the Paul Revere house in Boston during the course of restoration in 1907–1908. The effect of paneling was achieved by the imposition of stiles and rails (now missing) on the surface of this single board door, and the space so defined was painted to simulate two widely feathered panels of oak (figure 270). Traces of this same oak graining were found on the frame underneath the later eighteenth-century casing, together with imitation hardwood panels on the plastered side walls, two of which survived over the door leading into the ell until the time of the restoration.[60] The house itself, erected about 1680, belonged originally to the merchant Robert Howard, who died in 1718, and the character of the trompe l'oeil painting of the door would suggest that it had been executed during his lifetime, perhaps when the house was first built. If so, it is the earliest surviving bit of painted decoration in architecture at Massachusetts Bay.

For the exterior our knowledge is even more severely limited, and scraping through accumulated layers of paint seldom reveals satisfactory evidence. When the French-Andrews house in Topsfield was restored during the summer of 1919, an Indian red paint or stain was found behind a later cornice on the board covering the plate. The same kind of evidence was found concealed at the cornice level of the General Sylvanus Thayer birthplace in Braintree, ca. 1720, and a few other examples of an exterior red color are known, among all of which it is clear that the stain had been applied to the trim only and not to the clapboards.

In any event, we recognize that by the end of the first quarter of the eighteenth century the house painter's trade, with its diversity of colors and range of decorative effects, was firmly established in Boston. The time had now come for a more rapid spread of painters and formal painting techniques to the country. And this pivotal moment between the maturing of urban developments and rural beginnings coincides in broad terms with the transition in provincial Massachusetts from the postmedieval to academic styles in vernacular building, and marks as well the conclusion of the first century of building activity.

CHAPTER X

Toward an American Architecture

IN EVALUATING THE houses built by English immigrants at Massachusetts Bay during the first century of settlement we are concerned with the product of a provincial culture significantly removed from its parent source. The culture was a homogeneous one because its constituents, though of differing geographic backgrounds in old England, were nevertheless members for the most part of a single social order. The two fundamental questions for the student of architectural history are: How quickly did the process of Americanization occur? What was the full extent of its force? These questions have been raised more than once as we examined the origins of the immigrant carpenters and their response to a new, heavily forested environment as it affected every aspect of the building process.

The first English colonists in New England were mostly young and venturesome. Whether they had ever been to sea or not, the trans-Atlantic crossing was nevertheless an experience of profound impact, with ministers, farmers, craftsmen, and a sprinkling of the gentry alike crowded into small ships, their future in many respects an open question. While whole families and small clusters of neighbors huddled together for reassurance, the really important experience for most was the ultimate mingling and interaction of persons drawn from many English counties with their own individual dialects and social customs, to say nothing of quite perceptibly different patterns of building.

We have drawn attention to the homogenization of distinctive English habits in construction and the reduction of many of them to a merely vestigial status. At the same time, certain of the more striking regional features retained a strong degree of identity. This was particularly true of the common purlin roof, which though representative of practices among a lesser majority of the first settlers and though modified by them, yet soon became a preferred structural system because of its ready adaptability to the New England experience. There emerged also at Massachusetts Bay during the later years of the seventeenth century a variety of architectural expressions which qualify, in turn, as native regionalisms. Thus we recognize the distribution of the transverse ground-story summer beam in the communities north of Boston and the presence of stone chimneys and of roof frames composed entirely of principal rafters in Middlesex County. The reasons for these concentrations are by no means complex when we observe the degree to which some of the English regional habits did indeed maintain the force of their individuality, coupled with the natural tendency for certain predelictions to perpetuate themselves within a given area once they have become firmly established.

Herein we may read the tenacious persistence of inherited traditions among the transplanted Englishmen. These were deeply ingrained traditions which they managed to communicate successfully to their sons and grandsons, thereby confirming popular notions about the characteristic British reluctance to depart from time-honored custom. While the process of innovation and adaptation begins almost at once, the English and New English carpenter seldom stray into unorthodox ways. In only one instance have we discovered a feature inspired obviously by common sense but almost comic in its defiance of conventional framing methods. At a house dating to about 1700 owned by the Greenwood Kennels on North Street in Topsfield, the builders, in capping a range of wall, have selected for the plate a timber with a branch growing at just the right forty-five degree angle to furnish a corner brace as well, which at its lower end is tenoned into the post. Over and beyond such eccentricities, and with respect to technical functions, we have pointed to a number of features in construction which suggest contemporaneous communication between

England and America throughout the entire period of our study, the presence, if you will, of a carpenters' grapevine by which craftsmen on both sides of the Atlantic kept themselves tuned in to current levels of progress at a comparable level of building.

On the other hand, the effect upon the structures of the physical environment and the ready availability of materials is dramatically apparent almost at once. The rapid adoption of clapboards and shingles for covering and sawn pine for planking, sheathing, and other details of finish radically altered the appearance of an otherwise English-looking dwelling. The impact of the new social order upon the colonists is much harder to gauge. Many of the settlers in Massachusetts, whether minister or mechanic, were dissenters, who, whatever their dissatisfaction with economic conditions at home or with the evolving system of English land tenure, had also found the religious climate uncongenial. Given the practical problems of establishing civil government and planting new communities in the wilderness under the umbrella of a single dominant church (for the most part, to be sure, of their own choosing), how much in the way of sumptuary influence can we discern in the first permanent homes erected? That these newcomers perpetuated the building forms most familiar to them is clear and unarguable. Thus Thomas Dudley, it could be maintained, was quite unmindfully following a normal inclination when it came to the finish of the house he built in Cambridge, while Governor Winthrop, on the other hand, was reacting to new social conditions when he rebuked him and said "that he did not well to bestow such cost about wainscotting and adorning his house, in the beginning of a plantation."[1]

Among the early seventeenth-century English houses that parallel most closely those erected by the founders of Massachusetts Bay, the basic similarities are more marked than any differences. It would be difficult, in fact, in light of such comparisons, to argue that the American builder was inhibited by Puritan "sobriety" or had been very deeply affected by the precepts implied in Winthrop's rebuke. Robert Cushman had indeed written to the Pilgrims at the outset of the plantation at Plymouth that "Our riches shall not be in pomp, but in strength. . . . You may see it amongst the best politics that a commonweal is readier to ebb than to flow, when once fine houses and gay clothes come up."[2] Yet the relatively modest Fairbanks house, built within a year or two of the first settlement at Dedham, is not only sturdy and sound, but its surfaces within are consistently finished with a traditional regard for niceties. We can point to contemporary English houses of the same relative size and socioeconomic status that are not one bit more elaborate, and in some cases even less so. On balance, one should be prepared to exercise great caution in developing any theory that strong religious influences at Massachusetts Bay significantly affected the form and finish of the houses erected for the farmers and artisans from the smaller rural English communities which fed the Great Migration.

In broader terms, however, the story of architecture in New England throughout the seventeenth century is one of change and Americanization. Recent historians have sought to illustrate the ways in which imported political institutions and concepts of land tenure once introduced into New England began to change almost at once in response to new conditions—and so it was with the buildings. The question is largely one of degree. While the proportions and profile of the dwellings erected by the first and second generation remained quite reminiscent of those in old England, with outshots and lean-tos in varying relations to the overall mass, there was a discernible drift toward standardization which would culminate in the fourth quarter of the seventeenth century in that outspokenly American development, the integral lean-to house. No matter how derivative in terms of plan, its compact arrangement of rooms and utterly practical solution to the technical problem of roofing both the principal rooms and the lean-to reveal at the same time the New Englander's inventiveness and fully matured adaptation to his surroundings. And in its very standardization and lack of variety it expresses the leveling tendencies in the social system which had marked increasingly the general progress of the New England experiment.

For the earliest years one is faced at once with a realization of the impact upon the first generation of the phenomenal challenge of new housing. Thousands of persons had to be sheltered literally within a matter of months, and in any effort to imagine the appearance of the house itself and the aggregate of structures which made up a given community during the first decade of settlement, we would perhaps have been more startled with a sense of the newness of it all and the ever-present reminders of the frontier than with the range and variety of English house forms or, for that matter, socioeconomic differences.

Quantitative data exist which supplement the material evidence of the buildings themselves and enable us to reconstruct the physical reality of the seventeenth century in something more than the necessarily fragmented pieces presented in our text. Dedham is an unfailing source of documentary information, as well as the site of the oldest framed house at Massachusetts Bay. We find here, fortuitously, not one but five tax rates between 1648 and 1676 giving the value of dwellings during the mid-century period. Thus we are informed how one community at least took physical shape, and learn something further about the range in quality. The earliest rate for 1648 lists eighty houses. The minister not unexpectedly heads the list and owned the most expensive dwelling, assessed at some £45. He was followed closely by a single fellow townsman whose house was considered to be worth £40. Three houses were valued between £31 and £34, twelve between £21 and £30 (including Jonathan Fairbanks's, appraised at £28), sixteen between £11 and £20, and the remainder, thirty-nine in number, ranged in value from £2 to £10. The figures reflect clearly the initial investments of a youthful community when compared with ensuing valuations, which show a consistent pattern of depreciation as the years passed. This is particularly evident in "The valuation of Houses" for 1674. More or less as before there is but a single house valued at £40 and a sizeable majority of eighty-two dwellings now classified in the £1 to £20 bracket, the Fairbanks house being entered at £9. The most startling fact to emerge from the later rate, however, is not the qualitative range but an almost total absence of growth. There are now, after twenty-six years, only eighty-six houses, an increase of no more than six over 1648.[3] We are reminded that the ongoing story of the seventeenth century was one of sons and grandsons leaving the parental homestead and pushing beyond the central confines of the original communities once the first allotted lands had all been taken up.

While the Dedham records illustrate the depreciation of the first-built structures over a period of time, there is also evidence that demonstrates a rapid growth in the value of new-built houses as the decades wore on. With the rigors of first settlement a thing of the past, the quality of housing seems to have improved dramatically. An analysis of probate inventories in Essex County for the 1640s and 1650s reveals, in terms of monetary value for dwellings appraised singly or lumped together with outbuildings and no more than two acres of land at most, a range as follows: for the decade 1640–1649, £3 to £16, averaging £7 per house; and for the decade 1650–1659, £10 to £48, with a median value of £27.[4]

And yet, qualitative differences are not always easy to identify. In our study of the house frame we have emphasized the varying levels of technological sophistication and the greater and lesser degrees of finish enrichment that have survived. Three hundred years of change have substantially modified the appearance of many of our seventeenth-century houses. Even as England experienced a time of "great rebuilding" during the reign of the Tudors, so New England has undergone successive waves of prosperity and cultural change which have left their mark, none more radical than the universal period of rebuilding after the American Revolution, and the even more devastating changes of the nineteenth century following the Industrial Revolution.

Particularly revealing is a comparison of the seventeenth-century house in New England before and after restoration. Photographs of the Appleton-Taylor-Mansfield house in Saugus, ca. 1680, for example (figures 271-274), taken before its restoration by Wallace Nutting in 1915, show the typically steep roof of the original frame raised and flattened to cover later additions at the rear; leaded casement windows replaced by double-hung sash; unpainted clapboards long since exchanged for newer ones painted white; two façade gables removed (a common fate for seventeenth-century houses); and a two-story porch at the front shorn off and its place taken by a nineteenth-century veranda. Indoors, in the left-hand parlor at least, the original walls were built out and papered, the frame for the most part cased, the exposed ceiling plastered, and the first wide fireplace reduced in size and furnished with a mantelpiece of the Federal period. As for the Turner house in Salem, the celebrated House of the Seven Gables, few school children today would be able to identify this familiar literary shrine from photographs taken before it was restored in 1909-1910 (figure 275). Even more significant, restoration in some cases has resulted in a curious distortion of architectural fact. Different components, no matter whether correctly restored, have been made to bear a visual relationship to one another which they never had borne at any given moment in their history (figure 276).

If we recognize profound changes in the name of fashion and convenience, and acknowledge as well nearly a century of brisk restoration activity, with wishful thinking often the only guide to the recreation of original details, then we have some feeling for the extraordinary importance of the more easily altered features that have nevertheless come through the years intact. Much of our effort, in fact, has been directed at finding and evaluating these ephemeral elements of finish trim or the proof of their former existence.

While now deprived of what must have been quite superior framed houses in Boston, we do nevertheless have such structures as the Turner and Corwin houses in Salem to convey some sense of the architectural refinements enjoyed by the mercantile elite. And we can observe, also, that a majority of the existing houses built by the average seventeenth-century citizenry at Massachusetts Bay fall within the broader middle and lower middle limits of the Dedham tax rates. Lacking altogether, however, is any physical evidence for the lowest part of the spectrum. There is reference in 1687 in Woburn to a "Hovell with a Seller in the Side hill,"[5] and although falling outside the limits of Massachusetts Bay, we have Madam Sarah Knight's illuminating description in 1704 of a "little cottage" in nearby Rhode Island on the banks of the "Paukataug River," which she further qualifies for us as "one of the wretchedest I ever saw a habitation for human creatures."

> It was suported with shores enclosed with Clapboards, laid on Lengthways, and so much asunder, that the Light come throu' every where; the doore tyed on with a cord in the place of hinges; The floor the bear earth; no windows but such as the thin covering afforded, nor any furniture but a Bedd with a glass Bottle hanging at the head on't; an earthan cupp, a small pewter Bason, A Bord with sticks to stand on, instead of a table, and a block or two in the corner instead of chairs. The family were the old man, his wife and two Children; all and every part being the picture of poverty. Notwithstanding both the Hutt and its Inhabitance were very clean and tydee: to the crossing the Old Proverb, that bare walls make giddy hows-wifes.[6]

Whatever the extremes in finish, we are dealing with the houses of people removed from us now by some three centuries. Philosophical differences in their approach to the question of aesthetics can be assumed as a matter of course. One should not be concerned to find that chamfers occasionally run into an adjoining beam without the refinement of a "stop," or that the bark edge of an otherwise neatly dressed structural member will sometimes remain exposed to view, even in the best of houses. Clearly, these aberrations represented no affront to seventeenth-century sensibilities. Nor should one be upset by the juxtaposition of fine chamfers with plain, unmolded sheathing. These contradictions *could* represent

Figure 271. Appleton-Taylor-Mansfield house (Ironworks House, so-called), Saugus, Mass., ca. 1680, unrestored. *Photo, Sullivan L. Holman, ca. 1900.*

Figure 273. Appleton-Taylor-Mansfield house. Parlor, unrestored. *Photo, Wallace Nutting, ca. 1915.*

Figure 272. Appleton-Taylor-Mansfield house, restored. *Photo, C. Parke Pressey, 1923.*

Figure 274. Appleton-Taylor-Mansfield house. Parlor, restored. *Photo, William W. Owens, Jr., 1974.*

Toward an American Architecture

Figure 275. Turner house, Salem, Mass., ca. 1668, with seventeenth-century addition. *Photo, ca. 1888–1897.*

tionship of posts and studs with the closely spaced members of the ceiling frame. There is a peculiar attraction for twentieth-century eyes. We appreciate the finely handcrafted surfaces and the harmonious proportions—what the engineer would call a pleasing aspect ratio among the individual structural elements. We must credit this almost entirely to tradition and to long-evolved respect for the intrinsic beauties of timber, with which the English had been fabricating their dwellings for over a thousand years. The Captain Thomas Fiske house is proof enough that the builders gave some thought to the overall aesthetic appearance of their product. How much of this was conscious deliberation is another matter. With our limited knowledge of the seventeenth-century carpenter and his thought processes, it is hard to imagine him discussing artily with client or colleague the decorative possibilities inherent in the rhythmic repetition of floor joists! Yet the effect is undeniable, and has become such a popular hallmark of the earliest interiors that many an overzealous restorer has exposed rough-hewn pine joists of a later period that had been ceiled with plaster from the outset and were never destined to play any other than a purely supportive role in the structure.

It is perhaps much more to the point to ask whether the seventeenth-century builders vocally rationalized among themselves the increasingly wider spacing of floor joists as the century wore on, moving from the lavish, close positioning noted at the close of Elizabeth's reign to a two-foot interval by the end of our period. This is an easily proved and consistent evolution, and one which among other progressive manifestations readily demonstrates a conscious experimental concern with the engineering dynamics *and* the economics of floor framing.

The houses erected at Massachusetts Bay during the seventeenth century and in rural areas at least throughout the first quarter of the eighteenth century constitute a homogeneous style group. We have considered the buildings of the entire period, therefore, as a unified whole. Where regional derivations from one or another

little parsimonies, although it is just as likely that they simple imply a different aesthetic gestalt!

It is enough that New Englanders, in perpetuating under "frontier" conditions an inherited house form that grew directly from functional needs, did not neglect pure decoration as well: chamfering and stopping of the frame units, molding the edges of boards, pilastering the masonry surface of the chimney, and affixing ornamental drops and brackets. We can be further grateful that these embellishments included such comely refinements as the serpentine braces of the Captain Thomas Fiske house in Wenham (figure 211). Here, as elsewhere, the contrast of dark wood against white plaster is agreeable, and is greatly enhanced by the forthright angular rela-

area in England can be discovered they have been enlarged upon, and evolutionary developments have been put forward as well. We must disagree with Fiske Kimball when he states that there is little sense of evolution in the seventeenth century,[7] for there are indeed measurable differences in style and technology between the buildings of 1650 and 1700, as we have seen. To argue, however, for flagrant stylistic extremes would seem unwise in light of the surviving structures themselves. The earliest framed houses were added to almost as soon as they were finished, and the process of change and improvement went on continually, culminating in a "high" period at the end of the seventeenth century as the homes of ministers, merchants, and prosperous farmers blossomed forth with boldly projecting overhangs, pyramided gables, and ornamental brackets and drops. They remained fundamentally postmedieval in form and finish, however, and it is probably much more to the point to distinguish as the crowning "evolutionary" developments of the period the emergence of the integral lean-to, or saltbox house, and the introduction of elaborate joiner's trim during the first quarter of the eighteenth century.

Where still exposed and uncovered, the house frame as an art form, having begun after 1700 to lose luster, preserved its postmedieval character until the middle of the eighteenth century in conservative situations. The well-documented addition at the east end of the Stanley-Lake house in Topsfield about 1750, for example (figure 277), aside from its applied trim, is still very much in the seventeenth-century tradition, both in the size and chamfered finish of its timbers, their jointing and arrangement, and in the exposure (when first erected) of whitewashed joists in the chamber. Nearly always, however, with respect to such recessive expressions, there will be features present of the same build which betray a later date. At the thoroughly backward-looking Boardman-Howard house in Saugus, for example, despite the starkly simple and only partially finished interiors which reflect a house of modest pretensions (figures 229 and 278), the late period of its

construction—almost certainly in the 1740s—is disclosed in the reduced width of otherwise seventeenth-century appearing fireplaces and in its single concession to ornament, a turned newel post for the original staircase (figure 279).

What then do we learn from the whole? The fully developed seventeenth-century house as it has come down to us has an important role to play with other forms of material culture in helping to dispel a classic myth of the dour, austere Puritan. Among even the more modest houses "austerity," if indeed present, can be argued only in much modified terms. These buildings, more-

Figure 276. Balch house, Beverly, Mass., seventeenth century. (Right-hand portion and windows restored to earlier appearance.) *Photo, George Brayton, 1922.*

Toward an American Architecture

Figure 277. Stanley-Lake house, Topsfield, Mass. Detail of post, plate, and end tie beam, east chamber, ca. 1750. *Photo, Richard Merrill, 1967.* (Above)

Figure 278. Boardman-Howard house, Saugus, Mass. Parlor chamber, ca. 1740–1750. *Photo, Richard Merrill, 1954.*

over, are immensely readable documents. If we look beyond the mechanics, the technical message of the exposed frame of a Gedney house, for example, we begin to see other things as well. We discover that it is an expensive house. Its young builder, an up-and-coming shipwright, had married the sister of one of the town's richest men, and the lavish show of finely wrought timber in the frame is an affirmation of Gedney's becoming status and aspirations.

An equally important lesson to be learned from the fully exposed frame of the Gedney house is that of sufrace finish. We are never closer to the seventeenth century (in feeling at least) than when we rip out later trim and expose original

walls and ceilings. But they are always shabby and stained, having been covered over by later generations for just such reasons. When restored and furnished with the correct period accessories we may regain some impression at least of how these rooms looked at first (figure 280). Even in the absence of period furnishings the inventories can help to conjure up a picture that is rich in texture and color and far from austere.

Edward Johnson wrote at mid-century that "there are not many Towns in the Country, but the poorest person in them hath a house and land of his own, and bread of his own growing, if not some cattel."[8] This was the end of a long journey which had begun in the harbor at Southamp-

Figure 279. Boardman-Howard house. Detail of staircase. *Photo, Richard Merrill, 1954.*

Figure 280. Story house, Essex, Mass. Hall, ca. 1684, as installed in the Henry Francis du Pont Winterthur Museum. *Photo, Gilbert Ask, 1960.*

ton a generation earlier. It was largely a success story, one of beginnings and experimentation and adaptation to a new way of life. If the unpainted, darkly time-stained houses of the seventeenth century have seemed dour and austere to a later generation, then the evaluation has been superficial. Color was there, surface ornament was there, human interest was there. If these houses have been dismissed as simple, boxlike shelters, primitive in their inspiration and crudely fabricated by a group of rough-and-ready pioneers, then the evaluation is actually in error. We have sought to explain that while four-square and uncomplicated in form, the early house frame embodies nevertheless a highly complex and sophisticated array of structural concepts, climaxing a

thousand years of English experience in building with timber. There has been little need to get caught up in the current argument over whether or not, as a further elaboration of the theme, carpenters' joints can be used as an absolute dating device.[9] The real point, it would seem, is not that joints date, in and of themselves, but that a technological progression can indeed be demonstrated, at least in very general terms. This is as easily seen, in fact, as the clearly established regional derivations, and forms the very core of our thesis that the immigrant English carpenters were forced from the first moment of their landing to come to grips with a new environment and to find technical solutions for new problems. Behind the clapboards and the many later surface

changes, the fundamental interest of the seventeenth-century house continues to be its knowingly engineered frame which keeps pace with experiment and growth in the mechanics of fashioning a new social order in the American wilderness. Looking back at the broad sweep of our period, which begins with the first settlements at Boston and Salem and concludes with the end of the first quarter of the eighteenth century and the introduction of a new Renaissance vernacular style in New England, the essential message is clear: the structures erected at Massachusetts Bay during these vital years not only link the old world with the new but also establish distinctive patterns of building which have become a deeply imbedded part of the American tradition.

Appendix
Notes
Index

APPENDIX TABLES

TABLE 1. OVERALL DIMENSIONS FOR DWELLING HOUSES RECORDED IN
CONTEMPORARY DOCUMENTS AT MASSACHUSETTS BAY, 1637–1706.

| Year | Location | For private individuals | | For ministers | Other |
		Length of 27 feet and less	Length over 27 feet		
1637	Ipswich		$30 - 35 \times 16 - 18$		
1640	Boston	16×14			
ca. 1650	Sudbury		30×16		
1653	Braintree		30×18		
1653 – 4	Ipswich		$30 \times -$		
1655	Boston		ca. $28 \times -$		
1657	Ipswich				16×12[a]
	Beverly			38×17	
1659	Ipswich	18×18[b]			
1661	Marlborough			37×18	
1662	Reading	27×18			
1663	Bradford		34×16		
1664	Boston		$42 \times -$		
1665	Cambridge	ca. 16×16			
1666	Cambridge	ca. $24 \times -$			
1667	Dorchester	$18 - 20 \times 18 - 20$			
	Salem (?)	25×16			
1668	Acton		40×18		
1669	Dedham		$40 - 50 \times 18 - 20$		

TABLE 1. (continued)

| Year | Location | For private individuals | | For ministers | Other |
		Length of 27 feet and less	Length over 27 feet		
1669	Dorchester			38 × 20	
	Salem (?)	23 × 18			
1670	Boston	— × 16[b]			
	Ipswich	16 × 16			
	Ipswich	18 × 18			
1671	Ipswich	20 × 20			
	Ipswich	18 × 18			
	Ipswich	16 × 16			
	Dorchester	ca. 20 × 18			
1673	Cambridge	12 × 12			
	Cambridge	ca. 20 × —[b]			
	Dorchester	ca. 24 × 16 − 18			
	Dorchester	ca. 16 × 14			
	Wenham			18 × 18[b]	
	Salem	26 × 18			
	Lynn-Reading	26 × 18			
	Lynn-Reading	24 × 20			
	Danvers			28 × 20[c]	
1677	Dorchester	ca. 26 × 18			
1678	Cambridge	ca. 16 × —[b]			
	Salem		35 × 20		
	Salisbury (?)	24 × 20			
1679	Boston		34 × 20[c]		

TABLE 1. (continued)

Year	Location	For private individuals		For ministers	Other
		Length of 27 feet and less	Length over 27 feet		
1679	Boston		30 × ca. 27		
	Dorchester	18 × 16			
	Salem	24 × 18			
1680	Cambridge	18 × 15			
	Cambridge	26 × —			
1681	Danvers			42 × 20	
	Haverhill		48 × 20		
1682	Cambridge	26 × —[c]			
1684	Cambridge		35 × 18		
	Cambridge	16 × 16			
1685	Watertown			40 × 20	
1687	Cambridge	20 × —[b]			
	Salem	18 × 15			
1691	Topsfield	25 × 20			
1692	Watertown	14 × 14			
1696	Island in Boston harbor	20 × 16			
1699	Manchester			42 × 18	
ca. 1700	Medford			38 × 29	
1700	Wenham		40 × 20		
	Wenham	26 × 18			
1701	Boxford			48 × 20[c]	
	Boston				40 × 20[d]

TABLE 1. (continued)

| | | For private individuals | | | |
| | | Length of 27 | Length over | | |
Year	Location	feet and less	27 feet	For ministers	Other
1705	Charlestown	20 × 18			
	Charlestown	20 × 18			
	Charlestown	20 × 18			
1706	Boxford				30 × 14[e]
	Charlestown	22 × 18			
	Groton			38 × 18[c]	

Source: Building contracts, timber allowances, deeds, and so forth.

a. For town pauper.

b. Addition to existing house.

c. Lean-to or ell specified as well.

d. For schoolmaster.

e. Poorhouse.

TABLE 2. TIMBER GRANTS FOR THE TOWN OF CAMBRIDGE, 1646–1687

	New houses, additions, enlargements	Repairs and individual frame members (including house covering)	Buildings, unspecified, and out-buildings	Total
January	12	57	26	95
February	18	40	32	90
March	15	53	16	84
April	10	11	9	30
May	14	29	13	56
June	1	9	3	13

TABLE 2. (continued)

	New houses, additions, enlargements	Repairs and individual frame members (including house covering)	Buildings, unspecified, and out-buildings	Total
July	1	0	0	1
August	1	1	3	5
September	0	3	3	6
October	6	5	1	12
November	8	29	17	54
December	15	16	28	59

TABLE 3. ROOM-BY-ROOM INVENTORIES FOR ESSEX, MIDDLESEX, AND SUFFOLK COUNTIES, MASSACHUSETTS, 1630–1660, INTERPRETED AS REFLECTING HOUSE PLANS.

At least one ground-floor room, with or without chambers above[a]	Place	Date	Value (in pounds)
Hall (cooking equip., drink vessels) Chamber over hall (best bed) Little chamber within (bedg., grain)	Dorchester	1642	52.6.8
Lower room (best bed, cooking equip.) Chamber (grain)	Boston	1643	70.10.0
Lower room (bedg.) Chamber (best bed)	Braintree	1643	671.3.0
Hall* (cooking equip., best bed)	Boston	1651	246.17.9
Parlor (bedg.) Chamber above (bedg.)	Dorchester	1654	82.10.8½
Chamber (best bed, flax) Hall or low room* (cooking equip.)	Dorchester(?)	1658	64.6.8
At least one ground-floor room, with unlocated chamber			
Chamber (best bed) Kitchen (cooking equip.)	Cambridge	1643	15.13.2

TABLE 3. (continued)

	Place	Date	Value (in pounds)
Chamber (best bed) Loft (grain, wool, flax) Fire room (cooking equip.) Cellar	Newbury	1647	153.9.8
Parlor (best bed) Chamber (bedg., grain)	Braintree	1647	75.13.0
Chamber (bedg., grain) Parlor (best bed, cooking equip., dairy and drink vessels)	Lynn	1653	135.9.10
Hall (cooking equip., best bed) Chamber (bedg., grain)	Woburn	1656	163.0.0
Hall* (cooking equip.) Chamber* (best bed)	—	1658	25.0.1
Hall* (best bed, cooking equip.) Chamber (bedg., grain, wool) Cellar (prov.)	Boston	1660	—

At least two ground-floor rooms,
  with or without chambers above

	Place	Date	Value (in pounds)
Hall* (cooking equip., dairy vessels) Parlor* (best bed) Chamber over parlor (bedg.)	Ipswich	1646	287.2.1
Parlor (best furn.) Hall* (bedg., cooking equip., churn, cotton, meat)	Roxbury	1646	112.8.8
Parlor* (bedg.) Kitchen* (cooking equip.) Chamber over parlor* (best bed) Chamber over kitchen (bedg.)	Ipswich	1648	—
Parlor (best bed) Chamber over parlor (bedg., churn, drink vessels) Kitchen (bedg., cooking equip.)	Dorchester	1649	184.12.6
Hall chamber* (best bed) Hall Kitchen (cooking equip.)	Boston(?)	1652	—

TABLE 3. (continued)

	Place	Date	Value (in pounds)
Hall (best bed, cooking equip.) Cellar Lean-to	Woburn	1653	—
Parlor (best bed) Hall (cooking equip., bedg., meat, grain)	Ipswich	1654	318.19.11
Hall Cellar* (cooking equip., drink vessels) Hall chamber (best bed) Garret (bedg.) Shop chamber Shop (goods)	Boston	1654	524.6.1
Parlor chamber Hall (cooking equip.) Parlor (best bed)	Boston	1655	185.0.0
Great chamber over hall (best bed) Closet next great chamber Chamber over kitchen* (bedg., grain) Garret (bedg., grain) Hall* Kitchen* (cooking equip.) Cellar (prov., cooking equip., butter, drink)	Boston	1655	1506.14.7½
Parlor* (best bed, cooking equip.) Kitchen	Marblehead	1656	74.10.6
Lodging room (best bed) Chamber over lodging room (bedg., grain) Chambers over kitchen (bedg., hemp, prov.) Kitchen (cooking equip.) Cellar (meat)	Hingham	1658	419.13.6
Chamber over shop (bedg.) Chamber over hall (bedg.) Garret Hall* Cellar	Boston	1658	719.10.0
Chamber over hall (bedg.) Hall* (best bed) Kitchen (cooking equip., wool, bedg.)	Boston	1659	225.13.0

TABLE 3. (continued)

	Place	Date	Value (in pounds)
Parlor (best bed) Room over parlor (bedg.) "Staire head" of parlor (bedg.) "Ovr ye hall" (bedg.) Room next street (bedg., cooking equip.)	Boston	1660	105.10.6

At least two ground-floor rooms, with unlocated chambers

	Place	Date	Value (in pounds)
Hall (cooking equip., drink vessels) Cellar (meat, prov.) Upon the chamber (bedg., grain) Lodging chamber (bedg., wool) Other lodging room (bedg.)	Watertown	1645	—
Lower room* (cooking equip., bedg.) Milk house (dairy vessels) Upper room (best bed) Chamber (grain)	Watertown	1645	—
Hall (cooking equip., dairy vessels, powdering tub) Chamber (grain, flax, prov., bedg.) Little room (best bed)	Ipswich	1646	83.1.10
Hall* (cooking equip.) Parlor (best bed) Little chamber (bedg.) Same room(?) (dairy vessels)	Roxbury	1647	166.4.0
Chamber (best bed) Parlor* Kitchen* (cooking equip., powdering tub)	Ipswich	1648	89.15.6
Hall* Kitchen (cooking equip.) Chamber (best bed, wool) Garret (bedg., grain)	Dorchester	1650	254.4.7
Hall* (cooking equip., bedg.) Cellar (cooking equip.) Chamber* (best bed) Shop (goods)	Boston	1650	—

TABLE 3. (continued)

	Place	Date	Value (in pounds)
Hall*	Boston	1650	681.2.1
Kitchen (cooking equip.)			
Chamber (best bed)			
Inner chamber (bedg.)			
Garret			
Great chamber (bedg.)	Boston	1652	236.3.2
Little chamber (best bed)			
Garret (bedg., grain)			
Hall* (cooking equip.)			
Shop			
Cellar			
One upper chamber (best bed)	Cambridge	1654	141.1.0
Another chamber (bedg.)			
Another upper chamber (bedg.)			
Another room(?) (cooking equip., powdering tub)			
Hall*			
Hall or fire room* (cooking equip.)	Dedham	1654	164.9.10
Cellar (powdering tubs, drink and dairy vessels)			
Bed chamber (best bed)			
Buttery			
Chamber (grain, meat)			
Fire room* (cooking equip.)	Dorchester	1656	151.12.8
Inner room (bedg.)			
Cellar (meat, drink vessels)			
Chamber (best bed?, grain)			
Parlor (best bed)	Rumney Marsh	1656	—
Closet			
Kitchen* (cooking equip.)			
Chamber			
Bed chamber (bedg.)	Dedham	1657	—
Lean-to (bedg.)			
Chamber (grain)			
Shop (tools of trade)			
Cellar			

TABLE 3. (continued)

	Place	Date	Value (in pounds)
Great chamber*	Boston(?)	1658	337.9.0
Chamber (bedg.)			
Over the kitchen (bedg.)			
Great lower room* (best bed)			
Kitchen* (cooking equip., grain)			
Cellar (meat, drink vessels)			
Parlor*	Concord	1659	1302.0.11[b]
Parlor chamber (best bed)			
Hall chamber (bedg.)			
Kitchen chamber (bedg., wool, yarn)			
Garret (bedg., grain)			
New chamber* (bedg.)			
New room* (cooking equip.)			
Parlor* (best bed)	Newbury	1659	737.0.0
Kitchen* (cooking equip., drink vessels, churn, powdering tubs)			
Chambers (bedg.)			
Other chamber (bedg., grain, wool)			
First chamber (best bed)	Roxbury	1659	34.4.1
Second chamber (bedg.)			
Garret chambers (bedg., grain)			
Another room(?) (cooking equip.)			
Hall			
Cellar (drink vessels)			
Hall* (best bed, cooking equip.)	Braintree(?)	1660	512.0.0
Chamber* (bedg.)			
Garret			
Buttery			
Cellar			
Parlor (best bed)	Boston	1660	132.11.4
Kitchen* (cooking equip.)			
Cellar			
Chamber (bedg., wool)			

At least three ground-floor rooms

	Place	Date	Value (in pounds)
Chamber over parlor (bedg., grain)	Dorchester	1637	168.5.0
Room within parlor* (bedg., cooking equip.)			
Parlor (best bed)			
Chamber over cellar (bedg., churn)			

TABLE 3. (continued)

	Place	Date	Value (in pounds)
Hall (best bed) Chamber over hall Chamber over kitchen Kitchen (cooking equip.) Milkhouse (dairy vessels) Room over milkhouse (grain)	Charlestown	1637	405.16.0
Hall* Parlor* (best bed) Chamber over parlor (bedg.) Lean-to (cooking equip., butter, cheese, grain)	Ipswich	1642	296.19.6
Hall* Parlor (best bed) Buttery (cooking equip., dairy and drink vessels) Parlor chamber (bedg., cheese, grain) Hall chamber (grain, wool)	Dedham	1652	—
Parlor (bedg.) Kitchen (cooking equip.) Cellar chamber (best bed, cooking equip., dairy vessels) Parlor chamber (bedg.) Kitchen chamber (bedg.)	Newbury	1652	164.4.0
Parlor (best bed, wool) Little room (within?) (bedg.) Kitchen* (cooking equip., dairy and drink vessels)	Newbury	1653	166.14.6
Parlor* (best furn.) Inward parlor (bedg.) Hall* (best bed, cooking equip.) Chamber over parlor (bedg.) Chamber over hall (bedg.)	Boston	1653	—
Hall* (best bed, prov.) Hall chamber* (cooking equip., bedg., prov.) Garret (bedg.) Shop (grain) Cellar* (prov., cooking equip.) Little room (meat vessels)	Dorchester	1654	373.16.0

TABLE 3. (continued)

	Place	Date	Value (in pounds)
Lean-to Fire room* (cooking equip.) Lodging room (best bed) Upon the chamber (bedg., grain) Cellar (meat, drink vessels)	Watertown	1655	181.16.0
Parlor* (best bed) Lodging room (bedg.) Hall (cooking equip.) Cellar (meat, dairy and drink vessels) Upon the chamber (grain, hemp)	Watertown	1655	—
Kitchen* (cooking equip.) Room next kitchen (bedg., meat, grain) Parlor (best bed) Room over kitchen (wool, hemp, flax) Room over parlor Another upper room	Dorchester	1657	550.1.8
Hall* Parlor* (best furn.) Parlor chamber* (best bed?) Hall chamber (bedg.) Garret over parlor chamber (bedg.) Kitchen* (cooking equip., dairy vessels)	Cambridge	1659	903.19.8
Shop, warehouse, chamber (part of dwelling?) (goods) "His Closet" Garret (bedg.) Hall chamber* (best bed) Shop chamber* (bedg.) Hall* Kitchen* (cooking equip.) Kitchen chamber (bedg.) Cellars (butter, drink vessels)	Boston	1659	8528.8.3
Cellar under hall* (cooking equip.) Hall* Little room (bedg.) Other little room* (bedg.) Closet Hall chamber* (best bed) Garret (bedg.)	Boston	1660	4239.11.5

TABLE 3. (continued)

	Place	Date	Value (in pounds)
At least three ground-floor rooms, with unlocated chambers and/or study			
Upon the chambers (bedg., grain) Parlor* (bedg.) Hall* (bedg.) Lodging chamber (bedg.) Dairy (dairy vessels) Another room(?) (cooking equip.)	Watertown	1644	—
Hall Parlor (bedg.) Great chamber Closet Hall chamber (best bed) Chamber over kitchen* (bedg.) Garret (bedg., grain) Kitchen (cooking equip.) Cellar	Salem	1647	586.2.2
Hall* Parlor (bedg.) Chamber (bedg.) An outward room (bedg.) Entry	Boston(?)	1649	—
Garret over parlor (hemp, tow) Garret over hall (Garret?) over porch (bedg.) Hall chamber (bedg.) Porch chamber (bedg.) Parlor chamber Stairway Parlor (best bed) Hall Entry Kitchen* (cooking equip.) Cellar (still) Study	Boston	1649	103.10.11[c]
Parlor (best bed) Hall* Kitchen (bedg.) Chambers (bedg., grain)	Cambridge	1653	—

TABLE 3. (continued)

	Place	Date	Value (in pounds)
Shop (goods) Lower warehouse Upper warehouse Cellar (prov., hops) Kitchen* (cooking equip.) Chambers* (best bed) Garret (grain)	Boston	1653	439.17.5½
Hall* (cooking equip.) Lodging room (best bed) Inner room (bedg.) Chamber	Boston	1653	120.8.0
Hall (best bed) Chambers (bedg.) Parlor (bedg.) Cellar (dairy and drink vessels) Kitchen	Concord	1653	—
Parlor (best bed) Closet Hall* Kitchen (cooking equip., dairy vessels) Cellar (powdering tubs) Kitchen chamber (bedg.) Parlor chamber (grain) Study (books)	Newbury	1656	597.11.4[b]
Parlor* (bedg.) Hall Study chamber (bedg.) Parlor chamber (best bed?) Kitchen (cooking equip.)	Boston	1657	—
End of lean-to (bedg.) Other end of lean-to (bedg.) Hall (best bed) Little chamber (bedg.) Upper chamber (bedg.) Corn chamber (bedg.) Cellar	Woburn	1658	—

TABLE 3. (continued)

	Place	Date	Value (in pounds)
Parlor*	Dedham	1658	1820.18.8
Parlor chamber (best bed?)			
Hall chamber (best bed?)			
Parlor garret (bedg.)			
Hall garret (bedg., prov.)			
Hall* (cooking equip., wool)			
Buttery (butter, dairy and drink vessels)			
Cellar			
Buttery chamber (grain)			
Lean-to chamber (wool, hemp, prov.)			
Parlor (best bed)	Dedham	1658	392.10.0
Lean-to (bedg.)			
Hall* (dairy vessels, cooking equip.)			
Bed chamber (bedg.)			
Cellar (powdering tubs, drink vessels, prov.)			
Chamber (grain, wool, hops, bedg.)			

At least four ground-floor rooms

	Place	Date	Value (in pounds)
Parlor (best bed)	Watertown	1644	553.2.9[b]
Hall*			
Kitchen* (cooking equip.)			
Dairy (dairy vessels)			
Parlor chamber (bedg.)			
Kitchen chamber (bedg.)			
Parlor chamber (bedg.)	Charlestown	1647	100.0.0
Parlor			
Hall			
Lean-to			
Cellar (meat, dairy vessels)			
Kitchen (cooking equip.)			
Hall* (best bed)	Dedham	1649	54.15.4
Bed chamber (bedg.)			
Buttery (cooking equip., drink vessels)			
Meal house			
Hall chamber			
Chamber over bed chamber			
Garret (grain)			

TABLE 3. (continued)

	Place	Date	Value (in pounds)
Parlor*	Boston	1650	328.17.0
Parlor chamber (best bed?)			
Kitchen chamber (bedg.)			
Garret			
Kitchen* (cooking equip.)			
Buttery (cooking equip.)			
Cellar chamber (bedg.)			
Lean-to (bedg., meal)	Charlestown	1654	—
Cellar (fish, drink and dairy vessels)			
Hall			
Parlor (best bed)			
Hall chamber (bedg., grain)			
New room* (bedg., cooking equip., dairy vessels)			
Chamber overhead (bedg.)			
Dairy chamber (meat, prov., flax, hops)			
Parlor* (best bed?)	Watertown	1657	—
Upon the chamber (bedg., grain, wool)			
Lodging room (bedg.)			
Hall* (cooking equip.)			
Lean-to (dairy vessels)			
Cellar (meat, dairy vessels)			
Hall*	Boston	1658	1339.1.1
Parlor* (some cooking equip.)			
Kitchen* (cooking equip.)			
Shop			
Hall chamber (best bed)			
Closet			
Shop chamber (bedg.)			
Porch closet			
Warehouse chamber			
Garret			
Two other garrets			
Kitchen chamber			
Cellar			
Parlor (bedg.)	Boston	1658	251.14.1
Kitchen (cooking equip.)			
Hall*			
Hall chamber (best bed)			
Shop (liquors, wool, hops)			
Cellar (still)			

TABLE 3. (continued)

	Place	Date	Value (in pounds)
At least four ground-floor rooms, with unlocated chambers and/or study			
Hall* (bedg.) Lean-to (dairy vessels) Parlor (bedg.) Kitchen (cooking equip.) Chamber (best bed)	Braintree(?)	1638	170.19.10
Shop (tools) Hall Buttery An other buttery Little chamber (bedg.) Hall chamber Shop chamber (bedg.)	Boston	1643	133.0.6
Great chamber (bedg.) Little chamber (best bed?) Inner chamber over hall (bedg.) Outward chamber over hall (bedg.) Hall Kitchen* (cooking equip.) Shop (tools) Back kitchen Little chamber at stairhead	Boston	1646	255.3.8
Garret (grain, bedg.) Chamber (bedg.) On the other side* (best bed?) Parlor Kitchen* Buttery (cooking equip.) Cellar (prov., drink) Counting house	Boston	1652	998.9.4
Parlor* Inward parlor (bedg.) Hall chamber (bedg.) Parlor chamber (best bed) Meal chamber (bedg., grain) Garret over parlor (bedg.) Other garret (bedg., wool) Cellar (drink vessels, powdering tubs)	Roxbury	1653	1546.4.9

	Place	Date	Value (in pounds)
Kitchen* (cooking equip., dairy vessels)			
Wash house			
Corn chamber (mault, meat)			
Study (books, bedg.)			
Parlor (best bed)	Watertown	1655	—
Chamber (bedg., meat, grain)			
Buttery (cheese)			
Cellar (meat, drink vessels)			
Lean-to (cooking equip.)			
Hall*			
Shop (goods)	Boston	1657	972.15.8½
Another room(?)* (cooking equip.)			
Lean-to (cooking equip.)			
Parlor* (best bed)			
Chamber (bedg.)			
Lodging chamber (bedg., grain)			
Parlor* (best bed, cooking equip.)	Dorchester	1659	206.18.2
Hall or out fire room*			
Buttery (churn)			
Little lodging room (bedg.)			
Chamber (bedg., grain)			
Garret (bedg.)			
Cellar (meat and drink vessels)			
Chamber (bedg.)	Boston	1660	539.13.5
Kitchen* (cooking equip.)			
Lean-to (cooking equip.)			
Loom room			
Shop (goods)			
Cellar			
Hall* (cooking equip.)	Dedham	1660	405.6.0
Bed chamber (bedg.)			
Lodging room (best bed, flax)			
Cellar (meat and drink vessels)			
Parlor (drink, dairy, and meat vessels)			
Lean-to (cooking equip.)			
Several chambers and other places (bedg., grain)			

TABLE 3. (continued)

TABLE 3. (continued)

	Place	Date	Value (in pounds)
At least five ground-floor rooms			
Hall*	Boston	1653	2774.14.4
Chamber over parlor* (bedg.)			
Press (bedg.)			
Counting house (bedg.)			
Entry			
Parlor*			
Kitchen* (cooking equip.)			
Closet between kitchen and parlor			
Cellar			
Closet at stairhead			
Garret (bedg.)			
Little room (bedg.)			
"An Out house"			
Over kitchen (bedg.)			
Warehouse (bedg.)			
Parlor* (bedg.)	Roxbury	1657	812.7.6
Chamber over parlor (best bed)			
Chamber over hall (bedg.)			
Chamber over shop (grain)			
Meal chamber little parlor (bedg.)			
Shop (wool, flax)			
Hall			
Kitchen* (cooking equip., dairy vessels)			
Great cellar			
Old cellar			
Parlor* (best bed)	Boston	1658	434.13.5
Parlor chamber (bedg., grain)			
Kitchen chamber* (bedg.)			
Kitchen*			
Buttery (cooking equip.)			
Little parlor (bedg.)			
Shop chamber (bedg.)			
Out room			
Cellar (drink)			
Shop (tools)			
Parlor* (best bed)	Cambridge	1658	—
Little room out of the parlor			
Hall*			
Buttery (drink vessels)			

TABLE 3. (continued)

	Place	Date	Value (in pounds)
Cellar (dairy and drink vessels, flax)			
Kitchen (cooking equip., meat, cheese press)			
Parlor chamber (bedg., wool, hops)			
At least five ground-floor rooms, with unlocated chambers and/or study			
Shop (goods)	Roxbury	1646	2028.10.3
Hall			
Old kitchen* (cooking equip.)			
Cellar (dairy vessels)			
Kitchen			
Inner chamber (bedg.)			
Best chamber* (best bed)			
Study			
Upper chamber (bedg.)			
Little garret			
Little room behind kitchen (powdering tub)			
Little room behind Hall			
Little garret over shop (grain)			
New house chamber	Cambridge	1647	—
Kitchen			
Shop			
Lean-to			
Cellar			
Lean-to chamber			
Chamber			
Kitchen chamber			
Shop chamber			
Garret			
Counting house			
K. H. (cooking equip.)			
Little parlor* (best bed)	Boston	1653	1038.4.0[b]
Hall*			
Great parlor*			
Great chamber* (bedg.)			
Garret over great chamber (bedg.)			
Little chamber* (bedg.)			
Over porch (bedg.)			
Garret over little chamber and porch (bedg.)			
Garret over study (bedg.)			

Appendix Tables

TABLE 3. (continued)

	Place	Date	Value (in pounds)
Study* (books)			
Lean-to chamber (bedg.)			
Gallery ("1 bedsted")			
Lean-to parlor (bedg.)			
Kitchen* (cooking equip.)			
Larder cupboard			
Cellar (drink vessels)			
Hall	Ipswich	1653	158.15.3
Little parlor (best bed)			
Shop kitchen buttery* (tools, meat, butter, cooking equip.)			
Chambers (bedg., grain, wool, flax, hops)			
Parlor*	Boston	1658	577.5.0
Parlor chamber* (bedg.)			
Hall chamber (bedg.)			
Hall* (bedg.)			
Inner hall			
Lodging room* (bedg., cooking equip.)			
Lodging room within hall (best bed)			
Garret			
Study (books)			

Source: Registries of Probate for Essex, Middlesex, and Suffolk counties, in Salem, East Cambridge, and Boston, Mass., respectively.

a. Certain of the household contents, including provisions, have been summarized in parentheses when they define domestic functions which help to locate rooms within the plan as a whole. Thus, the presence of grain, hops, wool, flax, and so forth has been noted, since such items were apt to be housed in upper stories. The probable presence of a fireplace in any given room as suggested by fireplace equipment has been indicated by an asterisk.

b. Minister.

c. The governor.

TABLE 4. TIMBER BUILDING PERMITS FOR NEW DWELLING HOUSES AND ADDITIONS, BOSTON, 1707–1729.

Year	Length (feet)	Width (feet)	Stud (feet)	Roof	Remarks
1707	37	22	23	flat[a]	
	24	21	17	flat	Addition at rear, to replace part of house 21 × 14 feet, 10 feet stud

TABLE 4. (continued)

Year	Length (feet)	Width (feet)	Stud (feet)	Roof	Remarks
1707	42	20½ (front) 28½ (rear)	25	flat	To replace house 32 × 20½ feet
	20	18	22	flat	
	23	20	15	—	
	28	20	22	flat	Addition to east end of house, to replace existing construction
	40	20	17	—	
	31	24	17	—	With rear kitchen lean-to, 31 × 9 feet
	40	21	24	—	With attached kitchen, 20 × 16 feet, 16 feet stud
	40	19	22	flat	With attached kitchen, 18 × 12 feet, 15 feet stud
	23	18	16	—	
	17	15	14	—	Kitchen addition, to replace old kitchen, 16 × 9 feet
	19	18	15	flat	Detached kitchen, about 15 feet from house
	—	12	—	—	Kitchen addition, breadth of house
1708	20	13	14	—	Lean-to
	40	19	17	—	
	38	20	22	flat	
	40	20	18	—	
	12	12	7	flat	Lodging chamber over a passage between kitchen and dwelling house
	28	18	24	flat	
	30	20	22	flat	

TABLE 4. (continued)

Year	Length (feet)	Width (feet)	Stud (feet)	Roof	Remarks
1708	19	19	17	flat	Addition to side of house
	31	19	24	—	Addition to side of house
	32	26	22	flat	
	16	15	17	flat	Addition to end of house
	20	18	24	flat	Addition to side of house
	20	16	16	—	Addition to side of house, to replace old lean-to 20 × 12 feet, 8 feet stud
	14	11	14	flat	Kitchen addition to end of house
1709	39	20	32	flat	
	24	20	20	—	Addition to end of house, to replace old building, 24 × 12 feet
	21	16	19	flat	To replace old house, same dimensions
	17	12	16	flat	Kitchen addition to corner of house
	32	20	22	flat	To replace old house, 25 feet square
	40	20	18	—	To replace old house, 30 feet long
	18	17	21	flat	Addition to end of house, to replace old lean-to of about the same dimensions
	32	16	14	—	
	40	20	23	flat	
	25	18	17	flat	To replace old "building," 20 × 12½ feet
	18	14	9	—	Detached kitchen, 16 feet from house
	36	28	16	—	
	39	20	18	—	

TABLE 4. (continued)

Year	Length (feet)	Width (feet)	Stud (feet)	Roof	Remarks
1709	38	18	24	flat	
	30	21	26	flat	To replace old "building" about 24 × 16 feet
	30	16	26	flat	
	43	25	26	flat	To replace old house of about the same dimensions
1710	17	14	18	—	Kitchen addition to end of house
	23	17	21	flat	
	44	20	27	flat	
	26	13	14	—	Kitchen lean-to addition
	24	24	15	—	
	43	34	25	flat	
	36	24	18	—	
	42	18	26	flat	To replace old house, 38 × 18 feet, 18 square feet to be retained for kitchen at rear of new house
	48	19	—	—	Parsonage, "Three Stories high"
	24	20	18	—	With kitchen lean-to, 12 feet wide
	36	20	18	—	
	30	9	24	—	Addition to breadth of old house, to replace old building, same dimensions
	38	20	22	—	
	40	18	22	flat	
	72	36	28	flat	"Dwelling house and Shops"
	20	16	26	—	To replace old "building" of about the same dimensions

TABLE 4. (continued)

Year	Length (feet)	Width (feet)	Stud (feet)	Roof	Remarks
1710	32	20 (front) 16 (rear)	25	flat	
1711	21	17	22	flat	To replace old "building" 14 × 8 feet, 14 feet stud
	36	30	18	—	
	26	25	19	flat	
	39	18	17	—	To replace old "building" about as long
	34	32	22	flat	
	32	27	20	flat	
	32	27	20	flat	
	38	19	18	pitch	With attached kitchen 12 × 12 feet at one end
	48	30	17	—	
	38	19	16	—	
	40	20	27	flat	
	26	14	18	flat	Kitchen lean-to addition to end of house
	40	18	16	—	
	17	11	14	—	Cow house, to be moved and converted to a dwelling
	25	18	23	flat	
	20	12	16	—	"Part of a Dwelling house"
1713	40	38	24	—	To replace old house of about the same dimensions
	22	14	15	—	Detached kitchen
1714	20	16	12	—	Barn, to be moved and converted to a dwelling

TABLE 4. (continued)

Year	Length (feet)	Width (feet)	Stud (feet)	Roof	Remarks
1714	40	16	22	—	
	34	18	18	—	
	42	36	25	—	
	20	20	—	—	Kitchen addition to replace old kitchen 20 × 18 feet
	40	22	27	—	
	16	12	16	—	Addition to corner of parsonage, to replace old "building" 12 × 12 feet
	20	18	—	—	Addition to rear of house
	40	30	18	—	
	32	20	15	—	
	40	20	26	—	
	48	22	27	—	With kitchen addition 15 × 15 feet at one end
1715	22	6	24	—	Addition to breadth of house (22 feet) at one end
	35	35	18	—	
	50	21	18	—	
	40	20	18	—	
1717	30	20	18	—	
	40	30	20	—	
	55	30	20	—	With kitchen addition 20 × 20 feet
1718	15	11	14	—	Kitchen addition to middle of one side of house
	38	16	16	—	To replace old "building" of about the same dimensions

TABLE 4. (continued)

Year	Length (feet)	Width (feet)	Stud (feet)	Roof	Remarks
1719	30	20	16	—	
1720	18	18	16	—	Addition to end of house
	40	18	18	—	
1721	39	19	—	—	
	50	28	—	—	"Two storys hight"
	26	20	18	—	
1722	20	16½	8½	—	Kitchen, to be no more than a story high
1723	40	40	20	—	
1724	20	20	—	—	Addition to house "to make an even front to the said House which is now in the form of an L."
1725	34	16	18	—	
	34	18	18	—	"A small Kitchin behind"
	34	18	18	—	"A small Kitchin behind"
	22	18—20	18	—	
1726	58	35	19	—	
1727	66	21	21	—	
	44	32	18	—	
1728	38	19	18	—	With a "Small Kitchen" addition
	40	20	18	—	With a "small Kitchen" addition
	36	18	18	—	
1729	36	18—19	18	—	

Source: *A Volume of Records Relating to the Early History of Boston, Containing Miscellaneous Papers* (Boston: Municipal Printing Office, 1900), pp. 181—225.

a. William Leybourn, *A Platform for Purchasers* . . . (London, 1668). See plate, end of Second Book, where a "flat" roof is illustrated as one having a pitch of little more than twenty degrees.

TABLE 5. LENGTH OF BLADED SCARFS (OVERALL).

House	Date	Length of scarf (inches)
Fairbanks house, Dedham	ca. 1637	20¾
Pierce house, Dorchester	ca. 1650	19¾
Corwin house, Salem	ca. 1675	ca. 14
Appleton-Taylor-Mansfield house, Saugus	ca. 1680	ca. 27
Capen house, Topsfield	1683	ca. 25
Boardman house, Saugus	ca. 1687	18
Cooper-Frost-Austin house, Cambridge	ca. 1689	24
Ephraim Wheeler house, Concord	ca. 1700(?)	23¾
Platt-Bradstreet house, Rowley	after 1700	ca. 26
French-Andrews house, Topsfield	ca. 1718	ca. 18
Blanchard-Wellington house, Medford	ca. 1720	23¼
Parker Tavern, Reading	ca. 1725	22
Chaplin-Clark-Williams house, Rowley	ca. 1725	23¾

TABLE 6. SPACING OF FLOOR JOISTS.

Widest measurement (inches, on centers)

English examples (random sample)	Date	Approx. measurement (in.)
Lower Dairy Farm, Little Horkesley, Essex	1601	~17.5
House, Weathercock Hill, Chevington, Suffolk	1605	~17.5
Bailiff's House, Bewdley, Worcs.	1610	~17.75
Tanhouse Farm, Stoke Prior, Bromsgrove, Worcs.	1631	~18
Boring Mill Cottage, Coalbrookdale, Shrops.	1636	~17.5

Examples at Massachusetts Bay	Date	Approx. measurement (in.)
Fairbanks, Dedham	ca. 1637	~17
Blake, Dorchester	ca. 1650	~18
Pierce, Dorchester	ca. 1650	~18.25
Pickering, Salem (1)[a]	ca. 1651	~19.5
Austin Lord, Ipswich	before 1653	~18.5
Coffin, Newbury	ca. 1654	~19.5
Whipple, Ipswich (1)	ca. 1655	~18.5
Brown, Hamilton (1)	1662–1673	~17.75
Gedney, Salem	ca. 1665	~20.5
Bradstreet, No. Andover (summer beam)	ca. 1666	~18.5
Turner, Salem (1)	ca. 1668	~20.5
Swett-Ilsley, Newbury	ca. 1670	~18.9
Pickering, Salem (2)	ca. 1671	~20.5
Narbonne, Salem	ca. 1672	~18.9
Wilson-Appleton, Ipswich (1)	after 1672	~17.9
Corwin, Salem	ca. 1675	~20.5
Cushing, Hingham	1679	~17.9
Appleton-Taylor-Mansfield, Saugus	ca. 1680	~22.9
Paul Revere, Boston	ca. 1680	~18.9
Samuel Pickman, Salem	before 1681	~21.4
Whipple, Ipswich (2)	before 1683	~17
Capen, Topsfield	1683	~21.9
Story, Essex	ca. 1684	~21
Ward, Salem	after 1684	~21.9
Andrews, Hingham	1685–1690	~19.5
Quincy, Quincy (1)	ca. 1686	~18.9
Boardman, Saugus	ca. 1687	~21.9
Cooper-Frost-Austin, Cambridge	ca. 1689	~18.9
Browne, Watertown	1694–1701	~20
Capt. Thomas Fiske, Wenham	ca. 1698	~21.9
George Hart, Ipswich	ca. 1698	~21.9
Moody Bridges, No. Andover	ca. 1700	~21.4

George Giddings, Essex	ca.1700
Goldsmith-Pickering, Wenham	ca.1700
Knowlton, Ipswich	ca.1700
Wilson-Appleton, Ipswich (2)	1702–1718
White-Ellery, Gloucester	after 1703
Knight-Dimond, Marblehead (2)	before 1708
William Howard, Ipswich (2)	1709
John Allen, Marblehead	after 1709
Cottle, Newburyport	ca.1710
Parker-Orne, Marblehead	ca.1711
Parson Barnard, No. Andover	ca.1715
Hovey, Ipswich (1)	1718–1724
French-Andrews, Topsfield	ca.1718
Samuel Wilson, Needham	ca.1718
Abbot, Andover (2)	ca.1725
Burnham, Essex (2)	ca.1725
Chaplin-Clark-Williams, Rowley	ca.1725
Parker Tavern, Reading	ca.1725
Upton, West Andover	ca.1725
Hapgood, Stow	ca.1726

[a] Numbers in parentheses refer to first or second stage of building.

NOTES

INTRODUCTION

1. Bradford Torrey, ed., *The Writings of Henry David Thoreau, Journal* (Boston and New York: Houghton Mifflin, 1906), XII, 36.

2. The Reverend Nathan Chamberlain, *A Paper on New-England Architecture . . .* (Boston, 1858), pp. 4, 6.

3. Alvin Lincoln Jones, *Under Colonial Roofs* (Boston, 1894), p. iii.

4. Thomas F. Waters, "Some Old Ipswich Houses," *Publications of the Ipswich Historical Society*, V (1898), 39.

5. James Birket, *Some Cursory Remarks . . . in his voyage to North America, 1750–1751* (New Haven: Yale University Press, 1916), p. 15.

6. *The Diary of William Bentley, D.D. . . .* (Gloucester, Mass.: Peter Smith, 1962), III, 44.

7. See index to vols. XLIV–LXVII (1908–1931) of the *Essex Institute Historical Collections*, and vols. II–XIII (1898–1909) of *The Essex Antiquarian*.

I. THE ENGLISH BACKGROUND

1. Anthony N. B. Garvan, *Architecture and Town Planning in Colonial Connecticut* (New Haven: Yale University Press, 1951), p. 7.

2. J. Franklin Jameson, ed., *Johnson's Wonder-Working Providence, 1628–1651* (New York: Charles Scribner's Sons, 1910), p. 58.

3. Charles Edward Banks, *Topographical Dictionary of 2885 English Emigrants to New England, 1620–1650* (Philadelphia: Elijah Ellsworth Brownell, 1937), map facing p. xiii.

4. W. G. Hoskins, "The Rebuilding of Rural England, 1570–1640," *Past & Present*, no. 4 (November 1953), p. 50.

5. M. W. Barley, *The English Farmhouse and Cottage* (London: Routledge and Kegan Paul, 1961), table of contents.

6. *Public General Acts* (London, 1589), chap. 7.

7. Barley, *The English Farmhouse*, p. 67.

8. Raphael Holinshead, William Harrison, and others, *The Firste Volume of the Chronicles of England, Scotlande, and Irelande* (London, 1577), second book, chap. 10, p. 85.

9. Richard Carew, *The Survey of Cornwall* (London, 1602), p. 66.

10. *Winthrop Papers* (Boston: Massachusetts Historical Society, 1929–1947), III, 73.

11. James Savage, ed., *The History of New England from 1630 to 1649, By John Winthrop, Esq. . . . from his original manuscripts . . .* (Boston, 1853), I, 104.

12. Barley, *The English Farmhouse*, pp. 28, 43–44, 62–63, 77, 140.

13. Ibid., p. 75.

14. D/AER 17, f. 72v, Essex Record Office, Chelmsford, Essex.

15. Barley, *The English Farmhouse*, pp. 42, 45, 94–95, 139–141, 165.

16. Holinshead, *Chronicles of England*, second book, chap. 10, p. 85.

17. Barley, *The English Farmhouse*, p. 43n.

18. Daniel King, *The Vale-Royall of England . . .* (London, 1656), p. 19.

19. A. C. Edwards, *Elizabethan Essex* (Chelmsford, Essex: Essex County Council, 1961), fig. 13.

20. Harry Forrester, *The Timber-Framed Houses of Essex* (Chelmsford, Essex: Tindal Press, 1960), p. 7.

21. D/ABW 19/359, Essex Record Office, Chelmsford, Essex.

22. Peter Eden, "Smaller Post-medieval Houses in Eastern England," *East Anglian Studies*, ed. Lionel M. Munby (Cambridge, Eng.: W. Heffer & Sons, 1968), pp. 79, 91.

23. Sylvia Colman, "Two Small Mediaeval Houses . . . ," *Proceedings of the Suffolk Institute of Archaeology*, vol. 31, pt. 1 (1976), p. 65.

24. Ibid., p. 70.

25. Sidney O. Addy, *The Evolution of the English House*, 3d. ed. (London: Swan Sonnenschein, 1910), chap. 2; Garvan, *Architecture and Town Planning*, pp. 105–107; Barley, *The English Farmhouse*, pp. 19–20, 48, 79, 123, 151; M. W. Barley, "Rural Housing in England," *The Agrarian History of England and Wales*, ed. Joan Thirsk (Cambridge, Eng.: University Press, 1967), pp. 762, 765.

26. M. W. Barley, "Farmhouses and Cottages, 1550–1725," *Economic History Review*, 7 (April 1955), 294.

27. L. B. and M. W. Barley, "Lincolnshire Craftsmen in the Sixteenth and Seventeenth Centuries," *The Lincolnshire Historian*, vol. 2, no. 6 (1959), p. 21.

28. Barley, *The English Farmhouse*, pp. 70–71, 98, 140, 280–281, 143.

29. Holinshead, *Chronicles of England*, second book, chap. 10, pp. 84–85, and ibid., 1586 ed., second book, chap. 12, p. 188.

30. A. C. Edwards, *Essex Homes, 1066–1850* (Chelmsford, Essex: Essex County Council, 1965), fig. 10.

31. A. C. Edwards, "The Homes of Essex," label copy for exhibition mounted by the Essex Record Office, 1965.

32. Edwards, *Essex Homes*, figs. 11–12; and D/DP M1325, f. 596, Essex Record Office, Chelmsford, Essex.

33. Holinshead, *Chronicles of England*, second book, chap. 10, p. 85.

34. D/ABW 16/275, Essex Record Office, Chelmsford, Essex.

35. Forrester, *The Timber-Framed Houses of Essex*, p. 11.

36. Margaret Wood, *The English Mediaeval House* (London: Phoenix House, 1965), p. 221.

37. L. F. Salzman, *Building in England . . .* (Oxford: The University Press, 1967), pp. 430–432.

38. Wood, *The English Mediaeval House*, p. 222; Barley, *The English Farmhouse*, p. 29.

39. Barley, *The English Farmhouse*, p. 29.

40. Forrester, *The Timber-Framed Houses of Essex*, p. 13.

41. Barley, *The English Farmhouse*, p. 142.

42. Lord Francis Hervey, ed., *Suffolk in the XVIIth Century, The Breviary of Suffolk by Robert Reyce, 1618 . . .* (London: John Murray, 1902), pp. 50–51. Internal evidence suggests a date of about 1603 rather than 1618 for the original manuscript.

43. Forrester, *The Timber-Framed Houses of Essex*, p. 13.

44. Edwards, "The Homes of Essex," label copy. See also mimeographed reports on "Walker Field-Days," Essex Record Office, Chelmsford, Essex.

45. Banks, *Topographical Dictionary*, p. xv.

46. *Johnson's Wonder-Working Providence*, p. 50.

47. Ibid., pp. 21–22.

48. Bernard Bailyn, *The New England Merchants in the Seventeenth Century* (New York: Harper and Row, 1964), p. 16.

49. Alexander Young, *Chronicles of the First Planters of the Colony of Massachusetts Bay . . .* (Boston, 1846), p. 305.

50. Charles Edward Banks, *The Planters of the Commonwealth* (Baltimore: Genealogical Publishing Co., 1961), pp. 138, 143, 199, 161, 187.

II. FIRST SHELTERS AND INDIGENOUS BUILDING FORMS

1. William Wood, *New Englands Prospect* (London, 1634), pp. 2, 4, 7.

2. *The Boston Weekly News-Letter*, December 28–January 4, 1732/3.

3. *The Diary of William Bentley, D.D.* . . . (Gloucester, Mass.: Peter Smith, 1962), IV, 477.

4. J. Franklin Jameson, ed., *Johnson's Wonder-Working Providence, 1628–1651* (New York: Charles Scribner's Sons, 1910), p. 65; and Wood, *New Englands Prospect*, p. 50.

5. *Winthrop Papers* (Boston: Massachusetts Historical Society, 1929–1947), III, 138.

6. Alexander Young, *Chronicles of the First Planters of the Colony of Massachusetts Bay* . . . (Boston, 1846), p. 378.

7. James Savage, ed., *The History of New England from 1630 to 1649, By John Winthrop, Esq.* . . . *from his original manuscripts* . . . (Boston, 1853), I, 52–53. (Hereafter cited as Winthrop, *Journal.*)

8. Young, *Chronicles*, p. 378.

9. *Johnson's Wonder-Working Providence*, p. 65.

10. Young, *Chronicles*, p. 351.

11. Fiske Kimball, *Domestic Architecture of the American Colonies and of the Early Republic* (New York: Charles Scribner's Sons, 1922), p. 3.

12. C. F. Innocent, *The Development of English Building Construction* (Cambridge, Eng.: University Press, 1916), pp. 8–13.

13. E. B. O'Callaghan, ed., *Documents Relative to the Colonial History of the State of New-York* . . . (Albany, 1856–1883), I, 368.

14. *Johnson's Wonder-Working Providence*, pp. 113–114.

15. George B. Cheever, *The Journal of the Pilgrims at Plymouth* . . . (New York, 1848), p. 39.

16. Wood, *New Englands Prospect*, pp. 101, 99.

17. George Francis Dow, ed., *Records and Files of the Quarterly Courts of Essex County, Massachusetts* (Salem, Mass.: Essex Institute, 1911–1975), VI, 363. (Hereafter cited as Essex Quarterly Court Files, published.)

18. Winthrop, *Journal*, I, 43.

19. Young, *Chronicles*, p. 339.

20. George Francis Dow, "The Colonial Village Built at Salem, Massachusetts, in the Spring of 1930," *Old-Time New England*, ser. no. 65 (July 1931), p. 9.

21. *Johnson's Wonder-Working Providence*, p. 92.

22. Wood, *New Englands Prospect*, p. 96.

23. Don Gleason Hill, ed., *The Early Records of the Town of Dedham, Massachusetts, 1659–1673* . . . (Dedham, Mass., 1894), p. 85.

24. M. Halsey Thomas, ed., *The Diary of Samuel Sewall, 1674–1729* (New York: Farrar, Straus and Giroux, 1973), I, 162.

25. "Scituate and Barnstable Church Records," *New England Historical and Genealogical Register*, X (1856), 42.

26. Young, *Chronicles*, p. 374.

27. Nathaniel B. Shurtleff and others, eds., *Records of the Colony of New Plymouth in New England* (Boston, 1855–1861), II, 111. See also Richard M. Candee, "A Documentary History of Plymouth Colony Architecture, 1620–1700," *Old-Time New England*, ser. no. 218 (October–December 1969), pp. 38–39.

28. "Samuel Maverick's Account of New England in 1630," *Proceedings of the Massachusetts Historical Society*, second ser., I (1884–1885), 236.

29. Essex Quarterly Court Files, published, I, 28.

30. Innocent, *The Development of English Building Construction*, pp. 128–129.

31. C. F. Swift, ed., *Genealogical Notes of Barnstable Families Being a Reprint of the Amos Otis Papers* . . . (Barnstable, Mass., n.d.), I, 203.

32. Young, *Chronicles*, pp. 258–259.

33. Ibid., p. 379.

34. *Johnson's Wonder-Working Providence*, p. 211.

35. Young, *Chronicles*, pp. 380–381.

III. THE HOUSE PLAN

1. Edward Everett Hale, Jr., ed., *Note-Book kept by Thomas Lechford, Esq., Lawyer, in Boston, Massachusetts Bay, from June 27, 1638, to July 29, 1641* (Cambridge, Mass., 1885), p. 302.

2. Ibid., p. 56.

3. Suffolk County Probate Records, I, 77–78, Suffolk County Registry of Probate, Boston.

4. Essex Quarterly Court Files, VI, 70–71, Office of the Clerk of the Superior Court for Essex County, Salem, Mass. (Hereafter cited as Essex Quarterly Court Files, MS.)

5. *Winthrop Papers* (Boston: Massachusetts Historical Society, 1929–1947), IV, 11.

6. Essex County Probate Records, vol. 311, p. 338, Essex County Registry of Probate, Salem, Mass.; Essex County Deeds, vol. 100, p. 117, Essex County Registry of Deeds, Salem, Mass.

7. *Winthrop Papers*, IV, 11–12.

8. George Francis Dow, ed., *Records and Files of the Quarterly Courts of Essex County, Massachusetts* (Salem, Mass.: Essex Institute, 1911–1975), I, 198. (Hereafter cited as Essex Quarterly Court Files, published.)

9. Felicia Doughty Kingsbury, "A Roof-Tree that grew . . . ," *Old-Time New England*, ser. no. 139 (January 1950), p. 183.

10. Suffolk County Probate Records, XIII, 222.

11. M. W. Barley, *The English Farmhouse and Cottage* (London: Routledge and Kegan Paul, 1961), p. 109.

12. *The Diary of William Bentley, D.D.* . . . (Gloucester, Mass.: Peter Smith, 1962), IV, 127. (Hereafter cited as Bentley, *Diary.*)

13. See Abbott Lowell Cummings, "Notes on Furnishing a Small New England Farmhouse," *Old-Time New England*, ser. no. 171 (January–March 1958), p. 78.

14. Barley, *The English Farmhouse*, pp. 143, 135.

15. *Proceedings of the Massachusetts Historical Society*, second ser., XI (1896–1897), 4–6. (Not a probate inventory.)

16. Suffolk County Probate Records, I, 4 (new ser.).

17. Francis W. Steer, *Farm and Cottage Inventories of Mid-Essex* (London and Chichester: Phillimore & Co., 1969), pp. 194, 174, 165.

18. Suffolk County Probate Records, II, 29.

19. Ibid., I, 52–53 (new ser.).

20. Ibid., III, 218.

21. George Francis Dow, ed., *The Probate Records of Essex County, Massachusetts* (Salem, Mass.: Essex Institute, 1916–1920), I, 89, 310. (Hereafter cited as Essex County Probate Records, published.)

22. Middlesex County Probate Records, I, 107, Middlesex County Registry of Probate, East Cambridge, Mass.

23. Suffolk County Probate Records, V, 112.

24. Steer, *Farm and Cottage Inventories*, pp. 179–270.

25. Suffolk County Probate Records, I, 348; Essex County Probate Records, published, II, 63.

26. See, for example, James Savage, ed., *The History of New England from 1630 to 1649, By John Winthrop, Esq.* . . . *from his original manuscripts* . . . (Boston, 1853), II, 412. (Hereafter cited as Winthrop, *Journal.*)

27. *Winthrop Papers*, IV, 12.

28. Bentley, *Diary*, IV, 127.

29. *Note-Book kept by Thomas Lechford*, pp. 65–66.

30. Suffolk County Probate Records, III, 213, and II, 162.

31. Ibid., V, 113.

32. Suffolk County Court Records, docket no. 1833, Office of the Clerk of the Supreme Judicial Court for Suffolk County, Boston.

33. Suffolk County Deeds, IV, 37, Suffolk County Registry of Deeds, Boston.

34. Suffolk County Probate Records, XI, 190.

35. Middlesex County Probate Records, first ser., docket no. 5172.

36. Barley, *The English Farmhouse*, p. 95.

37. Middlesex County Probate Records, first ser., docket no. 5172.

38. Sidney Perley, ed., "Boxford Town Records, 1685–1706," *Historical Collections of the Topsfield Historical Society*, V (1899), 79.

39. *A Report of the Record Commissioners of the City of Boston, Containing the Records of Boston Selectmen, 1701 to 1715* (Boston, 1884), p. 11.

40. *The Records of the Town of Cambridge . . . Massachusetts, 1630–1703* . . . (Cambridge, Mass.: City Council, 1901), p. 257.

41. *Note-Book kept by Thomas Lechford*, p. 219.

42. Essex County Probate Records, vol. 302, p. 125.

43. Suffolk County Probate Records, II, 35, 41.

44. Barley, *The English Farmhouse*, pp. 134, 63.

45. Suffolk County Probate Records, I, 52–53 (new ser.).

46. Essex Quarterly Court Files, published, III, 119–120.

47. Suffolk County Probate Records, XXXVII, 162.

48. Barley, *The English Farmhouse*, p. 94.

49. Suffolk County Probate Records, I, 488 (new ser.).

50. Suffolk County Deeds, IV, 222.

51. *Second Report of the Record Commissioners of the City of Boston, 1877* (Boston, 1877), p. 146.

52. Essex Quarterly Court Files, MS, V, 51.

53. Ibid., VI, 86.

54. Essex County Probate Records, vol. 303, p. 98, and docket no. 28367.

55. Bentley, *Diary*, I, 26.

56. Suffolk County Deeds, V, 26.

57. Essex County Probate Records, published, I, 385.

58. Middlesex County Probate Records, XXII, 150.

59. Suffolk County Court Records, docket no. 1833.

60. C.O. 1/36, no. 34, Public Record Office, London.

61. Suffolk County Probate Records, V, 178.

62. Ibid., II, 106, and I, 85.

IV. The Builders and Their Resources

1. Erastus Worthington, *The History of Dedham . . .* (Boston, 1827), p. 38.

2. Don Gleason Hill, ed., *The Early Records of the Town of Dedham, Massachusetts, 1636–1659 . . .* (Dedham, Mass., 1892), pp. 30, 47–49 (hereafter cited as Dedham Town Records, 1636–1659); Charles Edward Banks, *The Planters of the Commonwealth* (Baltimore: Genealogical Publishing Co., 1961), pp. 162, 184, 187; Suffolk County Deeds, I, 326, Suffolk County Registry of Deeds, Boston; and *A Volume Relating to the Early History of Boston Containing the Aspinwall Notarial Records from 1644 to 1651* (Boston: Municipal Printing Office, 1903), p. 69.

3. John West, *Village Records* (New York: St. Martin's Press, 1962), p. 126.

4. *Second Report of the Record Commissioners of the City of Boston, 1877* (Boston, 1877), pp. 156–157.

5. Lane Family papers, privately owned.

6. Alexander Young, *Chronicles of the First Planters of the Colony of Massachusetts Bay . . .* (Boston, 1846), p. 261.

7. *Winthrop Papers* (Boston: Massachusetts Historical Society, 1929–1947), II, 161, 192.

8. William Wood, *New Englands Prospect* (London, 1634), p. 56.

9. *Winthrop Papers*, III, 124.

10. James Savage, ed., *The History of New England from 1630 to 1649, By John Winthrop, Esq. . . . from his original manuscripts . . .* (Boston, 1853), I, 138. (Hereafter cited as Winthrop, *Journal*.)

11. Nathaniel B. Shurtleff, ed., *Records of the Governor and Company of the Massachusetts Bay in New England* (Boston, 1853–1854), I, 74, 76, 84, 109, 159.

12. Winthrop, *Journal*, I, 246.

13. J. Franklin Jameson, ed., *Johnson's Wonder-Working Providence, 1628–1651* (New York: Charles Scribner's Sons, 1910), pp. 247–248.

14. Essex Quarterly Court Files, XXX, 116, Office of the Clerk of the Superior Court for Essex County, Salem, Mass. (Hereafter cited as Essex Quarterly Court Files, MS.)

15. George Francis Dow, ed., *Records and Files of the Quarterly Courts of Essex County, Massachusetts* (Salem, Mass.: Essex Institute, 1911–1975), VI, 91. (Hereafter cited as Essex Quarterly Court Files, published.)

16. *Town Records of Manchester . . .* (Salem, Mass., 1889), p. 98.

17. *A Report of the Record Commissioners of the City of Boston, Containing the Records of Boston Selectmen, 1701 to 1715* (Boston, 1884), pp. 11, 23, 28. (Hereafter cited as Boston Selectmen's Records, 1701–1715.)

18. Suffolk County Probate Records, XVI, 350, Suffolk County Registry of Probate, Boston.

19. *The Diary of William Bentley, D.D. . . .* (Gloucester, Mass.: Peter Smith, 1962), III, 263. (Hereafter cited as Bentley, *Diary*.)

20. Robert F. Trent, *The Joiners and Joinery of Middlesex County, Massachusetts, 1630–1730*, M.A. thesis, University of Delaware, May 1975, p. 69; "Col. Carrigain's Letter Respecting the Endecott Rock," *New England Historical and Genealogical Register*, I (1847), 312–313.

21. Dedham Town Records, 1636–1659, p. 74.

22. Middlesex County Court Records, folios 7 and 31, Office of the Clerk of the Superior Court for Middlesex County, East Cambridge, Mass.

23. Middlesex County Deeds, IV, 299, Middlesex County Registry of Deeds, East Cambridge, Mass.

24. William Barry, *A History of Framingham, Massachusetts . . .* (Boston, 1847), pp. 27, 11.

25. Middlesex County Deeds, XII, 607; Middlesex County Probate Records, first ser., docket no. 8130, Middlesex County Registry of Probate, East Cambridge, Mass.

26. Essex Quarterly Court Files, published, IX, 133.

27. Essex Quarterly Court Files, MS, VI, 70.

28. Henry W. Belknap, *Trades and Tradesmen of Essex County, Massachusetts . . .* (Salem, Mass.: Essex Institute, 1929), pp. 59, 55–56, 32.

29. Essex County Deeds, I, 30, Essex County Registry of Deeds, Salem, Mass.

30. Essex Quarterly Court Files, published, II, 92, and I, 290–291. See also Essex County Deeds, I, 62.

31. Curwen Family papers, I, 68, Essex Institute, Salem, Mass.

32. Curwen Family papers, American Antiquarian Society, Worcester, Mass.

33. Suffolk County Deeds, XII, 219; Suffolk County Court Records, docket no. 4399, Office of the Clerk of the Supreme Judicial Court for Suffolk County, Boston.

34. Edward Everett Hale, Jr., ed., *Note-Book kept by Thomas Lechford, Esq., Lawyer, in Boston, Massachusetts Bay, from June 27, 1638, to July 29, 1641* (Cambridge, Mass., 1885), p. 302.

35. William P. Upham and others, eds., "Town Records of Salem . . . ," *Essex Institute Historical Collections*, XLVIII (1912), 166. (Hereafter cited as Salem Town Records, *Essex Institute Historical Collections*.)

36. Suffolk County Probate Records, XIV, 144, and VI, 278 (new ser.).

37. Joseph Brown, Jr., Account Book, Essex Institute.

38. *Milton Town Records, 1662–1729* (Milton, Mass., 1930), p. 136.

39. Essex Quarterly Court Files, published, VI, 247.

40. Frances M. Caulkins, *History of New London, Connecticut . . .* (New London, Conn., 1852), p. 231.

41. Essex County Deeds, II, 96, and XII, 21.

42. Essex Quarterly Court Files, published, I, 82, 101; II, 1, 90; III, 106.

43. John Hull, Letterbook, typescript, p. 296, American Antiquarian Society.

44. *Note-Book kept by Thomas Lechford*, p. 303.

45. Essex Quarterly Court Files, published, VI, 6, 129; III, 393; VII, 385–386; Essex Quarterly Court Files, MS, XXXIII, 39.

46. *Re-Dedication of the Old State House, Boston, July 11, 1882*, 4th ed. (Boston, 1887), pp. 129–130.

47. Young, *Chronicles*, pp. 264, 266–267.

48. *Note-Book kept by Thomas Lechford*, p. 248.

49. Suffolk County Probate Records, I, 16, and II, 2–3.

50. George Francis Dow, ed., *The Probate Records of Essex County, Massachusetts* (Salem, Mass.: Essex Institute, 1916–1920), I, 64. (Hereafter cited as Essex County Probate Records, published.)

51. Suffolk County Probate Records, II, 7, 11, 15, 22; Middlesex County Probate Records, II, 54; III, 45.

52. See, for example, Charles F. Montgomery, ed., *Joseph Moxon's Mechanick Exercises . . .* (New York: Praeger Publishers, 1970); Henry C. Mercer, "Ancient Carpenters' Tools," *Old-Time New England*, ser. nos. 40 (April 1925)—53 (July 1928); and W. L. Goodman, *The History of Woodworking Tools* (London: G. Bell and Sons, 1964).

53. Henry C. Mercer, "Ancient Carpenters' Tools," *Old-Time New England*, ser. no. 40 (April 1925), p. 191 and fig. 28.

54. Essex County Probate Records, published, III, 205.

55. William H. Bowden, ed., "Marblehead Town Records," *Essex Institute Historical Collections*, LXIX (1933), 237.

56. Wood, *New Englands Prospect*, p. 55.

57. Middlesex County Probate Records, first ser., docket no. 8130.

58. Benno M. Forman, "Mill Sawing in Seventeenth Century Massachusetts," and Richard M. Candee, "Merchant and Millwright," *Old-Time New England*, ser. no. 220 (April–June 1970).

59. Dedham Town Records, 1636–1659, p. 39.

60. See, for example, Essex Quarterly Court Files, published, II, 363, and VIII, 377.

61. Don Gleason Hill, ed., *The Early Records of the Town of Dedham, Massachusetts, 1659–1673 . . .* (Dedham, Mass.,

1894), pp. 227–229, 13. (Hereafter cited as Dedham Town Records, 1659–1673.)

62. Essex Quarterly Court Files, published, I, 297–298.

63. See Marian Card Donnelly, "Materials in Early New England," *Old-Time New England*, ser. no. 224 (April–June 1971).

64. Wood, *New Englands Prospect*, pp. 16–18.

65. Charles Francis Adams, ed., *The New English Canaan of Thomas Morton* (Boston, 1883), p. 182.

66. Benno M. Forman, *The Seventeenth Century Case Furniture of Essex County, Massachusetts, and Its Makers*, M.A. thesis, University of Delaware, June 1968, pp. 7 and 95.

67. John Josselyn, *An Account of Two Voyages to New-England . . .* (London, 1674), p. 61.

68. John Evelyn, *Silva: or, a Discourse of Forest-Trees . . . delivered in the Royal Society the 15th of October, 1662 . . .*, 5th ed. (London, 1729), I, 56.

69. *The New English Canaan of Thomas Morton*, p. 183.

70. Boston Selectmen's Records, 1701–1715, pp. 162 and 164.

71. Wood, *New Englands Prospect*, p. 18.

72. *The New English Canaan of Thomas Morton*, p. 184.

73. Dedham Town Records, 1636–1659, pp. 157 and 140.

74. Josselyn, *An Account of Two Voyages*, p. 67.

75. *Fourth Report of the Record Commissioners of the City of Boston, 1880, Dorchester Town Records*, 2d ed. (Boston, 1883), p. 168; W. Noel Sainsbury, ed., *Calendar of State Papers, Colonial Series, America and West Indies, 1675–1676 . . .* (London, 1893), p. 467.

76. Essex Quarterly Court Files, published, VI, 323.

77. Wood, *New Englands Prospect*, p. 19.

78. M. W. Barley, *The English Farmhouse and Cottage* (London: Routledge and Kegan Paul, 1961), pp. 103, 118.

79. Bentley, *Diary*, II, 311.

80. Josselyn, *An Account of Two Voyages*, pp. 67–68.

81. Wood, *New Englands Prospect*, p. 18.

82. *Wenham Town Records* (Wenham, Mass.: Wenham Historical Society, 1930–1940), I, 177.

83. Ibid., I, 157.

84. J. W. Fortescue, ed., *Calendar of State Papers, Colonial Series, America and West Indies, 27 October, 1697–31 December, 1698 . . .* (London: His Majesty's Stationery Office, 1905), p. 537.

85. John Norden, *The Surveyors Dialogue* (London, 1607), p. 211.

86. Dedham Town Records, 1636–1659, pp. 25, 5, 14, 63, 15; Dedham Town Records, 1659–1673, pp. 173, 79, 167–169.

87. *Johnson's Wonder-Working Providence*, p. 116.

88. Suffolk County Deeds, II, 156, and IV, 50.

89. *A Report of the Record Commissioners of the City of Boston, Containing the Boston Records from 1660 to 1701* (Boston, 1881), p. 130.

90. *The New English Canaan of Thomas Morton*, pp. 180, 172–173.

91. *The Records of the Town of Cambridge . . . Massachusetts, 1630–1703 . . .* (Cambridge, Mass.: City Council, 1901), p. 162.

92. Oliver Rackham, "Grundle House: On the Quantities of Timber in Certain East Anglian Buildings in Relation to Local Supplies," *Vernacular Architecture*, III (1972), 3–8.

93. Salem Town Records, *Essex Institute Historical Collections*, IX (1868), 31.

94. Dedham Town Records, 1659–1673, p. 144.

V. ASSEMBLY AND REARING
OF THE HOUSE FRAME

1. Cecil A. Hewett, *The Development of Carpentry, 1200–1700, An Essex Study* (Newton Abbot, Devon.: David and Charles, 1969), p. 168.

2. Peter Nicholson, *An Architectural Dictionary . . .* (London, 1819), II, 704. See also Asher Benjamin, *The Builder's Guide . . .* (Boston and Philadelphia, 1839), p. 82.

3. T. N. Philomath [Richard Neve], *The City and Countrey Purchaser, and Builder's Dictionary . . .* (London, 1703). (Hereafter cited as Neve, *Builder's Dictionary*, 1703 or 1726 ed.)

4. Charles F. Montgomery, ed., *Joseph Moxon's Mechanick Exercises . . .* (New York: Praeger Publishers, 1970), p. 165.

5. Norman M. Isham, *Early American Houses* (Topsfield, Mass.: The Wayside Press, 1928), p. 23.

6. Suffolk County Deeds, II, 186, Suffolk County Registry of Deeds, Boston.

7. George Offor, ed., *Remarkable Providences . . . by Increase Mather* (London, 1890), pp. 52–53.

8. Hewett, *The Development of Carpentry*, p. 16, and conversations with the author.

9. *Joseph Moxon's Mechanick Exercises*, p. 163.

10. Dennis Family papers, Massachusetts Historical Society.

11. *Joseph Moxon's Mechanick Exercises*, p. 133.

12. *Winthrop Papers* (Boston: Massachusetts Historical Society, 1929–1947), IV, 12.

13. Henry A. Hazen, *History of Billerica, Massachusetts . . .* (Boston, 1883), p. 108.

14. Henry Wotton, *The Elements of Architecture* (London, 1624), p. 11.

15. See Isham, *Early American Houses*, fig. 19.

16. Franklin P. Rice, ed., *First Records of Marlborough, Massachusetts* (Worcester, Mass.: Franklin P. Rice, 1909), p. 13; *Fourth Report of the Record Commissioners of the City of Boston, 1880, Dorchester Town Records*, 2d ed. (Boston, 1883), p. 162.

17. *Winthrop Papers*, IV, 12.

18. John Mortimer, *The Whole Art of Husbandry . . .*, 2d ed. (London, 1708), p. 302.

19. Faulkner House, Acton, Mass., 1706–1709.

20. L. F. Salzman, *Building in England . . .* (Oxford: The University Press, 1967), pp. 206, 450, 205.

21. Edward Everett Hale, Jr., ed., *Note-Book kept by Thomas Lechford, Esq., Lawyer, in Boston, Massachusetts Bay, from June 27, 1638, to July 29, 1641* (Cambridge, Mass., 1885), p. 54; Neve, *Builder's Dictionary*, 1726 ed.

22. *A Report of the Record Commissioners of the City of Boston, Containing Miscellaneous Papers* (Boston, 1886), p. 136. (Hereafter cited as Boston Record Commissioners' Report no. 10.)

23. Ibid.; Essex Quarterly Court Files, VI, 70, Office of the Clerk of the Superior Court for Essex County, Salem, Mass. (Hereafter cited as Essex Quarterly Court Files, MS.)

24. *Joseph Moxon's Mechanick Exercises*, p. 160.

25. Jonathan Corwin, Account Book, vol. for 1656–1679, American Antiquarian Society, Worcester, Mass.; *The Records of the Town of Cambridge . . . Massachusetts, 1630–1703 . . .* (Cambridge, Mass.: City Council, 1901), p. 280.

26. *Joseph Moxon's Mechanick Exercises*, pp. 132–133 and plate 10.

27. *Winthrop Papers*, IV, 12.

28. *Joseph Moxon's Mechanick Exercises*, p. 163.

29. Essex Quarterly Court Files, MS, XXIV, 115.

30. Lane Family papers, privately owned.

31. Neve, *Builder's Dictionary*, 1703 ed., p. 30.

32. Boston Record Commissioners' Report no. 10, p. 136.

33. *Note-Book kept by Thomas Lechford*, p. 54.

34. Benjamin, *The Builder's Guide*, p. 82.

35. Peter Nicholson, *The Carpenter's New Guide . . .* (London, 1793), p. 54.

36. Batty Langley, *Ancient Masonry . . .* (London, 1736), dictionary index, see Beam.

37. Neve, *Builder's Dictionary*, 1703 ed., p. 30.

38. *Joseph Moxon's Mechanick Exercises*, p. 141.

39. M. Halsey Thomas, ed., *The Diary of Samuel Sewall, 1674–1729* (New York: Farrar, Straus and Giroux, 1973), II, 763.

40. *Winthrop Papers*, IV, 12.

41. *Wenham Town Records* (Wenham, Mass.: Wenham Historical Society, 1930–1940), I, 168.

42. Dennis Family papers, Massachusetts Historical Society.

43. Nicholson, *An Architectural Dictionary*, I, 263–264.

44. John Evelyn, *Silva: or, a Discourse of Forest-Trees . . . delivered in the Royal Society the 15th of October, 1662 . . .*, 5th ed. (London, 1729), I, 208–211.

45. Ibid., I, 212 (second of two pages so numbered).

46. Suffolk County Court Records, docket no. 1916, Office of the Clerk of the Supreme Judicial Court for Suffolk County, Boston.

47. Edith LaFrancis, "Barn-Raising Day: 1900," *Yankee* (September 1966), pp. 88–89.

48. Sidney Perley, ed., "Boxford Town Records, 1685–1706," *Historical Collections of the Topsfield Historical Society*, V (1899), 80.

49. Hewett, *The Development of Carpentry*, pp. 204–207.

50. *Joseph Moxon's Mechanick Exercises*, p. 165.

51. Edward Shaw, *Civil Architecture* . . . , 2d. ed. (Boston, 1832), pp. 189, 142.

52. Hewett, *The Development of Carpentry*, pp. 204–205.

53. *Massachusetts Gazette*, September 23, 1773.

54. See also Collections of the Museum of the City of New York for photograph of a painting of 1810 showing a house-raising on Grand Street, New York City.

55. A. N. Somers, *History of Lancaster, New Hampshire* (Concord, N.H., 1899), pp. 204–206.

56. Samuel G. Drake, ed., *The History of the Indian Wars in New England . . . from the Original Work, by the Rev. William Hubbard* (Roxbury, Mass., 1865), II, 239–240.

57. F. W. B. Charles, "Scotches, Lever Sockets and Rafter Holes," *Vernacular Architecture*, V (1974), 21.

58. George Francis Dow, ed., *Records and Files of the Quarterly Courts of Essex County, Massachusetts* (Salem, Mass.: Essex Institute, 1911–1975), II, 388.

59. William I. Davisson, "Essex County Wealth Trends . . . ," *Essex Institute Historical Collections*, 103 (1967), 304.

60. This scarf joint is illustrated and labeled "Blading" on p. 57 of the 1726 edition of Neve's *Builder's Dictionary*, with contemporary manuscript notes by Englishman Charles Hornby, Yale Center for British Art, New Haven, Conn.

61. Hewett, *The Development of Carpentry*, p. 185.

62. Cecil A. Hewett, "Some East Anglian Prototypes for Early Timber Houses in America," *Post-Medieval Archaeology*, III (1969), fig. 37.

63. J. T. Smith, "The Evolution of the English Peasant House in the Late Seventeenth Century . . . ," *Journal of the British Archaeological Association*, third ser., XXXIII (1970), 138.

64. A. C. Edwards, "The Homes of Essex," label copy for exhibition mounted by the Essex Record Office, 1965.

65. Richard M. Candee, "A Documentary History of Plymouth Colony Architecture, 1620–1700," *Old-Time New England*, ser. no. 218 (October–December 1969), pp. 39–47.

66. *Town Records of Manchester* . . . (Salem, Mass., 1889), p. 147.

67. Richard M. Candee, *Wooden Buildings in Early Maine and New Hampshire, A Technological and Cultural History, 1600–1720*, Ph.D. dissertation, University of Pennsylvania, 1976.

68. Benno M. Forman, "Mill Sawing in Seventeenth Century Massachusetts," *Old-Time New England*, ser. no. 220 (April–June 1970), pp. 117–119.

69. Henry W. Belknap, *Trades and Tradesmen of Essex County, Massachusetts* . . . (Salem, Mass.: Essex Institute, 1929), p. 40.

70. *Wenham Town Records*, I, 94.

71. Thomas F. Waters, *Ipswich in the Massachusetts Bay Colony* (Ipswich, Mass.: Ipswich Historical Society, 1905–1917), I, 77–78.

72. Essex County Probate Records, docket no. 26799, Essex County Registry of Probate, Salem, Mass.

73. "Military Committee's Report, March 29, 1676 . . . ," *Essex Institute Historical Collections*, XLI (1905), 355.

74. Thomas Hutchinson, *The History of the Colony of Massachusetts-Bay* . . . (Boston, Mass., 1764–1828), II, 67n.

75. Pynchon papers, vol. 5, pt. 2 (1672–1693), p. 384, Connecticut Valley Historical Museum, Springfield, Mass.

VI. ENGLISH REGIONAL DERIVATIONS AND EVOLUTIONARY TRENDS

1. William Hubbard, "A General History of New England . . . ," *Collections of the Massachusetts Historical Society*, second ser., V (1848), 193.

2. Charles Edward Banks, *The Planters of the Commonwealth* (Baltimore: Genealogical Publishing Co., 1961), pp. 138, 197; Charles Edward Banks, *Topographical Dictionary of 2885 English Emigrants to New England, 1620–1650* (Philadelphia: Elijah Ellsworth Brownell, 1937), pp. 63, 180, 182; Joshua Coffin, *A Sketch of the History of Newbury* . . . (Boston, 1845), pp. 25, 37, 40, 43, 48, 59, 306; *Vital Records of Newbury, Massachusetts, to the end of the year 1849* (Salem, Mass.: Essex Institute, 1911); Essex County Deeds, I (Ipswich), 188, Essex County Registry of Deeds, Salem, Mass.; George Francis Dow, ed., *Records and Files of the Quarterly Courts of Essex County, Massachusetts* (Salem, Mass.: Essex Institute, 1911–1975), IX, 132; VII, 165.

3. Don Gleason Hill, ed., *The Early Records of the Town of Dedham, Massachusetts, 1636–1659* . . . (Dedham, Mass., 1892), pp. 32, 33, 49 (hereafter cited as Dedham Town Records, 1636–1659); Don Gleason Hill, ed., *The Record of Births, Marriages and Deaths . . . in the Town of Dedham* . . . (Dedham, Mass., 1886), p. 127; Edward Everett Hale, Jr., ed., *Note-Book kept by Thomas Lechford, Esq., Lawyer, in Boston, Massachusetts Bay, from June 27, 1638, to July 29, 1641* (Cambridge, Mass., 1885), p. 180; Nathaniel B. Shurtleff, ed., *Records of the Governor and Company of the Massachusetts Bay in New England* (Boston, 1853–1854), I, 292 (hereafter cited as Massachusetts Bay Colony Records; Banks, *Planters of the Commonwealth*, p. 187.

4. Dedham Town Records, 1636–1659, p. 21; Frederick J. Kingsbury and Mary K. Talcott, eds., *The Genealogy of the Descendants of Henry Kingsbury* . . . (Hartford, Conn.: Chase, Lockwood and Brainard, 1905), p. 32 and chart facing p. 44; Suffolk County Probate Records, III, 349, IV, 86, Suffolk County Registry of Probate, Boston.

5. F. W. B. Charles, *Medieval Cruck-Building and Its Derivatives* . . . (London: Society for Medieval Archaeology Monograph Series, No. 2, 1967).

6. Massachusetts Bay Colony Records, I, 100; David Jillson, "Descendants of Capt. John Whipple, of Providence, R.I.," *New England Historical and Genealogical Register*, XXXII (1878), 403; *Fourth Report of the Record Commissioners of the City of Boston, 1880, Dorchester Town Records*, 2d ed. (Boston, 1883), p. 27 (hereafter cited as Dorchester Town Records); Suffolk County Deeds, III, 204, Suffolk County Registry of Deeds, Boston.

7. *A Volume Relating to the Early History of Boston Containing the Aspinwall Notarial Records from 1644 to 1651* (Boston: Municipal Printing Office, 1903), p. 106; *Births, Marriages and Deaths in the Town of Malden, Massachusetts, 1649–1850*, comp. Deloraine P. Corey (Cambridge, Mass.: The University Press, 1903); Lane Family papers, privately owned; Charles Henry Pope, *The Pioneers of Massachusetts* . . . (Baltimore: Genealogical Publishing Co., 1969), p. 277.

8. Banks, *Topographical Dictionary*, p. 145; "Notes and Queries," *New England Historical and Genealogical Register*, XLV (1891), 312; Dorchester Town Records, pp. 240, 309, 316; Suffolk County Probate Records, VI, 701.

9. *Note-Book kept by Thomas Lechford*, p. 345.

10. Lane Family papers, privately owned.

11. Alexander Young, *Chronicles of the First Planters of the Colony of Massachusetts Bay* . . . (Boston, 1846), p. 216; Banks, *The Planters of the Commonwealth*, p. 59.

12. Sidney Perley, *The History of Salem, Massachusetts* (Salem, Mass.: Sidney Perley, 1924–1928), I, 86.

13. Asher Benjamin, *The American Builder's Companion* . . . (Boston, 1806), p. viii.

14. Franklin P. Rice, ed., *First Records of Marlborough, Massachusetts* (Worcester, Mass.: Franklin P. Rice, 1909), p. 13.

15. Harry Forrester, *The Timber-Framed Houses of Essex* (Chelmsford, Essex: Tindal Press, 1960), p. 23.

16. Cecil A. Hewett, "The Development of the Post-Medieval House," *Post-Medieval Archaeology*, VII (1973), 78.

17. Cecil A. Hewett, in conversation with the author.

18. Ibid.

19. Cecil A. Hewett, "Some East Anglian Prototypes for Early Timber Houses in America," *Post-Medieval Archaeology*, III (1969), 101, 116.

20. See Appendix Table 6.

21. Cecil A. Hewett, *The Development of Carpentry, 1200–1700, An Essex Study* (Newton Abbot, Devon.: David and Charles, 1969), pp. 188–194.

22. Ibid., fig. 91.

23. Cecil A. Hewett, in conversation with the author.

24. Hewett, *The Development of Carpentry*, p. 184.

25. See Appendix Table 5.

26. *A Report of the Record Commissioners of the City of Boston, Containing the Boston Records from 1660 to 1701* (Boston, Mass., 1881), p. 17.

27. Hewett, *The Development of Carpentry*, p. 156.

VII. THE CHIMNEY

1. Jonathan Corwin, Account Book, vol. for 1656–1679, American Antiquarian Society, Worcester, Mass.

2. *A Report of the Record Commissioners of the City of Boston, Containing the Records of Boston Selectmen, 1701 to 1715* (Boston, 1884), p. 11. (Hereafter cited as Boston Selectmen's Records, 1701–1715.)

3. John Marshall, Diary, Massachusetts Historical Society.

4. Frank C. Brown, "Early Brickwork in New England," *Pencil Points*, XV (1934), pp. 165, 168.

5. T. N. Philomath [Richard Neve], *The City and Countrey Purchaser, and Builder's Dictionary* . . . (London, 1703). (Hereafter cited as Neve, *Builder's Dictionary*, 1703 or 1726 ed.)

6. Nathaniel B. Shurtleff, ed., *Records of the Governor and Company of the Massachusetts Bay in New England* (Boston, 1853–1854), V, 212. (Hereafter cited as Massachusetts Bay Colony Records.)

7. William Leybourn, *A Platform for Purchasers* . . . (London, 1668), p. 106.

8. Alexander Young, *Chronicles of the First Planters of the Colony of Massachusetts Bay* . . . (Boston, 1846), p. 39.

9. Ibid., p. 244.

10. *Second Report of the Record Commissioners of the City of Boston, 1877* (Boston, 1877), p. 81. (Hereafter cited as Boston Town Records, 1634–1661.)

11. Don Gleason Hill, ed., *The Early Records of the Town of Dedham, Massachusetts, 1636–1659* . . . (Dedham, Mass., 1892), p. 74.

12. Don Gleason Hill, ed., *The Early Records of the Town of Dedham, Massachusetts, 1659–1673* . . . (Dedham, Mass., 1894), p. 69.

13. J. Franklin Jameson, ed., *Johnson's Wonder-Working Providence, 1628–1651* (New York: Charles Scribner's Son, 1910), p. 248.

14. Sidney Perley, *The History of Salem, Massachusetts* (Salem, Mass.: Sidney Perley, 1924–1928), vols. I and II: John Beckford, Gregory Gibbs, John Mason, Thomas Maule, and Matthew Woodwell.

15. George Francis Dow, ed., *Records and Files of the Quarterly Courts of Essex County, Massachusetts* (Salem, Mass.: Essex Institute, 1911–1975), IV, 452 (hereafter cited as Essex Quarterly Court Files, published); Charles Henry Pope, *The Pioneers of Massachusetts* . . . (Baltimore: Genealogical Publishing Co., 1969), pp. 135, 337.

16. Massachusetts Bay Colony Records, V, 212, 451.

17. Photostats/1697/34, Massachusetts Historical Society.

18. Neve, *Builder's Dictionary*, 1703 ed.

19. Massachusetts Bay Colony Records, V, 451.

20. Edward Everett Hale, Jr., ed., *Note-Book kept by Thomas Lechford, Esq., Lawyer, in Boston, Massachusetts Bay, from June 27, 1638, to July 29, 1641* (Cambridge, Mass., 1885), p. 302.

21. *Winthrop Papers* (Boston: Massachusetts Historical Society, 1929–1947), IV, 11.

22. William P. Upham and others, eds., "Town Records of Salem . . . ," *Essex Institute Historical Collections*, IX (1868), 81.

23. James Savage, ed., *The History of New England from 1630 to 1649, By John Winthrop, Esq. . . . from his original manuscripts* . . . (Boston, 1853), I, 58. (Hereafter cited as Winthrop, *Journal*.)

24. George Offor, ed., *Remarkable Providences . . . by Increase Mather* (London, 1890), preface.

25. Essex Quarterly Court Files, published, III, 286.

26. Ibid., IV, 56.

27. See, for example, ibid., II, 366.

28. Curwen Family papers, American Antiquarian Society.

29. Ibid.

30. *Note-Book kept by Thomas Lechford*, p. 56.

31. Essex Quarterly Court Files, published, VI, 91.

32. Winthrop, *Journal*, I, 75–76.

33. John Josselyn, *An Account of Two Voyages to New-England* . . . (London, 1674), p. 46.

34. M. Halsey Thomas, ed., *The Diary of Samuel Sewall, 1674–1729* (New York: Farrar, Straus and Giroux, 1973), I, 376.

35. *Johnson's Wonder-Working Providence*, p. 232.

36. *Records of ye Towne Meetings of Lyn, 1691–1701/2* (Lynn, Mass.: Lynn Historical Society, 1949), p. 40.

37. Paul B. Jenison, "The Availability of Lime and Masonry Construction in New England: 1630–1733," *Old-Time New England*, ser. nos. 245–246 (Summer–Fall 1976), p. 24.

38. Caroline O. Emmerton, *The Chronicles of Three Old Houses* (Boston: Thomas Todd Co., 1935), pp. 26, 33.

VIII. EXTERIOR FINISH

1. Joseph Everett Chandler, *The Colonial House* (New York: Robert M. McBride & Co., 1916), p. 88.

2. James Savage, ed., *The History of New England from 1630 to 1649, By John Winthrop, Esq. . . . from his original manuscripts* . . . (Boston, 1853), I, 75–76. (Hereafter cited as Winthrop, *Journal*.)

3. George B. Cheever, *The Journal of the Pilgrims at Plymouth* . . . (New York, 1848), p. 55.

4. Winthrop, *Journal*, I, 104.

5. Suffolk County Deeds, I, 16, Suffolk County Registry of Deeds, Boston.

6. Don Gleason Hill, ed., *The Early Records of the Town of Dedham, Massachusetts, 1636–1659* . . . (Dedham, Mass., 1892), pp. 25, 45.

7. *Winthrop Papers* (Boston: Massachusetts Historical Society, 1929–1947), IV, 12.

8. *Second Report of the Record Commissioners of the City of Boston, 1877* (Boston, 1877), p. 70.

9. A. C. Edwards, "The Homes of Essex," label copy for exhibition mounted by the Essex Record Office, 1965.

10. M. W. Barley, *The English Farmhouse and Cottage* (London: Routledge and Kegan Paul, 1961), p. 144.

11. Adrian Oswald, "Excavations of a Thirteenth-Century Wooden Building at Weoley Castle, Birmingham, 1960–61," *Medieval Archaeology*, VI–VII (1962–1963), 116, 122.

12. R. T. Mason, in conversation with the author concerning Sussex.

13. *Fourth Report of the Record Commissioners of the City of Boston, 1880, Dorchester Town Records*, 2d ed. (Boston, 1883), p. 305. (Hereafter cited as Dorchester Town Records.)

14. Suffolk County Deeds, III, 398.

15. Suffolk County Court Records, docket no. 1833, Office of the Clerk of the Supreme Judicial Court for Suffolk County, Boston.

16. William Sumner Appleton, "The Repairs on the Cooper–Austin House," *Old-Time New England*, ser. no. 8 (February 1913), p. 13.

17. Edward Everett Hale, Jr., ed., *Note-Book kept by Thomas Lechford, Esq., Lawyer, in Boston, Massachusetts Bay, from June 27, 1638, to July 29, 1641* (Cambridge, Mass., 1885), p. 56.

18. Thomas Hutchinson, *The History of the Colony of Massachusetts-Bay* . . . (Boston, 1764–1828), I, 349n.

19. Nathaniel B. Shurtleff, ed., *Records of the Governor and Company of the Massachusetts Bay in New England* (Boston, 1853–1854), V, 240, 266–267. (Hereafter cited as Massachusetts Bay Colony Records.)

20. "Letter from the Rev. Dr. Belknap . . . ," *Collections of the Massachusetts Historical Society*, first ser., IV (1795) 189–190, reprint of 1835.

21. Cecil Headlam, ed., *Calendar of State Papers, Colonial Series, America and West Indies, 1700* . . . (London: His Majesty's Stationery Office, 1910), p. 469.

22. *Saturday Evening Gazette* (Boston), April 7, 1860.

23. Nathaniel B. Shurtleff, *A Topographical and Historical Description of Boston* (Boston, 1871), p. 644.

24. Caleb H. Snow, *A History of Boston* . . . (Boston, 1825), p. 167.

25. Shurtleff, *A Topographical and Historical Description of Boston*, p. 644.

26. Snow, *A History of Boston*, p. 167.

27. Museum Accession Records, Society for the Preservation of New England Antiquities, Boston.

28. Henry Wansey, *An Excursion to the United States of North America, in the Summer of 1794*, 2d ed. (Salisbury, 1798), p. 20.

29. *Note-Book kept by Thomas Lechford*, p. 57.

30. Massachusetts Bay Colony Records, II, 284.

31. Winthrop, *Journal*, I, 57–58.

32. Alexander Young, *Chronicles of the First Planters of the Colony of Massachusetts Bay . . .* (Boston, 1846), p. 339.

33. Winthrop, *Journal*, I, 147.

34. *Note-Book kept by Thomas Lechford*, pp. 157, 211.

35. Winthrop, *Journal*, II, 323.

36. Lane Family papers, privately owned.

37. Essex County Probate Records, vol. 307, p. 425, Essex County Registry of Probate, Salem, Mass.

38. George Francis Dow, ed., *Records and Files of the Quarterly Courts of Essex County, Massachusetts* (Salem, Mass.: Essex Institute, 1911–1975), VI, 420. (Hereafter cited as Essex Quarterly Court Files, published.)

39. Young, *Chronicles*, p. 244.

40. J. Franklin Jameson, ed., *Johnson's Wonder-Working Providence, 1628–1651* (New York: Charles Scribner's Sons, 1910), p. 71.

41. George Offor, ed., *Remarkable Providences . . . by Increase Mather* (London, 1890), p. 59.

42. William Wood, *New Englands Prospect* (London, 1634), p. 15.

43. Massachusetts Bay Colony Records, IV (pt. 1), 33.

44. M. Halsey Thomas, ed., *The Diary of Samuel Sewall, 1674–1729* (New York: Farrar, Straus and Giroux, 1973), I, 600. (Hereafter cited as Sewall, *Diary*.)

45. *The Records of the Town of Cambridge . . . Massachusetts, 1630–1703* (Cambridge, Mass.: City Council, 1901), p. 4.

46. *Winthrop Papers*, IV, 12.

47. William P. Upham and others, eds., "Town Records of Salem . . . ," *Essex Institute Historical Collections*, IX (1868), 81. (Hereafter cited as Salem Town Records, *Essex Institute Historical Collections*.)

48. *Note-Book kept by Thomas Lechford*, p. 302.

49. Dorchester Town Records, p. 200.

50. Ibid., p. 305.

51. John Josselyn, *An Account of Two Voyages to New-England . . .* (London, 1674), p. 67.

52. Charles F. Montgomery, ed., *Joseph Moxon's Mechanick Exercises . . .* (New York: Praeger Publishers, 1970), p. 165.

53. Salem Town Records, *Essex Institute Historical Collections*, LXVIII (1932), 210.

54. Peabody-Osgood Family papers, Unrecorded deeds, etc., 1721–1840, Essex Institute, Salem, Mass.

55. Essex Quarterly Court Files, XLI, 10, Office of the Clerk of the Superior Court for Essex County, Salem, Mass. (Hereafter cited as Essex Quarterly Court Files, MS.)

56. *The Acts and Resolves . . . of the Province of the Massachusetts Bay . . .* (Boston, 1869–1922), I, 212.

57. Bartlett B. James and J. Franklin Jameson, eds., *Journal of Jasper Danckaerts, 1679–1680* (New York: Charles Scribner's Sons, 1913), p. 275.

58. Henry A. Hazen, *History of Billerica, Massachusetts . . .* (Boston, 1883), p. 108.

59. Collections, Pocumtuck Valley Memorial Association, Deerfield, Mass.

60. *The Diary of William Bentley, D.D. . . .* (Gloucester, Mass.: Peter Smith, 1962), II, 26. (Hereafter cited as Bentley, *Diary*.)

61. Suffolk County Court Records, docket no. 1833.

62. *A Report of the Record Commissioners of the City of Boston, Containing the Boston Records from 1700 to 1728* (Boston, 1883), p. 103.

63. Suffolk County Probate Records, XIV, 144, Suffolk County Registry of Probate, Boston.

64. T. N. Philomath [Richard Neve], *The City and Countrey Purchaser, and Builder's Dictionary . . .* (London, 1703).

65. Essex Quarterly Court Files, MS, VI, 86.

66. Essex County Probate Records, vol. 331, p. 136. See also Essex County Deeds, vol. 103, p. 107, Essex County Registry of Deeds, Salem, Mass.

67. Young, *Chronicles*, p. 264.

68. Wood, *New Englands Prospect*, p. 55.

69. *Winthrop Papers*, III, 155, 171.

70. Alexander Young, *Chronicles of the Pilgrim Fathers . . .* (Boston, 1841), p. 237.

71. *Winthrop Papers*, IV, 12.

72. *Remarkable Providences . . . by Increase Mather*, p. 56.

73. Collections, Metropolitan Museum of Art, New York City.

74. *Johnson's Wonder-Working Providence*, p. 54.

75. Ipswich Town Records and Land Grants, 1634–1757, p. 146, Ipswich Town Hall, Ipswich, Mass.

76. Suffolk County Probate Records, XVIII, 133.

77. Franklin P. Rice, ed., *First Records of Marlborough, Massachusetts* (Worcester, Mass.: Franklin P. Rice, 1909), p. 13.

78. Essex Quarterly Court Files, MS, V, 51.

79. *A Report of the Record Commissioners of the City of Boston, Containing the Records of Boston Selectmen, 1701 to 1715* (Boston, 1884), p. 17.

80. Sudbury Town Records, I (1640–1695), 293, Sudbury Town Hall, Sudbury, Mass.

81. Suffolk County Court Records, docket no. 1833.

82. Essex Quarterly Court Files, MS, VI, 70.

83. *Joseph Moxon's Mechanick Exercises*, p. 159.

84. Chandlor, *The Colonial House*, pp. 87–88.

85. William Sumner Appleton, "A Description of Robert McClaflin's House," *Old-Time New England*, ser. no. 44 (April 1926), pp. 161–162.

86. Suffolk County Court Records, docket no. 1833.

87. *Joseph Moxon's Mechanick Exercises*, p. 143.

88. Collections, Society for the Preservation of New England Antiquities.

89. Ibid.

90. Essex Quarterly Court Files, published, II, 45n.

91. Harry F. Damon to Bertram K. Little, December 23, 1960, Correspondence Files, Society for the Preservation of New England Antiquities.

92. Collections, Essex Institute.

93. Collections, Society for the Preservation of New England Antiquities.

94. Charles F. Montgomery, "Thomas Banister on the New Sash Windows, Boston, 1701," *Journal of the Society of Architectural Historians*, XXIV (1965), 170.

95. Sewall, *Diary*, II, 762–763.

96. Peabody-Osgood Family papers, Unrecorded deeds, etc., 1721–1840, Essex Institute.

97. *Boston Gazette*, June 30/July 7, 1729.

98. Ibid., June 21/28, 1731.

99. Ibid., December 12, 1752.

100. Reminiscences of Colonel Timothy Pickering, December 4, 1828, Pickering Family papers, Pickering House, Broad Street, Salem, Mass.

101. Bentley, *Diary*, II, 115, 172.

102. The sash are preserved now in the collections of the Old Colony Historical Society, Taunton, Mass.

103. Edwin Whitefield, *The Homes of Our Forefathers . . . in Massachusetts*, 3d ed. (Boston, 1880), unpaged.

IX. INTERIOR FINISH

1. S. R. Jones and J. T. Smith, "Chamfer-Stops: A Provisional Mode of Reference," *Vernacular Architecture*, II (1971), 12–15.

2. See, for example, M. W. Barley, *The English Farmhouse and Cottage* (London: Routledge and Kegan Paul, 1961), p. 70, and N. W. Alcock, *Stoneleigh Villagers, 1597–1650* (Coventry, Warwickshire: Univeristy of Warwick, 1975), pp. 16–18.

3. See, for example, George Francis Dow, ed., *Records and Files of the Quarterly Courts of Essex, Massachusetts* (Salem, Mass.: Essex Institute, 1911–1975), IV, 57n. (Hereafter cited as Essex Quarterly Court Files, published.)

4. Charles F. Montgomery, ed., *Joseph Moxon's Mechanick Exercises* . . . (New York: Praeger Publishers, 1970), pp. 149–153.

5. Ibid., p. 150.

6. William Sumner Appleton, Notes on the Parson Joseph Capen House, Topsfield, October 5, 1913, Correspondence Files, Society for the Preservation of New England Antiquities, Boston.

7. Essex Quarterly Court Files, published, IX, 537.

8. Suffolk County Deeds, vol. 1900, p. 561, Suffolk County Registry of Deeds, Boston.

9. Staircase preserved now in the American Wing of the Metropolitan Museum of Art, New York City.

10. Bradford Torrey, ed., *The Writings of Henry David Thoreau, Journal* (Boston and New York: Houghton Mifflin, 1906), XII, 47. See also X, 279.

11. F. W. B. Charles, in conversation with the author.

12. Samuel Eliot Morison, ed., *Of Plymouth Plantation, 1620–1647, by William Bradford* (New York: Alfred A. Knopf, 1952), p. 363.

13. James Savage, ed., *The History of New England from 1630 to 1649, By John Winthrop, Esq. . . . from his original manuscripts* . . . (Boston, 1853), I, 88. (Hereafter cited as Winthrop, *Journal*.)

14. Essex Quarterly Court Files, published, I, 261–262.

15. Suffolk County Probate Records, XI, 190, Suffolk County Registry of Probate, Boston.

16. Ibid., V, 112.

17. Curwen Family papers, American Antiquarian Society, Worcester, Mass.

18. Winthrop, *Journal*, I, 88.

19. Nathaniel B. Shurtleff and others, eds., *Records of the Colony of New Plymouth in New England* (Boston, 1855–1861), XII, 26.

20. See Thomas F. Waters, *Ipswich in the Massachusetts Bay Colony* (Ipswich, Mass.: Ipswich Historical Society, 1905–1917), I, 390–391.

21. Ralph Ladd to author, February 27, 1954, Correspondence Files, American Wing, Metropolitan Museum of Art, New York City.

22. Benno M. Forman, *The Seventeenth Century Case Furniture of Essex County, Massachusetts, and Its Makers*, M.A. thesis, University of Delaware, June 1968, pp. 120–123.

23. George Francis Dow, ed., *The Probate Records of Essex County, Massachusetts* (Salem, Mass.: Essex Institute, 1916–1920), I, 158 (hereafter cited as Essex County Probate Records, published); Essex Quarterly Court Files, published, VII, 64.

24. *Joseph Moxon's Mechanick Exercises*, p. 160.

25. *A Report of the Record Commissioners of the City of Boston, Containing Miscellaneous Papers* (Boston, 1886), pp. 55–82; *A Volume of Records Relating to the Early History of Boston, Containing Miscellaneous Papers* (Boston: Municipal Printing Office, 1900), pp. 229–242; *A Report of the Record Commissioners of the City of Boston, Containing the Records of Boston Selectmen, 1701 to 1715* (Boston, 1884), pp. 122, 228 (hereafter cited as Boston Selectmen's Records, 1701–1715). See also Suffolk County Probate Records, I, 398; XVII, 138.

26. Arthur Welford, "Restoration of a XVI Century Farm House in Suffolk," *Proceedings of the Suffolk Institute of Archaeology and Natural History*, XXIV (1940–1948), 1.

27. "Order of Exercises . . . ," *Publications of the Ipswich Historical Society*, VI (1899), 39.

28. J. Franklin Jameson, ed., *Johnson's Wonder-Working Providence, 1628–1651* (New York: Charles Scribner's Sons, 1910), p. 96.

29. Suffolk County Probate Records, V, 172, 237.

30. Essex Quarterly Court Files, published, V, 37.

31. M. Halsey Thomas, ed., *The Diary of Samuel Sewall, 1674–1729* (New York: Farrar, Straus and Giroux, 1973), I, 339.

32. See *Oxford English Dictionary*: whitewash.

33. Don Gleason Hill, ed., *The Early Records of the Town of Dedham, Massachusetts, 1636–1659* . . . (Dedham, Mass., 1892), p. 147.

34. Essex County Probate Records, published, III, 53.

35. Suffolk County Deeds, XX, 147; XXXIV, 52; John Marshall, Diary, Massachusetts Historical Society.

36. Essex County Probate Records, vol. 302, p. 126, Essex County Registry of Probate, Salem, Mass.

37. George Francis Dow to Charles Over Cornelius, September 16, 1922, Correspondence Files, American Wing, Metropolitan Museum of Art, New York City.

38. Nina Fletcher Little, *American Decorative Wall Painting, 1700–1850* (New York: E. P. Dutton, 1972), p. 4.

39. Collections, Society for the Preservation of New England Antiquities.

40. William Sumner Appleton, Notes on the Blaney House, Swampscott, April 21, 1914, Correspondence Files, Society for the Preservation of New England Antiquities.

41. Massachusetts State Archives, vol. 246, p. 136, Boston.

42. *Johnson's Wonder-Working Providence*, p. 248.

43. Charles Edward Banks, *The Planters of the Commonwealth* (Baltimore: Genealogical Publishing Co., 1961), p. 136. See also Sidney M. Gold, "A Study in Early Boston Portrait Attributions . . . ," *Old-Time New England*, ser. no. 211 (January–March 1968), pp. 61–78.

44. Suffolk County Probate Records, IX, 191.

45. Massachusetts State Archives, XV B, 209.

46. Suffolk County Deeds, I, 136.

47. Ibid., VIII, 33.

48. Guildhall Library, London; Suffolk County Probate Records, IX, 239.

49. Henry Wilder Foote, *Annals of King's Chapel* . . . (Boston, 1882–1896), I, 89–90, 128.

50. David S. Greenough Collection, folder for 1653–1715, Massachusetts Historical Society.

51. Suffolk County Deeds, XV, 214, 126, 216; XVI, 107, 269–270.

52. See Abbott Lowell Cummings, "Decorative Painting in Seventeenth-Century New England," *American Painting to 1776: A Reappraisal*, Winterthur Conference Report, 1971 (Charlottesville, Va.: The University Press of Virginia, 1971), pp. 71–125.

53. "The Boston Stone," broadside, April 1, 1839, Collections, Society for the Preservation of New England Antiquities.

54. Joseph Buckley, Diary, Massachusetts Historical Society.

55. Boston Selectmen's Records, 1701–1715, p. 28.

56. Suffolk County Court Records, docket no. 7024, Office of the Clerk of the Supreme Judicial Court for Suffolk County, Boston.

57. Ibid.

58. *A Report of the Record Commissioners of the City of Boston, Containing the Records of Boston Selectmen, 1716 to 1736* (Boston, 1885), pp. 32–33.

59. Essex County Deeds, XLII, 74, Essex County Registry of Deeds, Salem, Mass.

60. Joseph Everett Chandler, "Notes on the Paul Revere House," *Handbook of the Paul Revere Memorial Association* (Boston: The Association, 1954), p. 19.

X. TOWARD AN AMERICAN ARCHITECTURE

1. James Savage, ed., *The History of New England from 1630 to 1649, By John Winthrop, Esq. . . . from his original manuscripts* . . . (Boston, 1853), I, 88.

2. Samuel Eliot Morison, ed., *Of Plymouth Plantation, 1620–1647, by William Bradford* (New York: Alfred A. Knopf, 1952), p. 363.

3. Don Gleason Hill, ed., *The Early Records of the Town of Dedham, Massachusetts* . . . (Dedham, Mass., 1892–1899), vol. for 1636–1659, pp. 153–154, 183–184; vol. for 1659–1673, pp. 86–87; vol. for 1672–1706, pp. 19–20, 45–46.

4. George Francis Dow, ed., *The Probate Records of Essex County, Massachusetts* (Salem, Mass.: Essex Institute, 1916–1920), vol. I.

5. Middlesex County Deeds, XIII, 121, Middlesex County Registry of Deeds, East Cambridge, Mass.

6. *The Journal of Madam Knight* (Boston: David R. Godine, 1972), p. 13.

7. Fiske Kimball, *Domestic Architecture of the American Colonies and of the Early Republic* (New York: Charles Scribner's Sons, 1922), p. 35.

8. J. Franklin Jameson, ed., *Johnson's Wonder-Working Providence, 1628–1651* (New York: Charles Scribner's Sons, 1910), p. 210.

9. See Cecil A. Hewett, *The Development of Carpentry, 1200–1700, An Essex Study* (Newton Abbot, Devon.: David and Charles, 1969).

INDEX

References to illustrations are in boldface type.